THE PROSPECT OF GLOBAL HISTORY

The Prospect of Global History

Edited by
JAMES BELICH
JOHN DARWIN
MARGRET FRENZ
and
CHRIS WICKHAM

OXFORD
UNIVERSITY PRESS

OXFORD
UNIVERSITY PRESS

Great Clarendon Street, Oxford, OX2 6DP,
United Kingdom

Oxford University Press is a department of the University of Oxford.
It furthers the University's objective of excellence in research, scholarship,
and education by publishing worldwide. Oxford is a registered trade mark of
Oxford University Press in the UK and in certain other countries

© Oxford University Press 2016

The moral rights of the authors have been asserted

First Edition published in 2016

Impression: 1

Published in the United States of America by Oxford University Press
198 Madison Avenue, New York, NY 10016, United States of America

British Library Cataloguing in Publication Data
Data available

Library of Congress Control Number: 2015942141

ISBN 978–0–19–873225–9

Printed in Great Britain by
Clays Ltd, St Ives plc

Preface

We envisage this volume as the first in a new series in global history which is characterized by historical depth, a wide geographical range, and the concrete application of different approaches to global history, engaging with multiple methodologies, coming from an interdisciplinary perspective, and teasing out connections and their limitations by asking challenging questions. Some of these ideas are explored in this volume.

The Editors

Acknowledgements

This publication arises from the conference 'New Directions in Global History', which took place at the University of Oxford from 27 to 29 September 2012, funded by the John Fell Oxford University Press (OUP) Research Fund. We thank them for their support. The editors would like to acknowledge the invaluable contribution of Claire Phillips of the Oxford Centre for Global History to the preparation of this volume, and of both her and Robert Fletcher to the organization of the conference from which it originates.

We are also grateful to Robert Faber, Rachel Neaum, and Cathryn Steele at OUP for their continued support.

Contents

List of Figures

List of Maps

List of Tables

List of Contributors

James Belich is Beit Professor of Commonwealth and Imperial History at Oxford University and a fellow of Balliol College. He previously taught in New Zealand, and has published several books on New Zealand history in global context. His latest book was *Replenishing the Earth: The Settler Revolution and the Rise of the Anglo-World, 1783–1939* (2009). He was director of the Oxford Centre for Global History from 2012 to 2014. His current research, on plague and expansionism in global history, was the subject of his GM Trevelyan Lectures at Cambridge University in late 2014.

Linda Colley is Shelby M.C. Davis 1958 Professor of History at Princeton University and a Fellow of the British Academy. Her work, which has been translated into ten languages, includes *Britons: Forging the Nation 1707–1837* (1992), *Captives: Britain, Empire and the World, 1600–1850* (2002), *The Ordeal of Elizabeth Marsh: A Woman in World History* (2007) and, most recently, *Acts of Union and Disunion* (2013) which was based on fifteen lectures commissioned and broadcast by BBC Radio 4. She is currently writing a new book, *Wordpower*, exploring the global histories of written constitutions after 1750.

John Darwin is Professor of Global and Imperial History at the University of Oxford, and Director of the Oxford Centre for Global History. His recent books include *After Tamerlane: The Global History of Empire* (2007), *The Empire Project: The Rise and Fall of the British World-System 1830–1970* (2009), and *Unfinished Empire: The Global Expansion of Britain* (2012). He is currently working on the role of port cities in the globalization era of 1830–1930.

Margret Frenz has been Lecturer in Global and Imperial History at the University of Oxford, and is a Fellow at the Nantes Institute of Advanced Study. Her previous publications include *Community, Memory, and Migration in a Globalizing World: The Goan Experience, c.1890–1980* (2014), *From Contact to Conquest: Transition to British Rule in Malabar, 1790–1805* (2003) and, (edited with Georg Berkemer) *Sharing Sovereignty: The Little Kingdom in South Asia* (2003; revised edition, 2015). She has also published articles in leading journals such as *Past & Present* and *Immigrants & Minorities*.

Antony G. Hopkins is Emeritus Smuts Professor of Commonwealth History at Cambridge and an Emeritus Fellow of Pembroke College. He holds a PhD from the University of London, Honorary Doctorates from the Universities of Stirling and Birmingham, and is a Fellow of the British Academy. He has written extensively on African history, imperial history, and globalization. His most recent books are *Globalisation in World History* (2001) and *Global History: Interactions between the Universal and the Local* (2006). He is currently completing a book entitled *American Empire: An Alternative History*.

Robert I. Moore is Professor Emeritus of Medieval History at Newcastle University. He is the author of *The First European Revolution, (c.970–1215)* (2001), *The Formation of a Persecuting Society: Authority and Deviance in Western Europe, 950–1250* (2nd edn, 2006) and *The War on Heresy* (2012), and series editor of *The Blackwell History of the World*, for which he is preparing *Foundations of the Modern World: A History of Eurasia, 750–1250*.

Matthew W. Mosca received his PhD from Harvard University (2008) and is currently Assistant Professor of Chinese History at the University of Washington. He has held research fellowships at the Center for Chinese Studies (University of California, Berkeley), the Hong Kong Institute for Humanities and Social Sciences (University of Hong Kong), and the Institute for Advanced Study. His first book, *From Frontier Policy to Foreign Policy: The Question of India and the Transformation of Geopolitics in Qing China* was published in 2013.

Kevin Hjortshøj O'Rourke is the Chichele Professor of Economic History at All Souls College Oxford. He is also Research Director of the Centre for Economic Policy Research. A Fellow of the British Academy, and Member of the Royal Irish Academy, he has taught at Columbia University, University College Dublin, Harvard, Trinity College Dublin, and Sciences Po Paris. He has served as an editor of the *European Review of Economic History*, as Vice President of the Economic History Association, and as President of the European Historical Economics Society. He has worked extensively on the history of the international economy.

Jürgen Osterhammel is Professor of Modern and Contemporary History at the University of Konstanz (Germany). His publications on world history include *The Transformation of the World: A Global History of the Nineteenth Century* (2014) and (with Jan C. Jansen) *Dekolonisation: Das Ende der Imperien* (2013). With Akira Iriye he is editor-in-chief of a six-volume *New History of the World*, published by Harvard University Press since 2012. He is a recipient of Germany's most prestigious academic award, the Georg Wilhelm Leibniz Prize, and a Corresponding Fellow of the British Academy.

Nicholas Purcell is Camden Professor of Ancient History. He has worked on many themes in Greek and Roman social and economic history, and is especially interested in environmental questions and how they relate to scale in historical analysis. His work (with the medievalist Peregrine Horden) *The Corrupting Sea* (2000) attempted to evaluate approaches to the history of the Mediterranean region over very long time frames. He is now working on the implications of that work for the ways in which Mediterranean histories may be situated in even larger geographical contexts. The present chapter derives from that work.

Francis Robinson has been the Professor of the History of South Asia at Royal Holloway, University of London, since 1990. From 2008–11 he was also Sultan of Oman Fellow at the Oxford Centre for Islamic Studies, Visiting Professor of the History of the Islamic World, Oxford, and a Fellow of Brasenose College. His interests are primarily in religious change in the Islamic world since the seventeenth century and more specifically in ulama and Sufis in South Asia. Amongst his recent publications are: 'Islamic Reform and Modernities in South Asia', *Modern Asian Studies* 2008; 'Strategies of Authority in Nineteenth and Twentieth Century Muslim India', *Modern Asian Studies* 2013; and, as editor, *Islam in the Age of Western Dominance, v. New Cambridge History of Islam*. He is currently writing a biography of Maulana Jamal Mian of Farangi Mahall.

Chris Wickham is Chichele Professor of Medieval History at the University of Oxford. He has written numerous books on Medieval Italy and, more widely, on Europe and the Mediterranean, up to 1250. He is a social historian, and also a comparative historian, committed to large-scale comparative work, as shown in his *Framing the Early Middle Ages* (2005). He has extended this comparative work widely, including to medieval China and the Islamic world.

PART I

CONCEPTUAL CONSIDERATIONS

Introduction
The Prospect of Global History

James Belich, John Darwin, and Chris Wickham

APPROACHES

Global history may be boundless, but global historians are not. Global history cannot usefully mean the history of everything, everywhere, all the time. There are various ways of usefully focussing the global approach, and the eminent contributors assembled in this volume innovatively deploy some of them. Here, the editors focus on three approaches that seem to us to have real promise. One is global history as the pursuit of significant historical problems across time, space, and specialism. This can sometimes be characterized as 'comparative' history, but it can be seen differently as well; it seeks answers to the same question in multiple sites. It is, of course, no easy art, and is discussed in the second section of this Introduction. Another is connectedness, including transnational relationships; these will be discussed in the third section. The third approach is the study of globalization, with which we begin. Globalization is a term that needs to be rescued from the present, and salvaged for the past. To define it as always encompassing the whole planet is to mistake the current outcome for a very ancient process.

GLOBALIZATION

Globalizing can be seen as the formation of trans-regional entities, extending beyond any single culture or polity, a process that began many millennia ago. Some simple typologies measuring the space, intensity, and vectors of globalization, may be useful. Globalization connected three categories of space: sub-global, semi-global, and pan-global. There have been only two cases of the last: the original spread of *homo sapiens* to all six habitable continents, and modern globalization, even if current scholarship unhelpfully dates this to 1492, 1800, the 1940s, and the 1970s. The 'semi-global' category stretches across a whole hemisphere. One remarkable example is the spread of Austronesian or 'Malayo-Polynesian' cultures, which in and around the first millennium AD spanned the whole Pacific and Indian Oceans, reaching East Africa and very probably the Americas. Another is the Arctic 'world system', circling the north of the planet, with specialized bio-technologies, ranging from domesticated reindeer and sled dogs to ice houses, toggle harpoons, and whale-hunting *umiak* boats. In the early centuries of the second millennium AD, a suite of these technologies enabled the Thule Inuit to migrate from Siberia to Greenland, via Canada, displacing the Paleo-Eskimo, Amerindian, and European (Viking) cultures that stood in their way. A third example, on which we concentrate below, is the semi-global system that stretched across Afro-Eurasia, the 'Old World', from the fourth millennium BC.

The sub-global category has sneaked into common usage in the form of sub-global 'worlds' as in 'Atlantic World', or 'Arab World'. Such worlds can emerge through the meshing of smaller systems, or can spin off a single mega-empire, but stretch beyond it in time and space. Japan and Ireland were part of Chinese and Roman worlds, but not empires. Hellenic and Mongol worlds survived the fragmentation of the relevant empires.

Europe was not a sub-global world in itself, but part of one. Its world also included the Middle East and North Africa. This macro-region's natural unity stemmed not from similar climate or terrain, but from shared boundaries of ocean, steppe, and desert, and a shared internal mix of land and water. It featured an unusual number of inland seas, enclosed or semi-closed by land. Historians have brilliantly demonstrated how the great Mediterranean linked its littorals and their histories.[1] But we have neglected the possibility that other seas did likewise, and that a whole constellation of seas could be connected. The Mediterranean was the flagship of a fleet that also included the Red, Black, Caspian, North and Baltic Seas, the Persian Gulf, and the Bay of Biscay. Straits connected the Baltic and North Seas, and also connected the Mediterranean to the Atlantic Ocean and the Black Sea. Rivers link, or almost link, the other seas. Interestingly, this 'world' has no accepted name— West Eurasia, though unfair to North Africa, is the best of a bad job. Whatever its name, it means that Europe is the wrong space in which to understand its own history.

The advent of sea-going boats, about ten thousand years ago, and the domestication of horses and camels, four or five thousand years ago, activated West Eurasia's connective potential, and while great differences persisted, some common history emerged. The whole region shared the Neolithic Levantine package of domesticated biota, the spread of Indo-European and Semitic languages, and the influence of the ancient Fertile Crescent civilizations. From 500 BC it also shared the influence of a series of tri-continental empires, each of which claimed the legacies of its predecessors: Persian, Hellenic, Roman, Arab, and Turkish. One can almost imagine a Chinese-style situation in which these were seen as successive dynasties of the same empire. A propensity to monotheism was a West Eurasian peculiarity: the Abrahamic religions of Judaism, Christianity, and Islam, to which one could

---

[1] Fernand Braudel, *The Mediterranean and the Mediterranean World in the Age of Philip II*, 3 vols. trans. Siân Reynolds (Berkeley: University of California Press, 1995); Peregrine Horden and Nicholas Purcell, *The Corrupting Sea: A Study of Mediterranean History* (Oxford: Blackwell Publishers, 2000); David Abulafia, *The Great Sea: A Human History of the Mediterranean* (Oxford and New York: Oxford University Press, 2011); Cyprian Broodbank, *The Making of the Middle Sea* (London: Thames and Hudson, 2013).

arguably add Zoroastrianism and Manichaeism. Finally, the 'One-God' world shared two great plague pandemics, further proof of its cohesion.[2]

This West Eurasian world was Europe's sub-global context; its semi-global context also included the Chinese, Indian Ocean, and steppe nomad 'worlds'— together the four 'Old Worlds'. To measure the intensity of connection within and between these worlds, we need our second typology. Mere *contact* is occasional and indirect, though it can be important in transferring biota and techniques. The second category, *interaction*, involves regular and on-going contact, exemplified by luxury trade. The next step up is *circulation*, exemplified by bulk trade. Finally, *integration* makes at least sections of a global system mutually dependent parts of a single economic or cultural whole.

The four old worlds, and the system linking them, were created by several vectors of connectivity. Here we deploy the last of our overarching typologies. Vector One is *diffusion*, where indirect long-range links are achieved by a series of transfers from neighbour to neighbour. Vector Two is *outreach*, a catch-all category including trade, religious evangelism, and long-range hunting or extraction, an important but neglected sub-type. Vector Three is *dispersal*, long-range migrations that reproduce the source society but do not necessarily remain connected to it. Austronesian and Thule migrations were of this kind, as were Bulgar and Viking conquest migrations in the late first millennium AD. Both of the latter pair formed several powerful but far-flung and largely unconnected polities. With Vector Four, *expansion*, the expanding entity remains connected to its point of origin. Great empires are the classic case, but not the only one. The empires of Alexander, Mahomet, and Chingis Khan quickly fell apart, but the parts remained expansive and connected for some centuries. Classical Greek, Phoenician, and modern European expansions were never unified into a single empire, but remained connected to their metropolis. Dispersal and expansion are the two forms of spread, in which the spreading culture dominates local folk, if any. They can be likened to a stretched rubber band, which either breaks into fragments (dispersal) or remains intact (expansion).

A fifth globalizing technique is to globalize through attraction, bringing things and thoughts to you via intermediaries rather than going to get them yourself. Finally, nodal places, regions, cultures, or networks linked two or more expansions or outreaches. An interesting form of nodality is the neutral resource region, unpopulated but used by multiple tribes or nations who have to negotiate shared access. An ancient example is the obsidian island, from Melos in the Eastern Mediterranean to Tuhua in the New Zealand archipelago. Both names mean 'obsidian', and were places where tribes met and mixed. A more modern example is the Newfoundland Bank, which from the sixteenth century hosted the cod fishing fleets of several European nations. Nodes are the lynchpins of globalization, and in turn depend on it (see section, 'Connectedness').

In this context, the question of *divergence* becomes something more than an international beauty contest in which the winner always looks rather like the judge.

---

[2] See ch. 6.

If one part of a global system hits upon some development considered advantageous by the rest, they will seek to adopt it, or raid or trade for it. If the advantage facilitates dispersal or expansion, they may have little choice. Eventually the divergent advantage will disseminate to at least the urban clusters within the global system. Thus divergence will lead to some convergence until another divergence arises. Convergence is not intended to imply homogenization. What converged was a growing menu of bio-technological and cultural (e.g. religious) options, mixed and matched in locally very different ways. Divergences could also create or expand globalized zones. Europe's 'great divergence' was in fact the last of at least four stemming from the Old Worlds. One could easily add a fifth: the massive spread, through peaceful outreach, of Buddhism from India, mediated by the Kushan Empire from the first century BC, and stretching from Japan to Samarkand, but that will not be discussed here.[3]

* * *

Ivory from an Asian elephant has recently been found in a Neolithic workshop in Spain, dated to 4,500 years ago,[4] and cloves from Southeast Asia were reaching the Euphrates less than a thousand years later.[5] These valuables were probably transferred by diffusion involving a sequence of land and sea transport. The first clear-cut divergence connecting and so creating the Old Worlds system did not come from towns or trades but from the domestication of the horse by the nomads of the Eurasian steppes. At first, from about 4,000 years ago, horses were used in twos and threes to pull chariots: from 3,000 years ago men rode them singly using compound bows. In the second millennium BC, horse nomads conquered and migrated their way deep into West Eurasia, Northern India, and Northern China, and their technology migrated even further to enable others to stop them, so linking and converging the four old worlds. Pulses of dispersal from the steppes, such as that of the Huns in the fourth century AD continued to afflict all three urbanized old worlds until the eighteenth century.

It is easy to underestimate the full historic importance of the horse-human alliance. Horses tripled human power, speed, and mobility. Equipped with Chinese horse collars, they helped revolutionize agriculture on heavy Northern European soils around 1000 AD. As late as 1850, horses supplied over half of all work energy in the United States.[6] Simply as transport, they provided a huge military advantage. They made possible long-range raiding, which reduced the risk of retaliation. They delivered fresh troops to the battlefield to face exhausted foot soldiers. When warriors learned to fight from chariots and horseback, the equestrian advantage

[3] Liu Xinru, *The Silk Road in World History* (Oxford: Oxford University Press, 2010), ch. 4; Liu Xinru, 'Silks and Religions in Eurasia, c.AD 600–1200', *Journal of World History* 6, 1 (1995), pp. 25–48.

[4] F. Nocete et al., 'The Ivory Workshop of Valencina de la Concepcion (Seville, Spain) and the Identification of Ivory from Asian Elephant on the Iberian Peninsula in the First Half of the 3rd Millennium BC', *Journal of Archaeological Science* 40, 3 (2013), pp. 1579–92.

[5] Richard L. Smith, *Premodern Trade in World History* (London and New York: Routledge, 2009), p. 85.

[6] Joel A. Tarr, 'A Note on the Horse as an Urban Power Source', *Journal of Urban History* 25, 3 (1999), pp. 434–48, pp. 435 and 445 (note 4).

multiplied. Chariots were quite a complex technology, a basket on metal-rimmed wheels weighing as little as 35 kilograms, whose horse team and charioteers required complex training. With compound bows and mass-produced cast metal arrowheads, trained archers could fire ten arrows a minute from horseback, even when retreating—the Parthian shot.

Both chariot and mounted archer bio-technologies were state-of-the-art, and sedentary states were forced to emulate them if they could. This was an enduring problem for China and India, whose ecologies did not suit the breeding of large horses. Here, sedentary states were compelled to acquire horses regularly from nomads through trade or alliance. Unlike most Sino-Indian imports, fresh horses were a necessity, not a disposable luxury. The advent of guns around 1300, in China then Europe, did not eliminate the horse archer advantage. Horse nomads would not wait around to be shot by cannon, and hand-held firearms were too short-range and cumbersome to be much of a threat to them until the later nineteenth century. Qing China crushed the last Mongol empire, that of the Zhungars in Central Asia, a century earlier, but only by a sustained, massive, and hugely expensive overland projection of force. Europeans in the Americas had to wait until the advent of repeating firearms in the 1870s to overcome the horse nomad empires of the Sioux, Comanche, and the Araucanians of the Argentine Pampas. Until then, European expansion had transferred its own antidote—horses.

The horse nomads connected the old worlds, at first through contact and dispersal, and then, with various Turkic and Mongol empires from the third century BC, through expansion and interaction. A second great divergence was anchored in China and India and based on the export of fine coloured textiles of silk and cotton. Beginning with diffusion and sporadic contact before 1000 BC, it moved into regular and substantial interaction in the last centuries BC, via the Silk Road, with nomad assistance, or via a monsoon-driven maritime route centred on the Indian Ocean.[7] By the early centuries AD, Chinese silk and Indian cotton had reached the Atlantic coast of West Eurasia.

Immanuel Wallerstein might deny the label 'world system' to this vast interaction on the grounds that it lacked an axial division of labour.[8] Manuel Castells might contest the label 'globalization' because a shared and self-perpetuating body of information was absent.[9] Yet there was a fundamental and resonant division of labour. China and India did the manufacturing, and the rest of the world paid in non-manufactures, such as spices, dyestuffs, horses, furs, and, especially, bullion. And there was a complementary set of semi-globally shared and self-perpetuating information and valuations. All cultures within the system agreed that bright silks and cottons, later joined by Chinese porcelain, were the most desirable of manufactures. 'For over a thousand years, Chinese porcelain was the most universally

[7] David Christian, 'Silk Roads or Steppe Roads? The Silk Roads in World History', *Journal of World History* 11, 1 (2000), pp. 1–26.

[8] Immanuel Wallerstein, *The Modern World-System*, 3 vols (Berkeley, Los Angeles, and London: University of California Press, 2011).

[9] Manuel Castells, *The Information Age: Economy, Society, and Culture*, 3 vols, (Oxford: Blackwell, 1996–8).

admired and most widely imitated product in the world.'[10] It was also internationally agreed that silver and gold, intrinsically the most useless of metals, were similarly valuable. From Pliny the Elder in the first century AD, through Armenian and Ottoman commentators in the fourteenth and seventeenth centuries, to the governors of the British East India Company in the early nineteenth century, we hear the same complaints about the one-way flow of bullion from West Eurasia to China and India.[11]

In the debate on 'the' Great Divergence—of Europe from the rest of the planet—those who argue that China and India had an economic edge as late as 1800 have been accused of over-correcting the Eurocentric pendulum, even of 'Euro-envy', in Eric Jones' pungent term.[12] Yet the evidence of bullion flows, like the reverse flow of Chinese techniques, seems impartial, and it survived 1,500 years of West Eurasian efforts at emulation. This Sino-Indian Great Divergence was not a matter of some intrinsic Asian dexterity. Rice, a highly productive super-crop, permitted dense populations and regional specialization in growing and weaving silk and cotton. Social complexity attuned textile producers to multiple and changing markets. Caste, clan, and lineage encouraged hereditary occupations in which children learned knack as well as skill. The Sino-Indian manufacturing divergence was also part of the answer to the question of why China and India did not expand overseas, though there were times when they could clearly have done so. The world came to them, bearing its valuables. They had no need to go to it, and globalized more by attraction than expansion.

From about 500 BC, West Eurasians could regularly buy Sino-Indian luxury textiles. Within a few centuries they could weave silks and cottons themselves from imported yarn. From about 500 AD, they could farm cotton bushes, mulberry trees, and silkworms and create the whole product themselves, though not, until about 1800, to quite the Sino-Indian benchmarks in quality and price. Tiny volumes of bright luxury cloth may seem unimportant, but this is deceptive. It could be used to express anything from individuality to uniformity, as well as status. The trade itself was light, but not small. Thirty square metres of fine cotton fitted within a coconut shell.[13] What economists would call its linkage effects was considerable—ten tons a year of silk or cotton fibre employed a thousand weavers in Genoa or Cologne. Above all, it drove emulation. The Lancashire cotton industry is widely agreed to have been crucial to English industrialization, and its main game was matching Bengal.

[10] Robert Finlay, 'The Pilgrim Art: The Culture of Porcelain in World History', *Journal of World History* 9, 2 (1998), pp. 141–87.
[11] Richard L. Smith, *Premodern Trade in World History* (London and New York: Routledge, 2009), pp. 97–8; Robert Bedrosian, 'China and the Chinese According to 5th–13th Century Classical Armenian Sources', *Armenian Review* 34, 1–133 (1981), pp. 17–24; Amita Satyal, 'The Mughal Empire, Overland Trade, and Merchants of Northern India, 1526–1707' (unpublished PhD thesis: University of California, Berkeley, 2008).
[12] Eric Jones, *The European Miracle: Environments, Economies and Geopolitics in the History of Europe and Asia*, 3rd edn (Cambridge and New York: Cambridge University Press, 2003), p. 247.
[13] Prasannan Parthasarathi, *Why Europe Grew Rich and Asia Did Not: Global Economic Divergence, 1600–1850* (New York: Cambridge University Press, 2011), p. 33.

West Eurasia probably achieved the shift from interaction to circulation around 100 BC, thanks largely to Roman expansion. The archetypal circulation was the grain trade, in which Egypt, Tunisia, and parts of the Black Sea coast fed Rome itself, its army, and eventually the second capital of Constantinople. There were other bulk trades: timber, marble, salt, wine, olive oil, and stranger trades too, notably the commerce in wild beasts, destined to be killed in arenas for the entertainment of Roman crowds. This last trade pushed out the edges of the Roman world, as Roman hunters or their agents searched for big beasts along the shores of the Baltic and deeper and deeper into Africa.[14] We can document at least two post-Roman periods of West Eurasian circulation corresponding to the two plague pandemics, 540s–760s and 1346–*c*.1800. A third, modern, pandemic, 1890s–1920s, covered much more space but killed fewer people. All three pandemics required bulk trade or circulation to spread and re-spread. Pandemics and intensifying globalization are good proxies for each other.

In the early seventh century, the third old world 'Great Divergence' took place: Islamic expansion. The astonishing initial conquests of the Arabs, unified by Islam, stretching from Spain to Sind in less than a century, were matched and extended by Islam's own equally astonishing outreach, through trade and conversion. The former reached India and China by sea in the eighth century AD; the latter voluntarily converted steppe nomads, including two Mongol khanates, and many trading partners. Muslim merchants in China were sufficiently numerous and rich to provoke massacres in 760 and 878.[15] But they kept coming. The famous Ming admiral Zheng He, whose great fleets reached East Africa and the Red Sea in the early fifteenth century, was Muslim. Where documents are lacking, Islam's penetration of South East Asia is mapped by the sudden disappearance of pork bones from middens.[16]

Though the Mongol legacy can be underestimated, Islamic expansion was more durable. The same is true of the fourth old world 'Great Divergence', that of Christian Europe, from 1400. As various historians have observed, Islam forced Christian expansion east and west, away from the more favoured south—the 'Great Diversion' of Europe. It is intriguing to note that the terrible twins of West Eurasia came from the same sub-global world and shared essentially the same god. A global approach makes it hard to see how their histories can continue to avoid each other.

[14] Michael MacKinnon, 'Supplying Exotic Animals for the Roman Amphitheatre Games: New Reconstructions Combining Archaeological, Ancient Textual and Ethnographic Data', *Mouseion* III, 6 (2006), pp. 137–61; Christopher Epplett, 'The Capture of Animals by the Roman Military', *Greece & Rome* 48, 2 (2001), pp. 210–22; Fik Meijer, *The Gladiators: History's Most Deadly Sport* (London: Souvenir Press, 2004 [2003]); George Jennison, *Animals for Show and Pleasure in Ancient Rome* (Philadelphia: University of Pennsylvania, 2005 [1937]).

[15] Hugh R. Clark, 'Frontier Discourse and China's Maritime Frontier: China's Frontiers and the Encounter with the Sea through Early Imperial History', *Journal of World History* 20, 1 (2009), pp. 1–33.

[16] Peter Vanderford Lape, 'Contact and Conflict in the Banda Islands, Eastern Indonesia 11th–17th Centuries' (unpublished PhD thesis: Brown University, 2000). See Francis Robinson, ch. 7, this volume, for further development of these points.

COMPARISONS

Kenneth Pomeranz may be right or wrong in dating 'the' Great Divergence, the fourth by our count, between (north-west) Europe and (central-southern) China to as late as 1800[17]—our authors themselves disagree about that—but the message of the foregoing is a different one. The range of these varied divergences, as already stressed, decentres the standard 'we-are-best' international grand narrative which concentrates on pan-global globalization, and on the fourth divergence listed above. The teleologies of power relationships, when they are posed as always having to lead to the Western conquest of most of the known world in the century and a half after 1750, or to the Western-dominated world economy of 1870–1970, are false. Global history must extend beyond them, and beyond the issue of divergence, to such issues as the globally focussed analysis of difference which underlies comparative history, and the globally focussed analysis of connectedness which underlies transnational history. Global history-writing also does not have to be restricted to the modern or modernizing world; there have always been globally directed developments of different types. We will come to connectedness in a moment, but let us look here at how to analyse what distinguished the various regions of the globe which did (eventually) connect with, or diverge from, each other, at how such differences can be compared, and at what such comparison is for.

Comparison can of course be done using any number of axes; what is essential is that it is done rigorously. And we would add reciprocally, using Pomeranz's terminology, that one side of the comparison should not be considered the 'norm' and the other the 'deviation'. This point is indeed widely accepted; it underlies the several discussions of comparison in the book which most closely parallels this one, *Writing the History of the Global*, edited by Maxine Berg.[18] It also underpins Max Weber's still-essential discussions of ideal types, which are invented constructs developed specifically for the purpose of neutral comparison, in that different real societies can be usefully analysed and compared according to how they fit, or fail to fit, the different elements in an ideal type, as long as it is set up properly.[19] Comparison can, however, be developed at various levels. Victor Lieberman's massive comparative volume sets whole political systems against each other, from Thailand to France, across a millennium of history up to 1800, and links state structures, economics, and culture in each as he does so. He also argues that much structural change in each of his case studies had a (very) broadly similar chronological phasing. He develops a precise argument from that similarity: that Eurasia as a whole tended to react in parallel ways to common stimuli, such as climatic shifts, and also, later, came together more and more in its development as a result

[17] Kenneth Pomeranz, *The Great Divergence: China, Europe, and the Making of the Modern World Economy* (Princeton: Princeton University Press, 2000).

[18] Maxine Berg (ed.), *Writing the History of the Global: Challenges for the Twenty-First Century* (Oxford: Oxford University Press, 2013), especially the contributions by M. Berg, P. Parthasarathi, R. B. Wong, K. Sugihara, and C. Clunas.

[19] Max Weber, 'Die Objektivität sozialwissenschaftlicher und sozialpolitischer Erkenntnis' (1904), in Max Weber, *Gesammelte Aufsätze zur Wissenschaftslehre*, 2nd edn (Tübingen, 1951), pp. 146–214, esp. pp. 190–200.

of the early globalization trends discussed above.[20] Alternatively, comparison can be more specific, as in Pomeranz's comparison, not of the whole of China, but of the lower Yangzi, with England in a single century, 1750–1850.

Similarly, at a more abstract level, Garry Runciman's major work of historical sociology, even though it looks to the whole world and to every historical period for its typologies, focusses on separable modes of power (production, coercion, and persuasion) when he makes his comparisons, and above all on 'the competitive selection of practices', such as patron–client relations as opposed to mass political parties, which led individual polities in history in one socio-political direction or another.[21] It must be added, and stressed, that comparison can be more focussed still: it can be restricted to individual features, which appear, in different contexts in each case, in a wide range of different societies, with the differences between the contexts then used to unpick and explain wider differences in development. In principle, almost anything could be used here as a way into such comparative analysis: the political role of fortifications, the training of officials, the extent of wage labour, the elements which go together to define political élites, the economic autonomy of religious organizations, the social role of literacy, the level of violence considered to be necessary to protect honour, the perceived immediacy of divine intervention, are all axes along which comparison could usefully be pursued in any period and across any geographical space.

Each of these levels of comparison can be defended for its usefulness; we certainly do not advocate one over another. But each contains risks. Lieberman's style of large-scale holistic comparison runs the risk of mixing incompatible elements together, or else, by focussing on whole political systems (China rather than the lower Yangzi), of implicitly privileging the political over the economic or cultural. But non-holistic comparison carries a risk too, of failing to understand properly the exact way in which the axis of comparison chosen might allow us to understand wider economic, social, political, cultural structures in each chosen region, without which the exercise is effectively useless. These risks need to be recognized explicitly, and constantly corrected for, in any global (or, indeed, non-global) comparison. There are other risks too: for example, failure to understand differences in our evidence-base—in both what it makes clear or ignores, and in the constraints of its genres—from place to place. That in itself tends to be a spin-off of the most substantial risk of all when undertaking comparative work: too great a reliance on prior work in the secondary literature. Such work will seldom have been done with a comparative eye, so will often fall into the traps which characteristically appear in non-comparative work, such as considering one's own field of study as normative, or else failing to confront (or even notice) the dominant grand narratives in

[20] Victor Lieberman, *Strange Parallels: South-East Asia in Global Context, c.800–1830, vol. 2: Mainland Mirrors: Europe, Japan, China, South Asia, and the Islands* (Cambridge: Cambridge University Press, 2009); for a detailed reaction, see Alan Strathern's review in *Journal of Global History* 7 (2012), pp. 129–42.
[21] Walter G. Runciman, *A Treatise on Social Theory*, 3 vols (Cambridge: Cambridge University Press, 1983–97); for a detailed reaction, see Chris Wickham, 'Systactic Structures', *Past and Present* 132 (1991), pp. 188–203.

the region one is focussing on. Scholars of 'world systems', and of divergence and convergence, must guard against this danger. Global yet focussed comparative history may be the best way to test, and if necessary undermine, grand narratives. But it will find it difficult to do so unless it recognizes their existence in most secondary work written on the area of study. The solution to this particular risk is hard, but usually necessary; it is to understand and rely on the primary sources above all. In global comparison, they will usually be in an uncomfortable variety of languages. So a properly conducted global comparative study will have to confront linguistic variety (and will thus, in practice, usually be collective): we may skitter over the surface of understanding if we do not.

Why do we do comparative history, given these risks? We would say, for three reasons. First, as has just been implied, to undermine—if possible, to destroy—inaccurate and self-serving national or international clichés, such as that 'Western feudalism' is a better preparation than 'oriental despotism' for the capitalist breakthrough (this is a terminology which no-one uses now, but it underpins a surprising array of more apparently scientific works), or, more specifically—and this claim is still made—that the security of property was too weak in Asian systems for capital accumulation to take place.[22] Second, to solve specific problems by looking at them comparatively, testing explanations against different examples of the same process. Print culture, for example, is often stated to be one of the elements which fuelled the spread of Protestantism in northern Europe, but it never had that effect in Italy, although Italy was a focus of early European printing and of a long tradition of autonomous lay piety; and print had no special links with dissent in China.[23] We look at Protestantism differently once we recognize that. Third, to get an idea of (and explanations for) the real inner structures of diversity, including in contexts of change and convergence. Thus, taking the example of a superficially convergent transnational structure, we need to recognize that the social and political role of the Christian church was very different in 1000 between Ireland, Italy, Byzantium, and Chinese Turkestan, as also is that of Islam today (even if it usually has no structure equivalent to a church) between Britain, Egypt, Iran, and Indonesia; and we will need to analyse both sets of differences comparatively if we wish to see why. In this context, it may indeed often be better to start with regions, not political systems, except when one is studying state structures; the political role of the church in Italy in 1000 was different between Rome and Milan too. It is also sometimes better to start with elements rather than wholes, as Linda Colley does in this book with the writing and reception of constitutions, for the different structurations of individual elements, again in a context of transnational connectivity, will give a more immediate idea of difference.

---

[22] This claim is efficaciously disposed of in a few pages in, for example, Pomeranz, *Great Divergence*, pp. 168–70.

[23] Though Chinese printing certainly did further intellectual developments: Kai-Wing Chow, 'Writing for Success: Printing, Examinations and Intellectual Change in Late Ming China', *Late Imperial China* 17, 1 (1996), pp. 120–57, and see in general that entire number of the journal for the cultural effects of early modern Chinese printing.

Let us take a brief example of a possible comparative study, one with little discernible evidence of transnational influences associated with it, the relation between military elites and civilian elites in pre-modern governments. (Here, the object of comparative attention has to be whole political systems.) All developed polities rely on organized military defence, and thus have armies which tend to dominate coercive power; military leaders are thus normally major political players. But all developed polities also need trained and expert officials to run them, whose careers are not typically focussed on the battlefield. Furthermore, all developed polities have various levels of landed aristocracy, which, particularly (but not only) in the pre-capitalist world, tend to have their own direct access to political power, thanks to their private wealth. How did all these interrelate in the past?

The Roman empire had two levels of landed aristocracy, focussed on the cities of the empire and on the capitals, which were both characterized for the most part by a very strong civilian culture, based on a literary education; both furnished the personnel for the civilian bureaucracy. The army, although perfectly capable of replacing emperors by coup, was relatively marginal to the standard career-structure of the other elites; although it was, as a result, rather more meritocratic too, wider social status depended more on wealth and education than on arms. Rome's Byzantine successor, however, although maintaining much the same form of state, after c.800 developed a military rather than a civilian aristocracy; as a result, given that aristocrats could and did gain education and civilian training as well, there was a much closer link between civil and military careers, and military expertise had a much higher status—even emperors composed manuals of military strategy. In China, often compared to Rome, the aristocracy was more military under the Han and Tang dynasties than it was later, under the Song and Ming. In China career bureaucrats were more often called to arms than under Rome, but a separation of roles is clear by 1000, in the Song period, with local aristocratic elites more directed to the bureaucratic career-structure, and civilian/educated ('mandarin') values, than to the military one, which was relatively culturally marginal—Song China being in this respect more similar to Rome than was the Han dynasty with which it is most often compared. The Arab caliphate and its medieval successors in the Middle East from Egypt to Iran, at least after c.860, was dominated politically by military leaders and their clients—themselves often future leaders—who had great power but rarely any landed base or élite origin; here the educated landed elites either provided bureaucrats who were subjected politically to army leaders, or restricted their political ambition to provincial-level politics. This did not lead to a hegemony of military values, however, but rather to two cultural and political worlds which had relatively little to do with each other, except at the interface between politico-military strategy and governmental expertise (the level at which military and civil were linked everywhere, that is to say). Finally, in the smaller and simpler polities of medieval Western Europe, where landed aristocracies were fully militarized and bureaucracies fairly sketchy until the thirteenth century, military values reigned supreme as secular status markers; even after c.1250, when states and thus their officials were more powerful, any secular leader needed to have a military training, and only a specifically ecclesiastical career (which usually excluded people from the highest levels of political leadership) could exempt the ambitious from it.

These five examples were all long-lasting and stable political systems (stability being here measured by the survival of the system, not of its individual leaderships—all these political systems in some periods and places, third-century Rome, tenth-century China, fourteenth-century Egypt, fifteenth-century England, had very short-term leaders, who died by violence). They had in many respects similar political structures—the most distinct was probably the medieval west, which had much simpler structures until the fourteenth century or so. The military vs. civilian balance was not, then, itself of structural significance for their durability: an observation which already runs counter to some of the local historiographies for each of these large regions. It should also be clear, even from these highly summary descriptions, that the involvement of the landed aristocracy in military activity, or its absence, was fundamental for determining the parameters of socio-cultural status in each of these systems. Only in the Islamic world, with its unusually total separation between the military and the civilian worlds (in some Islamic polities, ruling military elites were exclusively recruited from abroad), were the military values of non-landed groups not marginal to the rest of society; indeed, only in the Islamic world did landed aristocrats not dominate political practice and most political power. But we can also see that the varying association of much the same elements led to wider political practices whose dynamics were quite distinct. To push this further, we would of course have to add more parameters: the role of tax-raising in each system, or the level of centralization (how far did people look to the capital and the supreme ruler for advancement and cultural leadership in each system, and how important were provincial leaderships). We could of course also add more examples; Japan, the Guptas, the Khmers, the Aztecs, would all add variants on these basic patterns, to nuance our hypotheses and our explanations. But we can get a long way in posing, and sometimes answering, questions about how political systems worked in the past by developing just the examples presented here, in a comparative analysis.

Looked at with a comparative eye, every society of the past, across the globe, gives us a new set of questions to pose of other societies, and a new set of alternatives. The global becomes, indeed, an array of possibilities. Every society has paths not taken; which, and why? Comparison allows us to see which they might be, and in which ways the 'normal' can be refigured as the atypical. The grand narratives which dominate our historiographies will often dissolve as a result. Not always; some of them are strong enough to resist. But the proper testing of each of the storylines which historians like to construct for the past is a testing which encompasses all the possibilities which global comparison can bring.

CONNECTEDNESS

The history of connectedness, strictly, perhaps, of *uneven* or differential connectedness, is, finally, the most distinctive terrain of the global historian. It follows that global history must be centrally concerned with the history of *mobility*—the movement across space of people, goods, and ideas. Indeed, it might well be argued that one of the most compelling insights that global history has to offer is to insist that the systematic investigation of the forms of mobility is an indispensable part of historical inquiry in every place and period. If *l'histoire immobile* was the call to arms of one great school of history, for global historians the reverse must hold true: history is movement.

That this should be so may be explained by two exceptionally durable traits of human behaviour. It was Adam Smith who remarked on the human propensity to 'truck, barter and exchange'. Smith was thinking perhaps chiefly of goods. But a moment's thought will suggest how easy it is to extend that insight into the realm of ideas, information, beliefs, and practices—since few material goods travel far without some cultural freight. The long-distance traffic in objects that were thought to confer either cultural prestige or magical powers was probably the oldest kind of transcontinental trade in Afro-Eurasia. Indeed, much of that traffic must have assumed prior knowledge of the status of the goods sought out by their would-be consumers. Thus it was their alertness to the importance that the rulers of Middle Eurasia attached to the conspicuous display of gemstones that created the 'market' for rubies and sapphires in the courts of China.[24] Much the same might be said of the trade in relics and sacred texts that connected the Buddhist world, as it did the Christian. Belief and knowledge preceded 'demand'. Both were the product of the thirst for novelty—in equipment, possessions, or cosmological power—and for the advantages it might bring, that might be thought characteristic of most human societies, unless restrained by isolation, poverty, or prohibition.

The second great trait has been the urge to migrate, from the original migration 'out of Africa' some 70,000 years ago up to the vast flows of migrants, migrant labour, and refugees that make up the 'demographic globalization' of our own day. Migration in search of safety, survival, freedom, prosperity, or simply loot, has surely been one of the great constants of world history. It was the variations in the volume, velocity, direction, and motive of this 'world on the move', and in the regimes that have sought to contain or constrain it, that helped shape the (shifting) patterns of global connectedness as much, perhaps, if not more than those that arose from the exchange of goods and ideas.[25] Indeed, the two are not easy to separate, since both exchange and migration required human vectors; and while both contained the potential to reward those who entered the traffic, they could also subvert, demoralize, or even demolish the rulers and communities that they enveloped. We might note in passing that states and empires were invariably parasitic upon these forms of connectedness, and sought to extend and exploit them. But they were also fearful of their unwanted effects, and much of their administrative apparatus sprang up to surveille and proscribe 'undesirable' kinds of mobility. We will return to this point later on.

[24] Craig Clunas, Jessica Harrison-Hall, and Yu-Ping Luk (eds), *Ming China: Courts and Contacts 1400–1450* (London: British Museum Press, forthcoming 2016).
[25] For a valuable addition to this literature, Jan Lucassen and Leo Lucassen (eds), *Globalising Migration History: The Eurasian Experience (16th–21st Centuries)* (Leiden: Brill, 2014).

If exchange and migration required human vectors they also depended upon, and necessarily created, a more or less dense set of networks, the infrastructure of transmission. That infrastructure was determined in part by the constraints of the physical world, since networks need routes over land or sea (or through the air). Hence no historian of mobility can neglect the changing geography of roads, railways, sea-lanes, telegraph-lines or wireless transmissions, and the influence it exerted. Roads and railways disfavoured mountain, marsh, and jungle and sought out instead ridges, rivers, plateaux, and steppe.[26] The sea might have been a 'wide common over which men may pass in all directions'. But it was also one 'on which some well-worn paths show that controlling reasons have led them to choose certain lines of travel rather than others'.[27] In the sailing ship age, those paths were dictated in part by the seasonal pattern of winds and currents, and the constrictions imposed by navigational hazards.[28] On both land and sea, it was the supply of energy that ruled the volume of traffic. Draught animals needed grass (or a substitute); steamships and railways needed wood or coal; sailing ships needed wind. The result was that communications, and the networks that depended on them, have been channelled into corridors, and sucked towards junctions the alternatives to which were costly, inconvenient or dangerous. Human infrastructure was erected on these physical foundations. All networks required agents as well as principals, and some level of trust between them. They required a 'currency', whether of money, reputation, or faith, to reward their participants and discourage defection. Their institutional needs were governed by the size and shape of the traffic they served: thus (to name only three kinds) chambers of commerce and commercial exchanges; the Singapore doss-houses in which Chinese migrants were held while their indentures were sold; the mission-stations, monasteries, or sufi lodges (*zawiyas*) where the reservoirs of faith were filled up to irrigate the converted or swamp the infidel. Since institutions need resources, the capacity of a network would also depend upon its 'earning power' or its access to wealth or the wealthy.

For the global historian, the attractions of the network are obvious. They permit an escape from the historiographical domination of states and empires and their overbearing archives.[29] A network may evoke a world of artisans, dealers, and traders whose archival footprint is usually quite modest. Amongst elites, it may provide a social and cultural context that helps to explain their decisions and preferences.[30] Networks remind us that non-hierarchical, negotiated worlds coexist with those governed by regulation and rank. They can help us to grasp the scale of subaltern or

[26] Fernand Braudel, *The Mediterranean and the Mediterranean World in the Age of Philip II*, 2 vols, trans. Siân Reynolds (Berkeley: University of California Press, 1995), pp. 53–5; Jos Gommans, *Mughal Warfare: Indian Frontiers and High Roads to Empire, 1500–1700* (London and New York: Routledge, 2002), ch.1.

[27] Alfred T. Mahan, *The Influence of Sea Power upon History* (London: S. Low 1890), p. 25.

[28] For some impression of these, James Horsburgh, *India Directory, or, Directions for Sailing to and from the East Indies, China, New Holland, Cape of Good Hope, Brazil, and the Interjacent Ports*, 3rd edn, (London: Parbury, Allen and Co., 1827).

[29] For emphasis on this point, see Gagan Sood, 'Circulation and Exchange in Islamicate Eurasia', *Past & Present* 212 (2011), pp. 113–62, p. 162.

[30] A classic study is John F. Padgett and Christopher K. Ansell, 'Robust Action and the Rise of the Medici', *American Journal of Sociology* 98, 6 (1993), pp. 1259–319.

subversive movements and the reach of their influence.[31] They reveal, as is now almost commonplace, the permeability of borders, and the multiple (sometimes conflicting) allegiances of historical actors. It is easy to re-imagine a borderless globe populated not by states but by a pullulating mass of networks: administrative, commercial, financial, religious, migrational, scientific, educational, and military—all bound together by investments, remittances, bills of exchange, reports and despatches, telegrams, letters, parcels, newspapers and books, as well as by soldiers and sailors, merchants and salesmen, indentured labourers and slaves, peripatetic officials, wandering scholars, journalists, travellers, and tourists. But as the more rigorous practitioners of network analysis warn us, before we can judge the significance of a network (or even concede its existence) some hard questions must be asked. How extensive is the network? How frequent are the exchanges (of information, personnel, money, or goods) between the different parts of the network? How large is their volume and on what scale of intensity—that is, how important to its members are the exchanges between them? But this is only the start.

Perhaps the crudest distinction drawn between different kinds of network is between those that are 'weak' and those that are 'strong'. A 'weak' network might link a large number of 'nodes' or members, but as with those who lay claim to hundreds if not thousands of virtual 'friends', the bonds and solidarities between them might be fragile at best. We might be tempted to dismiss large 'weak' networks as useless or dysfunctional, and, where they have existed historically, as of little significance. That might be mistaken. Some network analysis suggests that large weak networks can be highly functional if the object is to maximize flows of information (a classic case might be our use of the Web). Those bound together by the circulation of newspapers might have had little else in common. Yet by their use and recirculation of the information received they might (dramatically) strengthen the cohesion of their other connections and networks. Moreover, there is no reason to assume that the conditions in which a network emerges remain constant. An event that promises political or social upheaval can galvanize a weak network, and endow it, if only temporarily, with an intense solidarity. Indeed, a weak network may have the capacity to transform by circulation, repetition, and 'translation' the significance of the event itself. The weak networks that helped mobilize the first crusade[32] or which ignited the 'Arab Spring' as a mass movement might serve as examples.

They might also suggest the importance of distinguishing networks by function, where different rules of connection might apply. Perhaps the obvious distinction lies between networks designed to inform and those intended to coordinate—for example, political, commercial, religious, or migrational action. In the 'real' world, the difference might seem more theoretical than real, since many—maybe most—networks combine both these functions in varying proportions. How effectively they do so (and how they do so) is likely to depend upon the wider 'ecology' of

[31] See Tim N. Harper, 'Singapore, 1915 and the Birth of the Asian Underground' *Modern Asian Studies* 47, 6 (2013), pp. 1782–811.
[32] On which see the suggestive essay by Marcus Bull, 'Origins', in Jonathan S. C. Riley-Smith (ed.), *Oxford History of the Crusades* (Oxford: Oxford University Press, 1999), pp. 15–34.

which a given network is part. The transmission of information, goods or people was always conditioned by at least three larger environmental constraints. The first was geopolitical: the ease or difficulty with which borders could be crossed; the safety or otherwise of long-distance travel; the reception of aliens or immigrants in a foreign jurisdiction; the extent to which movement was facilitated by the protection of large states and empires—the Pax Britannica or the Pax Mongolica. The second was technological: the ease and cost of movement, and (as we saw earlier) the influence that the technologies of movement exerted upon the circuitry of travel (which places were accessible, in what sequence, and in what season), and the realities of distance reckoned as time. The third was cultural, or perhaps primarily linguistic: the availability of a lingua franca and the status of linguistic intermediaries to manage the transition between language zones; the existence, or otherwise, of formal prohibitions such as those that long discouraged the development of printed publications and newspapers in the Ottoman Empire or prevented the circulation of information except that approved as 'Dutch knowledge' in pre-Meiji Japan; the extent to which a scribal elite could exercise a monopoly over the diffusion of information and knowledge.

We might want to ask what it is about a set of connections that would justify describing them as a 'global network'. In an influential article, S. M. Sindbaek contrasted the shape of early medieval networks of communication and exchange with their 'global' successors. The former, he argued, were characterized by the 'thinness' of their connections, and hence their vulnerability; the small number of 'hubs'; the paucity of travellers and the tendency for the same few persons to become 'specialized' travellers.[33] It is a useful reverse template for the global network, but perhaps one that flatters. A modern global network, like a missionary organization, might well depend upon little more than a handful of specialized travellers, some well known to each other. But a more important issue might be how many 'global' networks were or are actually global, in the sense of spanning the world. The changing constraints of geopolitics, technology, and culture were always likely to make them at best 'sub-global', capable of wide but not unlimited reach. That should point to the importance of 'nodes' in a network, and especially of those that functioned as 'choke points', 'bridgeheads', or 'gateways'. These were the locations on a network where it was forced to 'change gear'. They might offer a range of services: the storage and defence of valuable goods as in Saharan oases;[34] the negotiation between widely differing conventions of commercial practice including the forms of currency; the special transport expertise (on land or sea) required to enter unfamiliar or demanding environments; the provision of expertise in language or cultural lore needed for onward connection; or simply market information about regions with which contact was irregular. This kind of node served as a 'transformer', changing the 'voltage' that passed through the network, changing the medium through which its content was transmitted, and perhaps changing its message and substance as well.

---

[33] Søren M. Sindbaek, 'The Small World of the Vikings: Networks in Early Medieval Communications and Exchange', *Norwegian Archaeological Review* 40, 1 (2007), pp. 59–74.

[34] Judith Scheele, 'Traders, Saints and Irrigation: Reflections on Saharan Connectivity', *Journal of African History* 51, 3 (2010), pp. 281–300, p. 289.

We can see these functions most vividly at work in the history of port cities. Port cities existed to collect and distribute flows of goods, information, and people. They grew up at locations arranged along different maritime circuits and throve where long-distance seaborne traffic was most easily transhipped into smaller craft or forms of landward transport—caravan, ox-cart, railway, or lorry. Because they usually linked several different 'interiors' as well as the way stations on the sea-lanes that served them, they attracted a variety of different mercantile groups. Indeed, a striking feature of port cities was how often their merchant elites were drawn from distant locations and had few cultural ties with the local community. Since they traded in knowledge (including religious knowledge) as well as in goods, alongside their banks and exchanges, go-downs, and counting-houses, could be found centres of learning or religious instruction, as well as (in more modern times), post offices, telegraph offices, museums, geographical societies, and botanical gardens. They buzzed with rumour, correspondence, and the scribblings of news-writers. By the mid-nineteenth century, few lacked a printing press, churning out books and newspapers, some intended for faraway readerships strung out along their sea-lanes, river routes, railway lines, and roads.[35] Here was the setting in which multiple networks conducted their business, recruited new partners, and spied out the land.

But for those networks to flourish something more was required than the mutual attraction of their members and nodes. Their fate depended in part upon a larger 'ecology'. Among the most successful port cities were those that could profit from the 'overlap' between very large networks. In the nineteenth-century world, for example, the 'British world' (a zone made up of colonial possessions and the informal spheres where British influence predominated) shared large tracts of the globe with the 'Islamic world' and with the large maritime region occupied by settlers and sojourners from South China, the so-called *Nanyang*. Port cities like Aden, Bombay, or Singapore were outposts of British authority, and hubs in their system of steamships and mail-routes. But they were also key staging posts for the movement of Muslims whether on pilgrimage or in search of employment or learning. Singapore and Hong Kong formed the twin poles of the *Nanyang*: between them flowed a wide stream of migrants and remittances, commerce and philanthropy. It was 'overseas Chinese' in Singapore who helped to endow Hong Kong University and who dreamt of the modernization of China under 'Anglo-Chinese' auspices.[36] As these examples suggest, crucial to the success of port-city networks, and perhaps to global networks more generally, was the geopolitical regime to which they were subject. Those networks might flourish in the absence of empires or predatory states: perhaps the Indian Ocean before 1498 provides an example of this. But (as the same Indian Ocean *after* 1498 reminds us), they were vulnerable to the intrusion of armed interlopers on land or sea and the rivalries they brought with them. The richest merchant in Bengal before 1757 was part of

---

[35] See James Gelvin and Nile Green (eds), *Global Muslims in the Age of Steam and Print* (Berkeley: University of California Press, 2014), p. 13.

[36] See Michael R. Godley, *The Mandarin-Capitalists from Nanyang: Overseas Chinese Enterprise in the Modernization of China 1893–1911* (Cambridge: Cambridge University Press, 1981), p. 13.

the extensive Armenian mercantile network. Plassey ended his reign and he died in prison.[37] By contrast, a regime sympathetic to free movement and free trade, and with the power to enforce them (a parsimonious description of British imperialism) enabled the proliferation of innumerable networks and might even offer them legal protection. It was a Bombay colonial court that upheld the claim of the Aga Khan to the hereditary leadership of the far-flung Ismaili sect, and to the vast tithe income that came with it.[38]

Port cities thus functioned in part as 'vertical nodes': that is, they linked networks at different levels or scales. They connected a mass of 'unofficial' networks to the apparatus of authority and military power—the networks of empire and of the global order of which empires were part. They also serve to remind us that states and empires have many of the characteristics of a 'super-network'. Realistically viewed, empires (whether land-based or sea-borne) were typically a patchwork of tracts, precariously linked by a skein of routes and corridors, beyond which control was much less complete. '[A] *l'origine des grand pays, des grand corps nationaux, il y a toujours une "route"*', said Lucien Febvre.[39] Securing the corridors was the first priority of imperial rule: it was hardly surprising that the earliest forms of imperial map-making were so-called 'route-surveys' or itineraries.[40] Empires existed to exploit the opportunities created by mobility and to control its consequences—so far as they could. Unless they could do both, their time would be short.

* * *

Much of the historiography that we have inherited was fashioned for a world preoccupied with nation-making. It saw history as the rise of discrete and durable structures: constitutions, races, languages, literatures, 'advanced' economies full of railways, bridges, and banks, and, above all, states. The shock of the First World War began to unravel this historical fabric and set off a brief era of exceptional creativity in historical writing. But the uncertainty principle on which J. M. Keynes laid such emphasis in the mid 1930s—that flux and instability were the norm in human affairs—was checked by the outcome of the Second World War which licensed new histories of progress: Marxist, nationalist, liberal, and social democratic. Our own times have revived the sense of uncertainty. They encourage a view of world history as one swept by endless tsunamis of unpredictable change and irresistible force: climatic, epidemic, environmental, ideological, religious, technological, demographic, and geopolitical. The vehicle for many if not most of these is the incessant mobility of human societies. Tracking that mobility across the world through its complex circuits and networks may be the main contribution that

---

[37] Sushil Chaudhury, 'Trading Networks in a Traditional Diaspora: Armenians in India *c.*1600–1800' in Ina B. McCabe, Gelina Harlaftis, and Ioanna P. Minoglou (eds), *Diaspora Entrepreneurial Networks: Four Centuries of History* (Oxford: Berg, 2005).

[38] Nile Green, *Bombay Islam: The Religious Economy of the Western Indian Ocean 1840–1915* (Cambridge: Cambridge University Press, 2011), p. 173.

[39] Lucien Febvre, *La terre et l'évolution humaine* (Paris: Renaissance du livre, 1922), p. 409.

[40] Matthew H. Edney, *Mapping an Empire: The Geographical Construction of British India 1765–1843* (Chicago and London: University of Chicago Press, 1997), pp. 91–6; Ian J. Barrow, *Surveying and Mapping in Colonial Sri Lanka* (New Delhi: Oxford University Press, 2008), pp. 42, 81, 191.

'global' history can make to the wider discipline. But those circuits and networks should also remind us that for historians of every period and specialism understanding mobility is foundational. Why, asks a Saharan historian, should we give precedence to place over movement?[41] Why indeed?

THE ESSAYS IN THIS BOOK

The essays which follow are designed to develop the problematic of global history in different ways. We start with two general methodological discussions. Jürgen Osterhammel and Kevin O'Rourke look at the interrelationship between history and two of the social sciences in turn, historical sociology and economics, as guides for constructing a rigorous analysis of the global; both of them stress the weaknesses as well as the strengths of the contribution of the two social science disciplines in this field, but each shows how the combination with global historical practice strengthens both sides in the research process. Osterhammel sets out six alternative models for a theoretical global history, arguing, in effect, that none of them can work unless they are seen through a sociological lens, and that historical sociology is the best interlocutor: not only because it has a historical dimension by definition, and—importantly—not necessarily a teleological one, but also because it is less locked inside the 'arid idiom' of other strands of sociology. Sociology can add rigour and explanatory power to global history, while the latter can add fluidity and source-based problem-solving to sociology. O'Rourke is impatient both with the lack of interest in history in economics and with the parochialism of much economic history; he sees the advantage of global history precisely as being its capacity to undermine the current trend to national-focussed economic history, in that it recognizes that all states are part of larger-scale, and, already by 1600 (to an extent) global, economic systems. Conversely, economic analysis (he gives the example of price convergencies) can add rigour to historians' vaguer analyses. These two are genuine challenges to historians' assumptions; they also remind us that a key, essential, role for social theory of all kinds, in any analysis done by a historian, is its focus on the parameters of proper—again, rigorous—comparison.

From here, we move in a more 'historical' direction, and chronologically. Nicholas Purcell, Bob Moore, and James Belich discuss ancient and medieval global history. Purcell takes the ancient incense trade, which connected the Mediterranean, east Africa, and south Arabia (with links eastward from there) from at least the sixth century BC, as a model for what he calls 'soft globalization', following de Vries: as a set of more localized interrelationships through nodal points, with few if any traders moving across the whole trade route. He also stresses the degree to which this trade depended on culturally contingent assessments of value and rarity, and thus that economic and cultural history are less separable than many assume, not least when seen with a global perspective. Moore focusses on the importance of the urban revolution of the period 1000–1250 and, above all, the intensification of socio-political

[41] Scheele, 'Saharan Connectivity', p. 284.

relationships and socio-economic practices across the whole of Eurasia in the period 500–1500; he does not believe in the usefulness of the concept of 'medieval' when seen in global terms, but he pinpoints some common features of the 'medieval' centuries nevertheless. Belich offers a transnational case study of the effect of the Black Death on European socio-economic activity. He argues that the plague led to a surge in European commerce, and stresses the importance of multinational migrant groups such as sailors and mercenaries, in what he calls an 'expansion kit'—ships, cannon, smallpox, racism, and risk-taking—which all facilitated European (including Russian, Ottoman, and Moroccan) advances outside the home continent after 1500.

Matthew Mosca and Francis Robinson discuss the early modern world. Both of them look at the issue of the global from non-European perspectives, Qing China and the Islamic world, arguing that each are pivots for understanding global relationships, and globalization in general, perhaps the principal ones until 1800. Mosca makes a strong case for the centrality of Qing China to the globe, given that it had the largest population in the world by far, given that it was the main centre of east Asian trade up to at least 1800 (and with extensions outwards from that), and given that it was the cultural focus for surrounding societies as well. He parallels some of Kenneth Pomeranz's arguments here, although his focus and evidence-base is entirely different. Robinson stresses how the Muslim expansion between the eighth and the eighteenth century was the largest-scale—indeed, the most 'global' if one excludes the Americas—in human history before the eighteenth century; Islamic polities were the pivot of all long-distance economic, religious/legal, and scientific transnational connectivity in those centuries. After 1800, indeed, western conquest helped extend and entrench Islam (and non-religious cultural practices associated with it) still further, in India, Africa, Indonesia, and even America. These two contributions are excellent examples of the decentring of European-focussed historical metanarratives which has been one of the stated aims of global history from the outset; they show us the directions it can take in the future too.

The final two papers offer case studies in how to approach later modern global issues. Antony Hopkins argues against US exceptionalism in its imperial experience, and shows how the United States, particularly after 1898, in fact had just the same sort of empire and colonial experience that the European powers did. For her part, Linda Colley takes on the issue of constitution-making after 1750. Constitutions spread by 'contagion', largely to impress others, initially in the context of the American and French revolutions, then as an image of early nineteenth-century liberalism, and then, dramatically and competitively, everywhere in the world after 1860 or so. She shows clearly how not just economic history, but also political and institutional history, can and must be seen in transnational and global terms as well.

We entirely agree. As the foregoing makes clear, everything can be seen in global terms; and the possibilities and advantages of a global approach are as great in the medieval and early modern periods as they are in the nineteenth and twentieth centuries. The essays offered here show that the prospect of a complex, many-sided, global history of every period is bright.

1

Global History and Historical Sociology

Jürgen Osterhammel

GLOBAL HISTORY'S NEED FOR THEORY

The vision of global history shared by many contributors to the present volume is far from that of an insular sub-discipline settling down into complacent self-sufficiency. It is important to emphasize this point since the growth and internal professionalization of a new field, and especially a successful one, tend to strengthen its sense of autonomy. The very ability to draw upon one's own intellectual resources seems to be the hallmark of emancipation from a paternal master discipline. Yet, as this chapter will argue, such proud independence reflects only in part the achievement of maturity. In more than one sense it is an illusion. Global History[1] has to feed on conceptual inputs from outside its own purview. A major source of theoretical inspiration is historical sociology.

This diagnosis partly results from the situation of Global History in Germany, to some extent also in Austria and Switzerland, a situation that may be representative of a much greater number of countries.[2] Reconstructing the development of Global History only in view of the Anglophone experience provides a somewhat distorted picture. In the German-speaking countries, Global History has evolved neither from imperial history, as in Britain, nor from Western Civilization courses, as in the United States. The old German tradition of world history, from the Göttingen Enlightenment— with August Ludwig Schlözer as its main representative—to the Weimar Republic,[3] was virtually defunct by the late 1980s, and Marxist approaches—the most important alternative route to a universal view of history—were thoroughly discredited after the collapse of communist East Germany where historical materialism remained the

---

[1] 'Global History' written with capital letters denotes the academic discipline and its various discourses, 'global history' its object of study. In the case of 'Historical Sociology' such ambiguity is unlikely to occur; capitals are used only for reasons of symmetry.

[2] Dominic Sachsenmaier, *Global Perspectives on Global History: Theories and Approaches in a Connected World* (Cambridge: Cambridge University Press, 2011), ch. 3; Jürgen Osterhammel, 'Global History in a National Context: The Case of Germany', *Österreichische Zeitschrift für Geschichtswissenschaft* 20 (2009), pp. 40–58.

[3] No individual author can be named for this period. Its main achievement was a cooperative work: Walter Goetz (ed.), *Propyläen-Weltgeschichte: Der Werdegang der Menschheit in Gesellschaft und Staat, Wirtschaft und Geistesleben*, 10 vols (Berlin: Propyläen, 1931–3).

binding party line to the very end.[4] Given this lack of an unbroken tradition, Global History had to be imported, or rather *re*-imported, in the 1990s, to some extent via less ambitious historiographical programmes such as transnational history or *histoire croisée*.[5] Too weak in numerical terms to form a viable sub-discipline it is nowadays increasingly successful with a lay readership, but still finds limited support in school or college curricula, and continues to struggle for acceptance in research and academic teaching beyond a handful of universities.[6] This institutional fragility, however, offers at least one major advantage: it compels practising Global Historians to look for academic allies and to insert their activities as far as possible into cross-disciplinary research. A lack of discursive autarchy and a shallow rootedness in mainstream historiography turn an interdisciplinary orientation into a daily necessity. Global History is never alone.[7]

The situation in Germany, as well as other countries where a 'global turn' is far from being accomplished, highlights the general relationship between Global History and theory. It is important to state that by 'theory' I do not mean the all-encompassing 'grand' theories that claim to hold the answers to almost every problem under the sun, such as Marxism, Niklas Luhmann's theory of social systems, or a comprehensive Foucauldian view of the world.[8] Nor do I have postmodernist Theory (with a capital 'T') in mind—often a peculiar rhetoric rather than a coherent way of reasoning.[9] The extent to which Global History might commit itself to any of those grand theories and attempt, for example, to devise a comprehensive systems theory view of world history[10] is an intriguing matter, but not one to be considered at the moment.

Theory, as the term will be used in this chapter, is a coherent set of explicitly defined concepts—as well as ideas about the application of those concepts to the interpretation and explanation of observable phenomena. Historical observation involves the study of sources and relics, in the broadest possible sense, in the light—and by means—of established and newly emerging tools and methods of research.

---

[4] Jürgen Osterhammel, 'World History', in Axel Schneider and Daniel R. Woolf (eds), *Oxford History of Historical Writing, vol. V: Historical Writing since 1945* (Oxford: Oxford University Press, 2011), pp. 93–112.

[5] For a careful distinction between these (and other) approaches see Margrit Pernau, *Transnationale Geschichte* (Göttingen: Vandenhoeck & Ruprecht, 2011), pp. 36–66.

[6] Hans-Heinrich Nolte, 'Zum Stand der Weltgeschichtsschreibung im deutschen Sprachraum', *Zeitschrift für Weltgeschichte* 8 (2008), pp. 89–113; Matthias Middell and Katja Naumann, 'Global History 2008–2010: Empirische Erträge, konzeptionelle Debatten, neue Synthesen', *Comparativ* 20 (2010), pp. 93–133.

[7] But see the plausible observation that new fields in History seem to renege on their initial interest in theory once they have attained a certain degree of acceptance and routine: Gary Wilder, 'From Optic to Topic: The Foreclosure Effects of Historiographic Turns', *American Historical Review* 117, 3 (2012), pp. 723–45, esp. p. 731.

[8] On the notion of 'grand theory' see Quentin Skinner (ed.), *The Return of Grand Theory* (Cambridge: Cambridge University Press, 1985).

[9] In the critical sense of Daphne Patai and Will H. Corral (eds), *Theory's Empire: An Anthology of Dissent* (New York: Columbia University Press, 2005).

[10] The best starting point for such a venture would be the theory of 'world society' elaborated by one of Luhmann's disciples, Rudolf Stichweh, *Die Weltgesellschaft: Soziologische Analysen* (Frankfurt a.M.: Suhrkamp, 2000).

The main argument to be developed in the following pages will run as follows: Even more than other branches of history, Global History cannot be satisfied with mere description. Whether more explanatory or more interpretive in its general inclination, it always requires theoretical input—usually input it has not generated itself. This is not to resuscitate a sharp dichotomy between sociology as an explanatory, generalizing science and history as a descriptive, particularizing craft oblivious to larger intellectual vistas and destined to carry grist to the sociologists' mills. Still, interdisciplinarity presupposes a cognitive division of labour. Historians are very rarely ambitious and competent originators of big ideas. They look for theoretical inspiration beyond the boundaries of their own turf, and when they borrow theoretical concepts, as William H. Sewell, Jr—who has a foot in both camps—has put it, 'we often find that the concepts don't quite fit, that they need to be adjusted, nuanced, or combined with concepts from other, apparently incompatible, theoretical discourses in order to be useful in historical research'.[11] One major source of such inspiration is, or should be, a special branch of sociology known as Historical Sociology.[12] Before developing that argument, a few words are necessary about Global History and theory in general.

CONCEPTS AND CONSTRUCTIONS IN GLOBAL HISTORY

By its very nature, Global History is a theoretical enterprise. It involves reflection and requires decisions far beyond the needs of ordinary historical casework. None of its parameters can be treated as given or sanctioned by tacit conventions among the community of scholars. At least three such parameters demand constant attention and fine-tuning: time, space, and the mix of analytical approaches.

(1) Time frames and periodization are open to the constructivist intentions—though not the unbridled fancy—of the historian since the accustomed temporalities of national or continental (for example, European) history will no longer do. Global history challenges the temporal imagination.[13]

[11] William H. Sewell, Jr, *Logics of History: Social Theory and Social Transformation* (Chicago and London: University of Chicago Press, 2005), p. 5.
[12] The best introductions are Charles Tilly, 'Historical Sociology', in Neil J. Smelser and Paul B. Baltes (eds), *International Encyclopedia of the Social and Behavioral Sciences*, vol. 10 (Amsterdam: Elsevier, 2001), pp. 6753–7; Richard Lachmann, *What Is Historical Sociology?* (Cambridge: Polity Press, 2013); Theda Skocpol (ed.), *Vision and Method in Historical Sociology* (Cambridge: Cambridge University Press, 1984); Dennis Smith, *The Rise of Historical Sociology* (Cambridge: Polity Press, 1991); Craig Calhoun, 'The Rise and Domestication of Historical Sociology', in Terrence J. McDonald (ed.), *The Historic Turn in the Human Sciences* (Ann Arbor: University of Michigan Press, 1996), pp. 305–37; Gerard Delanty and Engin F. Isin (eds), *Handbook of Historical Sociology* (London: Sage, 2003); Rainer Schützeichel, *Historische Soziologie* (Bielefeld: Transcript, 2004); Walter L. Bühl, *Historische Soziologie: Theoreme und Methoden* (Münster: LIT Verlag, 2003).
[13] See the chapter on time in Jürgen Osterhammel, *The Transformation of the World: A Global History of the Nineteenth Century* (Princeton and Oxford: Princeton University Press 2014), pp. 45–76. Two important articles are William A. Green, 'Periodization in European and World History', *Journal of World History* 3, 1 (1992), pp. 13–53; Jerry H. Bentley, 'Cross-Cultural Interaction and Periodization in World History', *American Historical Review* 101, 3 (1996), pp. 749–70. On the undermining of schematic periodization by more flexible 'temporalities' see Helge Jordheim, 'Against Periodization:

(2) Likewise, the spaces of Global History are anything but self-evident. One of its great attractions to those fleeing the iron cage of conventional thinking and research about the past is the almost infinite variety of spatial units and levels at the global historian's disposal. Only a vulgar misunderstanding could accuse Global History of being inexorably drawn towards the largest possible picture. Global History is not to be confused with 'macro history', that is, the history of vast spaces, long periods of time, and colossal issues.[14] To quote the famous title of Donald R. Wright's study on the Kingdom of Niumi in The Gambia: the world *and* 'a very small place in Africa' (or anywhere else) can be accommodated within one and the same analytical framework.[15]

(3) A third dimension requiring decisions that do not spontaneously emerge from carefully contemplating the sources is the plurality of approaches in the repertoire of the global historian and the specific mix of those approaches. The vehement battles between social and cultural historians that marked the 1980s and 1990s look dated when held against the flexible combination of purportedly contradictory approaches in the better class of global history literature. In a similar vein, a history of discourses and a history of material culture do not seem to be as incompatible as many, until recently, were wont to believe. While Global History is not a sponge waiting to absorb anything that comes its way, it basically assumes a multi-faceted point of view and rejects crude alternatives: society vs. culture, structure vs. agency, and so on. Yet, combining different aspects—and sub-disciplines within historical scholarship—in a more than additive way entails careful considerations that one should not hesitate to call 'theoretical'.[16] If Global History is a special, cross-cutting or lateral way of devising questions, these questions can rarely be answered from within conventional self-contained discourses. To give just one example: a global economic history can even less afford to ignore 'culture', in the sense of knowledge, rules of conduct, or value orientations, than economic history in a national mould. In that sense, the questions themselves should have some theoretical content.

Koselleck's Theory of Multiple Temporalities', *History & Theory* 51, 2 (2012), pp. 151–71; from a different theoretical angle: Jon May and Nigel J. Thrift (eds), *Timespace: Geographies of Temporality* (London and New York: Routledge, 2001). A stimulating collection is Chris Lorenz and Berber Bevernage (eds), *Breaking up Time: Negotiating the Borders between Present, Past and Future* (Göttingen: Vandenhoeck & Ruprecht, 2013), including the chapter 'Globalisation and Time' by Lynn Hunt (pp. 199–215).

[14] Which again is different from Big History; a history of unlimited temporal depth linking the history of mankind with that of nature as such. On macro history see Charles Tilly, *Big Structures, Large Processes, Huge Comparisons* (New York: Russell Sage Foundation, 1984), and a collection of chapters on various historical topics: Randall Collins, *Macrohistory: Essays in Sociology of the Long Run* (Stanford, CA: Stanford University Press, 1999).

[15] Donald R. Wright: *The World and a Very Small Place in Africa: A History of Globalization in Niumi, The Gambia* (Armonk, NY and London: Sharpe, 2010). There are now numerous examples linking (in concrete detail) what sociologists differentiate schematically as 'macro', 'meso', and 'micro' levels. An interesting discussion is Lara Putnam, 'To Study the Fragments/Whole: Microhistory and the Atlantic World', *Journal of Social History* 39, 3 (2006), pp. 615–30.

[16] However, Sebastian Conrad in his superb mapping of the field argues that the very catholicity and inclusiveness of Global History has blunted efforts to provide it with a clear-cut theoretical profile: *Globalgeschichte: Eine Einführung* (Munich: C. H. Beck, 2013), p. 88.

But where does theory come from? Usually, historians are importers, consumers, and appliers of concepts generated within non-historical disciplinary contexts. They are rational and discriminating shoppers at the marketplace of theory. The terms and concepts they use are borrowed and derivative: obtained from sociology, anthropology, economics, philosophy, political science, religious studies, or whatever else might be pertinent to the study of a given problem. There is nothing objectionable about that. History can tolerate the pleasures of controlled eclecticism. It suffers whenever it is chained to theoretical orthodoxy. At the other extreme, it becomes dull when practised in the spirit of a craftsman-like empiricism, disdaining any kind of broader intellectual aspiration. Global History should steer clear of both dogma and of the kind of superficial *naiveté* that is content with a good 'global' story expertly told or, worse, with a jumble of facts and images.

When historians use other people's theories, they seldom simply apply them in a straightforward way. They mostly prefer what the American sociologist Dietrich Rueschemeyer has called 'usable theory' or 'empirical social theory'[17]—concepts that do not inhabit a space totally sealed off from the real world. They make those theories even more useful by adapting them to specific analytical purposes. In a way, theory comes into its own by being used for goals that lie outside its own auto-referential circle. Historians defer to the theorists' superior powers of abstract construction. But their handling of language tends to be more subtle and flexible than is often the case in today's systematic social sciences—with the partial example of anthropology and certain kinds of sociology where literary ambition has not been entirely forsaken. Historians embed variables and generalities into narratives. Rather than the antithesis of theory, narration is a potent medium of theoretical integration.

Conceptual innovation ought to constitute a major aim of the humanities under *any* circumstances. Global History can proudly display an assortment of novelties of that kind ranging from the 'settler revolution' (James Belich) and the 'Eurasian revolution' (John Darwin) to the 'mosquito empire' (John R. McNeill). Still, concepts such as these rarely form part of systematic theory-building. Historians may generate and successfully promote concepts or models of medium-range validity—J. G. A. Pocock's 'language of politics', Eric Hobsbawm and Terence Ranger's 'invention of tradition', Alfred Crosby's 'Columbian exchange' or Jan de Vries's 'industrious revolution' are celebrated examples—but they seldom propose entire terminologies or *systems* of terms and propositions, in other words, theories. In world history writing, one counts only three heroic attempts at creating a new language—if not necessarily a fully articulated 'theory'—to accompany a novel approach to history: by Arnold J. Toynbee in the earlier volumes of his *A Study in History*,[18] by the now forgotten German world historian Kurt

---

[17] Dietrich Rueschemeyer, *Usable Theory: Analytic Tools for Social and Political Research* (Princeton, NJ and Oxford: Princeton University Press, 2009), p. 1.
[18] Arnold J. Toynbee, *A Study of History*, 12 vols (London: Oxford University Press, 1934–61), esp. vols 1–2 (1934); see William H. McNeill, *Arnold J. Toynbee: A Life* (New York and Oxford: Oxford University Press, 1989).

Breysig (1866–1940),[19] and by the Australian economist and systems theorist Graeme Donald Snooks.[20] All three of them failed to win a conspicuous number of followers, at least among historians.[21] Historians seem to be ill equipped to enter the competition for comprehensive theorizing.

GLOBAL HISTORY AND HISTORICAL SOCIOLOGY: A FEW SHARED INTERESTS

Historical Sociology is only a marginal sub-discipline within sociology, in any country located at some distance from the centre of the profession. It is as peripheral as Global History continues to be within historical studies in many national systems of research and education. So why is it attractive as an interlocutor for Global History—regardless of the fact that historical sociologists may have an interest in Global History for their own reasons? Five points are of special importance.

(1) An excellent Italian overview of the classics of Historical Sociology carries the title *La storia comparata*.[22] Indeed, Historical Sociology, counting scholars like Max Weber and the German historian Otto Hintze among its founding fathers, boasts a long experience with comparison and its methodology.[23] At a time when historians still frowned upon comparison, or were at most willing to consider *two* national paths within a common analytical framework, historical sociologists developed intricate procedures of macro-historical comparison. This kind of literature—represented by Barrington Moore, Charles Tilly, Theda Skocpol, Jack Goldstone, or Michael Mann—achieved prominence during what has been called a 'second wave' of Historical Sociology—after the 'first wave' of the classics of Weber's and Hintze's

[19] Breysig's monumental works are difficult to read—even for Germans—and one is grateful for an overview: Bernhard vom Brocke, *Kurt Breysig: Geschichtswissenschaft zwischen Historismus und Soziologie* (Lübeck: Matthiesen, 1971).

[20] Graeme Donald Snooks, *Longrun Dynamics: A General Economic and Political Theory* (Basingstoke and London: Macmillan, 1998); Graeme Donald Snooks, *The Laws of History* (London and New York: Routledge, 1998); Graeme Donald Snooks, *Global Transition: A General Theory of Economic Development* (Basingstoke and London: Macmillan, 1999). For an essay on how economic and global historians could learn from each other, see O'Rourke in this volume.

[21] A global historian who is particularly sensitive towards questions of terminology and naming is Hans-Heinrich Nolte. See, for instance, his innovative *Weltgeschichte des 20. Jahrhunderts* (Vienna, Cologne, and Weimar: Böhlau, 2009).

[22] Pietro Rossi (ed.), *La storia comparata: Approci e prospettive* (Milan: Il Saggiatore, 1990).

[23] On the history of comparative macro-sociology see Jürgen Osterhammel, 'Transkulturell vergleichende Geschichtswissenschaft', in Heinz-Gerhard Haupt and Jürgen Kocka (eds), *Geschichte im Vergleich* (Frankfurt a.M. and New York: Campus, 1996), pp. 271–313, reprinted in my book *Geschichtswissenschaft jenseits des Nationalstaats: Studien zu Beziehungsgeschichte und Zivilisationsvergleich*, 2nd edn (Göttingen: Vandenhoeck & Ruprecht, 2002), pp. 11–45; Jürgen Osterhammel, 'Gesellschaftsgeschichte und Historische Soziologie', in Jürgen Osterhammel, Dieter Langewiesche, and Paul Nolte (eds), *Wege der Gesellschaftsgeschichte* (Göttingen: Vandenhoeck & Ruprecht, 2006), pp. 81–102.

generation at the beginning of the twentieth century, lasting from the late 1960s to the early 1990s.[24]

(2) Historical Sociology has for a long time been far less Eurocentric than mainstream historiography. While some of the greatest protagonists of Historical Sociology, Norbert Elias foremost among them,[25] largely disregarded the non-European world, others followed in the footsteps of Max Weber whose comparative studies on, for example, the city, capitalism, music, or the world religions set standards for a sociology of universal scope.[26] Representatives of such a truly cosmopolitan vision include Shmuel N. Eisenstadt, Jóhann Páll Árnason, or the sociologist of religion Robert N. Bellah—all three of them, interestingly, students of Japan. They provide models for transcending the West or, more generally, for overcoming *any* kind of parochialism, including that of area studies or oriental philologies.

(3) One outcome of such a globalizing attitude has been the attempt to pluralize the sociological mainstream's pet concepts of modernization and modernity. The idea of *multiple* modernities is chiefly associated with Eisenstadt's later work,[27] but it had already been implicit in a few earlier contributions to Historical Sociology. A long-term consideration of different developmental paths and a respect for the empirical historical record cast doubt on unilinearity and homogeneity in the course of societal evolution. Global Historians have much to contribute to this discussion.[28]

(4) Historical Sociology has shared the general infatuation of social scientists with the idea of globalization ever since the pioneering days when that concept was elaborated by a startling generation of original thinkers.[29] However,

---

[24] On the second wave see Julia Adams, Elisabeth S. Clemens, and Ann Shola Orloff, 'Introduction: Social Theory, Modernity, and the Three Waves of Historical Sociology', in Julia Adams, Elisabeth S. Clemens, and Ann Shola Orloff (eds), *Remaking Modernity: Politics, History, and Sociology* (Durham, NC: Duke University Press, 2005), pp. 1–72, at pp. 15–22.

[25] Followers of Elias later extended the master's scope, especially Johan Goudsblom and his school.

[26] Even those early 'cosmopolitan' authors, from Karl Marx to Fernand Braudel, are, of course, Eurocentrically biased if judged by very strict standards. See Jack Goody, *The Theft of History* (Cambridge: Cambridge University Press, 2006). For most of what global historians need to know about Weber see Stephen Kalberg, *Max Weber's Comparative-Historical Sociology* (Cambridge: Polity Press, 1994).

[27] Shmuel N. Eisenstadt, 'Multiple Modernities', *Daedalus* 129, 1 (2000), pp. 1–30; Shmuel N. Eisenstadt, 'Some Observations on Multiple Modernities', in Dominic Sachsenmaier, Jens Riedel, and Shmuel N. Eisenstadt (eds), *Reflections on Multiple Modernities: European, Chinese and Other Interpretations* (Leiden: Brill, 2002), pp. 28–41; and the essays collected in Shmuel N. Eisenstadt, *Comparative Civilizations and Multiple Modernities*, 2 vols (Leiden: Brill, 2003). A good discussion is Thomas Schwinn, 'Multiple Modernities: Konkurrierende Thesen und offene Fragen. Ein Literaturbericht in konstruktiver Absicht', *Zeitschrift für Soziologie* 38, 6 (2009), pp. 454–76. Therborn made the interesting suggestion to distinguish between different modernities not by institutions and values but according to their concepts of time: Göran Therborn, 'Entangled Modernities', *European Journal of Social Theory* 6, 3 (2003), pp. 293–305.

[28] See also Wolfgang Knöbl, *Die Kontingenz der Moderne: Wege in Europa, Asien und Amerika* (Frankfurt a.M. and New York: Campus, 2007), pp. 70–110.

[29] For summaries of the path-breaking work of that first generation of globalization studies see David Held, Anthony McGrew, David Goldblatt, and Jonathan Perraton, *Globalization: Key Concepts* (London: Foreign Policy Centre, 1999); David Goldblatt, and Jonathan Perraton, *Global*

at a time when only a handful of historians made themselves heard in the surging debate, historical sociologists were among the first to warn against exaggerated fantasies of the unprecedented novelty of 'global modernity' and the blessings of a futuristic 'global age', ungrounded in any previous human experience.

(5) Finally, one particular name has to be mentioned. Nobody has been more influential in building bridges between incipient global perspectives in history and sociology than Immanuel Wallerstein—a sociologist who developed a very serious involvement with historical research and who gained the respect of one of the greatest historians of the twentieth century, Fernand Braudel.[30] Whatever one may think of Wallerstein and his unwavering theoretical quest[31]—he served as an eye-opener and inspiration to many, especially among a generation that had become alerted to new or persisting inequalities on a global scale in the wake of decolonization. Wallerstein reinvigorated historical sociology in the early 1970s by taking, as one of his most perspicacious critics has put it, 'the long historic view, one that identifies enduring cycles, tendencies, structures, and the patterns of structural change',[32] he added historical depth to the emerging studies of global connections 'after empire'.

Today, Historical Sociology is not a homogenous field. It went through a 'third wave' during the 1990s when new authors, new sensibilities, and new subjects came to the fore, when comparison was attacked in the name of more relational approaches, when postmodernist aspersions were cast on the preference for vast master narratives, and when the battle between culturalists and adherents of rational choice unsettled the placid structuralism of an earlier generation of scholars. Three authoritative collections of articles, published in the first decade of the new century, projected quite different images of Historical Sociology—ranging between the allegedly polar opposites of explanation vs interpretation, structure vs agency, and macro vs micro levels.[33] For historians, this kind of plurality should be

Transformations: Politics, Economics and Culture (Cambridge: Polity Press, 1999); Jan Aart Scholte, *Globalization: A Critical Introduction* (Basingstoke and New York: Palgrave, 2000); Roland Robertson and Kathleen E. White (eds), *Globalization: Critical Concepts in Sociology*, 6 vols (London and New York: Routledge, 2003).

[30] Wallerstein's own reflections are to be found in Immanuel Wallerstein, 'From Sociology to Historical Social Science: Prospects and Obstacles', *British Journal of Sociology* 51, 1 (2000), pp. 25–35; Immanuel Wallerstein, 'Wegbeschreibung der Analyse von Weltsystemen, oder: Wie vermeidet man, eine Theorie zu werden?' trans. Hans-Heinrich Nolte, *Zeitschrift für Weltgeschichte* 2, 2 (2001), pp. 9–31 (from an unpublished English manuscript).

[31] Volume IV of his tetralogy 'The Modern World System' seems to have (so far) gone almost unnoticed. It is not really the 'global' interpretation of the nineteenth century many of his adherents had hoped for: Immanuel Wallerstein, *The Modern World-System, vol. IV: Centrist Liberalism Triumphant, 1789–1914* (Berkeley, Los Angeles and London: University of California Press, 2011).

[32] William I. Robinson, 'Globalization and the Sociology of Immanuel Wallerstein: A Critical Appraisal', *International Sociology* 26, 6 (2011), pp. 723–45, at p. 742, see also Immanuel Wallerstein's response: 'Robinson's Critical Appraisal Appraised', *International Sociology* 27, 4 (2012), pp. 524–8.

[33] James Mahoney and Dietrich Rueschemeyer (eds), *Comparative Historical Analysis in the Social Sciences* (Cambridge: Cambridge University Press, 2003); Delanty and Isin, *Handbook of Historical Sociology*; Adams et al., *Remaking Modernity*. For a comparison and classification of current approaches, see Willfried Spohn, 'Historical and Comparative Sociology in a Globalizing World', *Historická*

welcome rather than troubling. It testifies to the vitality of a field where no single theoretical orientation has gained the upper hand.

SIX TYPES OF GLOBAL HISTORY: THEIR SPECIFIC NEEDS FOR THEORY

Global History is no unitary and monolithic discourse either.[34] Practising Global Historians are likely to find it difficult to agree on a definition that goes beyond the claim that Global History is an approach to the past that is non-Eurocentric and focussed on long-distance connectivity across national and cultural boundaries. Under such a spacious roof, several different historiographical styles live in peaceful coexistence. A cursory glance at the leading journals and at the shelves of any well-stocked academic bookshop will already reveal divergent types of Global History or world history.[35] They also differ in their need of and demand for theory, as the six types identified below demonstrate.

Comprehensive histories. This first type needs very little theory since it does not aim at explanation and is often limited to a collection of data and materials fitted into a rough temporal framework of periods and stages. These are histories of 'something' on a worldwide canvas: a commodity, an institution, an idea, and so on (*Alcohol in World History*, or *A World History of the Family*).[36] This kind of literature can offer fascinating insights. If expertly done, it requires a certain technical 'field knowledge'. To take up the examples just mentioned, it would be impossible to write about alcohol or the family in world history without a good understanding of oenology or demography. But what one does *not* need for considering any given topic in a 'world historical'—in other words, a comprehensive—perspective, is a more general brand of theory that accounts for patterns and prime movers of change.

Universal histories. A second type of Global History is made up of reconstructions of the evolution of humankind as a whole and its cultural ecumene, including ideas of global unity and a common human destiny. As a continuation of the

---

Sociologie 1 (2009), pp. 9–27, at pp. 10–13. For an entirely different typology of strands within Historical Sociology, see Tilly, 'Historical Sociology', p. 6753.

[34] This becomes apparent in any survey of the field: Conrad, *Globalgeschichte*; Sachsenmaier, *Global Perspectives on Global History*; Andrea Komlosy, *Globalgeschichte: Methoden und Theorien* (Vienna, Cologne, and Weimar: Böhlau, 2011); Sebastian Conrad, Andreas Eckert, and Ulrike Freitag (eds), *Globalgeschichte: Theorien, Ansätze, Themen* (Frankfurt a.M. and New York: Campus, 2007); Jürgen Osterhammel, 'Globalgeschichte', in Hans-Jürgen Goertz (ed.), *Geschichte: Ein Grundkurs*, 3rd edn (Reinbek: Rowohlt, 2007), pp. 592–610; Patrick Manning, *Navigating World History: Historians Create a Global Past* (New York: Palgrave, 2003).

[35] German authors tend to distinguish between Global History as a history of connectedness and World History as a more general history of civilizations, whereas international usage seems to conflate the two terms preferring a broader concept of global history—or what the Enlightenment called 'general' history.

[36] Two recent examples chosen at random: Gina Hames, *Alcohol in World History* (London and New York: Routledge, 2012); Mary Jo Maynes and Ann Waltner, *The Family: A World History* (Oxford and New York: Oxford University Press, 2012). The multi-volume *New Oxford World History* (to which the Maynes and Waltner volume belongs) seems to take such a line.

Enlightenment's 'history of man' and of nineteenth-century evolutionism, this kind of rejuvenated 'universal history' makes considerable demands on theory. It presupposes a material philosophy of history or even, in the case of 'big history', of cosmological development in the very long run.[37] Philosophies of such a 'neo-Hegelian' kind are rarely offered by philosophers today,[38] but they are sometimes advanced by sociologists.[39] They have to address the question of what constitutes the overall unity of history during the period of the unification of the globe, but preferably also in earlier ages when planetary awareness was still lacking. One possible answer is the idea of 'world society' as the largest possible horizon of human activity.[40] Professional historians seldom dare to step on such treacherous ground. But the public from time to time demands sweeping visions of where we come from and which way we are heading. The popularity of authors such as Jared Diamond or Ian Morris testifies to these expectations.

Movement histories. A third type is composed of histories of transnational and global movements: political movements of global reach such as socialism, communism, feminism, or anti-colonialism,[41] but also the rise of globally adopted (and adapted) practices such as organized sports.[42] This approach, which is mostly organizational history with a firm rooting in institutional sources, in spite of its descriptive proclivities, is likely to profit from concepts of transfer, of translation, and of agency in varying contexts.

Competition histories. A fourth type comprises histories of material progress and backwardness and of the translation of materiality into power.[43] Any writings dealing with the European Miracle, the Great Divergence, the rise of Asia, or hegemonic cycles come under that heading. This type is rigorously comparative and thus closely related to 'second wave' Historical Sociology. All authors share a concern with progress and backwardness, with power differentials and with actual or

---

[37] On Big History see the brief sketch Fred Spier, 'Big History', in Douglas Northrop (ed.), *A Companion to World History* (Malden, MA, Oxford, and Chichester: Wiley-Blackwell, 2012), pp. 171–84.

[38] An exception was Ernest Gellner, *Plough, Sword and Book: The Structure of Human History* (London: Collins Harvill, 1988).

[39] Stephen K. Sanderson, *Social Transformations: A General Theory of Historical Development* (Oxford: Blackwell, 1995); Niklas Luhmann, *Theory of Society*, vol. 2, trans. Rhodes Barrett (Stanford, CA: Stanford University Press, 2013 [first German edition 1997]), pp. 27–131.

[40] A good survey of concepts of world society (especially John W. Meyer, Niklas Luhmann, and his school) is Theresa Wobbe, *Weltgesellschaft* (Bielefeld: Transcript, 2000).

[41] For example Robert Strayer, *The Communist Experiment: Revolution, Socialism, and Global Conflict in the Twentieth Century* (Boston, MA: McGraw-Hill, 2007); Gerd Koenen, *Was war der Kommunismus?* (Göttingen: Vandenhoeck & Ruprecht, 2010); with relatively little historical depth: Pierre Hamel, Henri Lustiger-Thaler, and Jan Nederveen Pieterse (eds), *Globalization and Social Movements* (Basingstoke: Palgrave, 2001).

[42] Allen Guttmann, *The Olympics: A History of the Modern Games*, 2nd edn (Urbana, IL and Chicago: University of Illinois Press, 2002); David Goldblatt, *The Ball Is Round: A Global History of Football* (London: Viking, 2006); Maarten van Bottenburg, *Global Games*, trans. Beverley Jackson (Urbana IL and Chicago: University of Illinois Press, 2001).

[43] There is probably no need for detailed references here. A good overview is Peer H. H. Vries, 'Global Economic History: A Survey', in Axel Schneider and Daniel R. Woolf (eds), *Oxford History of Historical Writing*, vol. V (2011), pp. 113–35, and also Peer H. H. Vries, *Escaping Poverty: The Origins of Modern Economic Growth* (Göttingen: Vandenhoeck & Ruprecht, 2013), which is partly a detailed critique of all the major authors in the field.

virtual rivalry between civilizations or economic regions. History is basically seen as jockeying for the top position in a global ranking competition. Several prominent combatants in the ongoing debate have a disciplinary background in sociology, though the majority are (economic) historians. Even the economic historians do not directly import concepts from the theory of economic growth. Most of them reject mono-causal reasoning and excessively general models and strive for their own personal version of 'a giant combination lock'[44] that might offer access to the secrets of Europe's ascendancy in modern times. The state of the art is presently an economic and ecological interpretation incorporating political/institutional and cultural aspects, 'culture' mostly meaning a religiously driven work ethic in the Weberian tradition.

Of the six types of Global History distinguished here, this has been the most successful in generating its own syncretistic theory, in many cases based on paradigms from classical 'political' economy (Adam Smith, Thomas R. Malthus, Joseph A. Schumpeter, et al.). Where it is manifestly dependent on sociology and anthropology is in determining the units of comparison. This makes the issue of 'civilizational arenas' almost unavoidable. Nowadays, the concept of 'civilization'—understood as a bounded macro-unit—has fallen out of favour, although the booming 'varieties of capitalism' literature is contributing to a modest revival, and books on 'Islamic capitalism' or 'Confucian capitalism' enjoy undiminished popularity. Comparisons are preferably drawn between sub-national regions such as Southern England and the Lower Yangzi. Still, whenever 'the West' and its competitive record make an appearance,[45] the issue of 'civilization' is at stake and resists an answer in terms of mere common sense. Even in economic history, reflections on civilizational boundaries and identities cannot be dismissed as pedantic trifles.[46] Global Historians owe clarity to their readers.

Network histories. A fifth type are histories of expansion, or to put it in less old-fashioned terms, histories of large-scale systems-building: of huge, often transcontinental, empires, migration systems, technical networks of communication, city networks, the world economy or, as *sub*systems of the world economy, of global trade, or a global financial system. The key term here is the 'network'. What is needed, therefore, is a non-technical approach to network analysis that makes it possible to describe networks and tell stories about their members without foregoing the advantages of a limited amount of quantification and formalism: networks always presuppose a multiplicity of participants and a certain degree of order and

---

[44] Eric L. Jones, *The European Miracle: Environments, Economies and Geopolitics in the History of Europe and Asia*, 3rd edn (Cambridge: Cambridge University Press, 2003), p. 238.

[45] This occurs less frequently now than in the past, but see Jack A. Goldstone, *Why Europe? The Rise of the West in World History, 1500–1850* (Boston, MA: McGraw-Hill, 2008); Niall Ferguson, *Civilization: The West and the Rest* (London: Allen Lane, 2011).

[46] There is a lot of material but little analysis in Brett Bowden, *The Empire of Civilization: The Evolution of an Imperial Idea* (Chicago and London: University of Chicago Press, 2009); a concise discussion is Bruce Mazlish, *Civilization and Its Contents* (Stanford: Stanford University Press, 2004). On the concept of the West see Alastair Bonnett, *The Idea of the West: Culture, Politics and History* (Basingstoke: Palgrave Macmillan, 2004); Jacinta O'Hagan, *Conceptualizing the West in International Relations: From Spengler to Said* (Basingstoke: Palgrave Macmillan, 2002).

regularity in the interaction among them.[47] If it chooses to ignore such an approach, history misses a bridge towards the systematic social sciences. Whether, and to what extent, general theories of 'globalization' are helpful to the historian is a related but distinct topic.[48]

Connection histories. Finally, a growing share of Global History literature is made up of histories of transfers and connections—perhaps in numerical terms this is the most significant class of studies today. Unlike the previous type, they do not necessarily involve two-dimensional systems and networks. Analysing a complex commodity chain is already a considerable challenge, even if it is not embedded in a truly systemic configuration.[49] The focus of connection histories is narrower than that of network histories. This enables them to identify and trace specific causal relationships. A good example is Lynn Hunt's attempt to be as precise as possible in inserting a global element into the usual internalist interpretations of the outbreak of the French Revolution of 1789.[50] Connection histories are frequently to be found in studies of migration and diasporas as they follow a group of migrants from their place of origin to their destination. They also play a considerable role in the global history of ideas where dissemination, especially in early stages, often occurs through individual contacts rather than by way of elaborate networks that demand 'a wider investigation than any single point of interface'.[51]

'Connectivity' has emerged as the signature concept of the sixth approach. If a plenary assembly of Global Historians were asked to choose the one central concept defining the field, the majority is likely to vote for 'connectivity'. In contrast to 'network histories' this category has received little theoretical attention and is mostly used in a casual way. Describing connections is not particularly demanding in terms of theory. But when the aim is explanation, things become more difficult. From an infinite number of connections in the universe, we are then interested in a much smaller number of *effective* connections with causative power. Therefore, connectivity is, or should be, a concept encompassing explanation.

In the cases of familiar mega-events such as the French Revolution or early industrialization, Global History has detected a wider context of impacting factors. The French Revolution, for a long time seen as a domestic conflict in Paris

[47] See, for example, John Scott, *Social Network Analysis*, 3rd edn (Los Angeles: Sage, 2012); John Scott and Peter J. Carrington (eds), *The SAGE Handbook of Social Network Analysis* (Los Angeles: Sage, 2011); a more formal approach in David Easley and Jon Kleinberg, *Networks, Crowds and Markets: Reasoning about a Highly Connected World* (Cambridge: Cambridge University Press, 2010).
[48] But see as a preliminary statement: Jürgen Osterhammel, 'Globalizations', in Jerry H. Bentley (ed.), *Oxford Handbook of World History* (Oxford: Oxford University Press, 2011), pp. 89–104.
[49] Steven C. Topik and Allen Wells, 'Commodity Chains in a Global Economy', in Emily Rosenberg (ed.), *A World Connecting, 1870–1945* (Cambridge, MA and London: Harvard University Press, 2012), pp. 593–812.
[50] Lynn Hunt, 'The Global Financial Origins of 1789', in Suzanne Desan, Lynn Hunt, and William Max Nelson (eds), *The French Revolution in Global Perspective* (Ithaca, NY and London: Cornell University Press, 2013), pp. 32–43.
[51] Samuel Moyn and Andrew Sartori, 'Approaches to Global Intellectual History', in Samuel Moyn and Andrew Sartori (eds), *Global Intellectual History* (New York: Columbia University Press, 201), pp. 3–30, at p. 13.

and the provinces, is now regarded as part of a wider Revolutionary Atlantic with repercussions from the distant 'periphery' on the metropole.[52] The Industrial Revolution is inserted into the vast scenarios of a global history of cotton textiles or of a transcontinental concatenation of coerced and (more or less) free labour.[53] In a different field, Global History undermines Western claims to matchless cultural originality by demonstrating the non-European origins of innovations such as perspective in painting, which the German art historian Hans Belting believes to be based on Arabic conceptions of light.[54]

Transfers such as the transmission of optical knowledge from the Near East to early Renaissance Italy—or the activities along any commodity chain—rarely just 'happen'. Their close description and, even more, their explanation raise all sorts of intricate issues. One way of linking up with current sociological theory would be to experiment with the concept of 'mechanism' that occupies a central role in so-called 'analytical sociology'.[55] That concept, still lacking a unanimous definition, covers only a small range of human motivation and will always remain suspicious to humanistic historians. At the same time, it has the great advantage of identifying and isolating for analytical purposes the 'typical' combinations of causes that bring about certain outcomes with a high degree of likelihood and regularity.[56]

In a similar vein Reinhart Koselleck, the great German theorist of time and historical semantics, urged historians to pay attention to recurrences and 'structures of repetition' (*Wiederholungsstrukturen*).[57] Koselleck would have been the last person to deny historical individuality. What he meant to say was that between strict determinism ('laws of history') and the total freedom of individual choice lies a wide intermediate space where the repetitive logics of limited spheres—such as markets, bureaucracies, churches, ecosystems—are brought together in ever-changing combinations to produce 'history'. It would be worthwhile to look at transfers, transmissions, and other forms of connectivity in the light of such considerations.

[52] David Armitage and Sanjay Subrahmanyam (eds), *The Age of Revolutions in Global Context, c.1760–1840* (New York: Palgrave Macmillan, 2010); Wim Klooster, *Revolutions in the Atlantic World: A Comparative History* (New York and London: New York University Press, 2009).
[53] Joseph E. Inikori: *Africans and the Industrial Revolution in England: A Study in International Trade and Economic Development* (Cambridge: Cambridge University Press, 2002); Giorgio Riello and Prasannan Parthasarathi (eds), *The Spinning World: A Global History of Cotton Textiles, 1200–1850* (Oxford and New York: Oxford University Press, 2009); Giorgio Riello, *Cotton: The Fabric that Made the Modern World* (Cambridge: Cambridge University Press. 2013); Sven Beckert, *Empire of Cotton: A New History of Global Capitalism* (London: Allen Lane, 2014).
[54] Hans Belting, *Florence and Baghdad: Renaissance Art and Arab Science*, trans. Deborah Lucas Schneider (Cambridge, MA: Harvard University Press, 2011).
[55] Peter Hedström, *Dissecting the Social: On the Principles of Analytical Sociology* (Cambridge: Cambridge University Press, 2005); Peter Hedström and Richard Swedberg (eds), *Social Mechanisms: An Analytical Approach to Social Theory* (Cambridge: Cambridge University Press, 1998); Peter Hedström and Peter Bearman (eds), *The Oxford Handbook of Analytical Sociology* (Oxford: Oxford University Press, 2009).
[56] I am paraphrasing Peter Hedström and Peter Bearman, 'What Is Analytical Sociology All About? An Introductory Essay', in Hedström and Bearman, *Oxford Handbook of Analytical Sociology*, pp. 3–24, at p. 5.
[57] Reinhart Koselleck, 'Einleitung', in his *Zeitschichten: Studien zur Historik* (Frankfurt a.M.: Suhrkamp, 2000), pp. 9–16, at p. 12.

KEY ISSUES OF HISTORICAL SOCIOLOGY

Historical Sociology is not a visibly demarcated discourse with an established grid
of themes and a characteristic toolbox. During its 'second wave', from the 1960s
to the 1980s, it defined itself as comparative sociology in the long run. Since then,
the focus on comparison has been somewhat attenuated and the clear identity
of the field thrown into doubt. Ironically, the ascendancy of globalization studies
and Global History has contributed to a growing insecurity among historical sociologists. When everything in the world is seen to be moving and flowing, when
boundaries are constantly undermined, shifted, and transgressed, it is difficult to
'freeze' units for analytical purposes: a logical prerequisite of comparison.
Moreover, traditional notions of 'society' have been destabilized on two different
fronts: on the one hand, a microsociology interested in rational action by individuals and small groups has little use for overall social structures; on the other hand,
cultural sociologists have shifted the emphasis from the objective and observable
markers of class, gender, and race to meaning, symbolism, emotion, and the social
imaginary.

This multiple challenge to Historical Sociology may enhance its openness towards
a dialogue with Global History. But what can Global History in turn expect from
Historical Sociology? A good starting point for a discussion of the linkages between
Global History and Historical Sociology is the venerable question of the concept
of civilization. That issue has vexed world history almost from its beginnings. Since
the nation state is obviously a very late phenomenon and an inappropriate spatial
unit for comprehending pre-modern history, the larger framework of a cultural
ecumene—'*la personnalité collective la plus grande qu'on connaisse*' (as Émile
Durkheim and Marcel Mauss put it in a path-breaking passage)—offered itself.[58]
It has the additional advantage of being a mode of *self*-description under a wide
variety of historical circumstances: The Western term 'civilization' has semantic
equivalents in many languages, and the opposition between 'Us the Civilized' and
'Them the Barbarians' is an almost universal grid of asymmetrical classification.
Since Oswald Spengler's and Arnold J. Toynbee's time, the category of civilization
has percolated from the summits of world history writing down to the level of a
popular literature that uses it in a casual and offhand way.

Samuel Huntington's controversial resuscitation of the concept as a vision of
antagonistic combat units in world politics has not enhanced its standing among
historians. Global History's hallmark has been that of an approach that avoids the
carving up of humankind into clearly demarcated macro-communities whose
coherence or identity is mainly guaranteed by shared religious beliefs. In other
words, Global History has positioned itself as world history liberated from the
straightjacket of 'civilization'. One of its characteristic features has been a penchant

---

[58] The greatest classical text for the theory of civilization was first published in 1913: Emile
Durkheim and Marcel Mauss, 'Note sur la notion de civilisation', in Marcel Mauss, *Œuvres, vol. II:
Répresentations collectives et diversité des civilisations*, ed. Victor Karady (Paris: Minuit, 1969),
pp. 451–5.

for *multi*-civilizational spaces of interaction: the Atlantic, the Indian Ocean, the Pacific, Eurasia, and so on.

However, the problem cannot be simply wished away. While nobody wants to return to a history of five, six, or seven 'Great Civilizations', it is impossible to dispense, in a radical way, with ideas of civilizational arenas. Whenever, for example, the term 'the West' is used in a way not explicitly restricted to geopolitics, it resonates with meanings of a 'Western *civilization*', of norms, values, institutions, and social rules that are distinctive attributes of European and neo-European societies. The debate about manifestations of modernity in the region between Manchuria and Hong Kong is largely conducted in terms of 'Chinese' modernity. Though much more ambiguous, the framing term 'Islamic world' is routinely used by many social scientists and historians when referring to an enormous range of heterogeneous phenomena. In this situation, conceptual awareness could be raised by referring to the work of Jóhann Páll Árnason and of the late Shmuel Noah Eisenstadt. In the writings of both authors, who place themselves in a broadly conceived Weberian tradition, we find an elaborate concept of civilization.[59] Eisenstadt summed up a lifetime of thinking about civilization(s) in a definition that sees a specific civilization as a characteristic 'combination of ontological or cosmological visions, of visions of trans-mundane and mundane reality, with the definition, construction, and regulation of the major arenas of social life and interaction'. Such regulation comprises institutional formations (political rule, the economy, kinship, etc.) as well as collective identities.[60]

One of the great virtues of refined concepts of 'civilization' is that they transcend the fruitless dichotomy between essentialism and constructivism. Historians, as contemporaries of, and sometimes participants in, the 'cultural turn' and as readers of anthropological literature, have learned to be wary of any 'essentialist' branding of human collectives. We are all constructivists now. At the same time, projecting present-day perceptions of cultural hybridity and infinitely malleable identities back onto the past is a less than satisfactory general approach for global historical studies. The ideas that human groups form about themselves, their neighbours, and enemies are certainly products of creative 'social imaginaries'.[61] However, such image-creating activities are not entirely arbitrary and contingent. They are partly shaped by traditions and social and cultural 'path-dependencies'; they are closely tied to institutions; and they produce effects that can, under certain circumstances, transform imagination into reality. The complex notion of 'civilization' as developed

[59] Jóhann Páll Árnason, *Civilizations in Dispute: Historical Questions and Theoretical Traditions* (Leiden: Brill, 2003); see also Wolfgang Knöbl, 'Contingency and Modernity in the Thought of J. P. Arnason', *European Journal of Social Theory* 14, 1 (2011), pp. 9–22.

[60] Shmuel N. Eisenstadt, 'Civilizations', in *International Encyclopedia of the Social and Behavioral Sciences*, vol. III (Amsterdam: Elsevier, 2001), pp. 1915–21, at p. 1916. See also Knöbl, *Kontingenz der Moderne*, pp. 62–70. A good discussion of Eisenstadt's later work is Willfried Spohn, 'An Appraisal of Shmuel Noah Eisenstadt's Global Historical Sociology', *Journal of Classical Sociology* 11, 3 (2011), pp. 281–301.

[61] The theory of social *imaginaries* comes in various shapes, especially related to Cornelius Castoriadis, *The Imaginary Institution of Society* (Cambridge: Polity Press, 1997 [French 1975]); Charles Taylor: 'Modern Social Imaginaries', *Public Culture* 14, 1 (2002), pp. 91–124; Charles Taylor, *Modern Social Imaginaries* (Durham, NC and London: Duke University Press, 2004).

by theorists like Eisenstadt on the basis of Durkheim, Mauss, and Weber goes far beyond the crude essentialism of authors of the Huntington school while not succumbing to the other extreme of denying any structural constraints of the collective imagination.

A second—and related—topic in need of careful and theory-guided consideration is the significance of the idea of 'fluidity' and 'flows' for Global History. Where earlier versions of world history tended to stress the different internal logics of macro-societies and civilizations, Global History prefers to see mobility or, in the fashionable plural form, 'mobilities'. This reflects a more general shift of sensibility. The social history of the 1960s and 1970s, at least on the European continent, neglected migration; it focussed on stratification, class conflict, and, following in E. P. Thompson's footsteps, on the connections between material life, class consciousness, and collective protest. The history of migration was mainly left to historical demography. At most, social history took an interest in *dramatic* instances of mass relocation; for instance, the transatlantic emigration from Europe during the second half of the nineteenth century or the forced translocations of populations after the two world wars.

Meanwhile, preferences have been turned upside down. When reading certain kinds of Global History literature these days, it is hard to avoid the conclusion that mobility is treated as the normal state of affairs. Social history dissolves into movement—movement of nomads and warriors, of slaves and convicts, of coolies, refugees, and frontiersmen, of gentleman travellers, and mass tourists.[62] Research of impressive quality has shown how travel, trade, gift exchange, or religious and literary communication constituted long-distance sociability and created spaces of interaction.[63] Yet, little is left of social history once mobility is subtracted, and the diaspora looks like a universally dominant form of social organization. Enamoured with what the sociologist Zygmunt Bauman calls social 'liquidity',[64] Global History appears to develop a mobility bias. It tends to be indifferent to *non*-migrant forms of social life: the sedentary peasantries that formed the bulk of numerous societies for the past millennia, or the many millions of townspeople who were stuck in their little communities and never set their sights on a metropolis or the all-connecting ocean.[65]

This may not be a serious problem, and it probably only compensates for a long and inexcusable neglect of mobility in mainstream historical scholarship. But it raises a couple of theoretical issues. Global History may be in danger of losing a sense of proportion by underestimating social structure and hierarchy; these are, after all, the foundations and preconditions of many kinds of movement and also

---

[62] See Valeska Huber, 'Multiple Mobilities: Über den Umgang mit verschiedenen Mobilitätsformen um 1900', *Geschichte und Gesellschaft* 36, 2 (2010), pp. 317–41.

[63] One recent example is Gagan D. Sood, 'Circulation and Exchange in Islamicate Eurasia: A Regional Approach to the Early Modern World', *Past & Present* 212 (2011), pp. 113–62. A magisterial overview is Dirk Hoerder, *Cultures in Contact: World Migration in the Second Millennium* (Durham, NC and London: Duke University Press, 2002).

[64] Zygmunt Baumann, *Liquid Modernity* (Cambridge: Polity Press, 2000).

[65] Symptomatic of this is Rosenberg, *A World Connecting*, a portrait of the period 1870 to 1945 that contains a chapter on migration but none on social structures.

the crystallizations of past mobility.[66] The early and path-breaking theorists of globalization, scholars such as Arjun Appadurai, Manuel Castells, and Ulf Hannerz, coined and elaborated the term 'flow', and a great number of monographical studies testify to its usefulness.[67] Sociology and anthropology have provided an innovative language to account for social dynamics at various spatial levels and along finely graded temporal scales. The success of this new way of framing the social is stunning. Yet one should beware of lopsidedness. From recent American social science textbooks, for example those written and edited by the prolific George Ritzer,[68] one gathers the impression that sociology in general and globalization studies in particular have abandoned any notion of a minimally stable social order.

Coming from a background in anthropology, Stuart Alexander Rockefeller has raised a number of important objections to the unchallenged popularity of 'flow think'.[69] One does not have to approve of all of his arguments, but when Arjun Appadurai, responding to Rockefeller, endorses his colleague's critique of 'recent excesses of the anthropology of flow',[70] the historian feels reminded of similar tendencies in Global History. Rockefeller castigates 'flow' as 'an image of agentless movement with no starting point and no telos',[71] and he is also right in claiming that common usage puts the emphasis on the flow rather than on the substance that is flowing.'[72] Moreover, metaphors of fluidity are likely to evoke an unrealistic impression of smooth, continuous, and unimpeded movement. By contrast, the habitually myopic historian is trained to look for variations of speed, resistance, failure, changes of context and their impact, the coordination (or lack thereof) of the activities of numerous actors, and so on.[73] When he or she reads, as one does with increasing frequency, that something—a commodity, a germ, or an idea—'circulated around the globe', the first reaction is amazement at such an improbable feat.

One can immediately add two further observations, one concerning the concept of 'space', the other of the 'network'. Global History has contributed enormously to a sharpened sense of space and place in historiography in general. Hardly more than a decade ago, the call for a return of space into historiography caused a stir.[74] Meanwhile, Global Historians have thoroughly digested the

---

[66] John Urry, 'Mobilities and Social Theory', in Bryan S. Turner (ed.), *The New Blackwell Companion to Social Theory* (Malden, MA: Wiley-Blackwell, 2009), 475–95. See also the Journal *Mobilities* published since 2006 and edited by John Urry et al.

[67] See the chapters on these authors in Matthias Middell and Ulf Engel (eds), *Theoretiker der Globalisierung* (Leipzig: Leipziger Universitätsverlag, 2010); see also Andrew Jones, *Globalization: Key Thinkers* (Cambridge and Malden, MA: Polity Press, 2010).

[68] See, most recently, George Ritzer, *Globalization: The Essentials* (Chichester: Wiley-Blackwell, 2011).

[69] Stuart Alexander Rockefeller, ' "Flow" ', *Current Anthropology* 52, 4 (2011), pp. 557–78.

[70] Arjun Appadurai, quoted in Rockefeller, ' "Flow" ', p. 569 (comment).

[71] Rockefeller, ' "Flow" ', p. 558.

[72] Rockefeller, ' "Flow" ', p. 560.

[73] Rockefeller, ' "Flow" ', p. 567.

[74] Jürgen Osterhammel, 'Die Wiederkehr des Raumes: Geopolitik, Geohistorie und historische Geographie', *Neue Politische Literatur* 43 (1998), pp. 374–97; Karl Schlögel, *Im Raume lesen wir die Zeit: Über Zivilisationsgeschichte und Geopolitik* (Munich: Hanser, 2003).

'spatial turn'[75] and, alerted by a neo-Braudelian *géohistoire*, they have refined their toolkit for spatial analysis. Where they evince some insecurity is in using spatial categories for purposes of *social* analysis. The more macro-sociology retreated from notions of social structure and social order, the more spatial metaphors were employed to describe social relationships—even if their distribution in space was not the prime focus of attention. 'Urban space' replaced 'urban society' even in those analytical contexts where forms of hierarchical subordination rather than mappable patterns of segregation were at stake. It would be preposterous to advocate a reversal of something that might be a wholesale paradigm change. Yet, Global History should enter into a dialogue with historical—and other—sociology about the spatialization of our analytical language, its gains and its limits. This should be done in view of a global social history that retains the full panoply of conceptual instruments accumulated ever since the beginnings of social history, sociology, and ethnology.

As far as the other master metaphor of global studies is concerned, the concept of the 'network', already mentioned above, begs all sorts of questions. It has rapidly become indispensable. All Global Historians use it: as economic historians, as historians of empires, as historians of the family. But how does one describe networks? How do we come to grips with their usually asymmetrical and irregular configurations? How do we avoid neglecting the holes between the nodes and connections? How do we add a third dimension to the network: the vertical dimension of hierarchy and power? How do we measure quantities and intensities? How do we grasp the meta-networking among different networks, their entanglement at the edges? How do we tell stories about the rise and fall, the life and death of networks? And who are the insiders and outsiders, the activists and the victims, the winners and the losers, the friends and the foes of networks?

Presently, the theory of networks is a rather formal branch of sociology, sometimes verging on mathematics. An influential creator of versions accessible to ordinary historians is Harrison C. White, the author of the classic work *Identity and Control: How Social Formations Emerge* (1992): a book—though not commonly regarded as a contribution to Historical Sociology—that is historically well informed and squarely re-inserts the figure of the actor into models of networks from which individual and collective agency had almost entirely disappeared.[76] Even in Harrison White's hands, however, sociological network analysis remains too formal to invite immediate application to topics of Global History. But a glance at the sociological literature ought to dissuade us from an undisciplined and arbitrary use of a term that is everyone's favourite and yet, upon closer inspection, reveals a treacherous polymorphism of meaning.

A fifth and final point relates to the kind of dynamics relevant to history and sociology. Social history and Historical Sociology were particularly close when a

---

[75] There is now a huge literature. The most important text remains Henri Lefebvre, *The Production of Space* (Oxford: Blackwell, 1991 [first French edition 1974]).

[76] Harrison C. White, *Identity and Control: How Social Formations Emerge*, 2nd edn (Princeton and Oxford: Princeton University Press, 2008).

'building-block view of social structure' (William H. Sewell, Jr)[77] enjoyed general popularity and when both disciplines were focussed on the same robust macro-processes: rationalization, secularization, industrialization, state-building, bureaucratization, urbanization, revolution, and so on: processes that are now discussed with less assurance and naiveté.[78] From the very beginning, however, Historical Sociology with its ingrained interest in pre-industrial societies was reluctant to identify 'society' with the bounded nation state. At the same time, it extended its comparative scope beyond Europe and North America, including Asia and some-times, via ethnological research, also Africa and the Pacific in its wide-ranging considerations. When History 'went global', it moved in a direction already familiar to Historical Sociology. Both share a concern for 'global variability'.[79]

The processes studied by Historical Sociology were not entirely domestic. In her influential book *States and Social Revolutions* Theda Skocpol made the point that a country's position in the international system was an independent variable that determined the development and outcome of revolutionary conflict.[80] Charles Tilly emphasized the importance of war-making for the development of European states.[81] At the same time, Historical Sociology lacked the analytical tools to come to grips with the multi-layered and multi-directional constellations that Global History would discuss so enthusiastically under headings such as 'entanglement' or 'hybridization'.[82] It is indicative that none of the leading representatives of Historical Sociology has made an original contribution to the study of colonialism.[83]

Where Historical Sociology and Global History could mutually benefit is in reflecting on the various concepts of change presently available—and conceivable in the future—to describe and explain processes at different temporal scales. The more numerous the connections and entanglements discovered by Global Historians, the greater the need to discriminate between them along parameters such as duration, intensity, rhythm, reversibility, causative power, and so on.[84] There is a danger that Global History degenerates into long, and somewhat trivial,

[77] Sewell, *Logics of History*, p. 329.

[78] Wolfgang Knöbl, 'Social History and Historical Sociology', *Historická Sociologie* 1 (2013), pp. 9–32, at pp. 24–5.

[79] Göran Therborn, 'At the Birth of Second-century Sociology: Times of Reflexivity, Spaces of Identity, and Nodes of Knowledge', *British Journal of Sociology* 51, 1 (2000), pp. 37–57, at p. 50.

[80] Theda Skocpol, *States and Social Revolutions* (Cambridge: Cambridge University Press, 1979); see also Stephen Hobden and John M. Hobson (eds), *Historical Sociology of International Relations* (Cambridge: Cambridge University Press, 2002).

[81] Charles Tilly, *Coercion, Capital, and European States, AD 990–1990* (Oxford: Blackwell, 1990).

[82] But see an attempt to integrate these aspects: Zine Magubane, 'Overlapping Territories and Intertwined Histories: Historical Sociology's Global Imagination', in Adams, Clemens, and Orloff, *Remaking Modernity*, pp. 92–108. An excellent survey of many forms of 'mixing' is Peter Burke, *Cultural Hybridity* (Cambridge and Malden, MA: Polity Press, 2009).

[83] The most important sociological analyses of colonialism came from a sociological tradition that was closer to ethnology than to history. A good example is the work of Georges Balandier.

[84] A little-known effort in this direction was made long ago in Peter Laslett, 'Social Structural Time: An Attempt at Classifying Types of Social Change by Their Characteristic Paces', in Tom Schuller and Michael Young (eds), *The Rhythms of Society* (London and New York: Routledge, 1988), pp. 17–36. A highly relevant sociological contribution to the theory of time and change (especially good on 'turning points') is Andrew Abbott, *Time Matters: On Theory and Method* (Chicago and London: University of Chicago Press, 2001).

lists of spaces, people, and events that are somehow linked to each other.[85] However, connections alone do not suffice to get to grips with the major institutions of the modern era, especially states and the structures of global capitalism. States and, by extension, empires are more than mere networks, as historical sociologists from Otto Hintze to Charles Tilly and Michael Mann have impressively shown.[86] And global capitalism cannot be reduced to market integration and commodity flows, disregarding the 'mercantilist' intervention of states, the effects of war and the agency of entrepreneurs, workers, and consumers.[87] Historical Sociology with its antennae for power and violence, and the processual dynamics of both, can remind Global History that the world has never been as 'flat', two-dimensional and peaceful as some theorists of globalization tend to suggest.

One might go on assessing the convergence and divergence between Global History and Historical Sociology in many different fields. There are topics of Global History that cannot be handled in a responsible manner without some familiarity with the relevant social science literature. It is hardly possible, for example, to work on the global history of the family in ignorance of the rich scholarly traditions in the sociology and anthropology of kinship and gender. In other instances, sociologists (and political scientists) will not be able to tell historians much they do not already know. Thus while a few political scientists are authorities on the theory of empire, the most important elements of that theory were elaborated by historians—since the time of Edward Gibbon.

CONCLUSION: AMBIVALENCE

The strengths and weaknesses of the respective disciplines vary from topic to topic. In general, Historical Sociology is strong on the methodology of explanation—which is generally not Global History's forte, while Global Historians in their practice of writing frequently come up with reasonable solutions for problems that seem daunting and intractable in theory, for instance the relationship between processes and institutions.[88]

The relationship between Global History and Historical Sociology is an ambivalent one. Neither of those two minority fields enjoys comfortable acceptance by its home discipline, and neither is institutionally stable and self-contained. They are both in search of thematic relevance, intellectual attractiveness, and scholarly stature. Cooperation between the two could be genuinely beneficial, not just a

[85] The same concern was voiced from a sociologist's point of view by Wolfgang Knöbl in his opening remarks at the workshop 'Macrosociology and World History Writing', Freiburg Institute of Advanced Study, Freiburg i.Br. (Germany), 10 to 11 February 2012 (unpublished manuscript, p. 4).
[86] See, above all, Michael Mann, *The Sources of Social Power*, 4 vols (Cambridge: Cambridge University Press, 1986–2013); the most relevant volume for theoretical purposes continues to be vol. I. A highly original discussion of the history of the state from a global history angle is Charles S. Maier, *Leviathan 2.0: Inventing Modern Statehood* (Cambridge, MA and London: Harvard University Press, 2014).
[87] See as a wide-ranging survey Larry Neal and Jeffrey G. Williamson (eds), *The Cambridge History of Capitalism*, 2 vols (Cambridge: Cambridge University Press, 2014).
[88] On that see Karen Barkey, 'Historical Sociology', in: Hedström and Bearman, *Oxford Handbook of Analytical Sociology*, pp. 712–33.

PRICES, QUANTITIES, AND PAROCHIALISM

While there have always been economic histories of individual countries, there was also a time when economic history was grand, sweeping, and international in scope: maybe not global, but at least (in Europe) pan-European. Perhaps it was easier to be geographically broad in the days when we knew less, but efforts to write economic history that was truly European also reflected a certain intellectual ambition. But then our horizons started shrinking. A symbol of this is the successive volumes of the *Cambridge Economic History of Europe*. Earlier volumes contained chapters on various aspects of the European economy taken as a whole— agriculture, fisheries, trade, and so on. Volume VII on the other hand, which covered the spread of modern industrialization in the nineteenth century, was essentially a collection of country studies.

Volume VII was published in 1978, and contained contributions from several famous cliometricians, as well as from quantitative economic historians who would probably have eschewed the 'cliometrics' label—Charles Feinstein, Maurice Lévy-Leboyer, Peter Temin, and others.[2] It was precisely around this time that economic history was becoming more quantitative, and more influenced by economics, and it is no surprise that it became more national in its focus as well. Quantitative economic history quantifies, and economists like measuring GDP. For this, data on outputs in different sectors are required, or of the incomes of land, labour, and capital, or of the expenditures of consumers, investors, the government, and foreigners. The raw material for such calculations is typically provided by the statistical agencies of well-developed states. And so there was a phase when cliometrics became more parochial, more focussed on country studies, and more focussed on the modern period. To be sure, Mokyr compared the economies of Belgium and the Netherlands in his dissertation,[3] and O'Brien and Keyder compared Britain and France,[4] but these comparative exercises, conducted for neighbouring pairs of European countries, were the exception rather than the rule. As for pan-European or global history: while this was the sort of thing that a Braudel or a Wallerstein might go in for, it was hardly suitable fare for a well-trained cliometrician. Apart from anything else, there simply was not the data.

Fortunately the balance has been shifting back again in recent decades. Paul Bairoch and, especially, Angus Maddison started compiling cross-country data, which despite its flaws had the hugely beneficial effect of making quantitative economic historians

[2] Charles Feinstein, 'Capital Formation in Great Britain', in Peter Mathias and Michael M. Postan (eds), *The Cambridge Economic History of Europe from the Decline of the Roman Empire, vol. 7: The Industrial Economies: Capital, Labour and Enterprise* (Cambridge: Cambridge University Press, 2008), pp. 28–96; Maurice Lévy-Leboyer, 'Capital Investment and Economic Growth in France, 1820–1930', in Mathias and Postan (eds), *The Cambridge Economic History of Europe from the Decline of the Roman Empire, vol. 7*, pp. 231–95; Robert M. Solow and Peter Temin, 'Introduction: The Inputs for Growth', Mathias and Postan (eds), *The Cambridge Economic History of Europe from the Decline of the Roman Empire, vol. 7*, pp. 1–27.
[3] Joel Mokyr, *Industrialization in the Low Countries, 1795–1850* (New Haven: Yale University Press, 1976).
[4] Patrick K. O'Brien and Caglar Keyder, *Economic Growth in Britain and France, 1780–1914: Two Paths to the Twentieth Century* (London and Boston: G. Allen & Unwin, 1978).

think in comparative and global terms again.[5] A lot of cliometric work is now explicitly comparative, either comparing pairs of regions, or countries, or cultures, in a case study manner, or using wider datasets including information on many countries over long periods of time. In 2010 Cambridge University Press published a pan-European economic history textbook modelled on Floud and McCloskey and its successors, containing thematic rather than country-specific chapters.[6]

There has even been a trend towards work that can reasonably be described as global in scope. Cliometricians have been working on the history of globalization, both in the context of the Atlantic economy, and of the world more generally. And more recently there has been a plethora of studies trying to pin down the timing of, and explain, both the Great Divergence between Europe and Asia, and the Little Divergences that occurred within both continents.[7]

In part this is a result of economists' natural tendency to generalize, which is what distinguishes us most from historians. Generalization requires data on as many units of observation as possible, so why deprive oneself of data from different periods or countries, when these are available? Computer technology and international scholarly networks, often funded by the European Commission, have been invaluable in helping us put together such pan-national datasets. In part, however, the move towards comparative, regional and global economic history is a consequence of economists reverting to a data source much prized by previous generations of economic historians, such as Braudel and Spooner: prices.[8]

In order to measure the total quantity of coal produced in a country in a given year, someone had to be counting it, and as noted earlier this 'someone' was often a modern developed state. This limits our ability to obtain data on economic quantities, both across space and over time. On the other hand, in order to obtain good price data all that is needed is an institution that was buying and selling whatever it is that you are interested in—and if it was important enough for economic historians to be interested in it, then someone was certainly buying or selling it. It is just a question of whether sellers and buyers left suitable records behind. Fluctuating borders make long-run GDP series deeply problematic in many parts of the world, but they do not alter the validity of a price series for a particular commodity in a particular market town. Even better, prices may be available for periods when borders bore no resemblance whatsoever to today's. Best of all, a lot of these prices were collected in the 1920s and 1930s, as a result of the efforts of Lord Beveridge, Edwin Gay, and their colleagues in the International Scientific Committee on Price

[5] Angus Maddison, *The World Economy: Historical Statistics* (Paris: Development Centre of the Organisation for Economic Co-operation and Development, 2003).

[6] Roderick Floud and Donald N. McCloskey (eds), *The Economic History of Britain since 1700* (Cambridge and New York: Cambridge University Press 1981); Stephen N. Broadberry and Kevin H. O'Rourke (eds), *The Cambridge Economic History of Modern Europe, vol. 2: 1870 to the Present* (New York: Cambridge University Press, 2010).

[7] For a representative contribution, see Stephen N. Broadberry, 'Accounting for the Great Divergence', LSE Department of Economic History Working Paper 184 (2013).

[8] Fernand Braudel and Frank Spooner, 'Prices in Europe from 1450 to 1750', in Edwin E. Rich and Charles H. Wilson (eds), *The Cambridge Economic History of Europe from the Decline of the Roman Empire, vol. 4: The Economy of Expanding Europe in the Sixteenth and Seventeenth Centuries* (Cambridge: Cambridge University Press, 1967), pp. 374–486.

History,[9] and there are many more price data available to be collected for other countries and other periods. This means that there is both an extensive margin and an intensive margin on which price history can still make major advances.

Prices provide an excellent way to measure the incomes of real people, who earned wages and used them to buy things, which is arguably more useful than measuring statistical artefacts such as GDP per capita. In addition, technological progress in the economy as a whole can be measured, if the analysis is sufficiently well grounded.[10] Furthermore, the integration of the international economy can be measured, as will be demonstrated in the next section.

TRACKING GLOBALIZATION OVER TIME

By when does it make sense to speak of a world economy? It depends on what is meant by a world economy, which in turn probably depends on what scholars are interested in.[11] For some historians, discovering that particular people were trading a particular commodity over a particular route at a particular time might be a very useful piece of information, for various reasons. Flynn and Giráldez are quite right to point to 1571 as being a turning point in the history of the world economy, since from then on all continents were in direct trading contact with each other.[12] But it remains legitimate to ask whether these connections were sufficiently deep to have mattered economically.

Mattered economically in what way? Different researchers will emphasize different things, depending on what they are interested in and their theoretical frameworks. O'Rourke and Williamson argue that one way in which nineteenth-century intercontinental trade was different from anything that had gone before was that it had big implications for European income distribution,[13] for what economists call 'Heckscher-Ohlin' reasons, but others might have entirely different yardsticks to measure the impact of trade by.[14] For example, if inflation is analysed, then the

[9] Arthur H. Cole and Ruth Crandall, 'The International Scientific Committee on Price History', *Journal of Economic History* 24, 3 (1964), pp. 380–6.
[10] Pol Antràs and Hans-Joachim Voth, 'Factor Prices and Productivity Growth during the British Industrial Revolution', *Explorations in Economic History* 40, 1 (2003), pp. 52–77.
[11] Which is why I now believe that the question of 'when did globalization begin?' is not a very sensible one. Jeff Williamson and I asked it in 2002 (Kevin H. O'Rourke and Jeffrey G. Williamson, 'When Did Globalisation Begin?' *European Review of Economic History* 6, 1 (2002), pp. 23–50), and I am pleased that we did, since it led to a productive debate that significantly advanced our understanding of the history of market integration. But questions whose answers depend on definitions are ultimately unsatisfactory.
[12] Dennis O. Flynn and Arturo Giráldez, 'Born with a "Silver Spoon": The Origin of World Trade in 1571', *Journal of World History* 6, 2 (1995), pp. 201–21.
[13] Kevin H. O'Rourke and Jeffrey G. Williamson, 'From Malthus to Ohlin: Trade, Industrialisation and Distribution since 1500', *Journal of Economic Growth* 10, 1 (2005), pp. 5–34.
[14] Kevin H. O'Rourke and Jeffrey G. Williamson, *Globalization and History: The Evolution of a Nineteenth-Century Atlantic Economy* (Cambridge, MA: MIT Press, 1999) were primarily concerned with the effects of late nineteenth-century globalization on income distribution, à la Heckscher-Ohlin, which is why O'Rourke and Williamson, 'When Did Globalisation Begin?' laid such stress on intercontinental trade in bulk, 'competing' commodities. But you might quite legitimately be interested in something else.

bullion flows from Latin America to Europe after 1500 clearly mattered, and the trade in silver is what Flynn and Giráldez emphasize.[15] The same authors' point that it did not take a lot of trade to transfer species such as potato between continents, with huge economic implications, is well taken.[16] So for now let us focus on one very simple question: was trade sufficient that it led to markets in different continents being well integrated with each other, or at least becoming better integrated with each other? To what extent did trade lead to markets in different continents behaving as though they were in fact part of a single, global market?[17]

Prices, rather than quantities traded, are exactly what you need to answer this question, since the hallmark of a single market is a unified price structure. Burger joints on the same street corner tend to charge a single price, unless some burgers are better than others. Similarly, in a single international market, prices for identical commodities will only differ across locations to the extent that trade costs of all sorts (not just transport costs, but tariffs and other import barriers, costs associated with different currencies, costs associated with the risks of trading across long distances, and so forth) make arbitrage expensive.

One indication that markets are integrated is when they have prices that are correlated with each other. Such a correlation could be spurious—in the case of grain prices it could be due to correlated weather shocks for example—but it could also reflect trade occurring in order to arbitrage away bigger-than-usual price differences, where those 'usual' differences reflect trade costs. Rather than declare that markets are integrated when price correlations exceed a certain arbitrary threshold value (they will certainly never be perfectly correlated), it makes sense to track these correlations over time, and ask whether markets were becoming better or less well integrated.

An even more compelling indication that markets were becoming better integrated, however, is if these 'usual' price gaps, reflecting trade costs, were falling over time. (Once again, it makes more sense to ask whether price gaps were *falling* than to ask whether they were lower than some arbitrarily defined threshold.) Falling price gaps lead (other things being equal) to falling prices in importing regions, and to rising prices in exporting regions. Falling prices in importing regions will lead to the production of the goods concerned contracting, while rising export prices will lead to export sectors expanding. This reallocation of resources will have an impact on aggregate economic welfare—the general presumption is that this will be positive, although there are several well-known exceptions to this general rule—and it will also have an impact on income distribution. Globalization produces losers as well as winners.

---

[15] Flynn and Giráldez, 'Born with a "Silver Spoon"'.

[16] Dennis O. Flynn and Arturo Giráldez, 'Path Dependence, Time Lags and the Birth of Globalisation: A Critique of O'Rourke and Williamson', *European Review of Economic History* 8, 1 (2004), pp. 81–108.

[17] It needs to be borne in mind (1) that earlier evidence for market integration can be found when exploring markets that are closer together than when exploring markets that are further apart; and (2) that earlier evidence for long-distance integration can be found for high value commodities such as silver than for bulkier commodities such as wheat. To keep the discussion manageable, I will focus on long-distance market integration in what follows.

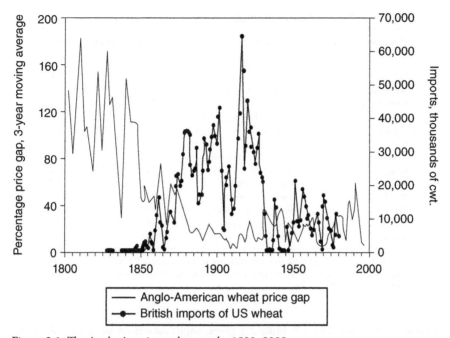

Figure 2.1 The Anglo-American wheat trade, 1800–2000
Source: Kevin H. O'Rourke and Jeffrey G. Williamson, 'From Malthus to Ohlin: Trade, Industrialisation and Distribution since 1500', *Journal of Economic Growth* 10, 1 (2005), pp. 5–34, p. 10.

Just as price correlations across markets could be spurious, so declining price gaps could in principle be unrelated to trade: however unlikely it may sound, it could be the case that, for some unknown reason, autonomous movements in supply and demand in two unconnected regions were working to bring the prices in each closer together. However, when price gaps fall at the same time as transport costs fall, and trade volumes rise, then this is compelling evidence that globalization is occurring.

For example, Figure 2.1 shows unmistakable evidence of declining transatlantic trade costs during the nineteenth century. The Anglo-American wheat price gap fluctuated considerably before 1840 or so, around a roughly constant trend. It then started a sharp decline, at about the same time that shipping costs started to fall, a result of the introduction of the steamship on long-distance routes.[18] The price gap had almost vanished by 1914. At precisely the same time, the volume of wheat shipped across the Atlantic exploded.

The example of the transatlantic trade in wheat is not an isolated one. International price gaps fell sharply on many routes and for many commodities

---

[18] C. Knick Harley, 'Ocean Freight Rates and Productivity, 1740–1913: The Primacy of Mechanical Invention Reaffirmed', *Journal of Economic History* 48, 4 (1988), pp. 851–76.

Table 2.1 Anglo-American price gaps, 1870–1913

Commodity traded	Markets in which quoted	1870	1895	1913
	A. Commodity detail			
Wheat	Liverpool vs Chicago	57.6	17.8	15.6
Meat and animal fats	London vs Cincinnati	92.5	92.3	17.9
Cotton textiles	Boston vs Manchester	13.7	3.7	−3.6
Iron bars	Philadelphia vs London	75.0	43.4	20.6
Pig iron	Philadelphia vs London	85.2	46.9	19.3
Cotton	Liverpool vs New York	13.3	11.2	9.7
Coal	New York vs London	−16.9	−2.0	8.8
Copper	Philadelphia vs London	32.7	13.6	−0.1
Hides	Boston vs London	27.7	16.6	8.7
Wool	Boston vs London	59.1	65.8	27.9
Tin	New York vs London	15.9	5.3	−2.3
Coffee	New York vs London	−18.1	−3.5	8.2
Sugar	New York vs London	50.9	74.2	91.0

Source: Kevin H. O'Rourke and Jeffrey G. Williamson, 'Late Nineteenth-Century Anglo-American Factor-Price Convergence: Were Heckscher and Ohlin Right?' *The Journal of Economic History* 54, 4 (1994), pp. 892–916, p. 900.

between 1815 and 1914.[19] Table 2.1 gives Anglo-American price gaps for a variety of commodities between 1870 and 1913. In the case of agricultural commodities such as wheat and animal products, British prices were higher than American ones, so the price gaps are the percentage by which the former exceeded the latter. In the case of industrial commodities such as cotton textiles or iron bars, American prices were higher than British ones, so the price gaps quoted are the percentage by which prices in Boston or Philadelphia exceeded prices in Manchester or London. In nearly all cases (sugar is the outstanding exception) price gaps fell, indicating that transatlantic commodity markets were becoming better integrated. Nor was price convergence limited to the North Atlantic. Between 1873 and 1913, the Liverpool–Bombay cotton price gap fell from 57 per cent to 20 per cent; the London–Calcutta jute price gap fell from 35 per cent to 4 per cent; and the London–Rangoon rice price gap fell from 93 per cent to 26 per cent. Between 1846–55 and 1871–9, during which period Japan was opened up to trade with the rest of the world, the Japan–Hamburg nail price gap fell from 400 per cent to 32 per cent, and the refined sugar price gap fell from 271 per cent to 39 per cent.[20]

In the nineteenth century, such declining price gaps were ubiquitous, and often quite dramatic. They involved all continents, and manufactured goods as well as primary products. Exceptions are rare, and where these occur they involved, as often as not, the intervention of governments trying to substitute 'artificial oceans'

[19] O'Rourke and Williamson, *Globalization and History*.
[20] Ronald Findlay and Kevin H. O'Rourke, *Power and Plenty: Trade, War, and the World Economy in the Second Millennium* (Princeton and Oxford: Princeton University Press, 2007), pp. 404–5.

for the real thing, by means of tariffs and other barriers to trade.[21] And not only were price gaps declining everywhere, reflecting declining trade costs, but price correlations were rising, and trade volumes were booming.

In earlier periods, the evidence for market integration is patchier. To find evidence for market integration depends on how it is measured, on the routes looked at, and on the commodities concerned. The further back in time, the more likely it is that any long-distance price integration will involve goods with a high value-to-weight ratio: luxury goods, or precious metals. Markets for more basic commodities show evidence of integration later, or (in earlier periods) over shorter distances.

For example, there is evidence that wheat prices in London and Philadelphia were correlated with each other in the eighteenth century,[22] although the correlation broke down during the mercantilist wars that characterized that period. Also, there is evidence of grain exports from the US to Britain during this time, although it was sporadic, and pales into insignificance with what was to come in the nineteenth century: market integration was constantly interrupted during this period by mercantilist trade policies and wars.[23] A first point to note here is that not much trade is required to produce correlated prices—imports of grain during years of particular scarcity in Britain could produce co-movements of prices on either side of the Atlantic, and so could trade between both locations and a third market, for example the Caribbean. A second point is that when this type of evidence is offered for the eighteenth century, it typically involves coastal markets in the United States, not markets in the continental interior: since overland trade was costlier than waterborne trade, the distinction matters significantly. Railroads were probably a more important innovation for the nineteenth-century global economy than steamships, linking continental interiors with coastal ports. A third point is that notwithstanding evidence of transatlantic trade during this period, this was not sufficient to cause a wholesale collapse in European wheat prices, and as a consequence in European land rents, such as occurred from the 1870s or 1880s onwards. There were market connections between continents before the nineteenth century, even for bulky commodities like grain, but the nineteenth century was very different from what had gone before.

Wars were one important factor impeding market integration before 1815. Mercantilist trading companies were another, since their *raison d'être* was to monopolize trade routes and keep price gaps high. Price gaps for cotton textiles between Britain and India were suspiciously constant between 1660 and 1760, while the same is true of price gaps for pepper and cloves between Amsterdam and Southeast

[21] Paul Bairoch and Susan Burke, 'European Trade Policy, 1815–1914', in Peter Mathias and Sidney Pollard (eds), *The Cambridge Economic History of Europe from the Decline of the Roman Empire, vol. 8: The Industrial Economies: The Development of Economic and Social Policies* (Cambridge: Cambridge University Press, 1989), pp. 1–160, pp. 55–8.

[22] Allen, Robert C., *Global Economic History: A Very Short Introduction* (Oxford: Oxford University Press 2011), pp. 68–9.

[23] Paul Sharp and Jacob Weisdorf, 'Globalization Revisited: Market Integration and the Wheat Trade between North America and Britain from the Eighteenth Century', *Explorations in Economic History* 50, 1 (2013), pp. 88–98.

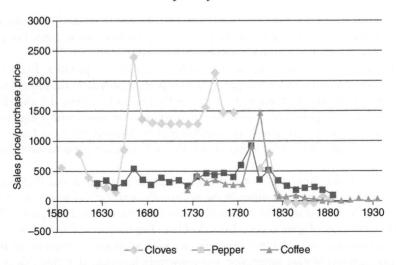

Figure 2.2 Spice and coffee price gaps, Amsterdam relative to Southeast Asia, 1580–1939
Source: Kevin H. O'Rourke and Jeffrey G. Williamson, 'When Did Globalisation Begin?' *European Review of Economic History* 6, 1 (2002), pp. 23–50, p. 33.

Asia (Figure 2.2). In the latter case, the large increase in the gap between prices in Amsterdam and Southeast Asia in the middle of the seventeenth century coincides with the Dutch obtaining a monopoly of the clove trade at that time, while the prominent spikes in the price gap coincide with the second Anglo-Dutch War and the Seven Year's War (and the spike in the coffee price gap coincides with the French Revolutionary and Napoleonic Wars). Not only the new steam technologies of the Industrial Revolution, but also an outbreak of comparative peace after Waterloo, and the collapse of the East India companies, were conspiring to increase global market integration in the nineteenth century.

The utility of price data comes through clearly when thinking about an earlier case of possible market integration. Did Vasco da Gama's voyages around the Cape of Good Hope help to integrate Eurasian markets, or is it rather true that '(t)he Portuguese carracks did not obtain any great significance as a connecting link between Europe and Asia'.[24] To contemporaries, and many historians since, the key issue raised by da Gama's exploits was the extent to which the Cape route would displace the traditional trades which had given Venice such a prominent role in the European economy. The fact that the traditional Mediterranean spice trade eventually made a comeback, and survived for the rest of the sixteenth century, suggests that Portuguese plans to monopolize this trade failed. This is the important fact that many historians have focussed on. But to go on to say that the Portuguese carracks had no significance in linking Europe and Asia economically is another matter entirely. When asking whether the Portuguese succeeded in their monopolistic aims, it makes sense to look at quantities and market shares; but

[24] Niels Steensgaard, *The Asian Trade Revolution of the Seventeenth Century: The East India Companies and the Decline of the Caravan Trade* (Chicago: University of Chicago Press, 1974).

when it comes to market integration, prices tell a very different story, although they have to be handled with care.

Frederic Lane is one of the rare traditional historians to have looked closely at the evolution of pepper prices before and after da Gama's voyages.[25] He noticed that the prices of pepper and other fine spices were falling during the fifteenth century, and rising in the wake of the Voyages of Discovery. His conclusion was that da Gama made no impact on European markets, since if anything pepper was becoming more expensive in his wake. But this conclusion ignores the fact that Europe was not only heading East during this period, but West as well, and that from the West Europe was importing vast quantities of silver, which was causing a general price inflation. If we look not at the nominal price of pepper or other spices, but at their real price (that is to say, their price relative to the general price level, or failing that, relative to a commodity like wheat), we see that pepper and other spice prices were in fact falling sharply throughout the sixteenth century, after a fifteenth century during which they had been, if anything, rising (Figure 2.3). Prices did briefly spike at the very beginning of the sixteenth century, presumably reflecting the impact of the initial disruption to trade routes; but once the Portuguese started importing more, prices came down again. And to the extent that the Venetians managed to get back into the spice trade, of course, this would have enhanced the economic impact of da Gama, since competition would have further forced down prices.

Prices can also be used to tell a good old-fashioned story. Edward Gibbon understood this, when he wrote that 'in the year 1238, the inhabitants of Gothia (Sweden) and Frise were prevented, by their fear of the Tartars, from sending, as usual, their ships to the herring fishery on the coast of England; and as there was no exportation, forty or fifty of these fish were sold for a shilling.... It is whimsical enough, that the orders of a Mogul khan, who reigned on the borders of China, should have lowered the price of herrings in the English market.'[26] Whimsical, but not surprising in an age when Europe was a backward appendage of Eurasia, and price shocks were something which were imposed upon it as a result of events happening in the centre of the world economy, rather than something which it imposed upon others. Take another look at those pronounced spikes in pepper prices which appear in both Flanders and England around 1410 (and which also show up in European price series for other Asian spices). They coincide with the voyages of Zheng He, which began in 1405 and as a result of which pepper became far more abundant, and cheaper, in China.[27] More spices imported into China, a

---

[25] Frederic C. Lane, 'Pepper Prices Before Da Gama', *The Journal of Economic History* 28, 2 (1968), pp. 590–7. Other examples include Eliyahu Ashtor, *Histoire des prix et des salaires dans l'Orient médiéval* (Paris: S.E.V.P.E.N., 1969); Eliyahu Ashtor, 'Spice Prices in the Near East in the 15th Century', *Journal of the Royal Asiatic Society (New Series)* 1 (1976), pp. 26–41; A. H. Lybyer, 'The Ottoman Turks and the Routes of Oriental Trade', *The English Historical Review* 30, 120 (1915), pp. 577–88.

[26] Edward Gibbon, *The History of the Decline and Fall of the Roman Empire* (New York: Fred de Fau and Co., 1907), p. 17.

[27] Findlay and O'Rourke, *Power and Plenty*, pp. 134, 141. For insights into the trade and circulation of aromatics in pre-modern Europe, see Purcell's chapter in this volume.

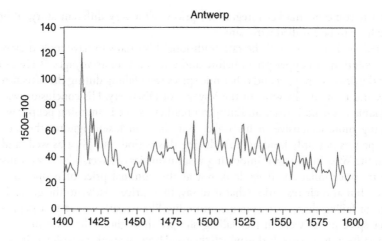

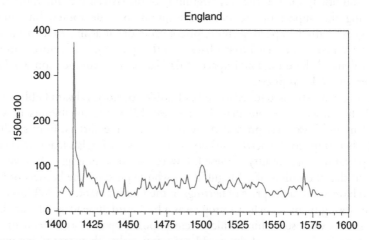

Figure 2.3 Real (CPI-deflated) pepper prices, 1400–1600

Source: Kevin H. O'Rourke and Jeffrey G. Williamson, 'Did Vasco da Gama Matter for European Markets?' *Economic History Review* 62, 3 (2009), pp. 655–84, p. 668.

huge consumer, meant a lot less available for Europe, which had only imported a tiny share of total production to begin with. In those days, the Asian dog was still wagging the European tail.

Economists' use of price data has a lot to offer traditional historians, therefore. At the same time, however, the former also have a lot to learn from the latter, for the simple reason that not everything that is important can be measured, and that not everything that can be measured is important. In the context of the seventeenth and eighteenth centuries, for example, there was a gradual shift towards long-distance trade in bulkier goods consumed by greater numbers of people. Silver, silk, and spices were gradually supplanted in importance by Indian textiles, sugar, tobacco, and other colonial goods. This shift in the composition of trade will not be picked up by price gaps for particular commodities, but it was clearly important, even for things that matter to economic historians. As consumption of these goods trickled down to ever-greater numbers of people, living standards rose in ways that are not captured by real wage indices (which assume that people consumed a constant bundle of goods). Hersh and Voth have recently quantified the impact: it was big.[28] By 1850, they conclude, 'the average Englishman would have been willing to forego 15 per cent or more of his income in order to maintain access to sugar and tea alone'. Furthermore, access to such commodities may have spurred an Industrious Revolution, with major implications for the British economy.[29] Just because it is difficult to quantify such effects does not mean that economists should dismiss them as irrelevant, and increasingly economists are not doing so.

The history of globalization has lessons for economists who are otherwise uninterested in history. There is by now a large body of evidence that shows a broadly U-shaped pattern in global commodity, capital, and labour markets over the past 200 years.[30] While the nineteenth century was a period of dramatic globalization, there followed a period of disintegration, before the world economy started to reintegrate in the late twentieth century. The ramifications of the First World War are obviously a major factor explaining interwar disintegration, but there were signs of an anti-globalization backlash during the late nineteenth century, in response to the distributional implications of market integration. The moral may be obvious to historians, but some economists can usefully be reminded of it: nothing is permanent, or can be taken for granted, and what politicians have done in the past, they can undo in the future.[31]

QUANTIFYING CONVERGENCE AND DIVERGENCE

One of the most basic aims of quantitative economic history is to establish what were the long-run trends in living standards in different parts of the world. There has been immense progress over the past couple of decades. A major part of it has involved constructing long-run series for real wages. This requires price information:

[28] Jonathon Hersh and Hans-Joachim Voth, 'Sweet Diversity: Colonial Goods and the Rise of European Living Standards after 1492', CEPR Discussion Paper 7386 (2009).

[29] Jan de Vries, *The Industrious Revolution: Consumer Behavior and the Household Economy, 1650 to the Present* (Cambridge: Cambridge University Press, 2008).

[30] Timothy J. Hatton and Jeffrey G. Williamson, *Global Migration and the World Economy: Two Centuries of Policy and Performance* (Cambridge, MA: MIT Press, 2005); Maurice Obstfeld and Alan M. Taylor, *Global Capital Markets: Integration, Crisis, and Growth* (Cambridge and New York: Cambridge University Press, 2004); Findlay and O'Rourke, *Power and Plenty*. International capital markets were extremely well-integrated in the late nineteenth century, disintegrated during the First World War and again during the Great Depression, remained disintegrated under the Bretton Woods settlement, and started to reintegrate from the late 1960s onwards, as capital controls were undermined by markets, before being abandoned by governments. International labour markets were arguably better integrated between 1870 and 1913 than at any time before or since, with falling transport costs interacting with relatively liberal laws regarding both emigration and immigration. Along this dimension, the world is probably less globalized now than it was in 1900.

[31] And who knows what rising fuel prices might imply for international market integration in the future?

on the nominal wages of workers, and on the prices of the goods that they consumed. It also requires information on how workers spent their incomes, so as to be able to compare wages with the price of a basket of goods that makes some sense historically. When constructing real wage series for a single country, researchers have used country-specific consumption baskets. When constructing real wage series that are comparable across countries as well as over time, they have had to use consumption baskets that are common across countries.

There have been two particularly influential contributions to this literature. Jeffrey Williamson constructed comparable real wage indices for fifteen Western European and New World countries between 1830 and 1988, focussing on the wages of unskilled building labourers.[32] He constructed budget shares for as many of these countries as possible, using contemporary sources, and then took an average of these when constructing his 'PPP-adjusted' (internationally comparable) real wages. His finding was that real wages in this small sample of relatively rich countries tended to converge in the late nineteenth century, diverged between 1914 and 1945, and converged again thereafter.

Robert Allen calculated real wages for a sample of European cities going back to the Middle Ages.[33] He got around the problem of comparability across countries by calculating real wages using standardized baskets of goods, taking account of the fact that different countries consumed different grains, or drank beer rather than wine, or used butter rather than olive oil. The paper showed a large income gap opening up between England and the Low Countries, on the one hand, and southern and eastern Europe on the other, with the former managing to hang on to a much larger share of their post-Black Death wage gains than the latter, despite increasingly rapid population growth during the seventeenth and eighteenth centuries. This divergence within Europe is sometimes referred to as the 'Little Divergence', thus distinguishing it from the better-known 'Great Divergence' between Europe and Asia.

Allen's paper has sparked an enormous literature, as well as an impressive international data-gathering exercise spanning all the inhabited continents, an example of cliometric collaboration at its best.[34] This effort was in part motivated by a desire to engage with the arguments of Kenneth Pomeranz, Prasannan Partasharathi, and others regarding when the gap in living standards between Europe and Asia first opened up, and extensive efforts have been made to compare real wages within and between continents.[35] Researchers have also constructed GDP per capita series for several countries, extending back to the Middle Ages in some cases.[36]

[32] Jeffrey G.Williamson, 'The Evolution of Global Labor Markets since 1830: Background Evidence and Hypotheses', *Explorations in Economic History* 32, 2 (1995), pp. 141–96.
[33] Robert C. Allen, 'The Great Divergence in European Wages and Prices from the Middle Ages to the First World War', *Explorations in Economic History* 38, 4 (2001), pp. 411–47.
[34] <http://gpih.ucdavis.edu> (accessed 30 January 2015).
[35] Kenneth Pomeranz, *The Great Divergence: China, Europe, and the Making of the Modern World Economy* (Princeton: Princeton University Press, 2000); Prasannan Parthasarathi, 'Rethinking Wages and Competitiveness in the Eighteenth Century: Britain and South India', *Past & Present* 158 (1998), pp. 79–109.
[36] For a recent survey, see Broadberry, 'Accounting for the Great Divergence'.

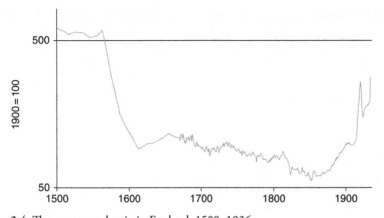

Figure 2.4 The wage-rental ratio in England, 1500–1936

Source: Kevin H. O'Rourke and Jeffrey G. Williamson, 'From Malthus to Ohlin: Trade, Industrialisation and Distribution since 1500', *Journal of Economic Growth* 10, 1 (2005), pp. 5–34, p. 8.

Real wages and GDP per capita sound as if they are measuring something similar—living standards—but of course they are not.[37] The real wages that we can measure over long periods of time are typically for male building labourers, although some authors have put together series for other types of labour—for example, masons or other skilled building workers—as well.[38] GDP per capita, on the other hand, measures average living standards in society as a whole. It includes not only the incomes of unskilled workers, but of landlords, peasants, capitalists, skilled workers, and anyone else earning an income. There is no reason why these two series should behave similarly, and lots of reasons to explore both, since doing so inevitably raises questions of income distribution that are fundamental in understanding both the process of economic development, and its social and political consequences.

For example, in a purely Malthusian world real wages might be expected to fluctuate around a roughly constant trend, while land rents gradually crept upwards as population pressure expanded. In such a situation GDP per capita (which includes land rents) might gradually increase, even though real wages remained static: the implication would be a society that was gradually getting more unequal over time. Figure 2.4 shows that this is precisely what happened in England between 1500 and 1840 or so: the ratio of wages to land rents fell more or less continuously. It is therefore no surprise that while the real wage data favoured by authors such as Allen and Clark show a Malthusian picture of English living standards that were remarkably stable over long periods of time, the most recent GDP data indicate a plateau between 1400 and 1650 or so (after the gains associated with the Black Death), followed by slow but steady growth.

---

[37] As is emphasized by O'Rourke and Williamson, *Globalization and History*.

[38] Humphries and Weisdorf have recently compiled long-run wage series for women in England: Jane Humphries and Jacob Weisdorf, 'The Wages of Women in England, 1260–1850', CEPR Discussion Paper 9903 (2014).

Table 2.2 GDP per capita in Europe and Asia, 725–1850 (1990 international dollars)

	England/GB	Holland/NL	Italy	Spain	Japan	China	India
725					483		
900					534		
980						1,247	
1086	754					1,204	
1120						1,063	
1150					603		
1280	679			957	560		
1300	755		1,482	957			
1348	777	876	1,376	1,030			
1400	1,090	1,245	1,601	885		960	
1450	1,055	1,432	1,668	889	554	983	
1500	1,114	1,483	1,403	889		1,127	
1570	1,143	1,783	1,337	990		968	
1600	1,123	2,372	1,244	944	791	977	682
1650	1,110	2,171	1,271	820	838		638
1700	1,563	1,403	1,350	880	879	841	622
1750	1,710	2,440	1,403	910	818	685	573
1800	2,080	1,752	1,244	962	876	597	569
1850	2,997	2,397	1,350	1,144	933	594	556

Source: Stephen N. Broadberry, 'Accounting for the Great Divergence', LSE Department of Economic History Working Paper 184 (2013), p. 23.

What has recent empirical work told us about the Great Divergence between Europe and Asia? On the one hand, it has confirmed one of the main arguments made by Pomeranz and others, namely that we should not compare all of China, say, with England, since there were large income gaps within both Europe and China (and India, and presumably the rest of Asia as well). We have already seen that real wages were much higher in England and the Low Countries than in the rest of Europe by the eighteenth century, since they did not fall there in response to rising population in the way that they did in the rest of the continent.[39] On the other hand, the literature has been critical of the claim that income gaps between Europe and Asia only opened up around 1800 or so. Broadberry and Gupta find that real wages in India and the Yangtze Delta were similar to those in the more backward parts of Europe during the European early modern period,[40] a finding confirmed by Allen et al. for the eighteenth century.[41]

GDP data confirm this picture of a 'Little Divergence' within Europe, and a relatively early 'Great Divergence' between Europe and Asia (Table 2.2). As already

[39] Pamuk has found further evidence in favour of the hypothesis of a 'Little Divergence' between northwest Europe and the rest of the continent in the wake of the Black Death, and extended the analysis to encompass Cairo and Istanbul as well: Şevket Pamuk, 'The Black Death and the Origins of the "Great Divergence" across Europe, 1300–1600', *European Review of Economic History* 11, 3 (2007), pp. 289–317.

[40] Stephen N. Broadberry and Bishnupriya Gupta, 'The Early Modern Great Divergence: Wages, Prices and Economic Development in Europe and Asia, 1500–1800', *Economic History Review* 59, 1 (2006), pp. 2–31.

[41] Allen, *Global Economic History*.

noted, GDP per capita was rising in England (and subsequently Britain) from the middle of the seventeenth century onwards, whereas real wages were constant, but again this led to living standards pulling ahead of those in Italy (the richest region among this group of countries in 1300) and Spain, as well as in China where per capita income shrank from the turn of the millennium onwards. The Great Divergence was a long time in the making, therefore. However, it remains true that income gaps exploded in the nineteenth century, with the onset of the Industrial Revolution: this remains a fundamental turning point in global economic history.

EXPLAINING CONVERGENCE AND DIVERGENCE

Figuring out what happened is hard enough; explaining it even harder. And yet the question of what led to the Great Divergence between Europe and Asia retains its fascination, even though it is difficult to see how it will ever be answered to everyone's satisfaction.

In 1990, David Landes memorably suggested that there have traditionally been two types of answer to the question 'Why are we so rich and they so poor?'

> One says that we are so rich and they so poor because we are so good and they so bad; that is, we are hardworking, knowledgeable, educated, well-governed, efficacious, and productive, and they are the reverse. The other says that we are so rich and they so poor because we are so bad and they so good: we are greedy, ruthless, exploitative, aggressive, while they are weak, innocent, virtuous, abused, and vulnerable.[42]

The evidence reviewed in the previous section has suggested to some that the former answer is more likely to be correct, and there has been no shortage in recent years of more or less monocausal accounts of what Europe got right, or what China, or India, or Islam, got wrong. Robert Solow's famous[43] remark in 1970 that 'Every discussion among economists of the relatively slow growth of the British economy compared with the Continental economies ends up in a blaze of amateur sociology'[44] applies in spades to discussions of Britain's initial relative ascent. It is to be welcomed that economists are now willing to engage with issues that traditionally lay outside their domain: science, culture, geography, politics, and so forth. But if they are going to do so, then they could usefully adopt some of the mental habits of historians, and be more nuanced and cautious in their historical judgements, and more willing to acknowledge both the complexity of the past, and the limits of our historical knowledge.[45]

Rather than embarking on yet another discussion of what explains Europe's take-off and the Great Divergence, let me focus on one key distinction between

---

[42] Landes, David S., 'Why Are We So Rich and They So Poor?' *American Economic Review* 80, 2 (1990), pp. 1–13.

[43] Thanks to Paul Krugman.

[44] Robert M. Solow, 'Science and Ideology in Economics', *Public Interest* 21 (1970), pp. 94–107, pp. 102–3.

[45] For further discussion on interdisciplinarity, see Osterhammel in this volume.

different arguments: those that emphasize developments within economies, and those that emphasize interactions between them.

I should begin by stating that I am biased, on account of my training as an international trade economist. It seems obvious to me that when countries interact with each other, this can have potentially enormous effects on their economies. Let me go back to Williamson's finding that wages in the Atlantic economy converged in the late nineteenth century, diverged in the interwar period, and converged again after the Second World War.[46] You may already have noticed a parallel between this stylized fact, on the one hand, and trends in international economic integration since the mid nineteenth century (outlined in section, 'Tracking Globalization over Time') on the other. Economic theory suggests that the similarity between these two sets of stylized facts (real wage convergence-divergence-convergence; globalization-deglobalization-reglobalization) is not a coincidence.

One of the main purposes of O'Rourke and Williamson was to make the connection between late nineteenth-century globalization, on the one hand, and real wage convergence (and factor price convergence more generally) on the other.[47] The attempt should resonate with global historians, since what we were reacting against was a tendency by growth economists, especially, to see growth within particular countries as being purely due to forces operating within those countries, as if each was isolated from all the others. There is a vast literature, following in the footsteps of key contributions such as Abramovitz, Barro, and Mankiw et al.[48] which asks whether poorer countries are growing more rapidly than, and thus converging on, richer countries. The overwhelming majority of this literature tries to answer this question by relating the growth experience of each country to features of that country—the education of its population, its income level, its savings rate, the quality of its government, its economic policies, and so forth. Sometimes its economic interactions with the rest of the world are taken into account, but the question that is typically asked is whether countries that are more open to trade in general grow more or less rapidly than countries that are more closed. But countries may be influenced, not just by their own exposure to trade in general, but by the types of countries they trade with, by the policies of their trading partners, and by the flows of labour, capital, and technology that link them.

O'Rourke and Williamson concluded that mass migration was the main factor leading to real wage convergence in the Atlantic economy during this period,[49] which is perhaps not surprising. International trade did not have as systematic an effect on international patterns of convergence or divergence, but was a powerful influence on the incomes of particular groups in particular countries during this period. For example, it can explain almost the entire decline in British land rents

---

[46] Williamson, 'The Evolution of Global Labor Markets since 1830'.

[47] O'Rourke and Williamson, *Globalization and History*.

[48] Moses Abramovitz, 'Catching Up, Forging Ahead, and Falling Behind', *Journal of Economic History* 46, 2 (1986), pp. 385–406; Robert J. Barro, 'Economic Growth in a Cross-Section of Countries', *Quarterly Journal of Economics* 106, 2 (1991), pp. 407–43; N. Gregory Mankiw, David Romer, and David N. Weil, 'A Contribution to the Empirics of Economic Growth', *Quarterly Journal of Economics* 107, 2 (1992), pp. 407–37.

[49] O'Rourke and Williamson, *Globalization and History*.

between 1870 and 1913, and about 40 per cent of the increase in British real wages. What is more, we only explored the impact of international linkages that are easily measured and whose effects can be calculated using standard economic models (that is, trade, migration, and capital flows). We did not consider the impact of multinational corporations or of international technology transfers, let alone of imperialism and other more political aspects of the international system of the time. Our conclusion was that globalization mattered significantly for late nineteenth-century economic outcomes, but we almost certainly understated its impact.

Economists tend to analyse history using the tools that they were taught at university (in my case, international trade theory). Sometimes this is helpful, at other times it is a handicap. Attempts to 'explain' the Industrial Revolution by reference to Britain's economic links with the rest of the world have often been stymied by the use of inappropriate theoretical frameworks. For example, attempts in the 1950s and 1960s to argue that the Industrial Revolution was 'caused' by overseas demand increasing British exports in some Keynesian fashion were easily disposed of by Joel Mokyr:[50] Keynes provided a theory of the business cycle, not long-run growth; British export prices fell during this period, rather than rising; in the long run growth is caused by innovation and investment; and so forth. The famous argument that slavery financed the investments that made the Industrial Revolution possible[51] may 'founder on the numbers',[52] but it also relies on classical growth theory with capital accumulation rather than innovation at its centre, which makes little sense on either theoretical or empirical grounds.

Marxist growth theory does not explain the Industrial Revolution, but it does not follow that slavery was irrelevant: apart from anything else, slaves produced the raw material used in one of the key sectors of the time, cotton textiles. Keynesian theory does not explain the Industrial Revolution either, but neither does it follow that exports did not matter, or that the entire demand side of the economy was of no importance. A counterfactual Britain without the capacity to export its manufactures, and to import food and raw materials, would have been a very different place indeed, and it would have been difficult or impossible to sustain the Industrial Revolution in such a world.[53] Gregory Clark et al. calculate that the welfare costs to the British economy of being shut off from the rest of the world would have been enormous by the middle of the nineteenth century, and this in the context of a fairly standard economic model which typically concludes that the welfare effects of trade are very small.[54]

[50] Joel Mokyr, 'Demand vs Supply in the Industrial Revolution', *Journal of Economic History* 37, 4 (1977), pp. 981–1008.

[51] Eric E. Williams, *Capitalism & Slavery* (Chapel Hill: University of North Carolina Press, 1944).

[52] Patrick O'Brien, 'European Economic Development: The Contribution of the Periphery', *The Economic History Review* 35, 1 (1982), pp. 1–18, p. 16.

[53] Findlay and O'Rourke, *Power and Plenty*, chapter 6.

[54] Gregory Clark, Kevin H. O'Rourke, and Alan M. Taylor, 'The Growing Dependence of Britain on Trade during the Industrial Revolution', *Scandinavian Economic History Review* 62, 2 (2014), pp. 109–36.

The Industrial Revolution, and the population explosion which accompanied it, made the British economy hugely dependent on trade. The path actually followed by Britain during this period required international trade; I would argue that trade was a necessary (but not sufficient!) condition for the Industrial Revolution that the world actually experienced in the late eighteenth and early nineteenth centuries. To argue that there were alternative, feasible, autarkic Industrial Revolutions available that would have been powered by forces internal to Britain (or even Europe) alone, strikes me as being closer to alternate history than to the more sober counterfactual exercises which economists usually engage in. The debate about the causes of the Great Divergence will continue, but it seems self-evident that the British economy of the late eighteenth and nineteenth centuries was just one part (if an unusually dynamic one) of a much bigger international system, and that recognizing this should be part of any explanation. Similarly, it doesn't make much sense to analyse economic growth around the world today without taking account of the ways in which different regions are interacting with each other.

POSTSCRIPT: THE BENEFITS OF A GLOBAL PERSPECTIVE

It often turns out that developments in one country are actually part of a much bigger story. Did Ireland really switch to protection in 1932 because of the arrival to power of Éamon de Valera in that year? Did it really switch back to a more liberal trade regime some three decades later because a particularly enlightened civil servant (T. K. Whittaker) convinced a particularly enlightened Minister and Taoiseach (Seán Lemass) that this was the right thing to do? This is hardly the entire story.

Consider the debate that has been raging since 2010 about the woes of the Eurozone. Is the crisis really due to a series of idiosyncratic, country-specific problems that, coincidentally, just happen to have occurred right around the periphery of the Eurozone, from Ireland to Portugal, Spain, Italy, Cyprus, and Greece? That was the dominant official narrative for much of the time. If instead the history of the Eurozone as a whole is analysed, a picture emerges of capital flows from the core to the periphery, channelled through local banks, leading to housing market bubbles, financial crises, and overpriced economies. Viewing the Eurozone as a system, rather than as a collection of individual countries, has profound implications for our diagnosis of what went wrong, and for what should be done about it.

Thinking about the world as a system is a useful habit of mind, not just for historians, but for economists and policymakers as well. Global history can help us to better understand the past; if it inculcates students with this habit of mind, it will help them to better understand the present as well.

PART II

GLOBAL CIRCULATIONS

3

Unnecessary Dependences
Illustrating Circulation in Pre-modern Large-scale History

Nicholas Purcell

GLOBAL HISTORY AND GLOBALIZATION

The rather various practices of history which call themselves 'global' fit awkwardly with the politically contested idea of globalization in our own times. Part of this interest derives from a novel historiographical development of the last decade or so, an enthusiastic and sometimes uncritical interpretation of pre-modern social and economic history and archaeology through the language, conceptual frameworks, problematics, and ideologies of modern economic analysis. This tendency can be ascribed in part to the normal swinging of the pendulum of polemic, as prevailing orthodoxies of the later twentieth century, Marxian, anthropologically inspired, socially embedded, and sometimes rather belligerent in tone, have found useful and fertile scholarly critiques. The trend is curious in one sense, in that these same years have seen a converse development in early modern social and economic history, in which conventional views of the genesis of economic modernity have been exposed to an equally imaginative and far-reaching revisionism. The zeal of contributors to both discussions suggests that more is at stake than the usual productive repositionings of scholarship from one generation to another. The right to historical legitimation, even from the ancient past, appears to matter. There is a related debate as to whether any periods of imperfect or questionable modernity can properly be said to have global histories. In the early days, it was possible to write 'global history, to state the first postulate, is contemporary history'.[1] That circumscribed view regards it as implausible to retroject the economic conditions of modernity. Though more recent writers have been less cautious, it remains interesting to explore how far there are other varieties of global history which can be used in epochs in which those conditions can really not be discerned. What modalities of interaction and interdependence might be proposed to meet the challenge of joining up local and regional histories on a sufficiently large scale? What are their histories like?

The brief study which follows originates in these discussions. It accepts that global history (or, if we take planet-wide inclusiveness to be a contingent condition, history

---

[1] Bruce Mazlish and Ralph Buultjens (eds), *Conceptualizing Global History* (Boulder, CO: New Global History Press, 1993), p. 2.

on a very large scale, the *histoire à très large échelle* of Roger Chartier)[2] is a rich and worthwhile discipline, not least because it can transform smaller-scale histories. It exhibits one case study, in which the modalities of inter-regional interaction may justify or demand a global scale of investigation, while calling for a toolkit of concepts and models rather different from those of the global history which is most inspired by the economic and political globalizations usually predicated of the last century and a half. It hopes, therefore, to be a small pointer to how global history can be independent of a globalization, about which it can remain agnostic.

In a recent paper on the limits of early modern globalization, Jan de Vries makes some rather helpful observations.[3] With an economic historian's precision (as well as a rather characteristic choice of adjectives), he defines 'hard' globalization demandingly. He will allow, in addition, a 'soft' globalization, for which only (in his words) 'evocations of a compressed and intensified world' may be called 'soft globalization'.[4] The strategy duly enables him to find serious limitations in early modern globalization (especially with reference to trade between Asia and Europe), which might still qualify for the softer variety. De Vries is reluctant to allow even soft globalization to be predicated of the pre-modern world. His 'compression and intensification' remain essentially connected with trade, and a particular vision of the nature of 'trade'. And while he fully accepts that there has been important trade since prehistory, he has a realistic description of it:

> These movements typically required the passage of goods through multiple nodal points, relays of international trade involving the sale of goods from one merchant community to another. Each such transfer raised costs and restricted flows of information, and, even more so, flows of people. As long as such regimes remained in place, the world's many regional economies had only indirect contact with each other and this contact necessarily lacked the intensity that could justify the term globalization.[5]

This paper embraces the multiple, fragmented, indirect negotiations so lucidly evoked by the great Dutch historian. While it can hardly be doubted that they diminish the profitability of commerce, it is precisely in their social and political complexity that they add up to another kind of connectedness. And it is in that area that we might find a hopeful way of extending the idea of global history to larger tracts of the discipline.

TRAJECTORIES OF A DESIRABLE PRODUCT:
THE ANCIENT *IMAGINAIRE* OF INCENSE

This paper concerns, at least as a starting-point, the 'passage of goods', to use De Vries' term. It focusses on a particular cluster of goods, the aromatic resins of trees

---

[2] Roger Chartier, 'La conscience de la globalité', *Annales HSS* 56, 1 (2001), pp. 119–23.
[3] Jan De Vries, 'The Limits of Globalization in the Early Modern World', *The Economic History Review* 63, 3 (2010), pp. 710–33.
[4] De Vries, 'The Limits', p. 711.
[5] De Vries, 'The Limits', p. 710.

endemic to south Arabia and the northern part of the Horn of Africa, which I shall loosely refer to hereafter as 'incense' (it is not possible to give even a full outline of a large and complex subject here; a bibliographical note follows at the end of this chapter).

Frankincense and myrrh are the most celebrated of these products. These resins have been highly esteemed for some three millennia. There are many similar substances: ladanum, mastic, and storax from Mediterranean shrublands, copal from Madagascar and Mozambique, gum benjamin from Indonesia, even amber (the fossil resin of extinct trees). But the product of the *Boswellia* and *Commiphora* species from the south Red Sea area has been (for whatever reasons) acknowledged superior throughout. Because these trees have a tightly defined ecological niche, and because their resins have distinctive aromatic properties, the goods at the core of the discussion have always had a reasonably clear and distinct character. Chemical analysis of archaeological resins has now become possible, adding an important dimension to the study of the subject.[6] The nature of the product is relatively simple. Around 500 grams of frankincense resin is collected by tree per season. The collection is very demanding neither of skill nor labour. The number of trees involved seems the principal control, but, for what the comparison is worth, the underdeveloped Ethiopian resin trade still managed 16,000 tonnes of export between 1996 and 2003.

To begin with, it will be helpful to note some conspicuous features of the representation of incense in Greek and Roman authors: here too my survey is inevitably brief and selective. No one will be surprised to hear that incense is the subject of poetic and mythological imagination. It is more surprising, and unusual, given the patina of ancient literary production, that the fantastic is paired with an unusually concrete register of description.

In Herodotus' history at the end of the fifth century BC, incense is among the materials with which an eastern world is portrayed. It is prominent in his account of Mesopotamia, and it certainly marks an exotic or alien counterpoint to the familiar Mediterranean world; but at the same time there is a geographically informed sense of the real location of the origin. Something similar is found in the tradition on the wars of Alexander; the incense-lands are a type of the unattainable, beyond the world in which real political conquest is possible, but the city of Gaza, where incense reached the Mediterranean, and where large stocks were stored, serves as a metonym for these remote places (Plutarch, *Life of Alexander* 25, 6–8). From the same period we have a very clear and well-informed account of the incense-lands in Theophrastus' botanical treatise. Both the more allusive and the more mundane detail elaborates and emphasizes the endemic rarity of incense. That, let us be clear, is a rhetorical choice. Incense is produced from truly endemic species, but there are many ways of presenting and developing that fact.

So it is not enough to note that incense is a type of the 'exotic'. Whereas many places on the fringe of the world were symbols of threatening danger, the scented groves of Arabia made it truly Happy, *eudaimon*, at once blessed by the gods and

---

[6] Richard P. Evershed et al., 'Archaeological Frankincense', *Nature* 390, 6661 (1997), pp. 667–8.

contented in the most serene and fulfilling manner. The Augustan historian Diodorus (3, 46) has a rapturous description of the incense groves, and the marvellous freshness of the summer perfumes which reach sailors passing along the coast. A few decades later, the elder Pliny, in his *Natural History*, presents incense as truly marvellous, but at the same time knows the most significant trajectory of incense towards the Mediterranean in the first century of our era in astonishing detail, specifying its length as 1485.5 miles in 65 camel-stages from Thomna of the Gebbanites in Hadramaut to Gaza (*Historia naturalis*, 12, 63), as well as giving contemporary prices for the product. A similar level of technical detail is to be found in the nearly contemporary text on the topography of sea-borne commerce in the Indian Ocean, the *Periplus of the Erythraean Sea*.

The extraordinary value of incense prompts ancient authors to reflect on the implications for political economy. Both the retail process and the institutions of each polity involved in controlling it receive detailed attention. Theophrastus (*Enquiry into Plants* 9, 4) was also struck by the political organization of the incense-growing regions of south Arabia, and by the conditions in which the product is sold. Well-informed botanically, he also claimed that, although some of the trees grew on private estates, it was the only product known that could not be cultivated. Incense becomes one of the goods which attracted ancient reasoning about the nature of sale and its conditions, a subject which, because sale was thought to require regulation, was seen as part of political philosophy. In the passage mentioned, Diodorus called the primary commercialization of incense in the lands of its production the most profitable exchange by weight against money known. The kings of Saba were extraordinarily wealthy, but the consequences for their own freedom and contentment were paradoxically dire.

The question of how the polities of south Arabia related to the demand for their unique resource is developed by other authors with the theme of sequences of communities through which incense is transported, and each of which seeks to control and profit from the produce in transit. This is a particular feature of the account of the geographer Strabo (*Geographica*, 16, 4, 19). Pliny too (12, 32) stresses the priests, scribes, guards, gatekeepers, and attendants who helped add up a strikingly precise (and very high) 668 sesterces of transaction costs per camel to set against the eventual profit, in a perfect illustration of De Vries' estimation of pre-modern trade. Communications, transport, and mobility all attracted reflection too—on the very large numbers of people and camels in the incense caravans, for instance, prompting a further political reflection: the dealers on the move could be taken for an army on an expedition (Strabo 16, 4, 23). But the descriptions involve a realistic plurality of routes, an intricate interweaving of land and sea transport, and the mobilization of participants from far afield. A stray geographical text of the early Hellenistic period refers to settlers in the 'blessed islands' (those around Bab al-Mandab) whose origins were as far away as Persia and Caramania. These observations amount to a surprising depiction of unfamiliar political geography, an outline, on a regional scale, of sets of communities with institutions and cultures sharing in their orientation towards the movement of valuable goods.

Both the scale and the nature of the analysis, and the crossovers between economic and political subject matter, are relatively uncommon in ancient literature.

Besides geographies of the exotic and the familiar, ancient texts on incense use it to ponder rarity and value, the scarce and the abundant, the cheap and the luxurious. Useful in tiny quantities, incense made possible specially grand displays of consumption. Herodotus (1, 183) already alleged the consumption of 30,000 kg of incense at the principal annual festival of Babylon. In the early imperial period more precise knowledge of the product is used to calibrate the excess: Nero burned more than an annual harvest of frankincense at Poppaea's funeral; Roman demand had led to a second annual incense-tapping on the shores of south Arabia. So extremely valuable was it that stories were told of the draconian security in the Alexandrian incense workshops (Pliny, *HN* 12, 59). This suggests a widespread familiarity with the idea of Roman state preoccupation with the security and maintenance of incense supplies, a preoccupation derived from the 25 per cent duty imposed by Rome on all such imports from beyond the empire, and reflecting and promoting the discourses of rarity and extreme expense to which incense was central.

Here, then, is a rather high-profile dossier, which has helped shape a subject of later historical reflection, variously described as 'the Incense Trade', or (by analogy with the 'Silk Road') the 'Incense Road'. There is enough intellectual construction and philosophical persuasion going on in any of them to make a historian wary. But some of what they foreground is supported by other evidence, three facets of which will now be presented briefly.

THE DOSSIER ON INCENSE TRANSFORMED

Perhaps unexpectedly, archaeology and epigraphy show that the fragmented polities of the ancient tradition are, by accident or through genuine knowledge, a feature of the real political geography of ancient Arabia and its neighbours. Redistributing aromatic resins mattered to, and transformed, the polities through which they passed. Controlling production and taxing transit became important, identity-conferring functions for early south Arabian communities, as for the Himyarite kingdom, the Aksumite state of late antiquity, or the Hadrami state of the Middle Ages.[7] In one celebrated instance, it was the development of control of the south–north routes which made possible the transition from desert pastoralism to complex statehood of the Nabataeans, and the eventual establishment of the city of Petra (Diodorus 19, 94, 4–5 is the key text).[8] Control and taxation of traders

---

[7] For later north-east African equivalents, see Fouad Makki, 'The Spatial Ecology of Power: Long-Distance Trade and State Formation in Northeast Africa', *Journal of Historical Sociology* 24, 2 (2011), pp. 155–85.

[8] See also Glenn Bowersock, *Roman Arabia* (Cambridge, MA: Harvard University Press 1983); David F. Graf, *Rome and the Arabian Frontier: From the Nabataeans to the Saracens* (Aldershot: Ashgate, 1997).

was likewise central to the Ghassanid polity in the sixth century.[9] One could hardly not allude to the debate on the part played by this web of historical structures in the history of Makka: much has changed in the thirty years since scholars vigorously questioned the idea that Hijaz trade in the age of Mohammed had been importantly connected with incense distribution.[10] The politics of incense movement was not limited to small states either. Large neighbouring hegemonies, also interested in the opportunities to levy proportionately higher duties, were involved too. The earliest case was the relocation of the neo-Babylonian monarch Nabonidus to the oasis of Tayma in the mid sixth century BC.[11] The extensive concerns of the Roman imperial state with Red Sea and Arabian communications have been spectacularly illustrated by the discovery of a routine dedicatory inscription relating to a detachment of the Roman army from Jordan carved in the second century AD on a rock face in the Farasan archipelago opposite modern Eritrea, just short of the Bab al-Mandab.[12]

There has been dazzling progress in the archaeology of land and sea redistribution. The harbour geography of the northern Red Sea has been considerably clarified, and the long elusive port of Leukos Limen identified; but the most important work has taken place in a series of port-settlements along the southern façade of the Arabian peninsula, at Al-Shihr, Qana', and Khohr Rori; and on the west coast of the Red Sea, especially at the two ports which the ancient Greeks of Egypt called Myos Hormos and Berenice.[13] Archaeology in adjacent regions has also provided fuller and more satisfactory matrices for the frankincense heartland. Ras Hafun in Somalia, the ports further south on the Swahili coast, Aqaba in Jordan, and various sites in the Gulf as well as new work in India, have changed the picture of western Indian Ocean connectivity completely. A special place must be accorded the finds from the island of Socotra, with the anaerobic conditions of the Hoq cavern which

---

[9] Irfan Shahid, *Byzantium and the Arabs in the Sixth Century*, vol. 2.2 (Washington, DC: Dumbarton Oaks, 2009).

[10] Patricia Crone, *Meccan Trade and the Rise of Islam* (Oxford: Oxford University Press, 1986); cf. the summary of Gene W. Heck, "'Arabia without Spices': An Alternate Hypothesis: The Issue of "Makkan Trade and the Rise of Islam"', *Journal of the American Oriental Society* 123, 3 (2003), pp. 547–76.

[11] Christopher Edens and Garth Bawden, 'History of Tayma: and Hejazi Trade during the First Millennium BC', *Journal of the Economic and Social History of the Orient* 32, 1 (1989), pp. 48–103.

[12] François Villeneuve, 'Une inscription latine sur l'archipel Farasân, Arabie Séoudite, sud de la mer Rouge', *Comptes Rendus de l'Académie des Inscriptions* 148, 1 (2004), pp. 419–29.

[13] See, respectively, Dario Nappo, 'On the Location of Leuke Kome', *Journal of Roman Archaeology* 23 (2010), pp. 335–48; Claire Hardy-Guilbert, 'Chihr de l'encens', *Arabian Archaeology and Epigraphy* 21, 1 (2010), pp. 46–70; Alexander Sedov, 'The Port of Qana' and the Incense Trade', in David Peacock and David Williams (eds), *Food for the Gods: New Light on the Ancient Incense Trade* (Oxford: Oxbow, 2007), pp. 71–111; Alessandra Avanzini, *A Port in Arabia between Rome and the Indian Ocean: Khor Rori* (Rome: L'Erma di Bretschneider, 2008); Marijke Van der Veen, *Consumption, Trade and Innovation: Exploring the Botanical Remains from the Roman and Islamic Ports at Quseir al-Qadim, Egypt* (Frankfurt: Africa Magna, 2011); Steven E. Sidebotham, *Berenike and the Ancient Maritime Spice Route* (Berkeley: University of California Press, 2011); also David Peacock, David Williams, and Sarah James, 'Basalt as Ships' Ballast and the Roman Incense Trade', in Peacock and Williams, *Food for the Gods*, pp. 28–70.

have preserved evidence of travellers from India and Palmyra.[14] The model excavations at Sumhuram in Oman have demonstrated connections between southern Arabia and India from the third century BC (a much earlier date than previously contemplated), so destabilizing our notions of the history of the circuits of Indian Ocean commerce.[15]

New evidence also displays the mobility of people around the distribution of incense and related goods, the numerous intermediaries between incense-producers and the polities of the distant consumers, a shifting tangle of conduits joining them, and crisscrossing west Asia from the Nile valley and the Red Sea to the Gulf, and north as far north as the Euphrates bend (Strabo 16, 3, 3) and the latitude of Antioch and Aleppo. The involvement of personnel from many different origins as mobile agents in the redistribution was clearly significant in adding complexity to the inventories of materials redistributed by the circuits for which aromatics were the principal reason and motor. The other redistributions which movements of resin catalysed included local routine and staple products. Recruitment to the various social and economic corollaries of the primary movements of aromatics thus had numerous effects on polities and communities adjacent to the paths followed by those movements, varying in detail as they did from time to time. Involvement in transit became part of the portfolio of opportunities available to peoples engaged in the perennial interplay of sedentary and mobile in arid and semi-arid areas, the formative social and political structures first modelled by Michael Rowton.[16]

There are two important respects in which the picture has changed from the basic vision of the Greek and Roman texts. First, we should now want to follow the *Periplus* in including the African side of the Red Sea fully in the picture, and in situating the land and sea northward distribution of endemic aromatics in tangles of movements including the east coast of Africa to far south of the Equator,[17] and the routes eastwards to the mouth of the Indus and the western facades of the Indian subcontinent. Second, and even more importantly, for all the peculiarity which is so crucial an attribute of the ancient construction of incense, the product of the south Arabian and African aromatics was both distributed and consumed in the company of a whole gamut of other aromatics of different qualities, value, character, and origin.

Herodotus was already alert to this. In a revealing passage (3, 107), he claimed that the poisonous flying snakes which protected the Arabian incense-trees could

---

[14] Zoltán Biedermann, 'An Island under the Influence: Soqotra at the Crossroads of Egypt, Persia and India from Antiquity to the Early Modern Age', in Ralph Kauz (ed.), *Aspects of the Maritime Silk Road: From the Persian Gulf to the East China Sea* (Wiesbaden: Harrassowitz, 2010), pp. 9–24; Ingo Strauch (ed.), *Foreign Sailors on Socotra: The Inscriptions and Drawings from the Cave Hoq* (Bremen: Ute Hempen Verlag, 2012).

[15] Alessandra Avanzini, *Eastern Arabia in the First Millennium BC* (Rome: L'Erma di Bretschneider, 2010).

[16] Michael B. Rowton, 'Autonomy and Nomadism in Western Asia', *Orientalia* 42 (1973), pp. 247–58; Michael B. Rowton, 'Enclosed Nomadism', *Journal of the Economic and Social History of the Orient* 17, 1–3 (1974), pp. 1–30.

[17] Thus also Philippe Beaujard, *Les mondes de l'océan Indien*, vol. 1 (Paris: A. Colin, 2014), p. 538.

only be deterred by burning the Mediterranean resin storax. Mediterranean resins and exotic ones were structurally entwined in his thinking. The rare product of a very limited region has always been the catalyst to the distribution of other, less exclusive, aromatics of lower value, with which the top-end materials are, covertly or transparently, combined. Eighty-five per cent of resins analysed from the eleventh-century southern Arabian port of Sharma, in the heartland of frankincense production, proved to be *Hymenaea* copal from Madagascar and the southern Swahili coast.[18] Here the Arabian production of frankincense catalysed the movement of a related material with very similar uses, mobilizing communications and production thousands of kilometres to the south. Medieval and early modern distribution systems also made available other resources endemic to the wider southern Red Sea area, of which coffee has been far and away the most successful.[19]

The central resin system thus gave direction and continuity and form to transport, commercialization and transfer of other materials. Some of those were products from far beyond the frankincense heartland, which simply had to pass through it (and including the spices of the larger Indian Ocean world, on their way to Mediterranean consumption). It is of course not at all unusual for goods on the move to travel in packages, to have congeners with which their meaning is entangled, to be conceived of and deployed in sequences and clusters. The extremely strong cultural identity of incense seems to have helped subordinate to it many subsidiary items in the changing weaves of circulation.

Enough has been said to suggest that the movement of incense has been historically intricate, and that it deserves careful study. But this could be said of many goods, and so far nothing I have said of the aromatics of the southern Red Sea zone so far justifies making more of it as a means of approaching global history than of any of these other materials. It is time to show how we might take that step.

UNNECESSARY DEPENDENCE: *CIRCULATION* INVOKED

The answer lies in another school of global-ish historiography, 'connected histories', *histoires connectées*,[20] and specifically in the development of this approach in the work done on *circulation* in early modern south Asian history by Markovits, Pouchepadass, and Subrahmanyam.[21] The emphasis is not on the material

---

[18] Martine Regert, Thibaut Devièse, Anne-Solenn Le Hô, and Axelle Rougeulle, 'Reconstructing Ancient Yemeni Commercial Routes during the Middle Ages Using Structural Characterization of Terpenoid Resins', *Archaeometry* 50, 4 (2008), pp. 668–95.

[19] See e.g. Michel Tuchscherer, *Le commerce du café* (Cairo: Institut français d'archéologie orientale, 2001).

[20] Natalie Z. Davis, 'Decentering History: Local Stories and Cultural Crossings in a Global World', *History and Theory* 50, 2 (2011), pp. 188–202; Sanjay Subrahmanyam, *Explorations in Connected History: From the Tagus to the Ganges* (Delhi: Oxford University Press, 2004); Michael Werner and Bénédicte Zimmermann, 'Penser l'histoire croisée: entre empirie et réflexité', *Annales HSS* 58, 1 (2003), pp. 7–36.

[21] Claude Markovits, Sanjay Subrahmanyam, and Jacques Pouchepadass, 'Introduction', in Claude Markovits, Sanjay Subrahmanyam, and Jacques Pouchepadass (eds), *Society and Circulation: Mobile*

commodity but, as the term 'circulation' suggests, on the social behaviours through which the movements of items, whether strictly commodities or not, are performed, and which are altered themselves by their engagement in the mobilities of people and goods.

The analysis of *circulation* is released from the contingencies which dominate the histories of particular items too narrowly defined. The study of circulation entails a certain degree of granularity, making a rich and fruitful counterweight to the large generalizations with which global history so often deals. It inevitably includes, alongside materialistic considerations, the social histories of all the people involved in the communities most affected by participating in circulation, and in the movements of ideas as well as the things which are the ostensible reason for the mobilities themselves. That is no minor matter, as such an enquiry must entail both the cultural construction of what moves and those who move it, as well as the engagement of participation of circulation in a gamut of other behaviours which can range from the management of primary production through to state-formation and ethnogenesis—a gamut which we can illustrate quite easily from the history of southern Red Sea aromatics. The historical landscape of distributing incense as I have outlined it strikingly matches the pictures both of inhibited trade and creative *circulation*. The social intricacy of the engagement of traders and other intermediaries in the complex of movements which centred on incense, as we have glimpsed it from archaeology, but above all from epigraphy, is especially relevant. We have observed the processes of formation, mutation, and disappearance of displacement and diaspora patterns of a sort that is especially suggestive for global history.[22]

But the principal appeal of this approach is that it releases the historian from the exclusively commercial interpretation of these exchanges and relationships (something which has occasionally approached parody).[23] Instead, our subject becomes the full range of social, political, and cultural behaviours entangled with the production and movement of incense and the other distributions which it galvanized. *Circulation* offers the global historian matrices for examining how areas—sometimes very extensive ones, as in the examples given above—were intertwined with each other, and, in particular, for observing how large-scale interdependence may co-exist with inhibited and poorly performing commerce. Though it offers a promising way of complicating the exclusively economic with the social and the cultural, it remains the case that—so far—a possible case of complex *circulations* has been outlined which may be of repeated local interest and significance, but which is no better than any other trajectory of a scarce resource at building up to a history where the models, rather than the contingent details, require analysis on the largest scale.

In south Asia, where the model was first applied, the perennial dialectics of tropical coastal lowland, riverine interior floodplains, and high plateaux, have been

---

People and Itinerant Cultures in South Asia, 1750–1950 (New Delhi: Permanent Black, 2003). See also Jürgen Osterhammel's explications on the six types of global history in this volume.

[22] Cf., for instance, Ina B. McCabe, Gelina Harlaftis, and Ioanna P. Minoglou, *Diaspora Entrepreneurial Networks: Four Centuries of History* (Oxford: Berg, 2005).

[23] As with Bradley Z. Hull, 'Frankincense, Myrrh, and Spices: The Oldest Global Supply Chain?' *Journal of Macromarketing* 28, 3 (2008), pp. 275–88.

invoked by the pioneers of *circulation* as the explanation for and the foundation of the patterns of circulation and their durability. These chains of interdependent social behaviours are patterned by physical, environmental, givens, but not determined by them. In the case of incense, it is not an ecology of the physical environment which determines the persistence, the longevity, of the movements, but a cultural ecology, in which it is not climate or soil which dictates consumption, but social behaviour, and above all, in this case, religious systems. It is the fact that these religious systems exhibit continua of comparable behaviour over the very long term and over truly vast distances that creates the social environments in which incense has been consumed, and it is in this that the trajectories of these aromatics can claim to be a tracer of a different kind of globalization.

If, over the last three millennia, these aromatic products have been distributed across a very wide area of the old world (though they have not always described equally extensive or similarly patterned geographies of distribution), and been repeatedly impressive in their capacity to stitch together large clusters of regions of apparently very different historical textures, that is because they have repeatedly played a role in social calibrations of scarcity, value-formation, as well as of the domestic and the exotic; and have fulfilled that role above all through their use in religious observance.

The rarity of south Red Sea aromatics has been counterpointed by extremely widespread patterns of everyday consumption, the circle being squared by the possibility of using very small quantities. But the sweet-smelling smoke of these products was a normal element in Mesopotamian and, from the archaic Greek period, in Greco-Roman religion, and had a role in flamboyant Roman public ceremonial which derived from it. Prominent in the religious practice of the Jerusalem Temple, it became a feature of Christian liturgy after the Peace of the Church (and quite soon after it, achieving an early prominence in the Syriac Christianity of the Levantine macro-regional contact-zone). It subsequently found several roles in Islam. The burning of aromatics in south Asian religious practice, with its diaspora eastwards and southwards, is a parallel structure, and the overlaps between the networks supplying the two, and the problematic of cultural crossovers which it suggests, are a further intriguing subject. With frankincense, then, we see a strange historical phenomenon. The esteem itself is an interesting subject. How variable have consumers' objectives been? What ranges of positive values are attributed to these sweet-smelling smokes? What part is played by discerning appreciation of the smell, what by convention and tradition, and what by the simple perception of the exotic? How do we relate the religious uses to the redistribution, and what effects does that inter-relationship have on other historical questions? The ultimate destination of incense in many contexts was destructive, as it was made an offering to the divine. The religious functions helped to locate it, as a material good, in a conceptual domain of gifts, offerings, and treasures, more than in more mundane contexts of routine commercial exchange.[24]

---

[24] See for instance Paul Freedman, 'Spices and Late-Medieval European Ideas of Scarcity and Value', *Speculum* 80, 4 (2005), pp. 1209–27 and Florin Curta, 'Merovingian and Carolingian Gift-Giving', *Speculum* 81, 3 (2006), pp. 671–99 for medieval cases.

The meaning, context and value of incense changed constantly as it was distributed away from the southern Red Sea. As it rose in price to accommodate the ever-rising transaction-costs, it came in some ways to resemble those ensembles of goods which we label 'luxuries', but the scale of its consumption and its religious connotations make that a tricky classification. The variety and the transience of elite consumption do make it difficult to fit in to global historical themes. The 'indispensable luxuries of everyday life'[25] may, however, because of their very wide distribution, from time to time, in the pre-modern world, constitute distributions large enough in volume and/or wide enough in their catchments to be attractive for global history (such patterns are important in Antiquity, a distinguishing feature of which is the presence of unusually large percentages of urban consumers by comparative pre-modern standards—even if the proportions are hotly debated and not absolutely very elevated). Pepper in both the Roman and later medieval period fits into this intermediate category. Incense is more complex. But at the same time it is essential to recognize that because incense could be consumed in very small quantities, it could both be luxurious and relatively familiar, something like a 'religious staple'. Type of expensive exoticism though it was, as the indispensable raw material of the most basic religious acts, it was included in the Roman-law concept of *penus*, the basic minimum for survival of the citizen (Gellius 4, 1).[26]

Materialism need not be reductive. Stuff itself is susceptible of meaning and value in many different registers, some rather unfamiliar today. The engagement of goods with the senses in the past is rightly attracting more attention, and there has been a good deal of interest in recent years in Greek and Roman olfactory history.[27] The subject turns out to have rich implications for major topics in intellectual or cognitive history, such as the understanding of sense-perception, itself, and of nature, more generally.[28] The approach intersects, in the case of incense, with the better-established spatial turn in history, itself well suited to the conceptual challenges of global history;[29] we have seen how important to the formation of ideas about and through south Arabian aromatics are the sense and character of the exotic. In combination with religious usages, incense came to evoke a cosmological, as well as a geographical, other—in the Abrahamic tradition, at any rate,

[25] Crone, *Meccan Trade*, p. 27.

[26] Cf. Giovanni Salmeri, 'Dell'uso dell'incenso in epoca romana', in Avanzini, *Profumi d'Arabia*, pp. 529–40.

[27] Giuseppe Squillace, *I giardini di Saffo: profumi e aromi nella Grecia antica* (Rome: Carocci, 2014); Alfredo Carannante and Matteo D'Acunto (eds), *I profumi nelle società antiche: produzione, commercio, usi, valori simbolici* (Salerno: Pandemos, 2012); Alessandra Avanzini (ed.), *Profumi d'Arabia* (Rome: L'Erma di Bretschneider, 1997).

[28] Béatrice Caseau, '*Euodia*: The Use and Meaning of Fragrances in the Ancient World and their Christianization (100–900 A.D.)', PhD dissertation, University of Princeton, 1994; Susan A. Harvey, *Scenting Salvation: Ancient Christianity and the Olfactory Imagination* (Berkeley: University of California Press, 2006).

[29] Angelo Torre, 'Un "tournant spatiale" en histoire: paysages, regards, ressources', *Annales HSS* 63, 5 (2008), pp. 1127–244; Matthias Middell and Katja Naumann, 'Global History and the Spatial Turn: From the Impact of Area Studies to the Study of Critical Junctures of Globalization', *Journal of Global History* 5, 1 (2010), pp. 149–70.

Paradise itself. Indeed, when we recall the evocations of Happy Arabia in Diodorus, perhaps we should not separate these two categories too rigidly.

Essentially ecologically derived histories of interdependence over the long term have certain characteristics. They generalize across intensification and abatement, and they exhibit complex patterns within which the particularities shift and recombine. In cultural ecology too there have been wanings as well as waxings, ruptures and discontinuities as well as long periods of convergence and comparability. But being able in pre-modern cases to examine the weakening of connective effects, and the breaking of links, and declines and ruptures as well as steady increases in global reach, enriches global history. Even in this brief account, certain diachronic questions need to be registered. Jewish, Mesopotamian, and Greek evidence for religious use of incense all starts (broadly) in the seventh century BC, and whether there was indeed some relatively sudden onset in that period remains controversial.[30] Positive climatic change around the millennium and the assertive, acquisitive, and extractive behaviours of the Neo-Assyrian polity in galvanizing interdependence should perhaps be linked.[31] It is also relevant that domesticated camels appear to have been widely used in south-west Asia only from around this date. South Arabian cultural affiliations in the first millennium BC point towards Mesopotamia, and there is no doubting the relevance of Mesopotamian cultural practice to both Jewish and Greek societies. The role of the Levant in mediating these connections is unmistakeable. Late Antiquity has posed another problem. The pagan-Christian transition has been seen as a caesura in the consumption of incense: but this no longer seems to be reflected by a decline in Arabian and Red Sea communications.[32] Incense was not one of the pagan observances most stringently prohibited by the newly Christian empire (*Codex Theodosianus* 16, 10, 12, AD 392), and early adoption by Christians now seems more plausible than it did in the past. Given the widespread and cross-cultural religious prominence of incense, major shifts in Eurasian religious history have undoubtedly had important effects on consumption of incense, but there remains much to be done.

INTIMATIONS OF THE GLOBAL

The circuits by which incense was distributed, then, certainly call for history *à très large échelle*. The pay-off of such attention to detail will not be limited to understanding the specifics of any one period-specific redistribution-system, or one set of regions through which it operated. The social and cultural effects of this dynamic reached far out into adjacent spaces, and not just through the wide consumption patterns of incense or the other items moved with it or by those who moved it. Redistributing resins, from the same limited areas, through relatively restricted

[30] Michal Artzy, 'Incense, Camels and Collared Rim Jars: Desert Trade Routes and Maritime Outlets in the Second Millennium', *Oxford Journal of Archaeology* 13, 2 (1994), pp. 121–47.

[31] Beaujard, *Les mondes de l'océan Indien*, vol. 1, pp. 506–14.

[32] R. K. Pedersen, 'The Byzantine-Aksumite Period Shipwreck at Black Assarca Island, Eritrea', *Azania* 43 (2008), pp. 77–94, cf. Richard Alston, 'Writing the Economic History of the late Antique East: A Review', *Ancient West and East* 3, 1 (2004), pp. 124–36.

communications corridors, over the long durations of mass demand, acted as a structure through which other mobilities or mobilizations could be realized. The processes by which the items in question were released into the continua of redistribution were extremely varied and historically contingent. But the two things which remain comparable across the different historical contexts, are the fact of the *circulation* in which aromatics were embedded, and the peculiar nature of incense, with its exaggeratedly high conceptual value, and its normal consumption as part of a system involving other aromatics, across very large cultural zones which are very different from each other in many respects.

These abutting 'zones' are, in their size, and in the fact of their complex interrelationship, suggestive of the project of history on the largest scale. They resemble what has been claimed of the similar potential of maritime histories.[33] The environmental givens of sea and ocean basins have, from the second millennium BC at least, often encouraged long-lasting continuities in patterns of contact or circulation, even if most of the relations have usually been subject to the de Vries strictures about fragmentation.[34] Where maritime spaces abut and intersect there have been particularly interesting patterns of contact and cultural exchange. In these cases, the durability of the connectivities is promoted by slow-changing environmental influences on the practicalities of seafaring. But it also owes a good deal to a second kind of environmental given, the ecological or geological distributions of items for which there is frequently widespread demand. That factor naturally applies to terrestrial and mixed circulations too.[35]

From the Red Sea as far north as Damascus and Antioch, the geography of the distribution of products from the resin heartland also mapped a complex and debatable zone, hard to control politically, and acting as a complex interface between the world of Mediterranean connectivity on the one side, and that of west Asia on the other. This hinge-zone was thus informed and shaped not just by the two large-scale domains to west and east, but by its functions as a cluster of conduits for movements from south to north. Its contacts and overlaps with the spaces on either side make it a notably hybrid place of constant change.[36] That zone, where very different cultural domains abutted, has also been implicated in religious

[33] Jerry H. Bentley, 'Sea and Ocean Basins as Frameworks of Historical Analysis', *Geographical Review* 89, 2 (1999), pp. 215–24; Maria Fusaro, 'Maritime History as Global History? The Methodological Challenges and a Future Research Agenda', in Maria Fusaro and Amélia Polónia (eds), *Maritime History as Global History* (St John's, Newfoundland: International Maritime Economic History Association, 2010), pp. 267–82; Gelina Harlaftis, 'Maritime History or History of *Thalassa*', in Gelina Harlaftis (ed.), *The New Ways of History* (London: I. B. Tauris, 2010), pp. 213–39; Nicholas Purcell, 'Beach, Tide and Backwash: The Place of Maritime Histories', in Peter N. Miller (ed.), *The Sea: Thalassography and Historiography* (Ann Arbor: University of Michigan Press, 2013), pp. 84–108.

[34] For this approach to the Indian Ocean, Markus P. M. Vink, 'Indian Ocean Studies and the "New Thalassology"', *Journal of Global History* 2, 1 (2007), pp. 41–62.

[35] For this approach to a new global history, see also Maxine Berg, (ed.), *Writing the History of the Global: Challenges for the Twenty-First Century* (Oxford: Oxford University Press, 2013).

[36] Cf. the approach to large-scale history of Serge Gruzinski, *Les quatre parties du monde: histoire d'une mondialisation* (Paris: Martinière, 2006); and for the Levant as a hinge between the Mediterranean world and west Asian circuits, Nicholas Purcell, 'On the Significance of East and West in Today's "Hellenistic" History: Reflections on Symmetrical Worlds, Reflecting through World Symmetries', in Jonathan R. W. Prag and Josephine C. Quinn (eds.), *Hellenistic West: Rethinking the Ancient Mediterranean* (Cambridge: Cambridge University Press, 2013), pp. 367–90.

innovation, which helps explain the density of its engagements with the social forms of religiosity far across the macro-regions which meet there.

The globalizations of economic modernity are the result of highly specific sets of *conjonctures*, and should be studied alongside many other kinds of structure which integrate histories on a very large scale. This paper has sought such a pattern in the more complex interdependences which are founded on the patterns of movements of locally rare raw materials and resources, and the social and cultural contacts, exchanges, and differentiations which result from them. Approaches of this kind offer an important alternative to the narrative of globalization, since the subjects exhibit abatement as well as intensification, and call also for explanations of dis-aggregation and declining connectivity. Perhaps, one might add, the history of contemporary, hard, globalizations will before long also be constrained to move in this direction, too. Being able to include lessenings as well as increases or inten-sifications, and trajectories of more than one directionality, greatly strengthens the historical enquiry, and, indeed, this is one of the great advantages of including as great a time-depth as possible in global history.

A further desideratum in global history met by this case study is the pursuit of granularity. Specializing in globality can sometimes be relatively unrewarding just when it avoids the crucial mix of scales which makes history interesting.[37] Global history, however wide its embrace, needs to operate with micro-histories, and to base itself on history *terre-à-terre*. If we undertake a history which concerns what joins things up, practically and conceptually, as well as what allows us sensibly to discriminate histories by region, period, or theme, then it will not suffice to operate at a level of generality and abstraction which matches the grand scale of the enter-prise. The spotlight of the history of incense thus shines on the micro-histories—of the dealers in copal at Sharma, as it might be. In particular, it is very easy to speak of flows without being at all transparent as to the mechanics of what movements are being covered by this metaphor. In this case, the obstacles, the inhibitors of free movement, are an ingredient in the construction of the commerce,[38] and serve the paradoxical purpose of evoking a movement which is both extraordinarily difficult and completely under cognitive and practical control.

Over my two and a half millennia, then, large-scale patterns of connectivity formed around, and to different extents derived their character from, the infra-structures by which the endemics of the greater Bab al-Mandab region were dis-tributed across Eurasia. These patterns resemble modern globalization in the extent which they could at some periods achieve, in the complexity of the distributions. These owed their origins and longevity to the scented resins and the prices which those could ultimately command, but came to include networks of local and long-distance movement of many other kinds of material. But the differences from contemporary globalization are as important to the historian. In worlds in which

---

[37] Jacques Revel, *Jeux d'échelles: la micro-analyse à l'expérience* (Paris: Gallimard, 1996) is the classic treatment.

[38] Eivind H. Seland, *The Indian Ocean in the Ancient Period: Definite Places, Translocal Exchange* (Oxford: Archaeopress, 2007).

the infrastructures were highly fragmented, the valuable commodities lent themselves not to the purposes of large centralized states or imperial hegemonies, but to social, economic, and political innovation which played a significant role in the very large processes by which Mediterranean, west Asian, northeast African, and Indian Ocean domains continued to abut along fault lines which have usually seemed, in one sense, peripheral, but in others were extremely central to the processes of political, economic, and cultural change across the widest spaces, and that is one of the counterparts of, the analogies for, globalization of the modern variety, which global history needs to include.

That the commodity at the heart of this congeries of processes should be one which was at many of these historical moments largely, principally or even exclusively used for regularity-enhancing, orthodoxy-promoting, everyday religious rites, rather than for elite conspicuous consumption or for necessary daily subsistence, also counterpoints the materialist calculuses of the study of modern globalization with something requiring a different set of historical approaches. Global history is only desirable if it liberates and enriches the historian: this example of how it might be attempted in a pre-modern Old World example offers the potential for both.

BIBLIOGRAPHICAL NOTE

There has been an explosion of work on incense and the southern Red Sea zone over the last generation. Among older syntheses, Nigel St J. Groom, *Frankincense and Myrrh: A Study of the Arabian Incense Trade* (London: Stacey, 1981) stands out; the most useful recent collection is David Peacock and David Williams (eds), *Food for the Gods: New Light on the Ancient Incense Trade* (Oxford: Oxbow, 2007: see the chapters by Gupta and Singer for general overviews). At the same time, archaeology and long-term history in the wider Indian Ocean have been transformed. From Federico De Romanis, *Cassia, Cinnamomo, Ossidiana: Uomini e merci tra Oceano Indico e Mediterraneo* (Rome: L'Erma di Bretschneider, 1996) on Roman trade, to the extraordinary collection of material on every aspect of premodern Indian Ocean history, Philippe Beaujard, *Les mondes de l'océan Indien*, vol. 1 (Paris: A. Colin, 2014, pp. 363–82 for Roman involvement in the Indian Ocean; pp. 383–91 for aromatics), there has been a series of useful general contributions, many of which include the aromatics which are the subject of this paper: out of many one might cite Gary K. Young, *Rome's Eastern Trade: International Commerce and Imperial Policy 31 bc–ad 305* (London: Routledge, 2001); John Keay, *The Spice Route: A History* (Berkeley: University of California Press, 2006); Eivind H. Seland, *The Indian Ocean in the Ancient Period: Definite Places, Translocal Exchange* (Oxford: Archaeopress, 2007); Roberta Tomber, 'Rome and Mesopotamia—Importers into India in the First Millennium AD', *Antiquity* 81 (2007), pp. 972–88; Raoul J. McLaughlin, *Rome and the Distant East: Trade Routes to the Ancient Lands of Arabia, India and China* (London: Continuum, 2010). More specific studies are referenced in the course of the text above.

4

A Global Middle Ages?

Robert I. Moore

INTRODUCTION

It is not only by origin that the idea of a Middle Age is a European one. The double discontinuity that defines it is quintessentially, irredeemably European. The end of antiquity is not a global idea, but it is certainly a Eurasian one. This chapter is about Eurasia. It touches on Africa, and some parts of its argument may be capable of extension to the Americas, but it will not stretch to Australasia or Oceania. Whatever difficulties we may now have with the end of antiquity—with its nature, its character, its chronology, the extent of continuity across it, and so on—the sedentary civilizations of Eurasia have all looked back since some time in the first millennium of the Common Era to a classical age of towering cultural achievement in which they located their origins. Separated from that age (though in varying degrees) by more or less clearly recalled catastrophe, they considered themselves directly or indirectly its heirs, and continued to draw on its legacy in ways they considered essential to their guidance and well being. There was thus nothing peculiarly European about proclaiming the glories of those heroic and classical pasts or representing current agendas as reassertions of their values and traditions.[1] By contrast, no such widely shared experience, development or perception was equivalent to the Renaissance in western European history and historiography, in Eurasia as a whole. The notion that the self-conscious recovery of antiquity and the conscious repudiation of the intervening millennium defined an epoch, with all that that notion has implied, has no resonance beyond Latin Europe and does not acquire it even by being linked, in Burckhardtian fashion, with transoceanic exploration or territorial acquisition.

'THE MIDDLE AGES' IN NON-EUROPEAN HISTORY

It is not surprising, then, that the tripartite periodization, Ancient, Medieval, Modern, divided around 500 and 1500, which has been conventional for European

[1] For instance, Sheldon Pollock, *The Language of the Gods in the World of Men: Sanskrit, Culture and Power in Premodern India* (Berkeley: University of California Press, 2006), Part 2; Marshall G. S. Hodgson, *The Venture of Islam: Conscience and History in a World Civilization*, 3 vols (Chicago: University of Chicago Press, 1974), vol. 2, pp. 293–328; Richard N. Frye, *The Golden Age of Persia: The Arabs in the East* (London: Weidenfeld & Nicolson, 1975), pp. 1–7.

history, generally makes little sense as a framing of non-European histories, widely used though it has been. Certainly, it does not serve to place regional histories in an agreed chronology. It is not unusual to find historians of India beginning the 'medieval' period with the establishment of Muslim conquest principalities in the thirteenth century, three centuries after some of their counterparts on China have announced a Renaissance under the Northern Song.[2] That is an extreme example. On the other hand, Chattopadhya's thoughtful discussion of the idea of the middle ages in Indian historiography sees periodization itself as a necessary counter to the stereotype of eternal changelessness. He finds 'early medieval' a better description than terms like 'late Hindu' or 'late classical' for the period from about the sixth to the twelfth century CE because it directs attention forwards, to continuities with what came later, rather than backwards to a much mythologized heroic past.[3] It is a fair point. This essay will make a similar case for treating the period between around 500 and 1500 as a distinct and coherent one in Eurasian history. Nevertheless, the word 'medieval' itself remains a hangover from the Eurocentric inheritance of modern historiography,[4] and reflects the widely and often rather vaguely held notion of a common historical trajectory which all societies, or civilizations, are presumed to follow. It raises the same difficulty as other efforts to fit the regional societies of Afroeurasia into a common developmental framework, more attractive to earlier generations than to this one, as in the long-lasting, wide-ranging, and in many respects fruitful discussion as to the extent to which or the terms on which several of them might properly be described as 'feudal'.[5] If European historians themselves have now for the most part either abandoned the word 'feudal' altogether or deploy it in very specific contexts, defined in correspondingly limited terms, rather than as a general characterization of whole societies, what is to be gained by prolonging its exposure in a wider world?

'THE MIDDLE AGES' IN PRACTICE

The same question might be asked no less pertinently of the term 'middle ages' itself.[6] If there are still historians of Latin or Western Europe who can perceive an

[2] For instance, Noboru Karashima, *South Indian Society in Transition: Ancient to Medieval* (New Delhi: Oxford University Press, 2009), pp. 1–23; Jean Gernet, *A History of Chinese Civilization* (Cambridge: Cambridge University Press, 1982), pp. 297ff.

[3] Brajadulal Chattopadhya, *The Making of Early Medieval India* (New Delhi: Oxford University Press, 1994), pp. 1–37, at 35–6.

[4] Ronald Inden, Jonathan Walters, and Daud Ali, *Querying the Medieval: Texts and the History of Practices in South Asia* (Oxford: Oxford University Press, 2000). I greatly regret that I have not been able to take account of Kathleen Davis, *Periodization and Sovereignty: How Ideas of Feudalism and Secularization Govern the Politics of Time* (Philadelphia: University of Pennylvania Press, 2008).

[5] Most recently, Eric Bournazel and Jean-Pierre Poly (eds), *Les féodalités* (Paris: Presses Universitaires de France, 1998); on its current use by historians of Europe, Charles West, *Reframing the Feudal Revolution: Political and Social Transformation between Marne and Moselle, c.800–c.1100* (Cambridge: Cambridge University Press, 2013), pp. 1–9.

[6] Cf. Timothy Reuter, 'Medieval: Another Tyrannous Construct?' *The Medieval History Journal* 1, 1 (1998), pp. 25–45, reprinted in Timothy Reuter, *Medieval Polities and Modern Mentalities*, ed. Janet L. Nelson (Cambridge: Cambridge University Press, 2006), pp. 19–37.

essential unity in the centuries between 500 and 1500 that sets them apart as a 'civilization' distinct from those before and after, it has a rapidly diminishing effect on their practice. As teachers of undergraduate and still more of graduate students, as organizers of research seminars, even, when commercial pressures permit, as writers of surveys and textbooks, they nowadays prefer to divide that millennium into three parts, though with only rough agreement among themselves as to where the dividing points may be. The middle (or, as we often say, 'central') one is still routinely called 'medieval', while those before and after shade with varying degrees of subtlety into the late antique and the early modern. This fragmentation is most obviously the result of the growth of knowledge, but also reflects conceptualization. That 'early' and 'later' middle ages are still widely preferred to the newer terminologies more often reflects reaffirmation of particular readings of those sub-periods themselves than championship of the essential unity of the entire millennium.[7]

All periodizations, of course, risk disguising continuities and inhibiting consideration of things that ought to be considered together. Conversely, they remain useful and vital for as long as they are capable of framing large questions that reward investigation and discussion, or are pressed on the academy by the curiosity of the wider world. It is hard to identify such questions about 'the middle ages' at or anywhere near the cutting edge of current or recent debate, either academic or popular. The idea has become for European history effectively useless, and, in most ways, a nuisance.[8] It serves mainly to distract attention from continuities with the periods before and after while legitimizing vacuous generalities spanning vastly different regions, societies, periods, and cultures. The depressing history of the word 'medieval' itself makes the point. Long discarded as a serious analytical category it clings to life as a considerable vested interest, and as a form of intellectual ghettoization that serves to excuse the ignorance of outsiders about what goes on inside its imagined boundaries, and of its devotees about almost everything else. It is a pretty safe rule of thumb, applicable equally whether it is used as a term of approbation or abuse, that the more someone uses the word 'medieval' the less they know about the middle ages.

It has not always been so. We like to remember that the idea of the middle age was invented by Petrarch and Leonardo Bruni in the fourteenth and fifteenth centuries and elaborated by Cellarius in the seventeenth,[9] but it did not catch on straight away. No British historian used the term 'Middle Ages' before Hallam, in

---

[7] For instance, David Rollason, *Early Medieval Europe 300–1050: The Birth of Western Society* (London: Routledge, 2012), explicitly at pp. 6–8; John Watts, *The Making of Polities: Europe, 1300–1500* (Cambridge: Cambridge University Press, 2009), pp. 9–42.

[8] For a comprehensive and sophisticated assault, to which I am very much in debt, Constantin Fasolt, *Past Sense: Studies in Medieval and Early Modern History* (Leiden: Brill, 2014), especially at pp. 545–96; Constantin Fasolt, 'Hegel's Ghost: Europe, the Reformation and the Middle Ages', *Viator* 39 (2008), pp. 345–86.

[9] For a convenient summary, see Willam A. Green, 'Periodization in European and World History', *Journal of World History* 3, 1 (1992), pp. 13–53. There is a certain irony in Green's conclusion that 1500 was no longer a useful dividing point for European history, but (largely under the impetus of world systems theory) had become an essential one for global history.

1818—Hume and Gibbon may be searched in vain—and it was Ruskin, in his *Lectures on Architecture* (1853), who formally defined the Medieval as falling between the Classical and the Modern, 'from the fall of the Roman Empire to the close of the fifteenth century'.[10] By that time the Victorian boom in romantic medievalism was well under way: four years later Trollope's Miss Thorne of Ullathorne would urge her Barsetshire neighbours to practise their jousting at the quintain.[11] A hundred years or so after that the pejorative sense of the word 'medieval' had become perhaps its commonest in general use. Merrill-Webster's third edition of 1961 gives as one of its meanings 'outmoded, antiquated'; the editions of 1909 and 1934 had not.[12]

It is worth pausing to recall the fortunes of Medieval History during the century or so, not a great deal longer, when its connotations were almost always positive, and when the influence of its specialists was at its height. Those fortunes were, of course, intimately bound up with the authentication and legitimation of the nation state that underpinned the historical movement of the nineteenth century,[13] and inextricably intertwined with the immense extension in size and influence of the professional middle class whose members were the nation state's leading architects, functionaries, celebrants, and beneficiaries. History's central role in the public education systems of the nascent modern state rested in large part on the indispensability of its medieval origins, real or imagined, to the authority and identity of the state itself, and on the universally acknowledged status of the medieval age as the soil—to borrow a favourite metaphor from this historiography—in which national institutions had taken root and flourished. National history from the early middle ages onwards was at the core of school and university curricula throughout Europe. As late as the 1950s, to offer a local example, if a British university or college had only one Professor of History it was as likely as not to be a medievalist. The fall when it came was precipitous. In 1965 the University of Warwick, one of the new generation of 'plateglass universities', became the first to establish a department of History that contained no medievalists, and to offer an honours degree in History that did not include the Middle Ages. The model was not immediately imitated, but this was a clear signal that times, for the Middle Ages, had changed. A more threatening manifestation was the rise of the social sciences, which in the 1960s moved out of their original strongholds, preeminently in Britain the LSE, to secure parity everywhere with the humanities both in numbers and (more slowly) in esteem. They either ignored History altogether or, seeing as how their essential business of modernization and industrialization classically

---

[10] John Ruskin, *Lectures on Architecture IV, 111*, cited from the Gutenberg edition, <http://www.gutenberg.org/files/23593/23593-h/23593-h.htm> (accessed 30 January 2015).

[11] Anthony Trollope, *Barchester Towers*, ed. John Bowen (Oxford: Oxford University Press, 2014), chs 22, 25–6.

[12] Fred C. Robinson, 'Medieval, the Middle Ages', *Speculum* 59, 4 (1984), pp. 745–56, at pp. 752–3. *OED*, tracing 'mediaeval' from 1807, had not recognized the alternative spelling or the pejorative usage by 1971.

[13] Patrick J. Geary, *The Myth of Nations: The Medieval Origins of Europe* (Princeton: Princeton University Press, 2002); Ian Wood, *The Modern Origins of the Early Middle Ages* (Oxford: Oxford University Press, 2013).

conceived, assumed that it was of no possible relevance to their concerns before 1750, or perhaps at the very earliest, 1500.

The broader narrative that remained the undisputed basis of academic history in the Western world right up to the 1980s offered a less secure refuge to the middle ages than narratives of national history had done. It told how human achievement had reached its peak in the liberal democracies of the industrial age. Both democracy and capitalist industrialism (which were taken to be inseparable in the authorized version, though not in the Marxist variant), were attributable to the special qualities of European, or Western, or Christian Civilization, and in particular to its synthesis of the rational and democratic traditions of the classical civilization of the ancient Mediterranean with the spiritual power and insights of the Judaeo-Christian legacy.[14] Since the achievement of that synthesis was held to be the special contribution of the Renaissance, the Middle Ages were correspondingly threatened with relegation to a passively preparatory role, the freezer, as it were, in which the meat of classicism was preserved, though inert, until the master chefs were ready for it. The medievalists tried to retaliate by pushing the Renaissance itself back to the twelfth century, or even, at their most daring, the ninth.[15] Nevertheless, the master narrative endorsed, albeit in attenuated form and often in the shape of Ecclesiastical or Church History, the presumption universal in Europe and the neo-Europes of the New World that the middle ages imparted a necessary legacy and continuity to 'our' history.

PERIODIZING GLOBAL HISTORY

To look back beyond the 1960s, into the world in which I began to grow up, is to gaze across a chasm that separates us from another age. The reasons have less to do with popular music, hallucinogenic substances, or even contraception than with the collapse of the great certainties of the Victorians and their children and grandchildren—not only nationalism and religion, but positivism, idealism, imperialism, orientalism (in the sense later identified by Edward Said).[16] That does not mean, of course, that nobody went on believing in those things, or that nobody had questioned them before. But in the 1960s they ceased to be certainties, to exercise a universal hegemony that marginalized those who had dissented from them, and provided solid foundations for a ruling culture and institutions, including the study and teaching of History. If there has been a single reason for the rise of world history, whose emergence as a rational, properly historical

[14] Culminating, perhaps, in David Landes, *The Wealth and Poverty of Nations: Why Some Are so Rich and Some so Poor* (New York: W. W. Norton, 1998); cf. Jack Goody, *The East in the West* (Cambridge: Cambridge University Press, 1996); Jack Goody, *The Theft of History* (Cambridge: Cambridge University Press, 2006).
[15] Charles Homer Haskins, *The Renaissance of the Twelfth Century* (Cambridge, MA: Harvard University Press, 1928); Erwin Panofsky, *Renaissance and Renascences in Western Art* (Stockholm: Almqvist & Wiksell, 1960).
[16] Edward Said, *Orientalism* (London: Routledge and Kegan Paul, 1978); Edward Said, *Culture and Imperialism* (London: Vintage Books, 1993).

discourse is also to be traced from that time,[17] it was the collapse of every alternative paradigm. The world had become too wide to be convincingly accommodated within the confines either of the prevailing historical narrative or of any of the metaphysical systems that that narrative had helped to unseat.

The power of the idea of the European middle ages to command a central place in the formation of academic history, and of the wider culture in which it flourished, had rested heavily on its ability to impart a sense of continuity between present and necessary past, and hence on the perceived unity of the period from 500 to 1500 itself. That perception no longer prevails among specialists in its study, and is no longer demanded outside their ranks. The question remains whether this periodization has anything useful to offer to world history, including global history, which has found itself in rather the same position at the end of the twentieth and beginning of the twenty-first centuries as academic history itself had done a hundred years or so before. To the extent that a commonly accepted periodization seems to be emerging the answer would appear to be not. Take, for example, that proposed by the late Jerry Bentley. He looked for periodization based on the history not of dominant regions or civilizations, but of cross-cultural interactions whose consequences went far beyond the individuals who took part in them, particularly mass migrations, campaigns of imperial expansion, and long-distance trade.[18] Before 1500 such interactions took place regularly within, though hardly at all between, three great regions—the Eastern Hemisphere (Afroeurasia), the Western Hemisphere and Oceania (Australasia and the Pacific). On that basis Bentley identified an age of classical civilizations, a post-classical age, and an age of transregional nomadic empires, respectively from 500 BCE to 500 CE, 500 to 1000 CE and 1000 to 1500 CE. Similarly, for the McNeills the year 1000 CE marks a point at which the thickening of their human web gathered significant pace, as for William H. McNeill twenty years earlier 1000 had seen the beginning of the economic revolution in Song China and the diffusion of its technology that launched an epoch-making period of growth and innovation throughout Eurasia.[19]

And so on. It is not my purpose here to conduct an opinion survey, and certainly not to deny the significance of the first centuries of the second millennium, which many now regard, and from many points of view, as a decisive period in world history comparable in importance to the so-called axial age in the ancient world, and to the coming of industrial society in the modern.[20] Indeed I could not do so without disavowing my own assertions that there was in those years an urban revolution, in

---

[17] Robert I. Moore, 'World History', in Michael Bentley (ed.), *Companion to Historiography* (London: Routledge, 1997), pp. 941–59.

[18] Jerry H. Bentley, 'Periodization in World History', *American Historical Review* 101, 3 (1996), pp. 749–70.

[19] John R. McNeill and William H. McNeill, *The Human Web: A Bird's-Eye View of World History* (New York: W. W. Norton, 2003), pp. 116 ff.; William H. McNeill, *The Pursuit of Power* (Chicago: University of Chicago Press, 1983), pp. 24–62. For China and economic revolution in the Song, see Mark Elvin, *The Pattern of the Chinese Past* (Stanford, CA: Stanford University Press, 1973).

[20] Jóhann P. Árnason and Björn Wittrock (eds), *Eurasian Transformations, Tenth to Thirteenth Centuries: Crystallizations, Divergences, Renaissances* (Leiden: Brill, 2004).

Gordon Childe's sense of the phrase,[21] in which the Europe we know became a
civilization in its own right, and that that revolution was itself part of a wider set
of crises in Afroeurasia in which the lineaments of the modern world became discernible.[22] Those propositions must be understood, and can only make sense,
however, in a wider context—and one which bears a surprising resemblance to
what we used to call the Middle Ages.

The argument proceeds from a very simple, not to say banal observation. History
begins with cities, because cities change, and indeed create their worlds.[23] The city
is most simply defined, notoriously, as a community that does not support itself. It
is therefore compelled to establish by persuasion or coercion regular and reliable
means of procuring from others what its inhabitants cannot, or will not, produce
themselves. For the present purpose we are concerned not so much with the urban
nucleus itself as with the supporting networks of production and exchange that
this necessity creates, and with their variation in density and complexity over space
and time. In the four millennia before the Common Era city life so understood
remained, saving a few tentative and ephemeral outliers, more or less restricted to
the areas of dense population and imperial pretensions to which it had spread from
its earliest sites, in the valleys of the Yellow River, and of the Indus, Nile, Tigris and
Euphrates. In the first centuries of the Common Era it faltered and in varying
degrees receded. Its recovery, visible in some regions by the fourth century, is evident
in most by the ninth. By around 1250 what turned out to be lasting city-based
civilization had been extended to many regions where it had previously been pre-
carious or non-existent, including Europe beyond the Alps, Russia, the Yangzi
basin and Szechuan, Japan, peninsular India, both mainland and island Southeast
Asia, central Asia, the African coast of the Indian Ocean, the valley of the Niger
and Meso-America—in fact, more or less everywhere where it has flourished since.
In other words, regions which had previously been incapable of sustaining cities
and their paraphernalia—priestly and warrior elites, high cultures and so forth—
over very long periods had acquired the economic, social, cultural, and governmental infrastructures that now enabled them to do so. Many of the inhabitants of
those regions had undergone what is universally acknowledged, along with industrialization, as the greatest transformation of human existence in its entire history,
that from hunter gathering or subsistence cultivation to organized agriculture, and
from simple, relatively undifferentiated ways of living to strictly hierarchical, dis-
ciplined, and sophisticated forms of social organization—a social conversion no
less momentous, at least in terms of this world, than the religious conversion which
so often accompanied it.

---

[21] V. Gordon Childe, *What Happened in History* (Harmondsworth: Penguin, 1942).

[22] Robert I. Moore, *The First European Revolution* (Oxford, 2001); 'The Eleventh Century in
Eurasian History', *Journal of Medieval and Early Modern Studies* 33, 1 (2003), pp. 3–21; Robert I.
Moore, 'Medieval Europe in World History', in Carol Lansing and Edward D. English (eds),
A Companion to the Medieval World (Oxford: Wiley-Blackwell, 2009), pp. 563–80.

[23] In this I am particularly influenced by Jane Jacobs, *The Economy of Cities* (New York: Random
House, 1969) and Kirti N. Chaudhuri, *Asia before Europe* (Cambridge: Cambridge University Press,
1990), pp. 338–74.

INTENSIFICATION AND RESILIENCE

In the 10,000-year trek from Marshall Sahlins' 'original affluent society',[24] however, the stage peculiarly characteristic of our millennium, 500 to 1500 CE, was
that most conveniently described as the transition from dispersed to intensive agriculture. Both are relative terms, but the latter generally includes a movement from
shifting to fixed patterns of cultivation and settlement, the appearance of enduring
village communities and the subordination and regimentation—the 'caging' as it
has been vividly described—of the cultivators to produce 'a broad-ranging increase
in society's material production (and, by various measures, productivity), primarily
agricultural but also artisanal',[25] accompanied by rapid commercialization and
urbanization. How far such development throughout the Eurasian rimlands, as
they are sometimes called (the peripheries of the ancient imperial heartlands and
beyond), is attributable to the revival of exchange within them, in the China Sea,
the Indian Ocean and the Mediterranean, and how far to long-term local intensification within the rimlands themselves remains debatable.[26] In either case its
momentum in the centuries around 1000 provided the foundation for the construction of autonomous polities and re-energized high cultures which became the
building blocks of modern world history. That in itself is sufficient to demand that
the years in which it occurred should be treated as a single period, irrespective of
whether or not we ascribe all those developments to a single set of causes.

   In the thirteenth and fourteenth centuries the citied civilizations of Eurasia were
beset on all sides by invasion from without and by ecological crisis, famine, disease,
and acute social conflict within—in short, by all the symptoms of the systems' collapse that had heralded the end of the ancient world.[27] Systems' collapse threatened, but it did not take place. Almost everywhere city life and the structures that
depended on it survived, to inaugurate another era of expansion and innovation
which issued in the modern world. As John Darwin remarks, 'the Ottomans, the
Mamluk state in Egypt and Syria, the Muslim Sultanate in northern India, and
above all China, were too resilient to be swept away by (Tamerlane's) lightning
campaigns'.[28] The political and social structures of Europe also survived essentially
intact. Only the absence of a general systems' collapse made it possible for Duby
to argue that the transformation of Europe in the eleventh and twelfth centuries
put in place the essentials of the Ancien Régime, or for Chaudhuri to describe the
eleven centuries 'from the rise of Islam to the beginning of European imperialism

---

[24] Marshall Sahlins, *Stone Age Economics* (Chicago: Aldine-Atherton, 1972), pp. 1–39.
   [25] Chris Wickham, *The Inheritance of Rome* (London: Allen Lane, 2009), pp. 529–51; Conrad
Totman, *A History of Japan* (Oxford and Maldon, MA: Blackwell Publishers, 2000), pp. 106–12,
140–58, quoted at p. 145.
   [26] Robert I. Moore, 'The Transformation of Europe as a Eurasian Phenomenon' in Árnason and
Wittrock (eds), *Eurasian Transformations*, pp. 77–98.
   [27] Walter Scheidel (ed.), *Rome and China: Comparative Perspectives on Ancient World Empires*
(Oxford and New York: Oxford University Press, 2009). See also James Belich on the 'spread of
Europe' in this volume.
   [28] John Darwin, *After Tamerlane: The Rise and Fall of Global Empires, 1400–2000* (London:
Penguin, 2007), p. 9.

in the 1750s' as 'a period during which the world saw the completion of an entire lifecycle for civilization in general'.[29] Those periodizations are entirely valid in their own terms and for their own purposes, but both assume the existence and the extent and survival of citied civilization itself.

It may seem perverse to insist on the fundamental significance of a periodization defined by something that did not happen. But the fact of that absence is not without interest to anyone who may wonder, in the second decade of the twenty-first century, whether modern society itself will prove able to display a similar resilience in the face of similar challenges on an even more comprehensively global scale. For the most part the agenda implied by explaining the absence of systems' collapse, the resilience of the systems, or at any rate the first round of questions that it poses, is fairly obvious. It is fairly obvious also that the answers to those questions cannot be confined either to the short term or to phenomena and activities that are recognizably 'cross-cultural'. Certainly, Bentley's mass migrations, campaigns of imperial expansion and long-distance trade, McNeill's 'encounters with bearers of another culture or civilization',[30] will always be necessary to any set of explanations. Their vicissitudes and permutations in the hands of Braudel or Wallerstein, Curtin, or Wolf, are the stuff of the last generation's most familiar and influential essays in global history.[31] Yet few will think such connectivities exclusively, or always even primarily responsible for the intensification of exploitation, both of people and resources, from which cities began, and which they are bound to sustain.

Understanding of these processes will always depend directly and indispensably on the primary monographic studies, closely bounded in place and time, which constitute the traditional staple of historical research. The chief difficulty of bringing their results to bear on the large-scale problems of world history is not their terrifying quantity and accelerating rate of production. It lies rather in the lack of the habit of comparison, and with it the identification of criteria for the selective deployment of primary studies on a basis more sophisticated than the lucky dip. That immediately demands the abandonment of the lumbering, grotesquely generalized spatial units, the continents and civilizations of the happily superseded 'West and the rest' discourse, which are geographical and cultural counterparts of 'the middle ages'. More fruitful are the precise regional and even micro-regional comparisons precisely selected for their purposes which enabled Kenneth Pomeranz and Chris Wickham to reframe and refresh the very old questions of why China did not industrialize before Europe, and what continuity there

---

[29] Georges Duby (most completely in) *The Three Orders: Feudal Society Imagined* (Chicago and London: Chicago University Press, 1980); Kirti N. Chaudhuri, *Trade and Civilisation in the Indian Ocean* (Cambridge: Cambridge University Press, 1985), p. 9.

[30] William H. McNeill, 'A Defence of World History', *Transactions of the Royal Historical Society* 5, 32 (1982), pp. 75–89, at p. 78.

[31] Fernand Braudel, *Civilization and Capitalism: 15th to 18th Century*, trans. Siân Reynolds, 3 vols (London: Fontana, 1981–4); Immanuel Wallerstein, *The Modern World-System*, 3 vols (Berkeley, Los Angeles, and London: University of California Press, 2011); Philip D. Curtin, *Cross-Cultural Trade in World History* (Cambridge: Cambridge University Press, 1984); Eric R. Wolf, *Europe and the People Without History* (Berkeley and London: University of California Press, 1982).

was in Europe between antiquity and the early Middle Ages.[32] The approach has been fully elaborated in precept and practice by Victor Lieberman, insisting on the necessity of such systematic comparison to explain not only the changes which occurred in different places, but why it has so often appeared that they did so in something approaching a common rhythm.[33]

The questions why and how regions that had previously been incapable of sustaining city life over long periods became capable of doing so addresses issues that have always been close to the concerns of historians, and even more of archaeologists. We know a great deal about the development and diffusion of species and of technology, the harnessing of labour and the mechanisms of coercion, persuasion, and exchange in most parts of the world, and we are rapidly learning more. Even so, there is plenty of scope for the systematic exposition and comparative analysis that would help us to understand all of them better. I am not aware, for instance—though, to make the confession of all-embracing ignorance that is always implicit in discussions like this, perhaps I ought to be—of a sustained examination of the implications of the fact that technology in Europe was mainly driven by the shortage of manpower, and almost everywhere else by the needs of water management.[34]

Or, to take a couple of examples from my own field of interest, we have striking, well-documented and familiar accounts almost everywhere of the ways in which temples and monasteries advanced the frontiers of cultivation, disseminating new crops and techniques, stimulating local exchanges, refining the division of labour, and drawing the people who lived around them into close and mutually productive relations by the lure of status and prestige, differentiated by caste or conversion from their coarser, perhaps still semi-pastoral neighbours.[35] The similarities are plain, but much might be learned from trans-regional and cross-cultural comparison searching enough to draw out the differences less obvious than those of religious affiliation. Again, we have in pilgrimage a phenomenon universal since the earliest times. Some locate its origin in the annual return of hunter-gatherers

[32] Kenneth Pomeranz, *The Great Divergence: China, Europe and the Making of the Modern World Economy* (Princeton: Princeton University Press, 2000); Chris Wickham, *Framing the Early Middle Ages: Europe and the Mediterranean, 400–800* (Oxford: Oxford University Press, 2005).

[33] Victor Lieberman, 'Transcending East-West Dichotomies: State and Culture Formation in Six Ostensibly Different Areas', in Victor Lieberman (ed.), *Beyond Binary Histories: Re-Imaging Eurasia to c.1830* (Ann Arbor: University of Michigan Press, 1999), pp. 19–102; Victor Lieberman, *Strange Parallels: South-East Asia in Global Context, c.800–1830, vol. 1: Integration on the Mainland, vol. 2: Mainland Mirrors: Europe, Japan, China, South Asia, and the Islands: Southeast Asia in Global Context, c.800–1830* (Cambridge: Cambridge University Press, 2003 and 2009).

[34] It does not seem to me that continuing occasional debate on Karl Wittfogel, *Oriental Despotism: A Comparative Study of Total Power* (New Haven: Yale University Press, 1957) constitutes an exception; it is, as Mark Elvin puts it, 'a seriously incomplete description, but not foolish or without perception': Mark Elvin, *The Retreat of the Elephants: An Environmental History of China* (New Haven and London: Yale University Press, 2004), p. 106.

[35] Burton Stein, *Peasant State and Society in Medieval South India* (Delhi: Oxford University Press, 1980), pp. 63–89; David Ludden, *Peasant History in South India* (Delhi: Oxford University Press, 1989), pp. 3–41; Jacques Gernet, *Buddhism in Chinese Society: An Economic History from the Fifth to the Tenth Centuries* (New York: Columbia University Press, 1995), pp. 94–116; Mikael S. Adolphsen, *The Gates of Power: Monks, Courtiers and Warriors in Premodern Japan* (Honolulu: University of Hawai'i Press, 2000), 21–74.

to the burial places of their ancestors. It is a custom universally acknowledged as a vital element in the rooting and replication of every civilization. It was funda-mental to the establishment of the universal religions of the modern world. Missionary zeal is usually presented, almost tautologically, as the first expression and defining vehicle of their rise and diffusion in the first millennium.[36] No doubt it was, but all of the world religions, old and new, were sustained in concrete form by pilgrimage, whose routes and networks, like those of the railway in the nine-teenth century, spread with ever-increasing density across the map of Eurasia—and which, like the railway, necessarily touched every kilometre that they crossed, changing old communities and creating new ones at the regular stopping places that they required for rest and refreshment. Its consolidating and acculturating effects are obvious enough to the briefest contemplation, but there is a dearth of specific comparative study. Yet if any single institution 'made' the Eurasian Middle Ages it was pilgrimage.[37]

Nothing would be easier than to continue down the list, topic by topic, to make the uncontentious but not entirely trivial point that we are still some way from a comprehensive and properly differentiated account of the global establishment of complex, cited society. The examples of the foundation of temples and monas-teries and of pilgrimage also bear however on the rather less familiar question of the sources and nature of the resilience that enabled the world that was constructed between 500 and 1250 to survive the calamities of the later thirteenth and four-teenth centuries. It can hardly be described as a new issue. Braudel's famous pages on Europe's moving brick frontier were written half a century ago, and Eric Jones laid much stress on the development of protection against recurring disaster; every textbook account of the Mongols in the Middle East is a reminder of the vulner-ability that arose from dependence on the sophisticated irrigation systems that once supported prosperity and diversity; William H. McNeill—again—and Alfred W. Crosby have classically underlined how devastatingly the transmission of people and goods can open the way for that of pests and pathogens.[38] But those examples also suggest that we are at present better at describing disaster than at under-standing what limits its effects and what enables recovery from it. That must surely point us inwards, towards the intimate workings of small communities, to assess the density of social as well as of market networks, and the nature and substance of the ties that bind them, and towards the quality and penetration of governance, at all levels but especially at those farthest removed from the reach of princes and

[36] For instance, Jerry H. Bentley, *Old-World Encounters: Cross-Cultural Contacts and Exchanges in Pre-Modern Times* (New York and Oxford: Oxford University Press, 1993), pp. 67–110.

[37] It may be suggestive that I am unable to identify a serious and comprehensive analytical discus-sion of pilgrimage as a social institution in any of the relevant cultures, still less a comparative one, despite the pioneering curiosity of Victor Turner and Edith Turner, *Image and Pilgrimage in Christian Culture* (Oxford: Basil Blackwell, 1978).

[38] Fernand Braudel, *Capitalism and Material Life* (London, 1973 [Paris, 1967]), pp. 193–5; Eric L. Jones, *The European Miracle: Environments, Economies, and Geopolitics in the History of Europe and Asia*, 3rd edn (Cambridge and New York: Cambridge University Press, 2003), pp. 22–40; William H. McNeill, *Plagues and Peoples* (Garden City, NY: Anchor Press/Doubleday, 1976); Alfred W. Crosby, *Ecological Imperialism: The Biological Expansion of Europe, 900–1900* (Cambridge: Cambridge University Press, 1986).

their servants. And since few things are more various than susceptibility to misfortune and the capacity to recover from it, such a survey points us inexorably towards systematic comparison.

CONCLUSION

If I were to seek a general term to characterize the claims on our attention of the millennium between 500 and 1500 I would plump for 'intensification'. It would serve, in the first place, to distance the discussion of global history from the bizarre but profoundly influential doctrine which held sway for so long, that intensive economic growth—the sustained increase of real income per head—had been attained only after 1500 and uniquely by Europe and its offshoots. It would remind medievalists that it is still, though now a good deal ameliorated, their characteristic weakness to pay insufficient attention to the material circumstances of the things they study. It would focus attention on the single most persistent agent of change at most times and in most places, at any rate among sedentary people, namely the securing and distribution of surplus and, more especially, on the necessarily disruptive impacts of its increase on social relations. But 'intensification' would not confine us to those things. It can frame questions that run well beyond them to every kind of increasing (or diminishing) complexity in society and culture as well as in material life. That includes, for example, the development and application of instruments of government, and their capacity to penetrate small communities and override or support local hegemonies;[39] the diffusion of literacy and the institutions to sustain it, both topographically and socially; the creation of communities and their forms of association and representation; the extension of priestly power and influence, the creation of ever-closer networks of shrines and pilgrimage routes and the inculcation of religious mentalities and practices;[40] the growth of 'gentry societies', their mechanisms of recruitment, exclusion, and mutual support,[41] or of merchant guilds or charitable associations.[42] All these can be described in their ways as forms of intensification. All might be considered, at every level, from the clearing of forests to the ruling of empires, from the point of

---

[39] West, *Reframing the Feudal Revolution*, pp. 109–69; James Heitzmann, *Gifts of Power: Lordship in an Early Indian State* (New Delhi: Oxford University Press, 1997).

[40] Glen Dudbridge, *Religious Experience and Lay Society in T'ang China* (Cambridge: Cambridge University Press, 1995); Valerie Hansen, *Changing Gods in Medieval China, 1126–1272* (Princeton: Princeton University Press, 1990); Edward L. Davis, *Society and the Supernatural in Song China* (Honolulu: University of Hawai'i Press, 2001).

[41] Leonora Neville, *Authority in Byzantine Provincial Society, 950–1100* (Cambridge: Cambridge University Press, 2004); Chase Robinson, *Empire and Elites after the Muslim Conquest: The Transformation of Northern Mesopotamia* (Cambridge: Cambridge University Press, 2000); Roy Mottahedeh, *Loyalty and Leadership in an Early Islamic Society*, 2nd edn (London: Tauris, 2001); Michael Chamberlain, *Knowledge and Social Practice in Medieval Damascus, 1190–1350* (Cambridge: Cambridge University Press, 1994); Robert Hymes, *Statesmen and Gentlemen: The Elite of Fu Chou, Chiang-si, in the Northern and Southern Sung* (Cambridge: Cambridge University Press, 1986).

[42] Hugh R. Clark, *Community, Trade and Networks: Southern Fujian Province from the Third to the Thirteenth Century* (Cambridge: Cambridge University Press, 1991).

view among others of whether and how they contributed to, or detracted from, the resilience of their society, its capacity to adapt to change, and to resist or survive the dangers that beset it.

It need hardly be added that everything I have said about this millennium in which the world learned to construct complex, citied civilization that did not collapse, including not least my use of the terms 'city', 'civilization', 'collapse', and of course 'intensification', is open to objection as speculative, tendentious, and lacking not only substance but definition. As the sniffier reviewers used to say, it offers more questions than answers. I certainly hope so. They seem to me questions which have at least some of the qualities that enabled the study and teaching of these centuries to contribute so handsomely to the shaping of our discipline and its hold on the public imagination in its formative years. They evoke a common past, shaped by a common engagement with problems and perils that confront us now as urgently as ever. For that reason I am confident that the Age of Global Intensification deserves and will command an essential place in the agenda of the Oxford Centre for Global History. I fear it is too much to hope that it will not be described as the Global Middle Ages.

5

The Black Death and the Spread of Europe

James Belich

GLOBALIZING EUROPE

A global approach need not be universal, but it should cross boundaries of discipline, time, and space. What follows stumbles across several of history's sub-disciplines, and even draws on science. The time frame merges the late Medieval and Early Modern eras, 1350–1800. The space consists of Europe, North Africa, and West Asia. This sub-global 'world' with no name actually shared a lot. It shared an unusually high sea-land ratio—not just the great Mediterranean but also other seas: the North, the Baltic, the Black and the Red, the Caspian and the Aral, as well as the Persian Gulf and the Bay of Biscay. Rivers linked, or almost linked, many of these seas, creating an Inner Seas World with great potential for interactivity. The region also hosted a continuous series of tri-continental empires: the Persian, the Hellenic, the Roman, the Byzantine and the Islamic. These empires claimed succession from their predecessors, and in China they might have been seen as successive dynasties. The region also shared an intriguing propensity to monotheism—Judaism and Zoroastrianism as well as Christianity and Islam—and the 'One-God World' is a possible name. The region also shared the Black Death. My immediate subject is Europe, but this unnamed world is the context in which European history needs to be re-set.

This chapter seeks fresh understanding of the *spread* of Europe, namely its expansion to 1800, when it had secured lodgements in all six inhabited continents. It does not address the *rise* of Europe, namely its industrialization after 1800. But I will not conceal my view that for the two to be unconnected would be a strange coincidence.

Many scholars still root Europe's propensity to spread in periods before 1345, often well before. Anthony Pagden traces it to early Christianity; others to the early or high Middle Ages.[1] Michael Mitterauer writes: 'There is a consensus in historical scholarship that many of the developments typifying Europe's 'special path' (*Sonderweg*) arose in the eighth and ninth centuries in the lands between the Seine and the Rhine, the heartland of the Carolingian Empire.'[2] It is true that medieval

---

[1] Anthony Pagden, *Worlds at War: The 2,500-Year Struggle Between East and West* (New York: Random House, 2008).

[2] Michael Mitterauer, *Why Europe? The Medieval Origins of its Special Path*, trans. Gerald Chapple (Chicago and London: University of Chicago Press, 2010 [German orig. 2003]), p. 1. Also see Eric L. Jones, *The European Miracle: Environment, Economics and Geopolitics in the History of Europe and Asia*, 3rd edn (Cambridge and New York: Cambridge University Press, 2003); David S. Landes, *The Wealth and Poverty of Nations: Why Some Are so Rich and Some so Poor* (New York: W. W. Norton, 1998).

Europe *tried* to spread outside its boundaries—Vikings to Greenland, Novgorodians across the Urals, Crusaders to the Levant. But these attempts all failed. If Europe did have a special path, it led nowhere in terms of expansion before 1345.

PLAGUE MYSTERIES

After 1345, Europe was beset by a terrible plague, known as the Black Death. Naturally, this catastrophe has generated an enormous literature, still going strong. But 666 years of scholarship have failed to achieve consensus on the most basic questions about the Black Death, such as what it was, where it was, and how many people it killed. Recent scholarly estimates of mortality vary between 5 per cent and 60 per cent, which is not much help to the generalist. Even *when* the Plague was is a surprisingly vexed question. To spare you my wanderings in the mazes of science, history, rat studies, and cosmic theory, I will cut to my tentative conclusions.

What was the Black Death? It was bubonic plague. Ten years ago, leading experts asserted emphatically that this was not so. 'The Black Death in Europe, 1347–52', stated Samuel Cohn, 'was any disease other than the rat-based bubonic plague.'[3] This view is understandable in the light of discrepancies between medieval and modern plague, but wrong. An increasing number of DNA studies of plague victims show *Yersinia Pestis, Y Pestis*, bubonic plague.[4]

Where was the Black Death? It is generally assumed to have hit China, and possibly India, in the mid-fourteenth century too. But the evidence for this has never been strong; some scholars have long rejected it; and recently George Sussman concluded: 'A close examination of the sources on the Delhi Sultanate and the Yuan Dynasty provides no evidence of any serious epidemic in fourteenth-century India and no specific evidence of plague among the many troubles that afflicted fourteenth-century China.'[5] This does not preclude a Chinese origin for the disease in the deeper past. But the immediate source of our Black Death was probably the steppes of West Central Asia.[6]

[3] Samuel K. Cohn Jr, *The Black Death Transformed: Disease and Culture in Early Renaissance Europe* (London: Arnold, 2002), p. 1.

[4] Stephanie Haensch et al., 'Distinct Clones of Yersinia Pestis Caused the Black Death', *PLoS Pathogens* 6, 10 (2010), pp. 1–8. Also see Sacha Kacki, Lila Rahalison, Minoarisoa Rajerison, Ezio Ferroglio, and Raffaella Bianucci, 'Black Death in the Rural Cemetery of Saint-Laurent-de-la-Cabrerisse Aude-Languedoc, Southern France, 14th Century: Immunological Evidence', *Journal of Archaeological Science* 38, 3 (2011), pp. 581–7; Kirsten I. Bos et al., 'A Draft Genome of Yersinia Pestis from Victims of the Black Death', *Nature* 478, 7370 (2011), pp. 506–10; Verena Schuenemann et al., 'Targeted Enrichment of Ancient Pathogens Yielding the pPCP1 Plasmid of Yersinia Pestis from Victims of the Black Death', *Proceedings of the National Academy of Sciences of the United States of America (PNAS)* 108, 38 (2011), pp. 746–52; Ingrid Wiechmann, Michaela Harbeck, and Gisela Grupe, 'Yersinia Pestis DNA Sequences in Late Medieval Skeletal Finds, Bavaria', *Emerging Infectious Diseases* 16, 11 (2010), pp. 1806–7; Michael Knapp, 'The Next Generation of Genetic Investigations into the Black Death', *PNAS* 108, 38 (2011), pp. 15669–70.

[5] George D. Sussman, 'Was the Black Death in India and China?' *Bulletin of the History of Medicine* 85, 3 (2011), pp. 319–55.

[6] Stuart J. Borsch, *The Black Death in Egypt and England: A Comparative Study* (Austin: University of Texas Press, 2005), p. 5. Also see Ole J. Benedictow, *The Black Death 1346–1353: The Complete History* (Woodbridge, Suffolk: Boydell Press, 2004), p. 50.

There is no simple answer to the question of Western Europe's 'Great Divergence' here. Mortalities in Eastern Europe, North Africa, and the Middle East seem similar, though the evidence is less strong. Michael Dols made this case for North Africa and the Middle East in 1977, and a fine crop of recent theses on the Ottoman Empire support it. Some claim that Eastern Europe was less hard hit, and this may be true of a few regions, such as Poland. But Eastern Europe's largest state, the Golden Horde, by now quite urbanized and sedentary, was hit as early as 1346, and frequently thereafter.[7] The Horde's vassals, the states of Christian Russia, were repeatedly swept by plague after 1352.[8] Suggestions that Bohemia and Finland escaped largely unscathed are not convincing, and it has long been clear that the Black Death ravaged the Balkans.[9]

How many people did the Plague kill? A death rate of around 30 per cent is accepted for Western Europe, but uneasily because modern plagues kill a maximum of 3 per cent. Yet, remarkably, recent research supports an average mortality of around 50 per cent for the first strike alone. Researchers have compiled quite numerous sets of figures, from such documents as records of the replacement of clergy and tenants. The rates vary, from 45.5 per cent in Italy and 49 per cent in France, to 60 per cent in Spain, but not by much. John Aberth averages the estimates for Spain, Italy, England, and France and comes up with 51 per cent.[10] Evidence of farm abandonment and reforestation across Europe supports such figures.[11]

These figures are hard to swallow, but they are possible. The last Western European bubonic plague outbreaks, in Marseilles in 1720–2 and Messina in Sicily in 1743, did kill half the population. The evidence for 50 per cent is better than that for 30 per cent, even for the first strike around 1350 alone. If we shift perspective from the first strike around 1350 to the first three strikes, 1347–75, the nightmarish

[7] Joseph P. Byrne, *Encyclopedia of the Black Death* (Santa Barbara: ABC-CLIO, 2012), p. 238; Janet Martin, *Medieval Russia 980–1584*, 2nd edn (Cambridge and New York: Cambridge University Press, 2007), p. 222.

[8] Martin, *Medieval Russia*, p. 300; A. B. Savinetsky and O. A. Krylovich, 'On the History of the Spread of the Black Rat (*Rattus rattus L.*, 1758) in Northwestern Russia', *Biology Bulletin* 38, 2 (2011), pp. 203–7; Charles J. Halperin, *Russia and the Golden Horde: The Mongol Impact on Medieval Russia* (Bloomington: Indiana University Press, 1987); John T. Alexander, *Bubonic Plague in Early Modern Russia: Public Health and Urban Disaster* (New York: Oxford University Press, 2003 [1980]); Nancy Shields Kollmann, 'The Principalities of Rus' in the Fourteenth Century', in Michael Jones (ed.), *The New Cambridge Medieval History, vol. VI, c.1300–c.1415* (Cambridge: Cambridge University Press, 2000), pp. 764–94.

[9] John V. A. Fine, *The Late Medieval Balkans: A Critical Survey from the Late Twelfth Century to the Ottoman Conquest* (Ann Arbor: University of Michigan Press, 1987), pp. 320–1; Robin Harris, *Dubrovnik: A History* (London: Saqi Books, 2003), pp. 210–11.

[10] John Aberth, *From the Brink of the Apocalypse: Confronting Famine, War, Plague and Death in the Later Middle Ages*, 2nd edn (London and New York: Routledge, 2010), pp. 91–4. Also see John Hatcher, *The Black Death: An Intimate History* (London: Weidenfeld & Nicolson, 2008), p. 152; Barney Sloane, *The Black Death in London* (Stroud, Gloucestershire: History Press, 2011). Benedictow (*The Black Death*) makes a strong case of 60% mortality throughout Europe.

[11] Dan Yeloff and Bas van Geel, 'Abandonment of Farmland and Vegetation Successsion Following the Eurasian Plague Pandemic of AD 1347–52', *Journal of Biogeography* 34, 4 (2007), pp. 575–82; Thomas B. van Hoof et al., 'Forest Re-Growth on Medieval Farmland after the Black Death Pandemic: Implications for Atmospheric CO_2 Levels', *Palaeogeography, Palaeoclimatology, Palaeoecology* 237, 2–4 (2006), pp. 396–409; Hans Antonson, 'The Extent of Farm Desertion in Central Sweden during the Late Medieval Agrarian Crisis: Landscape as a Source', *Journal of Historical Geography* 35, 4 (2009), pp. 619–41.

notion of demographic halving becomes really hard to avoid. Most of Europe was hit by one or more of the early strikes. Further aftershocks tended to run down the regions that had hitherto escaped.[12]

Some unusually good population statistics from England allow us to check these estimates over the longer term.[13] They indicate that the first strike alone reduced the number of English from 4.8 million in 1348 to 2.6 million in 1351, a decline of 46 per cent. Further strikes reduced the English to a nadir of 1.9 million in 1450, a decline on the 1348 figure of 60 per cent. Recovery did not begin until after 1500. England may not have been typical, but most of its exceptionality lay in the future and there is no reason to think that it was unusually susceptible to plague.

When was the Plague? As the above grim litany suggests, it was a single calamity around 1350 *and* an entire era, 1350–1800. The general halving of populations between 1346 and 1375, was followed by 25 lesser but substantial epidemics over the next four centuries. Each outbreak was followed by a spike in birth rates as survivors remarried and bred.[14] High fertility and high mortality raced neck and neck, with the former overhauling the latter in most regions by about 1450 or 1500. Mortalities declined and focussed more on cities. But demographic *upturn* was not demographic *recovery* to pre-Plague population levels; for most places, this came around 1570. From 1650 or so, the plague and its socio-economic effects declined, but its cultural afterlife, boosted by occasional epidemics, survived to 1800.

PLAGUE'S IMPACT

Several writers have claimed revolutionary effects for the plague, but often with more heat than light. Like Basques and Scots, the Black Death 'made the modern world'. A larger minority of scholars have argued more convincingly for specific effects. The plague abetted the rise of centralized states; introduced the 'European Marriage Pattern', resulting in long-term population control; or reshuffled relations between lord and peasant, resulting in the demise of un-free labour in Western Europe and the advent of 'second serfdom' in the east. Most historians pass over the plague quite lightly, remain ambivalent about its possible consequences, or simply avoid the issue.

The history profession is understandably suspicious of determinisms, master variables, and silver-bullet solutions to complex historical problems. This is especially so when the alleged silver bullets are 'exogenous', external to human history itself— think sunspots and comets. Yet the Black Death not only halved populations, but also doubled the average per capita endowment of *everything*—bullion, goods,

[12] Byrne, *Encyclopedia of the Black Death*, p. 110.
[13] Stephen Broadberry, Bruce M. S. Campbell, and Bas van Leeuwen, 'English Medieval Population: Reconciling Times Series and Cross-Sectional Evidence', University of Warwick Working Paper, 27 July 2010, <http://www2.warwick.ac.uk/fac/soc/economics/staff/academic/broadberry/wp/medievalpopulation7.pdf>.
[14] Christiane Klapisch-Zuber, 'Plague and Family Life', in Michael Jones (ed.), *The New Cambridge Medieval History, vol. 6, c.1300–c.1415* (Cambridge: Cambridge University Press, 2000), p. 139.

buildings, animals, land and so on. In this it differed from most disasters. Flood, fire, earthquake and war destroy things and animals as well as kill people. Even famine leads starving people to eat their breeding stock and seed-corn. If the halving of people and the doubling of everything else does not have a potentially revolutionary effect, what does? At what point does due caution about master variables and exogenous causes become a propensity to ignore the elephant in the room?

Let me now attempt a short summary of the post-plague political economy, before turning to possible spread-friendly effects. Several scholars have associated the Plague Era with the rise of the strong centralized state, and Stephen R. Epstein has linked this to both the growth of commerce and the expansion of Europe. 'The late medieval crisis, which impelled state formation in western Europe, may have marked the most decisive step in the continent's long trajectory to capitalism and world hegemony.'[15] Plague might indeed have given states a helpful nudge. It encouraged the adoption of guns, for reasons noted below, and gunpowder armies, and navies of specialized warships, eventually became so expensive that only large strong states could afford them. But when was eventually? The permanent rise of the centralized European state is not obvious before the later seventeenth century; we will see that a surge in European commerce began in the later fourteenth century; and expansion beyond Europe began in the fifteenth. In any case, recent work indicates that the rise of states was at best half the picture, 1350–1650.

These studies emphasize 'transnational' networks and diasporas of trade, credit, skills, and labour, operating through and across territorial states, strong or not. The Portuguese 'crypto-Jewish' or 'New Christian' merchant network has rightly received much recent attention.[16] It was these merchant tribes, not territorial states, that were called 'nations' at the time. David Parrott has recently questioned the notion that states dominated the business of war from the fifteenth century— private mercenaries, financiers, and contractors remained crucial to 1650 and perhaps beyond. Other research demonstrates the existence of transnational pools of maritime labour, in the North Sea for example, a finding extended below.[17]

The notion that city states declined while territorial states rose from the fifteenth century is also contestable or at least misdated. Venice, Genoa, and Lubeck flowered after the Black Death, exploiting the various transnational pools. They also developed what can be called 'virtual hinterlands', overseas town-supply districts, whose economies were transformed to fit their metropolis. Some virtual hinterlands were formally owned, as with Venice's Crete and Genoa's Corsica. Others were informal but quite tightly controlled, as with Lubeck's grip on parts of

[15] Stephan R. Epstein, *Freedom and Growth: The Rise of States and Markets in Europe, 1300–1750* (London and New York: Routledge, 2000), p. 69.

[16] Daviken Studnicki-Gizbert, *A Nation upon the Ocean Sea: Portugal's Atlantic Diaspora and the Crisis of the Spanish Empire, 1492–1640* (Oxford: Oxford University Press, 2007), p. 5.

[17] David Parrott, *The Business of War: Military Enterprise and Military Revolution in Early Modern Europe* (Cambridge: Cambridge University Press, 2012); Paul van Royen, Jaap Bruijn, and Jan Lucassen (eds), *'Those Emblems of Hell?' European Sailors and the Maritime Labour Market 1570–1870* (St John's, Newfoundland: International Maritime Economic History Association, 1997).

Scandinavia.[18] Another transnational technique, in which Genoa specialized, was to intertwine with larger states in a symbiotic relationship, somewhere between that of junior ally and puppet master. As with early hominids, this was a time when several species of political economy stalked the land.

Historians in the 1980s presented the post-plague era as one of economic depression, and this view persists in some quarters, but most historians would now accept that there was a consumption and trade upturn from the mid-fourteenth century, at least in per capita terms. At the root of this was an increase in arable productivity per worker. Grain farming retreated from the least fertile acres to the most fertile. There were countervailing factors, such as a decline in labour-intensive yield-enhancing practices like weeding. On the other hand, there were more work animals, more manure, cheaper wood, and cheaper iron. Surplus land was converted to pasture, which increased livestock still further, or allowed to revert to forest, which increased timber and fuel supplies. Grain prices dropped less in prime grains, wheat and barley, and more in lesser grains, rye and oats.

One might expect a turn to economic autarchy on the grounds that halved populations needed fewer imports, and this did happen in some regions. But in many regions, we find an increase in specialization and export. Some gave up growing grain, which was now cheaper and easier to import, and shifted to pastoral products, or industrial crops such as dye-plants and hops. The Spanish wool export industry, based on the semi-nomadic *mesta* system, emerged on acres cleared by the plague, as Braudel noted, and Hungarian long-range cattle droving can be traced to this period too.[19] 'Many western agricultural regions reduced grain monoculture', writes R. C. Hoffman, 'so promoting interregional market exchange of more diverse agricultural products from regional specialists.'[20]

After the first strike of plague around 1350, trade volumes declined, but much less than the population. English wool exports, whether as cloth or raw wool, only declined 17 per cent between 1351 and 1391,[21] a per capita increase of two-thirds, and Spanish wool exports began. From about 1400, the expansion of the wool trade became absolute, *before* significant upturns in population, let alone full recovery.[22] There was a similar curve in the trade in Eastern spices. Volumes dipped initially, and prices fluctuated, but volumes increased substantially during the

[18] David Kirby, *Northern Europe in the Early Modern Period: The Baltic World 1492–1772* (London and New York: Longman, 1990), p. 59; Justyna Wubs-Mrozewicz, 'Interplay of Identities: German Settlers in Late Medieval Stockholm', *Scandinavian Journal of History* 29, 1 (2004), pp. 53–67.

[19] Carla Rahn Phillips and William D. Phillips Jr, *Spain's Golden Fleece: Wool Production and the Wool Trade from the Middle Ages to the Nineteenth Century* (Baltimore and London: Johns Hopkins University Press, 1997); Lajos Racz, 'The Price of Survival: Transformation in Environmental Conditions and Subsistence Systems in Hungary in the Age of Ottoman Occupation', *Historical Studies* 24, 1 (2010), pp. 21–39.

[20] R. C. Hoffman, 'Frontier Foods for Late Medieval Consumers: Culture, Economy, Ecology', *Environment and History* 7, 2 (2001), pp. 131–67.

[21] John H. Munro, 'Medieval Woollens: The Western European Woollen Industries and their Struggles for International Markets, c.1000–1500', in David Jenkins (ed.), *The Cambridge History of Western Textiles*, vol. I (Cambridge: Cambridge University Press, 2003), p. 281.

[22] John Oldland, 'Wool and Cloth Production in Late Medieval and Early Tudor England', *Economic History Review* 67, 1 (2014), pp. 125–47; Richard A. Goldthwaite, *The Economy of Renaissance Florence* (Baltimore: Johns Hopkins University Press, 2009), p. 272.

fifteenth century.[23] The same pattern can be detected in other trades, as we will see. One key development was the emergence of permanent sea-links between the Mediterranean and North Sea trade circuits. Alum from Anatolia, brought mainly by Genoese ships, crucial for dyeing cloth, was traded at Bruges for cloth made by the Flemish from English wool. This trade had been intermittent before the Black Death; it became permanent only after it. Such link trades underwrote the well-known hybridization of Mediterranean and Atlantic shipbuilding techniques, which produced the long-range full-rigged ship.

The shift to a higher growth path in trade had a downside. It enhanced inter-activity and so seems to have encouraged the spread of lesser partners of the plague from the late fifteenth century, including typhus, smallpox, and influenza—as though *Y. Pestis* was not enough.[24]

Increasing specialization and trade, first per capita and then absolute, may be related to another, counter-intuitive, post-plague development—the sharpest rela-tive urbanization before the nineteenth century. Recent general estimates do show a slight fall in the urban proportion of the European population over the four-teenth century.[25] But these estimates overlook two factors. They are based on harder data, such as tax and militia records, for city populations than for the overall population, which are often calculated for 1400 simply by reducing Europe's population for 1300 by a quarter or a third—the old best guess for plague mor-tality. If we deflate by half, the new best guess, we find a significant rise in relative urbanization. We should also note that historical demographers use a set bench-mark to distinguish cities from towns—five or ten thousand people. A city reduced to town status by plague would disappear from the figures, even if it lost only a quarter of its population, and so increased relative to its hinterland.

Unlike its lesser partners, the plague was an unusual disease in that it initially hit country dwellers as hard as city dwellers. Labour-intensive grain farming no longer needed as many people, and to shore up their populations cities offered induce-ments to migrants such as quick access to citizenship, which explains increased urbanization. A few cities, such as Lubeck, Novgorod, and Genoa, actually grew in the fifteenth century. Many, perhaps most, lost much less than 50 per cent. Of Flanders' three great cloth towns, Ypres declined permanently, but Ghent and

[23] Kevin H. O'Rourke and Jeffrey G. Williamson, 'Did Vasco da Gama Matter for European Markets?', *Economic History Review* 62, 3 (2009), pp. 655–84; Filipe Themudo Barata, 'Portugal and the Mediterranean Trade: A Prelude to the Discovery of the "New World"', *Al-Masaq: Islam and the Medieval Mediterranean* 17, 2 (2005), pp. 205–19; Paul Freedman, *Out of the East: Spices and the Medieval Imagination* (New Haven and London: Yale University Press, 2008); David Bulbeck, Anthony Reid, Lay Cheng Tan, Yiqi Wu, *Southeast Asian Exports since the 14th Century: Cloves, Pepper, Coffee and Sugar* (Leiden and Singapore: KITLV Press/Institute of Southeast Asian Studies, 1998); C. H. H. Wake, 'The Changing Pattern of Europe's Pepper and Spice Imports, ca.1400–1700', *Journal of European Economic History* 8 (1979), pp. 361–403. Reprinted in Michael N. Pearson (ed.), *Spices in the Indian Ocean World* (Aldershot: Variorum, 1996); Frederic C. Lane, 'Pepper Prices before Da Gama', *The Journal of Economic History* 28, 2 (1968), pp. 590–7; Eliyahu Ashtor, 'The Volume of Mediaeval Spice Trade', *Journal of European Economic History* 9, 3 (1980), pp. 753–63.

[24] Kenneth F. Kiple (ed.), *The Cambridge World History of Human Disease* (Cambridge: Cambridge University Press, 1993).

[25] E.g. Paolo Malanima, *Pre-Modern European Economy: One Thousand Years (10th–19th Centuries)* (Leiden and Boston: Brill, 2009), pp. 246–9.

Bruges recovered quickly. The Black Death created 'a competitive market in human beings' in which cities were major players, with some losers and more relative winners.[26]

PLAGUE AND EXPANSION

In this context of labour shortage it is hardly surprising that the post-plague years witnessed an upsurge in labour-saving practices, including the mass-advent, though not invention, of blast furnaces and the proliferation of industrial milling. But to appreciate the true scale of this shift we have to extend our purview beyond machine technology to practices that saved time and training, extended working lives, and even saved lives. Improved armour and fortifications made fewer soldiers go further. The increased use of Arabic numerals made fewer notaries go further. For scribes and craftsmen, the mass-advent of spectacles increased working lives. The shift from oared ships to sailing ships, requiring far smaller crews, gathered pace after the plague, with the major exception of the Mediterranean galley. The use of the musket and its precursors also took off during the early plague era. It took far less time to train a musketeer than an archer competent in the use of long bows or compound bows, or even crossbows. Muskets were not more effective than longbows until about 1500, if then. But their use required ten years less to learn.

Despite these labour savings, the post-plague manpower crisis boosted real wages by 50 per cent or more. Most common folk were peasants not wageworkers and declining grain prices put downward pressure on their incomes. But greater productivity, larger holdings, and less onerous tenures probably compensated for this. For the first time since the fall of the Roman Empire, the buying classes extended beyond elites. Long sequences of sumptuary laws are one index of this. They tried to control elite as well as non-elite consumption, of flash clothing in particular, but their constant reiteration indicates that they failed. In desperation, the Venetian Senate declared in 1511 that 'all new fashions are banned'.[27] Another index is the emergence or percolation down the social hierarchy of 'lesser luxuries', 'semi-luxuries', or 'comforts'. The century or so after 1350 witnessed the flowering, though again not necessarily the invention, of long-lasting hopped beer, brandy, transportable hard cheeses, a non-elite market for copper pots, lighter woollens, and mix-cloths such as fustian, and 'the mass diffusion of linen underwear'.[28]

This modest 'golden age' for free workers and peasants ended around 1500, in serfdom in eastern Europe and low wages in western Europe. But it left some legacies. One was a modest permanent increase in the buying classes. Most peasants and workers were dragged back into poverty, but others became yeomen or their equivalents, and at least the relative number of craftsmen and out-burghers

---

[26] William P. Caferro, 'Warfare and Economy in Renaissance Italy, 1350–1450', *Journal of Interdisciplinary History* 39, 2 (2008), pp. 167–209.

[27] Alan Hunt, *Governance of the Consuming Passions: A History of Sumptuary Law* (Basingstoke; London: Macmillan, 1996), p. 37 and *passim*.

[28] Epstein, *Freedom and Growth*, p. 65.

increased. Another legacy was the social memory of a 'world we have lost', in which masters treated men with some respect, and food was abundant. This idea can be detected in English, Scandinavian, and Russian folk utopianism. It helped motivate far-settlement in the nineteenth century and perhaps before. A third legacy of the 'golden age', and of the great plague reshuffle in general, was the flowering of a type of labour that I call 'crews': wandering bands of workers engaged in mobile activities such as shipping, war, commercial hunting, and transhumance herding.

After 1350, as we have seen, regions in which grain growing was marginal abandoned it; imported their grain from more favoured regions, and turned to other activities such as pastoralism to pay for it. From about 1450, demographic upturn began and populations began to creep back up despite continuing bouts of plague. The reshaped local economy could not absorb the extra labour, which therefore looked elsewhere. If you had an existing martial or maritime tradition, you became a soldier in someone else's army or a sailor in someone else's fleet. The Swiss are a martial case in point. Between about 1400 and 1800, 'at a minimum, the entire mercenary emigration amounted to 1.2 million'. Only one-third returned so there was a net 'loss to the cantons of 800,000 men'.[29] Other mercenary-producing regions ranged from Scotland to Albania, which were equally mountainous and grain-deprived. Sailor-producing regions included the Basque Country, Dalmatia, the Greek islands, and Norway. Some crew regions supplied the international labour pool; others were embraced by growing states: Northern Portugal, Upland Castile, the Welsh Marches, and the Cossack Steppes.

Despite these varied origins, crews had characteristics in common. They were typically young single men who perpetuated their 'crew culture' by acculturating recruits, not procreation. They were orderly on the job and notoriously disorderly off it. Even on the job, there was a touch of golden age independence about crewmen. They accepted a master, but could make life difficult for him if he transgressed cherished norms. English sailors used 'round robin' petitions to state their grievances, a circle of marks and signatures in which no name came first. German mercenaries and Russian Cossacks alike held protest meetings in a circle with no one at the head. In no case was there a 'ring-leader'.[30] Crew were a semi-feral workforce; hired only when you needed them, but from whom you expected certain pre-existing skills. They were dangerous but useful.

Let me now return to trades, focussing on two pairs: the northern hunt for fish and furs, and the southern hunt for sugar and slaves. These dissimilar trades shared an addictive quality. Sugar is literally addictive, as some of us know all too well.[31] Intensive fishing and fur hunting were metaphorically addictive, in that they tended to deplete stocks in particular seas and regions, so pulling you on to the

---

[29] John Casparis, 'The Swiss Mercenary System: Labor Emigration from the Semiperiphery', *Review* (Fernand Braudel Center) 5, 4 (1982), pp. 593–642.

[30] Parott, *The Business of War*, pp. 62–3; Peter Earle, *Sailors: English Merchant Seamen 1650–1775* (London: Methuen, 1998), ch. 11; Shane O'Rourke, *The Cossacks* (Manchester and New York: Manchester University Press, 2007), p. 51.

[31] Alexis Conason, 'Is Abstinence the Best Treatment for Sugar Addiction?', *Psychology Today* (4 April 2012), available online at: <https://www.psychologytoday.com/blog/eating-mindfully/201204/sugar-addiction> (accessed 28 January 2015).

next. Victims of slave raids tend to flee, fortify, or federate, forcing slavers too to push on in search of fresh victims.

The North Atlantic herring and cod fishing trades, together with Basque whaling, were important before the Black Death, and contracted immediately after it. They resurged from the 1390s, and to unprecedented levels. The emergence of herring busses, which processed the fish at sea, and new gutting techniques, which enhanced their preservation, date to the late fourteenth century. In 1346, pre-plague cod fishing in Icelandic waters peaked at twelve ships.[32] In 1419 and 1491, twenty-five English and ninety Hanseatic cod fishing ships were lost in storms off Iceland.[33] Basques were also involved in this trade, as well as the whaling business. They were coastal whalers, but did not mind whose coast. They had whaling stations in Ireland in the fifteenth century and eventually in Iceland, where they are known from archaeology not documents.[34] By the late fifteenth century, depleted stocks and international rivalries were pushing the hunt for both cod and whales further into the North Atlantic.

Novgorod was the key player in the fur trade, before and after the Black Death, though other Russian principalities were also important. In the thirteenth century Novgorod itself was the size of London and its vast territory made it 'the largest state in all of medieval Europe'.[35] Until 1400, its fur exports were dominated by squirrel. Taken in the prime place and season, squirrel was no second-rate fur, but made robes 'fit for great lords'.[36] The squirrel trade seems to have taken the Black Death in its stride, with exports peaking at around half a million furs about 1400. It then declined, probably due to resource depletion. Novgorod responded by extending its hunt for even better furs, notably sable, renewing its efforts to extend its fur empire across the Urals in 1445.[37] In the 1470s, Novgorod was conquered by Muscovy, which took over its fur empire and pursued its Siberian project with more success. The permanent Russian presence in Siberia dates from the 1490s, not from a century later as Yermak's legend has it.

With its small contiguous hinterland, its chaotic politics, and its dire factional record of a coup or rebellion every four years, Genoa was an unlikely superpower, a nightmare for institutional determinists. City and *contado* combined had only 150,000 people around 1400, one-tenth the Venetian equivalent.[38] Yet the

[32] Ragnar Edvardsson, 'The Role of Marine Resources in the Medieval Economy of Vestfirdir, Iceland' (unpublished PhD thesis: City University of New York, 2010).

[33] Brian Fagan, *Fish on Friday: Feasting, Fasting and the Discovery of the New World* (New York: Basic Books, 2006), pp. 183, 186.

[34] Edvardsson, *The Role of Marine Resources*; Jean-Pierre Proulx, *Whaling in the North Atlantic: From Earliest Times to the Mid-19th Century* (Ottawa: Parks Canada, 1986).

[35] Roman Konstantinovich Kovalev, 'The Infrastructure of the Novgorodian Fur Trade in the Pre-Mongol Era (ca. 900–ca.1240)' (unpublished PhD thesis: University of Minnesota, 2003).

[36] Susan Mosher Stuard, *Gilding the Market: Luxury and Fashion in Fourteenth-Century Italy* (Philadelphia: University of Pennsylvania Press, 2006), p. 63.

[37] C. Raymond Beazley, 'The Russian Expansion towards Asia and the Arctic in the Middle Ages (to 1500)', *American Historical Review* 13, 4 (1908), pp. 731–41; Janet Martin, *Treasure of the Land of Darkness: The Fur Trade and its Significanc for Medieval Russia* (Cambridge: Cambridge University Press, 1986), p. 86.

[38] Tom Scott, *The City-State in Europe, 1000–1600: Hinterland, Territory, Region* (Oxford: Oxford University Press, 2012), p. 72.

Genoese led Europe in maritime, mercantile, and fiscal influence, and despite their close-run failure to conquer Venice in 1380, their informal empire flourished after the plague. Keys to Genoa's success included its synergistic relationship with Europe's interstate pool of labour, skill, and capital. The Genoese were themselves a merchant diaspora and a finance network, and also developed partnerships with larger states ranging from the Byzantine to the Spanish empires.

Genoa was a major player in many trades—the word 'jean' derives from 'Genoa', which indicates their prominence in cotton. They also led the sugar and slave trades. While the Genoese and Venetians had dabbled in sugar production in the crusader states in the thirteenth century, their main suppliers were Syria, Palestine, and especially Egypt. After the Black Death, sugar production collapsed in Egypt, perhaps due to disruption of the irrigation system, and declined in Syria and Palestine.[39] The Genoese took to developing plantations and mills in the few ecologically appropriate parts of southern Europe: first Cyprus, then Sicily, then southern Spain. David Abulafia has no doubt about what stimulated demand. 'This boom in sugar production, in both Spain and Sicily, reflects the expansion in demand for luxury and semi-luxury foodstuffs that followed the Black Death.'[40]

European slaving, near defunct, revived with the post-plague manpower crisis. Pioneered by Venice, Gypsy slavery became substantial in the Balkans; it lasted in Romania until the mid nineteenth century.[41] With their great slave mart of Caffa exporting 1,500 slaves a year around 1400, the Genoese were the leading Christian slavers, though Malta was also prominent. However, like Venice, Genoa faced a big and growing problem: the Ottoman Empire. Historians have noted that the Black Death facilitated the rise of the Ottomans from 1350. They were still seminomadic, and nomads were less prone to catch plague than sedentary people. But the Ottomans finessed the post-plague manpower crisis in more ways than this; they were masters of getting other peoples to work for them. They reconciled Jews and Christians to their rule, while incentivizing them to convert. They developed symbiotic relationships with junior partners, the Barbary States and Crimean Tartars, and, thanks partly to these partners, they took slaves.

My guess for average Ottoman slave imports between 1450 and 1700 is 20,000 a year, similar to though less lethal than the Atlantic slave trade. Only the *devirsme* or 'boy levy', which averaged a few hundred a year and provided the Janissaries, came from within the empire. The Barbary states and the Crimean Tartars provided most of the rest. The former drew white slaves from captured ships and coastal raids as far as Iceland, and black slaves from across the Sahara. The Tartars raided Poland and Russia. The Ottomans themselves traded with local slavers in

[39] Bethany J. Walker, 'From Ceramics to Social Theory: Reflections on Mamluk Archaeology Today', *Mamlūk Studies Review* 14 (2010), pp. 109–57; Eliyahu Ashtor, *Levant Trade in the Later Middle Ages* (Princeton: Princeton University Press, 1983).

[40] David Abulafia, 'Sugar in Spain', *European Review* 16, 2 (2008), pp. 191–210.

[41] George C. Soulis, 'The Gypsies in the Byzantine Empire and the Balkans in the Late Middle Ages', *Dumbarton Oaks Papers*, 15 (1961), pp. 141, 143–65; David M. Crowe, *A History of the Gypsies of Eastern Europe and Russia* (New York: St Martin's Press, 1995), ch. 4; Elena Marushiakova and Vesselin Popov, 'Gypsy Slavery in Wallachia and Moldavia', in Tomasz Kamusella and Krzysztof Jaskulowski (eds), *Nationalisms Today* (Oxford: Peter Lang, 2009), pp. 89–124.

the Caucasus and East Africa. The Ottomans took over the Genoese Black Sea coastal empire, and its slave trade, between 1453 and 1475, and were threatening it well before. The Greater Mediterranean was a single slave market,[42] and the Ottomans increasingly monopolized it in the fifteenth century.

Agile as ever, the Genoese shifted balance to the west, where they already had considerable assets: comprehensive mercantile and maritime penetration of Spanish Andalusia, Muslim Granada, and Portugal. Six Genoese were successive admirals of Portugal in the fourteenth century.[43] Genoese controlled the Granada and Valencia sugar plantations, in which slave labour featured though its dominance is contested.[44] As early as 1385, Genoa's Iberian proxies began raiding for slaves outside Europe, in the Canary Islands,[45] adding raids on the coast of Northwest Africa from 1420. As Berbers and Guanches fled inland or took to the mountains, these expeditions were pulled on to new islands and coasts in search of fresh victims. According to Malyn Newitt, the early Portuguese voyages to West Africa, allegedly 'of discovery', were 'openly and explicitly a series of raids designed to obtain slaves'.[46] Eventually it proved easier to plug into and indirectly expand the existing West African slave trade, whose circuits had the added attraction of providing gold. From about 1450, some Atlantic Islands, particularly Madeira, were converted to slave-worked sugar-lands. The Genoese controlled two-thirds of Madeiran sugar production in 1500.[47] As many have noted, prevailing winds induced ships sailing home from West Africa and the Islands to loop further and further out into the Atlantic.

By the late fifteenth century, with or without Columbus (who was of course Genoese), Europeans were on their way to the Americas on three trajectories: across the South Atlantic after slaves and sugar-lands, across the North Atlantic in pursuit of cod and whales, and across Siberia in search of furs.

If we draw these strands together, as some Europeans did at the time, we get what amounts to an expansion kit: a package of traits, transnationalisms, techniques, and trajectories that facilitated and encouraged long-range spread. Sailing ships mounting improving cannon; improving pulleys and pumps; hand-guns, siege cannon, and the art of cannon-proof fortification; all merged if not emerged in response to the post-plague labour crisis. All were portable ways of saving lives or saving labour and they permitted the projection of power by small crews. The

---

[42] Jeffrey Fynn-Paul, 'Empire, Monotheism and Slavery in the Greater Mediterranean Region from Antiquity to the Early Modern Era', *Past & Present* 205, 1 (2009), pp. 3–40.

[43] John Bryan Williams, 'From the Commercial Revolution to the Slave Revolution: The Development of Slavery in Medieval Genoa' (unpublished PhD thesis: University of Chicago, 1995).

[44] Mohamed Ouerfelli, *Le sucre: production, commercialisation et usages dans la Méditerranée médiévale* (Leiden: Brill, 2008); Abulafia, 'Sugar in Spain'; J. H. Galloway, *The Sugar Cane Industry: An Historical Geography from its Origins to 1914* (Cambridge and New York: Cambridge University Press, 1989); Alberto García Porras and Adela Fábregas García, 'Genoese Trade Networks in the Southern Iberian Peninsula: Trade, Transmission of Technical Knowledge and Economic Interactions', *Mediterranean Historical Review* 25, 1 (2010), pp. 35–51.

[45] Alfred W. Crosby, 'An Ecohistory of the Canary Islands', *Environmental Review* 8, 3 (1984), pp. 214–35.

[46] Malyn Newitt, *A History of Portuguese Overseas Expansion, 1400–1668* (London: Routledge, 2005), p. 15.

[47] Barata, 'Portugal and the Mediterranean Trade'.

Portuguese shipped pre-cut stone for forts to West Africa and the Indies, enabling tiny garrisons with numerous cannon to cling to populous coasts like leeches. The crews too were available, and the numbers involved in expansion were cumulatively not that small. My guess is that at least eight million crewmen sojourned outside Europe between 1450 and 1800. The transnational pools involved capital, technologies, and 'virtual hinterlands' as well as labour. This helps explain an apparent paradox of early European expansion: much of it was carried out by the tiny states of Portugal and the United Provinces, with populations of only one or two million. Their dwarfishness is part illusion. The Dutch marshalled resources and manpower from much of Eastern Europe. The Portuguese were kick-started into expansion by the Genoese, who marshalled capital and skills from much of the Mediterranean.

The expansion kit included biological weapons. Unlike the plague, the lesser diseases (typhus, smallpox, and influenza) seldom killed more than 25 per cent of a population, and surviving a dose conferred immunity. In cities, they survived as endemic diseases by targeting the newborn. As we all know, such diseases were transferred to the virgin populations of the Americas and elsewhere by European expansion—the terrible 'White Death' that burned a path for European expansion.[48]

The post-plague European expansion kit was not without software, a cultural dimension. I can touch on only two: racism and risk. While the earlier history of Europe is replete with xenophobia, persecution, and anti-Semitism, I can find few signs of hard racism before 1400. Hard racism involves the delusion that, however well assimilated or long assimilated into other cultures, people never lose core characteristics. This belief seems to have emerged first in Spain in the fifteenth century. It was associated with doctrines of the 'purity of the blood', and with the conviction that long-converted Muslim and Jewish families remained non-Christian at heart.[49] Whether it was linked to the Black Death, or to the effort to create a unified Spanish identity from disparate components I do not yet know. But the utility of racism as software for expansion seems clear.

First, it justified black African slavery even if Africans converted to Christianity. Previously, pagan potential slaves had been a diminishing resource for both Christianity and Islam, because conversion conferred at least theoretical protection. Muslim slaves were hard to catch; indeed, the boot was on the other foot.

Racism also facilitated white settlement and its reproduction. It encouraged white workers to side with white masters against black workers. It allowed settlers to incorporate some foreigners as white 'kindred races'. Long-range settlers were often thought to deteriorate away from their home environment. Racism gave them a counter-argument, enabling them to assert that they were virtual metropolitans. Racial virtues were conceptually more transferable than those derived from particular environments, particular institutions, or particular moments in history.

---

[48] Massimo Livi Bacci, *Conquest: The Destruction of the American Indios* (Cambridge: Polity Press, 2008 [2005]), p. 63.

[49] Miriam Eliav-Feldon, Benjamin Isaac, and Joseph Ziegler (eds), *The Origins of Racism in the West* (Cambridge and New York: Cambridge University Press, 2009).

Above all, perhaps, racism encouraged the inbreeding of settler populations, which did not melt into their subject cultures like male-only migrants. Endogamy permitted racial illusions to persist, and made settlers 'the perfect prefabricated collaborators' in European expansion, a self-opinionated but also self-perpetuating and self-motivating source of imperial labour.

Continued racial parity with metropolitans helped incentivize long-range settlement. Incentives were needed, because until the nineteenth century voluntary European family migration to distant regions, 'the little death', was very hard to trigger. Racism helped. So did folk memories of a golden age that might be reproduced on the frontier, as did previous experience of settling. Andalusians, Ulster Protestants, and Cossacks, who had already experienced migration within Europe, figured disproportionately in early Spanish, British, and Russian extra-European migration, among women in particular. The importance of 'second settlement' might extend further. Many sources tell us that the way to attract peasants to newly cleared, conquered or plague-depopulated areas in medieval Europe was to offer better conditions and greater liberties, a cachet settlement continued to carry.

Some two million Europeans migrated outside Europe before 1800, at most a quarter of them women. Frontier fertility meant that this delivered a settler population of close on ten million by 1800. As noted above, some eight million crewmen also left Europe. Though theoretically sojourners, half of them died abroad. Only 10 per cent of the 200,000 Portuguese crewmen leaving for the East Indies in the sixteenth century returned. Another 10 per cent survived in the Indies, where there were 16,000 live Portuguese in the 1570s.[50] Thus a voyage from Lisbon to Goa or Macao in the sixteenth century involved an 80 per cent chance of premature death. In the two centuries 1600–1795, the Dutch East India Company, or VOC shipped almost one million crewmen to Asia. To quote Victor Enthoven, 'VOC officials, including sailors and soldiers, had all contracted to stay in Asia for five years. The majority of them died during their stay abroad.'[51]

Most of these men were volunteers, and after the first few voyages, they knew their chances. Plague is the best candidate for causing this normalizing of high risk. During plagues, dicing with death was a fact of life and if you sailed for Goa or Batavia at least you threw the dice yourself. Once aboard and abroad, crews risked many diseases, but the Black Death was not one of them. A plague-driven shift in attitudes to risk is arguably also apparent in milder form: the emergence of popular lotteries in the fifteenth century.

A million-dollar question remains, of course: why did Eastern Europe and the Islamic World, which also suffered from plague, not share in Western Europe's expansion? One answer is that they did. Russia acquired one of the greatest empires outside Europe. Its Cossack crews used disposable boats rather than full-rigged

[50] Sanjay Subrahmanyam and Luís Filipe F. R. Thomaz, 'Evolution of Empire: The Portuguese in the Indian Ocean during the Sixteenth Century', in James D. Tracy (ed.), *The Political Economy of Merchant Empires: State Power and Word Trade 1350–1750* (Cambridge: Cambridge University Press, 1991), pp. 298–331.

[51] Victor Enthoven, 'Dutch Crossings: Migration between the Netherlands and the New World, 1600–1800', *Atlantic Studies* 2, 2 (2005), pp. 153–76.

ships, but pursued prey, accepted risk, and carried guns and diseases as well as any. Mughal expansion into India, Islam's America, might just be the greatest post-plague spread of all. Morocco, which did have plague and guns, conquered a large chunk of West Africa in the late sixteenth century, projecting its power over 1,700 kilometres.[52] Giancarlo Casale has recently demonstrated that the Ottoman Empire was not inactive or unsuccessful in the Indian Ocean in the sixteenth century, and it established substantial domains in East Africa.[53]

But the Ottomans already had a vast empire, including most of southeast Europe. Like China, it did not need to chase furs or fish; other peoples brought them to it. Unlike Europeans, it was not squeezed out of the Mediterranean slave market; it was doing the squeezing. Instead, it became the anvil on which European expansion had to hammer itself out.

[52] Roland Oliver and Anthony Atmore, *Medieval Africa, 1250–1800*, rev. edn (Cambridge: Cambridge University Press, 2001), p. 57.
[53] Giancarlo Casale, *The Ottoman Age of Exploration* (Oxford and New York: Oxford University Press, 2010).

6

The Qing Empire in the Fabric of Global History

Matthew W. Mosca

CHINA IN THE WORLD: COMPETING PERSPECTIVES

China's interactions with the outside world have been intensively studied. From an overwhelming early emphasis on diplomacy with European countries, this scholarship has now expanded to cover many periods, regions, and topics. The rise of global history presents an opportunity not only to reaffirm the significance and accelerate the pace of this research, but also to explore new approaches. This short essay will therefore consider what forms innovation might take, in light of established and emerging scholarship. It concentrates primarily on the early modern period, roughly 1500 to 1800, an era that has provoked conflicting judgements about China's influence on the world, and the world's influence on China.[1]

Current scholarship in English on early modern and modern China in the world evolved from the political history of Qing foreign relations with the West in the period after the Opium War.[2] Following an approach formulated in the 1941 article 'On the Ch'ing Tributary System' by John K. Fairbank and S. Y. Têng, scholars juxtaposed a 'traditional' mode of foreign relations, in which Ming and Qing emperors claimed ritual superiority over other monarchs, with one developed in Europe and progressively imposed on China after 1842.[3] Subsequent research concentrated on war and diplomacy, state-building and finance, education and missionary activity, and advances in science and technology, to see how this 'traditional' China, impelled by foreign demand and example, gradually assumed a new, 'modern' form. A smaller cohort of scholars looked back in time from the vantage of 1842, with most attention falling on western European embassies, conditions at Canton, and, to a lesser extent, early treaty-based relations with Russia.

[1] The author wrote this paper during his term as a Member of the School of Historical Studies, Institute for Advanced Study, funded by a Mellon Fellowship for Assistant Professors. He would like to thank Professor Nicola Di Cosmo for making this visit possible, and the College of William & Mary for granting him leave in the 2013–14 academic year. He also wishes to thank Fahad Bishara, David Brophy, Onuma Takahiro, and David Robinson for their assistance and insight.
[2] This brief review primarily concerns historiography in English. The relationship of this body of historiography with Chinese and Japanese scholarship is a complex topic outside the scope of this paper.
[3] J. K. Fairbank and S. Y. Têng, 'On the Ch'ing Tributary System', *Harvard Journal of Asiatic Studies* 6, 2 (1941), pp. 135–246.

This focus on the West then expanded to include more careful consideration of the application to non-Western countries of China's 'tribute system', a concept invented to embrace the various ritual, trade, and diplomatic policies that seemed to distinguish Ming and Qing foreign relations from European norms. China's priority, in this view, was stable, and predictable relations with its neighbours demonstrated the emperor's ritual superiority through the reception of submissive foreign embassies. This was taken to be a mode of international relations adapted to the cultural and political values shared in Asia, particularly East Asia. As studies of ideology and written regulations have yielded over time to more granular analysis of particular cases, researchers now have a clearer picture of tension and conflict within superficially harmonious relationships.[4] This undercuts any interpretation of Qing foreign relations based on a neat distinction between (East) Asian and European countries. Hamashita Takeshi has posited that a China-centred 'tribute trade system' knit Asia, especially East and Southeast Asia, into an integrated network of hierarchical economic and political ties. Because European traders were forced at first to adapt to this system, Hamashita suggests that important elements of it survived into the era of treaty ports and helped shape such 'modern' phenomena as Asian nationalism and Japanese industrial development.[5]

Research on commodities flowing through Chinese ports, silver above all, led to an even more dramatic reappraisal of China's role in the early modern world. Whereas scholarship on the tribute system typically limited attention to China's nearest neighbours and the West, this work sought to integrate China into a global system in which the New World played a key part. Whereas politically oriented studies stressed China's restrictions on external contact, studies of commodity flows emphasized a 'reversal of causality' by which China did more than Europe to shape the global economy.[6] Some went so far as to assert that in the early modern period 'the entire global economic order was—literally—Sinocentric'.[7] Even if these claims prove to be exaggerated, as some have argued,[8] studies of commerce in opium, tea, furs, ginseng, and other commodities leave no doubt that China's market stimulated numerous global trading ventures and helped finance expanding European power in Asia and the Americas. New appreciation of China's cornerstone role in global trade and domestic economic strength contributed to the influential thesis that parts of China rivalled parts of Europe as the world's most

---

[4] See, for instance, Andre Schmid, 'Tributary Relations and the Qing-Chosŏn Frontier on Mount Paektu', in Diana Lary (ed.), *The Chinese State at the Borders* (Vancouver: UBC Press, 2007); Seonmin Kim, 'Ginseng and Border Trespassing Between Qing China and Chosŏn Korea', *Late Imperial China* 28, 1 (2007), pp. 33–61; Yingcong Dai, 'A Disguised Defeat: The Myanmar Campaign of the Qing Dynasty', *Modern Asian Studies* 38, 1 (2004), pp. 145–89.

[5] Takeshi Hamashita, 'The Tribute Trade System and Modern Asia', trans. Neil Burton and Christian Daniels, in Linda Grove and Mark Selden (eds), *China, East Asia and the Global Economy: Regional and Historical Perspectives* (London: Routledge, 2008), pp. 12–26.

[6] Dennis O. Flynn and Arturo Giráldez, 'Born with a "Silver Spoon": The Origin of World Trade in 1571', *Journal of World History* 6, 2 (1995), pp. 201–21.

[7] Andre Gunder Frank, *ReOrient: Global Economy in the Asian Age* (Berkeley: University of California Press, 1998), p. 117.

[8] Kent G. Deng, 'Miracle or Mirage? Foreign Silver, China's Economy and Globalization from the Sixteenth to the Nineteenth Centuries', *Pacific Economic Review* 13, 3 (2008), pp. 320–58.

prosperous regions until separated by a Great Divergence around 1800.[9] Climate and the environment are now joining commodity flows as factors tying China to global trends.[10]

One strand of what has come to be dubbed New Qing History has developed comparable findings on very different terrain. Reacting against an earlier coastal bias that discounted pressing inland concerns of the empire's Manchu rulers, and against a conceptualization of the imperial worldview as monochromatically Sinocentric, this scholarship made Qing policies toward Inner Asia a political counterpart to revisionist work on China's place in world trade. Earlier findings had foregrounded indicators of China's decline and alienation from global trends before the Opium War. New Qing History scholars, by contrast, noted the achievements the Qing shared with other early modern empires: between 1600 and 1800 Manchu rulers greatly expanded the territory under their control; extinguished the formidable Junghar empire; pushed back Russian expansion by force and kept it at bay by diplomacy; won the cooperation of the Mongol aristocracy and Tibetan Buddhist clergy as well as the Chinese literati elite; and incrementally deepened centralized control over their subjects while implementing technological, bureaucratic, and logistical innovations.[11]

Parallels to this New Qing History can be identified in recent work on China's maritime frontier. Just as studying Inner Asia challenged a view of the Qing state as essentially Chinese, emerging scholarship on the 'Zheng Family Empire', which seized Taiwan from the Dutch and held it against the Qing until 1683, has come to see it as a maritime enterprise without an obvious Chinese precedent. Just as the Manchus held off Russian expansion, the Zheng state used diplomacy and military force to keep the Dutch at bay and protect trade routes stretching from Cambodia to Japan.[12] Nor did Qing victory mark the end of Chinese interaction with Southeast Asia. Although the vital economic role of overseas Chinese in Batavia, Manila, and other Southeast Asian outposts of European empires has long been appreciated, emerging studies are

---

[9] Kenneth Pomeranz, *The Great Divergence: China, Europe, and the Making of the Modern World Economy* (Princeton: Princeton University Press, 2000).

[10] William S. Atwell, 'Notes on Silver, Foreign Trade, and the Late Ming Economy', *Ch'ing-shih wen-t'i* 3, 8 (1977), pp. 1–33; William S. Atwell, 'Some Observations on the "Seventeenth Century Crisis" in China and Japan', *Journal of Asian Studies* 45, 2 (1986), pp. 223–44; Geoffrey Parker, *Global Crisis: War, Climate Change and Catastrophe in the Seventeenth Century* (New Haven: Yale University Press, 2013).

[11] The most compelling reconsideration of Qing imperialism is Peter C. Perdue's *China Marches West: The Qing Conquest of Central Eurasia* (Cambridge, MA: Harvard University Press, 2005); see also Laura Hostetler, *Qing Colonial Enterprise: Ethnography and Cartography in Early Modern China* (Chicago: University of Chicago Press, 2001). A slightly different approach to the 'colonial' expansion of Chinese farmers and merchants within the Qing Empire has also identified resonances with contemporary European expansion. See for instance, Emma Teng, *Taiwan's Imagined Geography: Chinese Colonial Travel Writing and Pictures, 1683–1895* (Cambridge, MA: Harvard University Asia Center, 2004).

[12] Cheng Wei-chung, *War, Trade and Piracy in the China Seas, 1622–1683* (Leiden: Brill, 2013), pp. 222–4; Tonio Andrade has recently called attention to this 'Zheng Family Empire' as a neglected Asian 'overseas empire': 'Beyond Guns, Germs, and Steel: European Expansion and Maritime Asia, 1400–1750', *Journal of Early Modern History* 14, 1–2 (2010), pp. 165–86.

illuminating the political role of overseas Chinese, even the presence of Chinese-dominated micro-states, in what is now Thailand and southern Vietnam.[13]

Reconsideration has extended to the intellectual, cultural, and religious connections between China and the outside world. Work on the Roman Catholic mission to China as both a scientific and religious enterprise, a perennial source of interest, is increasingly concentrating on the interactive nature of these encounters, in which both sides contributed jointly to forms of knowledge and religious practice that did not belong entirely to either.[14] Similar approaches have been taken to Islam in a Chinese context.[15] Intellectual connections within East Asia, linking China, Japan, Korea, and Vietnam, are drawing renewed attention, as is the cosmopolitan interaction between Chinese and Inner Asian cultural elements, in which 'Qing rule . . . fostered the crossing of boundaries, a mixing and fusion, and ultimately the creation of new forms that defined a distinctive Qing culture.'[16]

Aspects of new findings in all of these fields overturn most of the assumptions prevailing when the 'tribute system' model was first advanced. Where historians once wrote of China between 1500 and 1800 as myopically Confucian, isolated and aloof, and approaching a political and civilizational dead end, they can now (doubtless nudged partly by the precipitous rise of contemporary China) point to commonalities with other parts of a world under the rubric of 'early modernity': economic vitality, political achievement, and intellectual openness. Yet, by a sort of law of the conservation of decline, those challenging earlier conceptions of Qing failings often feel compelled by their awareness of the empire's nineteenth-century troubles to balance positive appraisals with countervailing reference to problems and stagnation in other spheres—typically, ones they have chosen not to study in detail. Consequently, our understanding of the Qing Empire as a whole remains fractured and contradictory, and how best to integrate these strands of scholarship remains to be determined. In the interest of brevity, this essay will discuss only one facet of these competing pictures of the Qing in the world, that involving different spatial scales of analysis.

[13] On Chinese as a political force in Southeast Asia long after 1683 see Masuda Erika, 'The Fall of Ayutthaya and Siam's Disrupted Order of Tribute to China (1767–1782)', *Taiwan Journal of Southeast Asian Studies* 4, 2 (2007), pp. 75–128; On the complex commercial, political, and religious legacy of post-Zheng-era overseas Ming loyalism see, for instance, Charles J. Wheeler, 'Buddhism in the Re-ordering of an Early Modern World: Chinese Missions to Cochinchina in the Seventeenth Century', *Journal of Global History* 2, 3 (2007), pp. 303–24.

[14] See, for instance, Nicolas Standaert's study of Chinese Catholics marshalling Confucian and Christian learning to support of the Jesuit position in the Rites Controversy (*Chinese Voices in the Rites Controversy: Travelling Books, Community Networks, Intercultural Arguments* [Rome: Institutum Historicum Societatis Iesu, 2012]); Henrietta Harrison's *The Missionary's Curse And Other Tales from a Chinese Catholic Village* (Berkeley: The University of California Press, 2013); and Catherine Jami on Kangxi's engagement with mathematics and natural science ('Western Learning and Imperial Scholarship: The Kangxi Emperor's Study', *East Asian Science, Technology and Medicine* 27 (2007), pp. 146–72, 166).

[15] Zvi Ben-Dor Benite, *The Dao of Muhammad: A Cultural History of Muslims in Late Imperial China* (Cambridge, MA: Harvard University Asia Center, 2005).

[16] Johan Elverskog, 'Wutai Shan, Qing Cosmopolitanism, and the Mongols', *Journal of the International Association of Tibetan Studies* 6 (2011), pp. 243–74, p. 245; on East Asia see for instance Benjamin A. Elman, 'One Classic and Two Classical Traditions: The Recovery and Transmission of a Lost Edition of the *Analects*', *Monumenta Nipponica* 64, 1 (2009), pp. 53–82.

A disjuncture remains between how China is treated at the regional, Eurasian, and 'truly global' scales. Much of what we know about Qing interaction with its neighbours comes from studies with a bilateral or, at most, regional focus. These show that the Qing Empire played a major economic and political role along virtually every sector of its frontier. Fitted together, this tissue of interaction assumes a continental scale. The political awareness of the Qing state extended at one time or another to almost every corner of Eurasia, including much of the Islamic world. In addition to its immediate neighbours, it conducted correspondence before 1800 with non-contiguous rulers in Europe, Central, and Southeast Asia, who collectively held territory from the Atlantic to Korea, and from Bengal to the Arctic Circle. This correspondence included negotiations on boundaries, alliances, terms of trade, and other issues of crucial economic and political concern. Within this vast ambit, the Qing state monitored military movements, political upheavals, and trade flows, expanding or constricting its range of contacts as seemed most prudent. Few historians of Qing history have probed the degree to which this continent-wide awareness added up to more than the sum of its many regional parts, particularly the question of how far the Qing state and non-official observers connected these various strands of activity into an integrated picture.[17]

If the Qing is increasingly recognized as an early modern Eurasian power, its 'truly global' role remains more ambiguous. Global history, named after a spatial unit, relies heavily on distance as a metric for evaluating global importance. If indeed the 'truly global' was created by sustained trans-Atlantic or trans-Pacific, then China was brought into global history by European maritime ventures that it may have partly inspired but that it did not directly encourage or plan. This America-centred criterion relegates China to a passive role, and promotes what might be called the vending machine model, in which China's global importance is limited to serving as an unconscious engine of world trade: foreigners came to insert silver into a stationary China and departed with its goods. This model gives license for a convenient division of labour. Historians of global trade flows can emphasize the vast sums slotted into the machine, and the distances its customers travelled, without needing to discuss how, or even whether, Qing rulers, officials, and scholars understood the global ramifications of their part in this exchange, still less how they may have tried to influence global developments. Historians of China, for their part, can concentrate on the inner workings of the machine by the study of China's domestic economic indicators. Thus, some of the most forceful revisionist claims for China's dominant role in a connected global economy have come from scholars who do not primarily study China or use Chinese sources. Historians of China seeking to place its economy in a global framework have overwhelmingly favoured a comparative

---

[17] For two recent studies on connections between distant sectors of the Qing frontier see John Herman, 'Collaboration and Resistance on the Southwest Frontier: Early Eighteenth-Century Qing Expansion on Two Fronts', *Late Imperial China* 35, 1 (2014), pp. 77–112; Matthew W. Mosca, 'The Qing State and Its Awareness of Eurasian Interconnections, 1789–1806', *Eighteenth-Century Studies* 47, 2 (2014), pp. 103–16.

approach.[18] Missing in this division of labour is the question of how aware Qing observers were of the world in which they were increasingly enmeshed.

If contact with the Americas is indeed the hallmark of the 'truly global', then it is worth considering whether early modern China can be studied at this scale except as inspiring and setting conditions for world-shaping enterprises of which Europeans were the sole conscious architects. One approach would be to study more closely the engagement of China and the New World before 1800. Although the Qing Empire neither possessed American colonies nor operated trans-Atlantic or trans-Pacific vessels, there were Chinese migrants and goods in the Americas, and Chinese officials and scholars were aware of the New World through maps and written accounts. Did this constitute an active engagement before the mid nineteenth century? A second approach would be to challenge the view that the 'truly global' required engagement with the Americas on the grounds that this criterion overemphasizes long-distance connections at the expense of other metrics of global significance. In the early modern world, vessels of European empires monopolized the longest-distance voyages, so measuring the global by distance perforce emphasizes the European role. Yet, as a populous and prosperous empire with many neighbours, the Qing Empire's position would by contrast be accentuated by a measure of global importance according more weight to the percentage of the world's population, economy, or total volume of trade influenced by, say, its trade policies or economic trends. How best to balance possible metrics is a matter of huge complexity; what some may see as a useful democratization of the criteria of global history may strike others as an attempt by early modern Asianists to tilt the playing field in their favour. At the very least, however, historians should ponder whether the label 'truly global' is too easily lent to transoceanic connections of all sorts, while economic, political, and cultural interaction between the Qing and its immediate neighbours—in an age when the Qing Empire had a larger population than Europe and the Americas combined—are viewed (through the lens of distance) as of merely regional importance.

When evaluations of the global engagement of the Qing Empire differ, they typically split along major historiographical fault lines of spatial and temporal scale and sub-disciplinary approach: contrasting Inner Asia with China, especially its coast; the successful High Qing before 1800 with the diminished Late Qing thereafter; and economic, political, and intellectual developments with each other. It would be unrealistic to suggest either that historians ignore or renounce these divides, which have been reaffirmed by generations of inquiry as sensible and convenient, or that they become expert in the minutiae of all the economic, political, religious, and intellectual strands tying the Qing Empire to the outside world across three centuries and thousands of miles of frontier. The linguistic requirements

[18] Kenneth Pomeranz, considering how to place Qing China in a global context between 1760 and 1840, finds that this is best done by (primarily economic) comparison and explicitly downplays the importance of 'global flows' or 'global currents' (208): 'Their Own Path to Crisis? Social Change, State-Building and the Limits of Qing Expansion, c.1770–1840', in David Armitage and Sanjay Subrahmanyam (eds), *The Age of Revolutions in Global Context, c 1760–1840* (Basingstoke: Palgrave Macmillan, 2010).

alone that such expertise would demand are staggering to ponder. A more modest goal for global history in a Qing context is to offer a complementary plane for pursuing phenomena that remain dimly understood precisely because they cut across these divisions.

GHOMBOJAB AND THE 'SONS OF CHAGHATAI'

Although this essay does not afford space for such a study, even in miniature, I would like to make a rough sketch of the contours of one case to show some of the possibilities, and attendant challenges, of attempting histories cutting across dominant research divisions. In 1725, the Mongolian nobleman Ghombojab completed a brief genealogy of the descendants of Chinggis Khan whom he, as a member of the ruling lineage of the Üjümücin tribe, regarded as his lineal ancestor. Little is known of his life before this point. In 1692, while quite young, he was granted the title of Bulwark Duke (*Fuguo gong*), and had five audiences with the Kangxi emperor by 1709, when he was given in marriage a member of the imperial clan. By 1715, for reasons unknown, Ghombojab was stripped of his dukedom. Because his correspondence with the throne over this matter was conveyed by officials in the imperial bodyguard, it is possible that he was then a member of that body and already resident in Beijing. Sometime around 1722, the year of Kangxi's death, Ghombojab was put in charge of the Tibetan School, where he worked alongside members of the Tibetan Buddhist clergy to train officials in the language skills needed for correspondence and scholarship. As his position suggests, he was known as someone with a remarkable mastery of languages.[19]

Tucked away in his genealogy, Ghombojab gave the following description of the progeny of Chaghatai, son of Chinggis Khan:

> The imperial prince Chaghatai became khan in the country of the white-hatted Muslims, and established his capital in the city of Yarkand. Among his five sons, the eldest Abdula Khan sat on his father's throne. His second son, Imamaquli, became khan in Central Asia and established his capital at Samarkand. Adaramamad became khan in India and established his capital at Balkh. The fourth son, Küngkür, ruled as khan in the country of Rum, and established his capital at Istanbul. The fifth son Temür ruled as khan in the Red-hatted Urunggh-a country and established his capital at Bukhara.[20]

[19] For details of Ghombojab's early life, see Wuyunbilige, 'Guanyu Qingdai zhuming Menggu wenren Wuzhumuqin gong Gunbuzhabu de jidian xin shiliao', *Qingshi yanjiu* (2009), pp. 119–23; for a summary of his multilingual writings and translations, see J. W. de Jong, 'O "Zolotoj knige" S. Damdina'; [review essay], *T'oung Pao*, 2nd Series, 54, 1 (1968), pp. 173–89.
[20] For these names I have followed the forms in L. S. Puchkovskiĭ (ed.), *Ganga-ĭin Uruskhal: Istoriia zolotogo roda vladyki Chingisa:—sochinenie pod nazvaniem 'Techenie Ganga'* (Moskva: Izdvo vostochnoĭ litry, 1960); slightly different Mongolian spellings are given in Coyiji (ed.) *Ghangha-yin urusqal* (Hohhot: Nei Menggu renmin chubanshe, 1980), pp. 55–7; Tibetan forms of these names are given in Ghombojab, *Rgya-nag chos-'byung/Hanqu Fojiao yuanliu ji* (Beijing: Zhongguo Zangxue chubanshe, 2005), pp. 208–9. This passage is translated in Johan Elverskog, *The Pearl Rosary: Mongol Historiography in Early Nineteenth Century Ordos* (Bloomington: The Mongolia Society, 2007), p. 48, n. 143. Elverskog's translation leaves several terms in their original form; my translation interprets *Quyici* as the Chinese *Huizi* (Muslim) and *Balaša* as Balkh. *Urunggh-a* perhaps derives from Urgench.

Setting aside its inaccuracies, this passage has two noteworthy attributes. First, from his vantage point in Beijing, Ghombojab's historical vision extended across Islamic Central Asia to India and Istanbul. Second, several of these names appear here for the first time in the Mongolian-language historical record. Where did he get his information?

As a point of departure, let us assume that Ghombojab encountered his informant or informants in Beijing, most likely within the orbit of the Qing court. In 1713, the Kangxi emperor informed his Grand Secretaries, and presumably other courtiers, that 'the Muslims (*Huizi*) of the northwest are of very many kinds, but all are descendants of Chinggis Khan'.[21] In an undated note, probably a record of these same remarks, the emperor elaborated that after Chinggis had conquered the 'countries of the Muslims' he had ordered his sons to rule them, and although with the passage of time they had gradually exchanged their Mongolian characteristics for the languages, behaviour, and customs of Muslims, the rulers of these tribes remained nonetheless descendants of the Yuan.[22]

Who in contact with the Qing court had information to offer about these territories, particularly Central Asia? One possibility were Russians, who in the early eighteenth century had some contact with most of the peoples of Central Asia. Conduits for information exchange intensified after 1676, as envoys, consuls, merchants, and clergy reached Beijing in larger numbers. Relations with Russia allowed the famous trans-Siberian mission of 1712–15, sent by the Kangxi emperor to the lower Volga to meet Ayuki Khan of the Torghut Mongols. Its member and chronicler Tulišen published an account of his travels in Chinese and Manchu, with a map depicting the Qazaqs, India, and the Ottoman Empire, as well as Moscow and Sweden.

The origins of Tulišen's mission, however, remind us that long-distance Eurasian contact did not rely solely on Russian mediation. In 1698, Ayuki Khan's nephew had gone on pilgrimage to Tibet via the territory of his kinsmen, the Junghars, but political tensions left him stranded and dependent on Kangxi's patronage. Could information about Ghombojab's 'sons of Chaghatai' have come from this closely connected Torghut (Kalmyk)-Junghar network? It is possible to tentatively identify three of those 'sons' as Abdullah, the Chaghataid ruler at Yarkand (r. 1638–67), Imam Quli Khan, a descendant of Chinggis's son Joci who reigned at Bukhara (r. 1611–42), and Nadhr Muhammad, another Jochid who ruled in this period in Balkh (1606/7–41) and subsequently at Bukhara. Küngkür probably refers here not to the Ottoman sultan but to his vassal, the Jochid khan of Crimea.[23] The first of these four had extensive contact with the Junghars, and the latter three had political contact with the Torghuts.[24] Their far-flung contacts made the Torghuts an

[21] *Qing shilu* (Beijing: Zhonghua shuju, 1985), vol 6, p. 505 (253.8a), KX52/2/6 (2 March 1713).
[22] Li Di (ed.), *Kangxi jixia gewu bian yizhu* (Shanghai: Shanghai guji chubanshe, 1993), p. 95.
[23] Zhong Han, 'Kongga'er shiliao pingzhu', *Minzushi yanjiu* 8 (2010).
[24] Onuma Takahiro and David Brophy offered me important advice in the search for these identifications. Puchkovskiĭ has already identified the reference to Imam Quli Khan: L. S. Puchkovskiĭ, *Mongol'skie, Buriat-Mongol'skie Rukopisi i Ksilografy Instituta Vostokovedeniia* (Moscow: Izdvo Akademii Nauk, 1957), p. 41. On relations with Abdullah see David Brophy, 'The Oirat in Eastern Turkistan and the Rise of Āfāq Khwāja', *Archivum Eurasiae Medii Aevi* 16 (2008/2009), pp. 5–28; on contact with Imam Quli Khan and Nadhr Muhammad, see Giorgio Rota, 'Safavids and Kalmyks in the 17th Century: A Preliminary Assessment', *Proceedings of the 5th Conference of the Societas Iranologica Europæa*, vol. 2 (2006), pp. 191, 194.

invaluable source of political intelligence to both the Qing court and the Tibetan Buddhist intellectual world. The Mongolian cleric and scholar Sum-pa Mkhan-po, who stayed in Beijing while Ghombojab was still active and was familiar with his list of the sons of Chaghatai, learned about the Ottoman Empire from a Torghut informant. This informant may also have supplied his information about Bukhara, Samarkand, and other parts of Central Asia.[25]

Behind this diplomacy with the Torghut lay the core interest of the Qing state in Central Asia: its prolonged conflict with the Junghars, first under Galdan and then under his nephew Tsewang Rabtan. Galdan had solidified Junghar domination over the Tarim Basin and campaigned into Central Asia. It was in the aftermath of his conquests that the Qing court made its first direct contact, in 1696, with a royal descendant of Chaghatai.[26] As early as 1697, Kangxi knew that Galdan dominated Muslim states to his west, including (he believed) Bukhara, Samarkand, and the Qazaqs as well as nearer cities like Yarkand and Turfan. Kangxi had no wish to aid or annex Central Asian lands, and rejected the offer of a high-ranking Chinese military officer to 'lead the Muslims (*Huizi*) to attack Galdan's rear'.[27] The proponent of this alliance with foreign Muslims was Ma Ziyun, a native of Shaanxi and himself a Muslim. In his private life, Ma had in 1686 summoned and patronized Khwaja 'Abd Allah (d. 1689), who instructed him in the Qadiriyya branch of Sufism. Little is known about how 'Abd Allah, said to be a descendent of the Prophet born in Medina and educated in Baghdad and Egypt, had reached China. By some accounts he arrived by sea, although there is evidence that he had travelled in Central Asia.[28] In the late seventeenth century, Sufi networks stretched across Eurasia, and some Sufis played an important role in Central Asian politics.[29] However, we have no way of knowing whether the scheme Ma put to Kangxi was based on information, or even strategies, supplied by his Sufi contacts.

Although Kangxi did not adopt Ma's plan, he remained well aware that the Junghars were clashing with enemies to their west. This knowledge was put to use by his son, the Yongzheng emperor, six years after Ghombojab wrote his genealogy. In preparation for his 1731 campaign against the Junghars, the emperor sent twin missions to Russia and the Torghuts, and broached the strategy of sending envoys back eastward from the lower Volga into Central Asia, to inform Bukhara and the Qazaqs of the planned Qing attack. For trustworthy agents 'perfectly familiar with Muslim affairs' and able to communicate with the Qazaqs, he sought assistance

[25] Sh. Bira, *Mongolian Historical Literature of the XVII–XIX Centuries Written in Tibetan*, trans. Stanley Frye (Bloomington: Tibet Society, 1970), 29.

[26] David Brophy, 'The Kings of Xinjiang: Muslims [sic] Elites and the Qing Empire', *Études Orientales: Revue Culturelle Semestrielle* 25 (2008), pp. 69–90, p. 69.

[27] *Qing shilu*, vol. 5, p. 955 (KX 183.2b–3a), KX36/4/5 (24 May 1697); vol. 5, p. 964 (KX 183.20b–21a), KX36/5/24 (12 July 1697).

[28] Ma Tong, 'A Brief History of the Qādiriyya in China', trans. Jonathan Lipman, *Journal of the History of Sufism* 1, 2 (2000), pp. 547–76; Ma Tong, *Zhongguo Yisilan jiaopai menhuan suyuan* (Yinchuan: Ningxia renmin chubanshe, 1986), pp. 83–92.

[29] For more on Sufi and Muslim networks, see Francis Robinson in this volume.

from recently surrendered subjects at Hami and Turfan.[30] The defeat of the Qing expedition that year, resistance by the Russians, and the emperor's death in 1735 halted this strategy.

Another source of information on Mongol Central Asia at the Qing court were the Jesuits, and indeed in 1729 Prince Yin-xiang turned to Fr. Antoine Gaubil for historical information about 'the irruption of Chinggisid Tartars (*Tartares Gengiscaniens*) in Asia and Europe'.[31] These missionaries also provided information about contemporary geopolitics that Qing statesmen used in conjunction with other sources. Between 1722 and 1729, the period in which Ghombojab composed his list of the sons of Chaghatai, Jesuit cartographers and their Qing counterparts were busy collecting sources and testimony to create maps integrating the Qing Empire, Russia, the Junghars, and other parts of Central Asia.[32] Antoine Gaubil mentioned in 1725 a map made in Beijing based on 'reports of Tartars come from beside the Caspian Sea'. In 1729, Gaubil noted that Yongzheng's brother, who pressed him for the latest news from Europe, was also collecting information about Central Asia. When the prince received such intelligence, Gaubil observed, he 'first consulted some Muslims here [Beijing], who know something of their history and of the geography of the Muslim countries'.[33] It is unclear whether the prince turned to some among the hundreds of 'Central Asian Turkic-Muslims' who came to Beijing as caravan traders, or, more likely, Chinese Muslims residing in the city permanently.[34] Whether or not Chinese Muslims in Beijing kept abreast of developments in the Islamic world by questioning foreign Muslims, they certainly did so by other channels. Around 1721 one of Ghombojab's colleagues in the Qing bureaucracy, a Muslim official named Zhao Shiying, recorded information about the Islamic world gleaned from a Jesuit, 'a man of the country of Italy, on the western outskirts of Arabia (*Tianfang*).'[35]

Jesuits used their presence in China to research Central Asia for their own ends. Over the course of the seventeenth century, they had systematically probed for a viable overland route from Europe to China. When the one via Siberia proved stubbornly closed to them, and the one via Persia, India, Tibet, and Xining too arduous, an ambitious plan was devised in the early 1690s to staff missions in

---

[30] Noda Jin, *Ro-Shin teikoku to Kazafu hankoku* (Tokyo: Tōkyō Daigaku Shuppankai, 2011), pp. 88–92; *Gongzhongdang Yongzheng chao zouzhe* (Taibei: Guoli Gugong bowuyuan, 1977), vol. 17, pp. 857–8.

[31] Antoine Gaubil, *Correspondance de Pékin, 1722–1759*, ed. Renée Simon (Geneva: Librairie Droz, 1970), p. 237.

[32] On this cartographic work see Matthew W. Mosca, *From Frontier Policy to Foreign Policy: The Question of India and the Transformation of Geopolitics in Qing China* (Stanford, CA: Stanford University Press, 2013).

[33] Gaubil, *Correspondance de Pékin*, p. 237.

[34] Onuma Takahiro, 'The Development of the Junghars and the Role of Bukharan Merchants', *Journal of Central Eurasian Studies* 2 (2011), pp. 83–100.

[35] According to Han Qi, this was an encounter between Zhao and Fr. Matteo Ripa: 'Cong Zhong-Xi wenxian kan Ma Guoxian zai gongting de huodong', in Michele Fatica and Francesco D'Arelli (eds), *La Missione Cattolica in Cina tra i Secoli XVIII–XIX* (Naples: Istituto Universitario Orientale, 1999), pp. 71–82, pp. 75–7. On Zhao Shiying see *Beijing lishi wenxian yaoji jieti*, ed. Han Pu (Beijing: Zhongguo shudian, 2010), vol. 2, p. 663.

Bukhara and Samarkand as a bridge between Persia and Gansu.[36] Although this project failed, Jesuits in Persia, relying in part on Armenian merchants, were able to augment overland itineraries from Isfahan to China via India and Siberia with a third running through Herat, Balkh, Bukhara, and Turfan.[37]

Another scholar sifting the various currents of information at Beijing in this period was Chen Lunjiong. His father, a Fujianese merchant with experience abroad, had advised the Qing court on how to capture Taiwan in 1683 and was rewarded with a high position in the Qing military. French Jesuits, in a 1717 letter home, described their debates with him over his fierce opposition to Christianity. Chen Lunjiong, whom he had once taken on a mission to Japan, served in Kangxi's bodyguard in the early 1720s and around the end of that decade composed an account of the eastern hemisphere. Although principally concerned with the maritime world, Chen's map and text described Central Asia, including the Caspian Sea, Siberia, and territories he described as 'Galdan' (the Junghars), 'Samarkand' (Muslim Central Asia), and Persia.[38] Chen seems to have had confidence in his knowledge of Central Asia, for in 1736 he memorialized about Siberia's important strategic position relative to the Junghars.[39] Chen's case reminds us that Inner Asian developments were by no means overlooked on the maritime frontier. Galdan's death in the foothills of the Altai on April 4, 1697, first reported to Kangxi on June 2, was reported at Nagasaki by a Chinese ship that had put to sea from Ningbo on July 14.[40]

Taken individually, none of the conduits of information reviewed here is a certain source for Ghombojab's list of the 'sons of Chaghatai'. This is perhaps not surprising. A year after Ghombojab completed his work in Beijing, another genealogy of the descendants of Chinggis, the *Histoire Généalogique des Tatars*, was published at Leiden. This was the work of Abu 'l-Ghazi Bahadur Khan (1603–63), ruler of Khiva, like Ghombojab a historian and descendant of Chinggis. The content of his work was gleaned over the course of a life in which he had travelled throughout Central Asia and lived in Persia and among the Qazaqs and Torghuts (Kalmyks). Originally written in Chaghatai Turki, the text was interpreted into Russian by a Muslim scholar, and then into German by Swedish prisoners of war. If it is, as the modern scholar Bertold Spuler has judged, 'widely defective for the earlier periods', this is surely due to the heterogeneous sources from which its author assembled it.[41] It seems likely that Ghombojab's work was formed by a comparable fusion of different sources of information ricocheting around the Qing Empire, particularly Kangxi and Yongzheng-era Beijing.

[36] For an overview of these Jesuit efforts see Felix A. Plattner, *Jesuits Go East*, trans. Lord Sudley and Oscar Blobel (Dublin: Clonmore & Reynolds, 1950), pp. 166–215.

[37] [Jacques Villotte], *Voyages d'un Missionaire de la Compagnie de Jesus, en Turquie, en Perse, en Armenie, en Arabie, & en Barbarie* (Paris: J. Vincent, 1730), pp. 643–5.

[38] Chen Lunjiong, *Haiguo wenjian lu* (no location: no publisher, 1730), 1.28a, 41b.

[39] *Qing shilu*, vol. 9, pp. 516–17 (QL 21.32b–33a), QL1/6/29 (6 Aug 1736).

[40] Hayashi Shunsai, *Ka-I hentai* (Tokyo: Tōyō bunko, 1959), vol. 3, p. 1921.

[41] Clifford E. Bosworth et al (eds), *The Encyclopaedia of Islam*, 2nd edn (Leiden: Brill, 1967), vol. 1, p. 121.

THE QING IN GLOBAL HISTORY

Pondering avenues of research that would establish the provenance of Ghombojab's list of the 'sons of Chaghatai', a small question in itself, raises larger issues about the scales at which it should be tackled. There are compelling reasons to study it in the context of Mongolian history, and indeed this is how Ghombojab and his works have most commonly been approached. After all, he was born in Mongolia, and his work, written in Mongolian, dealt with the descendants of Chinggis, a topic of special concern for the Mongolian aristocracy. His findings about the 'sons of Chaghatai' were influential within subsequent Mongolian- and Tibetan-language historical works. Yet even approached as Mongolian history, the bounds of inquiry are blurred. If Ghombojab was gleaning information from Torghut or Junghar informants that were in turn aware of the Chinggisid pedigree of other Central Asian dynasties, then Ghombojab could be seen as a member of a Mongolian diaspora with entangled genealogical and historical concerns stretching from the edge of Europe to the edge of Manchuria.[42] Since he likened the pedigree of the Mongol aristocracy to the 'flow of the Ganges', traced its earliest origins back to India, and had a deep engagement with Buddhism, we can also see him as a northern member of an Indo-Tibetan intellectual world.[43]

From another angle, however, the Mongolian and even Inner Asian scale of inquiry proves inadequate, and it seems more illuminating to place Ghombojab's findings in a Qing context that accentuates the role of Beijing and China. He and many others, from Manchu conquerors to Mongol aristocrats, Jesuits, Russians, Torghuts, and Bukharan merchants, converged on Beijing from beyond China proper because of China's size and significance as a market, mission field, or source of income and power. Many of those coming to Beijing were able to communicate with each other because they had, like Ghombojab, learned Chinese or Manchu for pragmatic ends, or were able to find another *lingua franca* like Latin or Mongolian. Based after 1722 in the Tibetan School, Ghombojab's duties led him to work at various times alongside Manchu, Chinese, Tibetan, and Mongolian colleagues. He reiterated his list of the sons of Chaghatai in a Tibetan history of China and Chinese Buddhism. He also translated Buddhist works into Chinese. As a polyglot with intellectual interests crossing the China-Inner Asia divide, he had much in common with other Qing contemporaries.

Although he and his writings can profitably be considered within these larger contexts, Ghombojab had assembled a particular pattern of knowledge that was not likely shared by other Qing subjects, other Mongols, or even other Mongol Qing officials in Beijing. His strikingly novel list of the 'sons of Chaghatai' was the

[42] I have borrowed this concept of a 'Mongolian diaspora' from David Robinson (personal communication).

[43] Matthew T. Kapstein has placed Sum-pa Mkhan-po's geographic scholarship within a 'generally Indianized cultural framework' and as part of 'transformations of South Asian knowledge systems': 'Just Where in Jambudvīpa Are We? New Geographical Knowledge and Old Cosmological Schemes in Eighteenth-century Tibet', in Sheldon Pollock (ed.), *Forms of Knowledge in Early Modern Asia: Explorations in the Intellectual History of India and Tibet, 1500–1800* (Durham, NC: Duke University Press, 2011), p. 336.

product of his unique engagement with different strands of Eurasian, if not global, currents. Equally singular elements would also be found if we considered the outlooks of, say, the Kangxi emperor, Chen Lunjiong, Antoine Gaubil, Ma Ziyun, Zhao Shiying, and other of Ghombojab's contemporaries active within the orbit of the Qing court. This variety of knowledge and experience would be yet more pronounced if we considered the full range of those whose places of birth lay scattered throughout the Qing Empire. Limiting attention to Han Chinese Qing subjects before 1800, one finds merchants sojourning in Java, labourers taken to work in Nootka Sound, Catholic seminarians sent to train in Naples, and Muslims going to the Middle East for *hajj* and study.

Individual particularities arising from the confluence of multiple institutions and networks, the likely origin of Ghombojab's list of the 'sons of Chaghatai', reveals tension between macro- and micro-historical scales of analysis when trying to relate Qing history to its global context. Historians specializing in the Qing Empire, were they inclined to do so, could sketch out intersecting networks of trade, correspondence, and human movement that linked individual Qing subjects to almost every corner of the globe even before 1800. Marshalling these cases as evidence of a large Qing 'global footprint' would likely be challenged by alternative interpretations. Historians of other empires, such as the British, Russian, or Dutch, or of other large-scale entities like the Catholic Church, or the Islamic or Tibetan Buddhist *oecumene*, might with equal justice claim some of these figures as stray Qing subjects whose global connections required the initiative and infrastructure of their own object of study. Historians specializing in China or other sub-imperial units might claim these figures for their own research by arguing that the Qing Empire's size and diversity meant that no common Qing identity meaningfully existed. Yet rejecting the Qing Empire as a unit of analysis in favour of components like China proper, Tibet, or Mongolia leaves those same components open to disaggregation on similar grounds. After all, residents of Shanxi, Gansu, Fujian, Yunnan, and other provinces had distinct patterns of sojourning beyond China proper, conducted various types of foreign trade, received different foreign visitors, and in the process accumulated distinct pools of local knowledge. The same could be said about Sinophone Christians and Muslims, or officials serving in Beijing. Demanding increasingly rigorous levels of internal cohesion could be used to shatter any group identity, leaving only an atomized constellation of individuals whose engagement with the larger world was to some extent unique and idiosyncratic.

Micro-historical attention to the ways in which various global forces, trends, and networks intersected in the lives of individual Qing subjects is one important supplement to scales of analysis already well established in the study of that empire's place in the world, notably the bilateral (e.g., Qing-Korea, Qing-Russia), sub-imperial (e.g., China proper, Tibet, Mongolia), Qing imperial, and greater regional (e.g., East or Inner Asia). For global history to produce novel findings, however, it is equally important to consider the reverse: how to reassemble the interactions of particular Qing subjects with others at the Eurasian, if not global level, in a way that illustrates dynamics cutting across the most common imperial or regional scales of research.

One brief example, drawn from the cartography of Central Asia in the late seventeenth and eighteenth centuries, can illustrate the interaction of individuals on a Eurasian level. It is well known that employees of the Qing state—Han Chinese, Manchus, Mongols, Jesuits, Tibetan Buddhist clergy—played a crucial role in this mapping. They were, however, only one part of a larger field of densely interwoven intellectual activity and information transmission. Russian relations with the Qing Empire stimulated the production of general maps of Siberia and surrounding territories.[44] Some copies of these Russian maps reached Beijing by 1689, where they were consulted by Jesuits and other Qing officials. In 1690, Antoine Thomas sent to Rome from Beijing an adaptation of one, covering not only Siberia but Central Asia, Persia, and India.[45] A Russian prototype also guided Tulišen's map of Eurasia, although he seems to have added information from Torghut informants. When Antoine Gaubil prepared his own personal manuscript map of Inner and Central Asia, his use of both Torghut and Russian place names, and particular Russian names in Chinese form (e.g. his *Touliessco* for the Chinese *Tuliyesike*, from Russian *Turetskoe* ['Turkish']) shows that he had read Tulišen's account, published around the time he reached Beijing. Gaubil's map also drew on recent European maps available in Beijing (which Chen Lunjiong also consulted around this time for his map of the eastern hemisphere). At the same time, Gaubil's draft map contained historical data, making reference to Chinggis Khan and Tamerlane. This shows that he was not only drafting it with reference to the official Qing project of mapping Russia and Central Asia, but also making notes for his personal project, commenced in 1725, of writing a history of the Mongols. When it was complete, this history referred to Chinese and Manchu sources, 'Tartar' informants, and works published in Europe.[46] Although Gaubil's history was finally published in Paris in 1739, his map remained in manuscript. Still, its depiction of Central Asian cities like Balkh and Bukhara was closely related to the 1734 map by Jean Baptiste Bourguignon d'Anville that was printed and widely circulated in Europe as part of Du Halde's celebrated description of China.[47] Another map consulted by d'Anville was a historical map of Central Asia produced for the French translation of Abu 'l Ghazi's history of the Mongols, published in 1726.[48] One of the figures instrumental in arranging that translation, Philipp Johann von

[44] Valerie Kivelson, '"Exalted and Glorified to the Ends of the Earth": Imperial Maps and Christian Spaces in Seventeenth- and Early Eighteenth-Century Russian Siberia', in James R. Akerman (ed.), *The Imperial Map: Cartography and the Mastery of Empire* (Chicago: University of Chicago Press, 2009), pp. 57–9.

[45] Anthony Florovsky, 'Maps of the Siberian Route of the Belgian Jesuit, A. Thomas (1690)', *Imago Mundi* 8 (1951), pp. 103–8.

[46] Christophe Comentale, 'Une Carte Inédite de Père Antoine Gaubil, S. J. : Chine et Tartarie', in *Chine et Europe: Évolution et Particularités des Rapports Est-Ouest de XVIe au XXe Siècle* (Paris: Institute Ricci, 1991), pp. 125–33.

[47] Theodore Foss, 'A Western Interpretation of China: Jesuit Cartography', in Charles E. Ronan and Bonnie B. C. Oh (eds), *East Meets West: The Jesuits in China, 1582–1773* (Chicago: Loyola University Press, 1988), pp. 236–7.

[48] *Carte de l'Asie septentrionale [...] du temps de la grande invasion [...] de Zingis-Chan, pour servir à l'histoire généalogique des Tatars* (1726), <http://gallica.bnf.fr/ark:/12148/btv1b84688533> (accessed 4 June 2014).

Strahlenberg, was a Swedish prisoner of war in Tobolsk between 1711 and 1722, and therefore presumably in that city when Tulišen sojourned there. Von Strahlenberg, like Tulišen, visited the Torghut territories and painstakingly produced his own maps of Central Asia.[49]

These cartographic interconnections, the details of which remain to be fully excavated, by no means represented a consciously collaborative endeavour. Still, not only was their content to some degree interdependent, but the circumstances in which they were created were shaped by interlocking political, commercial, intellectual, and religious currents. To arbitrarily segregate the analysis of these maps based on the languages they used, the empires within which they were composed, or the birthplaces and political or religious affiliations of their draughtsmen, would give at best a very partial picture of the dynamics by which people and information moved, merged, and influenced each other. Above all, these maps demonstrate certain interests, for instance in the geography of Central Asia, and in the history of the Mongols, that took particular forms in individual cases but were also expressions of research trends common across virtually all of Eurasia.

CONCLUSION

Several distinguished historians have recently shown how micro-histories can open new vistas on larger phenomena in global history, a conclusion with which this essay concurs.[50] Yet given the natural tendency of micro-history to gravitate toward cases chosen for their striking and unexpected features, it is worth emphasizing that *every* Qing subject, indeed every inhabitant of early modern Eurasia, had a unique engagement with global forces shaped by many factors, including place of residence, occupation, social connections, consumption, conversation and reading, and simply what they were curious about. Depending on what common denominators one selects as an organizing principle, whether state policies, prevailing languages and authoritative sources of knowledge, patterns of trade, religious beliefs, or institutional membership, these individual cases can be marshalled to support research calibrated to the scale of China, the Qing Empire, and entities greater or smaller. Yet when individual engagements with global forces are studied in pursuit of general conclusions about China or the Qing Empire in the world— conclusions, in other words, which aim at generalities about hundreds of millions

---

[49] On von Strahlenberg's activities, see John R. Krueger, *The Kalmyk-Mongolian Vocabulary in Stralenberg's Geography of 1730* (Stockholm: Almqvist & Wiksell International, 1975).

[50] An early recognition of this can be found in Sanjay Subrahmanyam, 'Connected Histories: Notes towards a Reconfiguration of Early Modern Eurasia', *Modern Asian Studies* 31, 3 (1997), pp. 735–62, p. 750; Bernhard Struck, Kate Ferris, and Jacques Revel, 'Introduction: Space and Scale in Transnational History', *The International History Review* 33, 4 (2011), pp. 573–84, p. 577, pp. 579–80; comments of Sebouh David Aslanian in 'How Size Matters: The Question of Scale in History', *American Historical Review* 118, 5 (2013), pp. 1431–72, pp. 1444–6. A particular successful micro-historical demonstration of 'the way in which the threads of local history are interwoven with global connections' (p. 9) is Harrison's *The Missionary's Curse and Other Tales*; see also Tonio Andrade, 'A Chinese Farmer, Two African Boys, and a Warlord: Toward a Global Microhistory', *Journal of World History* 21, 4 (2010), pp. 573–91.

of people—it is easy to set aside the experience of one, ten, or ten thousand people as an exception or mere curiosity.

Herein lies the value of pairing close attention to individuals with a global level of analysis aiming to relate these individuals to vast but diffuse patterns of engagement. Common interest in the geography of Central Asia or the history and genealogy of the Mongols, for example, can serve as organizing criteria to show what has been called the 'transnational co-production of knowledge' working itself out above the scale of empires, continents, or organized transnational networks like the Catholic Church.[51]

Much scholarship has addressed the question of how to fit the Qing Empire, China, or its constituent sub-regions into their global context, on the assumption that these are coherent and self-contained entities interacting (or not) with others holding similar properties. Before cutting out these familiar patterns for analysis, however, it is useful to peer closely at the individual threads constituting the fabric of global history. Connecting strands severed as a matter of course to juxtapose, say, the Qing and British empires, or China and Europe, could be kept intact if we chose to cut out different and less obvious patterns. Ghombojab could properly be labelled a Qing subject and official, resident of Beijing, Mongolian aristocrat, and Tibetan Buddhist. Any attempt to separate out those categories for analysis in global history would have to include him. Such an approach would, however, be unable to address adequately either the uniqueness of his list of the 'sons of Chaghatai', which in 1725 he was perhaps the only person in Eurasia to espouse in that precise form, or the complex ties that probably came together to inform his ideas. Perhaps paradoxically, then, historical research that does not frame itself as studying the place of China or the Qing Empire in the world may in fact better illustrate how deeply individual Qing subjects were woven into global developments.

---

[51] This phrase is taken from Sebastian Conrad, 'Enlightenment in Global History: A Historiographical Critique', *American Historical Review* 117, 4 (2012), pp. 999–1027, p. 1026.

PART III

GLOBAL NETWORKS

7

Global History from an Islamic Angle

Francis Robinson

THE ANGLE OF APPROACH

This subject is approached from the following background: an upbringing in the 1960s 'Expansion of Europe' tradition in Cambridge; a period in the 1970s spent with the late Freda Harcourt in developing a subject called 'World History since 1900' in the University of London;[1] a research life with a particular focus on the lives of learned and holy men and religious change in South Asia;[2] and a writing life which has, from time to time, reached beyond South Asia to embrace the Muslim world as a whole.[3] That remarkable Chicago historian, Marshall Hodgson, who died in 1968, has been a source of inspiration, as he has been to many others. He set out to write a world history but by the time he died had only succeeded in covering, incompletely, the Muslim world. There is much to be learned from his attitude of respect for his subject of study, manifest for instance in his notorious fastidiousness in the use of nomenclature. His history was published in 1974 under the title *The Venture of Islam: Conscience and History in a World Civilization.*[4]

From this background this chapter will address first the expansion of the Muslim world from the eighth to the eighteenth century as a global phenomenon and then its continuing expansion in the age of Western domination. This will be followed by comments on some specific phenomena of global reach and significance which flow from research on Muslim societies: the tales of storytellers which cross vast regions of the world; understandings of astrology and astronomy which have been widely shared; and particular commodities the impact of whose production and consumption has been of global significance. We will conclude by addressing the 'Protestant turn' in religious piety, experienced throughout Muslim societies in the nineteenth and twentieth centuries, but also experienced in other leading world

---

[1] Freda Harcourt and Francis Robinson, *Twentieth-Century World History: A Select Bibliography* (London: Croom Helm, 1979).

[2] A typical product of this interest is: Francis Robinson, *The Ulama of Farangi Mahall and Islamic Culture in South Asia* (Delhi: Permanent Black, 2001).

[3] See Francis Robinson, *Atlas of the Islamic World since 1500* (Oxford: Phaidon, 1982), and Francis Robinson (ed.), *The Cambridge Illustrated History of the Islamic World* (Cambridge: Cambridge University Press, 1996).

[4] Marshall G. S. Hodgson, *The Venture of Islam: Conscience and History in a World Civilization*, 3 vols (Chicago: University of Chicago Press, 1974).

faiths. Often its expression is entangled with modernities. Out of a discussion of these various themes, some signposts to future directions in global history should emerge.

THE MUSLIM WORLD AND GLOBAL HISTORY

Some may be reluctant to treat civilizations as worthy units of study for the global historian. This may flow from a desire to focus attention away from the expansion of the Western world system, which absorbed a great deal of scholarly energy in the second half of the twentieth century. It may also flow from a desire to escape from the essentialism implicit in Samuel Huntington's *Clash of Civilizations*.[5] Yet there are insights to be gained from studying the Muslim world system, which preceded the Western one, parts of which continue to operate beneath the sway of Western dominance.

The expansion of the Muslim world was a major global phenomenon. Muslims emerged from Arabia in the mid seventh century to defeat the Byzantine Empire and overwhelm the Sasanian Empire within a decade of the death of the Prophet in 632. This was followed by a further one hundred years of rapid expansion so that by 750 Muslims ruled from North Africa and Spain through to the Talus river in Central Asia and the Indus basin in South Asia. In the process they made the cities of West Asia great entrepôts of goods, new technologies, and new ideas from lands covering the Mediterranean basin, the Indian Ocean rim through to China. From the thirteenth century the Muslim world continued to expand into West Africa, South and Southeast Asia, preparing the way for the position today when more Muslims live east of the Hindu Kush than to the West. The Mongol invasions were initially a disaster, but were turned to advantage by the conversion of the Il Khans to Islam and the further expansion of the Muslim world into Central Asia. Up to the seventeenth century Muslim society was the most expansive in the Afro-Asian region and the most influential. It occupied the 'geographical pivot of history', as expounded by Halford Mackinder in his 'heartland thesis'.[6] China and Japan in the north east and Europe in the north west were on the periphery. China certainly exported important innovations such as paper and gunpowder, but also received a host of influences from the Muslim world, in particular through the Mongol Yuan dynasty, ranging from cartography and astronomy and medicine to a host of new crops. Europe, once Muslim civilization had absorbed its Hellenic gifts, was in its turn the receiver of influences from the Muslim world, which it still struggles to recognize in full. Such was the respect for Islamic learning as late as the second half of the seventeenth century that the Royal Society has several shelves of books in Arabic collected in the first ten years of its existence. Early fellows of the Society, like Robert Boyle and Christopher Wren, made a point of learning Arabic.

[5] Samuel P. Huntington, *The Clash of Civilizations and the Remaking of World Order* (New York: Simon and Schuster, 1996).
[6] Halford Mackinder, 'The Geographical Pivot of History', *The Geographical Journal* 23 (1904), pp. 421–37.

By this time the Muslim world, although still dominated by its three gunpowder empires—the Ottoman, Safawid, and Mughal—no longer seemed to have over-whelming power in its possession. Nevertheless, given its many centuries of dom-inance across the Afro-Asian world, and its influence on lands beyond, it must surely continue to be a subject for global historical study.

THE CONNECTEDNESS OF THE MUSLIM WORLD

One outstanding fact about the Muslim world was its connectedness. Over the past fifty years we have learned much about this; it has created a thirst for learning more. One aspect of this connectedness was the way the Muslim world was linked by trade, in particular the long-distance trade across land and sea (see Map 7.1); the shipping trade routes around the Indian Ocean rim which linked East Africa and Arabia to Iran, India, South East Asia, and China; the great caravan trade routes across land—the Silk route linking China to the cities of Central and West Asia, the routes across the Sahara from Cairo to the cities of trade and scholarship of North and West Africa (see Map 7.2). Symbolic of the connectedness of the medieval Muslim world was the way in which the Moroccan traveller, Ibn Battuta, was able to spend twenty-four years in the fourteenth century travelling amongst Muslim communities from West Africa to China. The widespread use of Arabic eased his passage; the widespread use of Islamic law enabled him from time to time to gain a post as a *qadi*.

A much more powerful dimension of the connectedness of the Muslim world was the way in which it was linked by the teacher–pupil relationships of the ulama (learned men) and the master–disciple relationships of Sufis (holy men). Ulama and Sufis were the men, although a surprising number of women were also in-volved, who studied the central messages of Islam, the Quran, and Hadith, and the wide range of skills needed to make them socially useful as law. Their relations with wielders of political power on the one hand, and society at large on the other, are the central threads of Islamic history.

A key requirement for such religious specialists was that they should travel in search of knowledge. And they travelled widely. The twelfth-century Sufi, Ibn Arabi, for instance, travelled from his birthplace Murcia in Spain to the great Islamic cities of Spain and North Africa, to Cairo, Jerusalem, and Mecca, and then to Baghdad, Damascus, and the leading cities of Anatolia. As the Sufi or *alim* (sin-gular of ulama) travelled—Sufi and alim were usually just two sides of one indi-vidual—they strove to sit at the feet of the leading religious specialists of their time. In the case of ulama they learned books from leaders in their field, and collected the *ijaza*s, or licences to teach, which gave them authority over these books, at the same time telling the scholar how this authoritative knowledge had been passed down from the original author of the book, through many teachers of the book, to him. Crudely, more *ijaza*s meant more authority. In bolstering the authority of a particular intellectual tradition, or town, or family, there grew the tradition of writing *tabaqat*s or *tazkirah*s, collective biographies, which would show both how

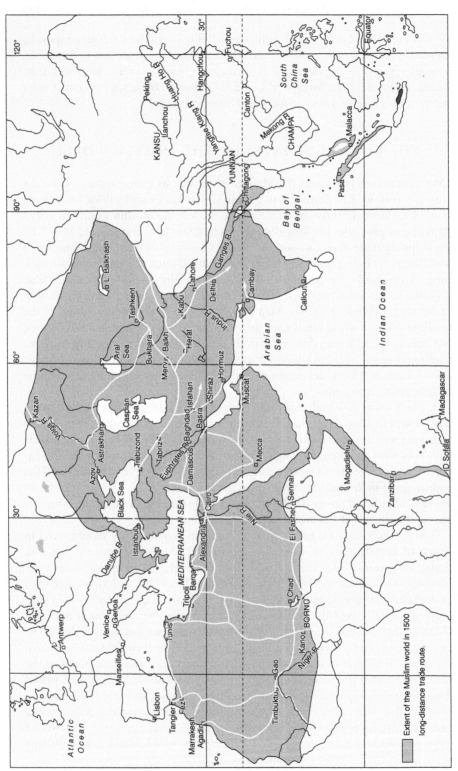

Map 7.1 Long-Distance Trade Routes and the Islamic World, c.1500

Extent of the Muslim world in 1500

long-distance trade route.

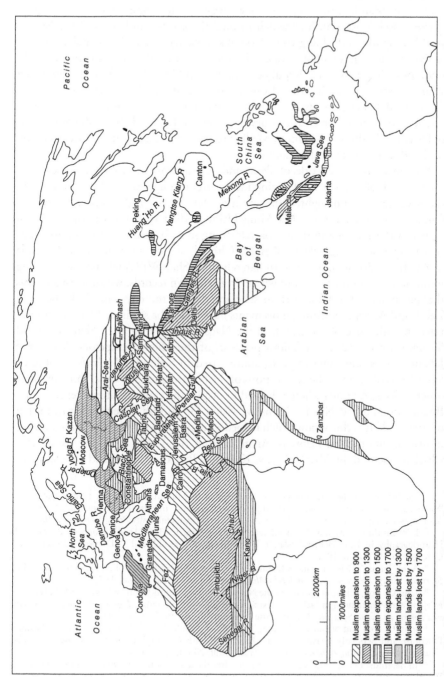

Map 7.2 The Expansion of Muslim States and Populations, 900–1700

Muslim expansion to 900
Muslim expansion to 1300
Muslim expansion to 1500
Muslim expansion to 1700
Muslim lands lost by 1300
Muslim lands lost by 1500
Muslim lands lost by 1700

1000 miles
2000 km

Pacific Ocean

Atlantic Ocean

Indian Ocean

Arabian Sea

Bay of Bengal

South China Sea

Java Sea

North Sea

Baltic Sea

Black Sea

Mediterranean Sea

Caspian Sea

Aral Sea

Red Sea

Cordova
Granada
Fez
Genoa
Venice
Vienna
Athens
Tunis
Constantinople
Moscow
Kazan
L. Balkhash
Samarkand
Bukhara
Tabriz
Baghdad
Damascus
Jerusalem
Cairo
Medina
Mecca
Basra
Isfahan
Herat
Kabul
Delhi
Lahore
Zanzibar
Timbuktu
Kano
Peking
Canton
Jakarta
Malacca

Volga R
Dnieper R
Danube R
Oxus R
Jaxartes R
Euphrates R
Tigris R
Persian Gulf
Nile R
Senegal R
Niger R
Chad
Indus R
Ganges R
Huang Ho R
Yangtse Kiang R
Mekong R

knowledge had been passed down through time and how it had been sought from across the Islamic world. For us they reveal the networks of teacher–pupil or master–disciple relationships which formed the arteries and veins of the Islamic world along which the life-giving blood of knowledge travelled.[7] They show us too, as Evrim Binbas has taught us to see, how such a fifteenth-century network might underpin what he terms a 'Republic of Letters' in Central and West Asia in which scholars wrote to each other from Cairo, Istanbul, Damascus, Isfahan, and Samarqand.[8] They show us, too, how a scholar might rely on the advice of a former teacher. So from seventeenth-century Sumatra, Abd al-Rauf al-Sinkili wrote to his old teacher Ibrahim al-Kurani in Medina to get a dispute about the interpretation of the ideas of Ibn al-Arabi resolved.[9]

We can see these networks of ulama and Sufis at work most vividly as they form the channels along which reforming ideas travel throughout the Muslim world in the seventeenth and eighteenth centuries. So, in the eighteenth century, the Chinese Muslim reformer, Ma Ming Hsin, studied with the Mizjaji family of ulama in the Yemen and then took reforming ideas back home, leading to major risings against Ching rule in Western China.[10] So the brilliant Iraqi, Murtada al-Zabdi, studied with the great Indian reformer, Shah Wali Allah, before travelling to the Yemen and then to Cairo where, from his own records, we know that he was the 'go-to man' for West African scholars visiting the city—the links between Zabdi and African reforming movements have still to be studied.[11] So, too, we can trace the influence of the assault of the Naqshbandi Sufi master, Shaykh Ahmad Sirhindi, on the eclectic religious practices of the Mughal emperors, Akbar and Jahangir. This reforming impulse, summarized in Sirhindi's *Maktubat* (collected letters) travelled along the connections of the Naqshbandi Sufi order into, amongst other regions, Anatolia where it helped to inspire the early twentieth-century Sufi, Bediuzzaman Saeed Nursi's alternative vision for Turkish development from that of Ataturk.[12] It is this vision which helped underpin the Kayseri phenomenon, the industrialization from below of Anatolia from the 1960s. It is this vision, too, which lies behind the AKP (Adalet ve Kalkınma Partisi, or Justice and Development

---

[7] For the role of these relationships in the making of Muslim societies see: Francis Robinson, 'Knowledge, its Transmission and the Making of Muslim Societies' in Francis Robinson (ed.), *Cambridge Illustration History of the Islamic World* (Cambridge: Cambridge University Press, 1996), pp. 208–49.

[8] I. Evrim Binbas, 'Sharaf al-Din Ali Yazdi (ca.770s–858/ca.1370s–1454): Prophecy, Politics and Historiography in Late Medieval Islamic Historiography' (unpublished PhD thesis: University of Chicago, 2009), pp. 76–107.

[9] A. H. Johns, 'Friends in Grace: Ibahim al-Kurani and Abd al-Rauf al-Singkili', in S. Udin (ed.), *Spectrum: Essays Presented to Sutan Takdir Alisjahbana* (Jakarta: Dian Rakyat, 1978).

[10] John O. Voll, 'Linking Groups in the Networks of Eighteenth-Century Revivalist Scholars: the Mizjaji Family in Yemen', in Nehemia Levtzion and John O. Voll (eds.), *Eighteenth-Century Renewal and Reform in Islam* (Syracuse, NY: Syracuse University Press, 1987), pp. 69–92.

[11] John O. Voll and Stefan Reichmuth, 'Murtada al-Zabidi (1732–91) and the Africans: Islamic Discourse and Scholarly Networks in the Late Eighteenth Century', in Scott S. Reese (ed.), *The Transmission of Learning in Islamic Africa* (Leiden: Brill, 2004), pp. 121–53.

[12] In the midst of a spiritual crisis in the years after the defeat of the Ottoman Empire in the First World War, Sirhindi's *Maktubat* showed him that his one true guide was the Quran. Sukran Vahide, Ibrahim M. Abu-Rabi (eds), *Islam in Modern Turkey: An Intellectual Biography of Bediuzzaman Said Nursi* (Albany: State University of New York Press, 2005), pp. 165–7.

Party), the moderate Islamist party which currently rules Turkey.[13] Azyumardi Azra's *The Origins of Islamic Reformism in Southeast Asia: Networks of Malay-Indonesian and Middle Eastern 'Ulama in the Seventeenth and Eighteenth Centuries* is a major step forward in charting the connections between reform and connectedness.[14] But there is still much work to be done to understand the Islam-wide reach of Muslim networks on the eve of the era of European dominance.

The question remains, what did Western power, which swept over the Muslim world from 1800, and which has continued to dominate it in one form or another ever since, do for spread of the Muslim world and its connectedness? One outcome was a continuing process of Islamization; the dynamics of Western Christian rule did much, for instance, to deepen the Islamic presence in Indonesia and in East and West Africa. A second outcome was a further expansion of Muslim peoples so that they came to have a truly global reach: Muslim sects such as the Ahmadiyya and the Nizari Ismailis took advantage of the British Empire to spread under its umbrella (see Map 7.3).[15] Muslims from the old Muslim world seized the economic opportunities offered by the West to establish themselves in Western Europe, North and South America, the Caribbean, South Africa, and Australia.[16] The old forms of connectedness continued, not least as ulama and Sufis came to represent their societies against their elites, who had been co-opted by the West. Sufis came to have notable international followings: the disciples of Baba Farid of Pakistan's Pak Pattan in Malaysia, of Bombay's Ghulam Muhammad in South Africa, of Hazrat Shah 'Zindapir' from Pakistan's northwest frontier in the English midlands, and of Lucknow's Bahr Ul-Ulum in California.[17] The teacher–pupil relationship underpinned the spread of the reformist activism of India's Deoband throughout Pakistan, but particularly to the troubled lands to the West where in the Northwest it informed the early development of the Taliban and in Iranian Baluchistan where it began to provide intellectual leadership to Muslims from Central Asia.[18] The teacher–pupil relationship also underpinned the growing

[13] ESI, 'Islamic Calvinists: Change and Conservatism in Central Anatolia', Berlin/Istanbul, 19 September 2005, <http://www.esiweb.org> (accessed 31 January 2015); M. Hakan Yavuz, *Islamic Political Identity in Turkey* (New York: Oxford University Press, 2003).

[14] Azyumardi Azra, *The Origins of Islamic Reformism in Southeast Asia: Networks of Malay-Indonesian and Middle East Ulama in the Seventeenth and Eighteenth Centuries* (Crows Nest, NSU: Allen & Unwin, 2004).

[15] Francis Robinson, 'The British Empire and the Muslim World', in Judith Brown and Wm. Roger Louis (eds), *The Oxford History of the British Empire: vol. IV, The Twentieth Century* (Oxford: Oxford University Press, 1999), pp. 398–420.

[16] Humayun Ansari, 'Islam in the West', in Francis Robinson (ed.), *The Islamic World in the Age of Western Dominance* (New Cambridge History of Islam V) (Cambridge: Cambridge University Press, 2010), pp. 686–716.

[17] Robert Rozehnal, *Islamic Sufism Unbound: Politics and Piety in Twenty-First Century Pakistan* (Basingstoke: Palgrave Macmillan, 2007), pp. 134–6; Nile Green, *Bombay Islam: The Religious Economy of the West Indian Ocean 1840–1915* (Cambridge: Cambridge University Press, 2011), pp. 208–34; Pnina Werbner, *Pilgrims of Love: The Anthropology of a Global Sufi Cult* (London: C. Hurst & Co, 2003), pp. 30–60.

[18] Stéphane A. Dudoignon, *Voyage au pays des Baloutches: (Iran oriental, an XVIII—XXI siècle—de la République islamique)* (Paris: Éditions Cartouche, 2009); Sana Haroon, 'The Rise of Deobandi Islam in the North-West Frontier Province and its Implication in Colonial India and Pakistan 1914–1996', *Journal of the Royal Asiatic Society* 18, 1 (2008), pp. 47–70.

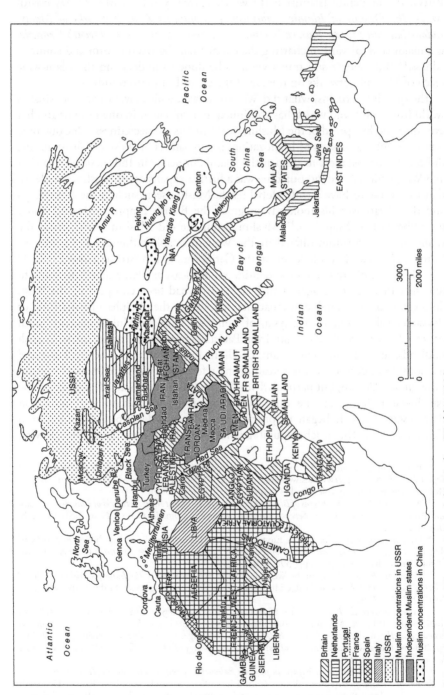

Map 7.3 European Domination and the Muslim World, c.1920

activism of the Shia of West Asia; it is not possible to understand Lebanon's Hezbollah without also learning of its leadership's teacher–pupil connections to the great *hawza*s of an-Najaf and Qum.[19] Connections such as these usually escaped British imperial administrators, as they may escape intelligence services today.

NEW FORMS OF CONNECTEDNESS

New forms of connectedness have come to mingle with and overlay the old ones. Transnational Islamist organizations have emerged. I think of the Muslim Brotherhood and the Jamaat-i Islami which currently challenge westernized elites for power in West Asian and South Asian states. I think of the Tablighi Jamaat, or preaching society, which is said to be the most widespread Muslim organization in the world. There are many other Muslim NGOs of which the most notable are the International Institute of Islamic Thought based at Herndon in Virginia and the Fethullah Gulen educational movement which, inspired at one remove by the teachings of Bediuzzaman Saeed Nursi, is based in over fifty countries. Beyond this there are state-based organizations such as the Saudi-funded World Muslim League and the Islamic Conference Organization. Modern connectivity, however, no longer rests just with person-to-person contact or on an institutional basis, it also exists in the media. This has grown from the development of the press in the nineteenth century, which helped Muslims to begin to conceive of their community of believers in pan-Islamic terms as a civilization to the emergence of wireless, television, and in the internet in the second half of the twentieth century, which have greatly enhanced the civilization-consciousness, the *umma*-consciousness, of the ordinary Muslim. Osama bin Laden was brilliantly successful in using these tools to reach out to the ordinary Muslim and to help turn the community of believers into a community of conscience.[20] There is real value in studying the connectedness of the Muslim world and the systems which support it, not just for the modern intelligence services but also for the global historian, who wishes to understand how this remarkable civilization has spread and held together over the past 1,400 years.

At this point there is one issue which needs to be addressed. Some might see a danger in paying special attention to religious knowledge and its transmitters in the working of Muslim societies as leading towards the Orientalist trap of essentialism. However, to ignore the role of ulama and Sufis, and their connectedness across the Muslim world, would be to turn away from a real understanding of how that world, and its constituent Muslim societies, works. Providing there is awareness of the dangers and no temptation to explain all developments in Muslim societies

[19] See Nicholas Noe (ed.), *Voice of Hezbollah: The Statements of Sayyed Hassan Nasrallah* (London and New York: Verso, 2007), especially the introduction by Nicholas Blanford.
[20] For an overall argument about modern connectedness see: Francis Robinson, 'The Islamic World from World System to Religious International', in Abigail Green and Vincent Viane (eds), *Religious Internationals in the Modern World: Globalization and Faith Communities since 1750* (Basingstoke: Palgrave Macmillan, 2012), pp. 111–35.

in terms of Islam, there should be no problem. Indeed, the religiously based systems of connectedness in the Muslim world are an important global story.

SHARED WORLDS OF KNOWLEDGE AND EXPERIENCE

In the following section, I will highlight those potential global history subjects which flow from research on the Muslim world: storytelling, astrology, and astronomy, and the impact of commodities.

The World of Storytelling

The world of storytelling, and widely shared stories and fables, is a possible line of enquiry for the global historian. The modern technologies of print, wireless, television, film, and electronic social networks have existed for the briefest of moments. For most of human time imaginations have been stretched, and senses been alternately delighted and terrified, by the art of the storyteller. This art, though a dying one in its face-to-face form, continues to the present day as a profession in the teahouses of Morocco, for instance, in the coffeehouses of Iran, and amongst the Wayang puppeteers of Java. As a private art it continues amongst families across the world; it has continuing capacity to delight children reminding us of its power through time.

There is a world of shared stories which reaches out from West Asia into Europe and North Africa, and also into South and Southeast Asia. It may well reach more widely; of this we need to know more. Two of the apparent starting points for stories are the Old Testament and the Epic of Gilgamesh which share themes, amongst them the Garden of Eden and Noah's Flood. But the Epic's influence ranges more widely than this. Martin West has demonstrated its considerable influence on Greek epic down to Homer.[21] Its influence on both the Hindu and the Muslim world of South Asia can be found in the presence of Khwaja Khidr, who is usually depicted as an old man dressed in green and standing on a swimming fish.[22] There are great Muslim epics whose origin and influences stretch across the region. There is the extraordinary Persian romance, *Vis and Ramin*, composed for the eleventh-century Seljuk court in Isfahan, whose origin reaches back to the Pahlavi Parthian past and whose influence is thought to have spread through the Seljuk court in Damascus, and contact with Crusaders, to become the basis of the European story of Tristan and Isolde.[23] There is the mystical romance, *Mirigavati* or the 'Magic Doe', composed by the Sufi Qutban Suhravardi in 1503 for the Sharqi Sultan of Jawnpur in what is now India's eastern Uttar Pradesh. In a

[21] Martin L. West, *The East Face of Helicon: West Asiatic Elements in Greek Poetry and Myth* (Oxford: Clarendon Press, 1997).

[22] 'Al-Khadir', in Clifford E. Bosworth et al (eds), *The Encyclopaedia of Islam*, 2nd edn (Leiden: Brill, 1978), vol. 4, pp. 902–5.

[23] Fakhraddin Gurgani, *Vis & Ramin*, trans. Dick Davis (Washington, DC: Mage Publishers, 2007), pp. viii–xl.

story, designed both for courtly delight and for the training of young mystics, the Sufi learns how through the conquest of desire, the self can be annihilated. In the process we have reflections of Homer's *Odyssey* and the tale of Sinbad the Sailor.[24] Then, there is the epic of the Prophet's uncle, *Amir Hamza*, so beloved of the Mughal emperor Akbar. This has had a life which probably began in the seventh century and runs down to the present. It has been cherished across the Indian Ocean region and in its nineteenth-century Calcutta-published version carries references ranging from the Sasanian court at Ctesiphon through to East India Company soldiers.[25] Arguably the peak of the Islamic storytelling tradition exists in the *One Thousand and One Nights*, which first came to light in full manuscript form in thirteenth-century Syria. In this collection we see how the Arabs drew on the storytelling traditions of the land and peoples they conquered—Greeks, Romans, Copts, Jews, Berbers, Persians. This has been an extraordinary source of folktales and stimulus to the imagination both for the West and the East. Indeed, the West has raided it for stories to be told in all media as hungrily as the Arabs raided the resources of their subject peoples.[26] Christopher Shackle has shown the remarkable impact of just one story, that of *Sayf al-Muluk*, as it travelled through a range of cultures in South Asia.[27]

It is possible that the global significance of folk literature was lost sight of once it came to be captured for nationalist purposes from the nineteenth century onwards. But there is much more to be learned from its connectivity across the Eurasian region, and indeed beyond that region. If in doubt, consider the impact of just one book, Martin West's *The East Face of Helicon: West Asiatic Elements in Greek Myth and Poetry*.[28] Arguably before he published this book it was still possible to consider the classical literature of Greece and Rome as a world unto itself. Now the young classicist wonders whether it might not be wise to learn an Oriental language or two.

Astrology

Astrology is a second area of shared knowledge and experience worthy of the attention of the global historian. There has been considerable reluctance until recently to consider its significance for understanding aspects of Muslim societies up to the nineteenth century. In this respect Muslim societies are little different from human societies at large. From the beginning of time humans have sought to find meaning

---

[24] Aditya Behl and Wendy Doniger (eds), *The Magic Doe: Qutban Suhravardi's Mirigavati: A New Translation by Aditya Behl* (New York: Oxford University Press, 2012), especially Behl's introduction, pp. 9–38.

[25] Musharraf Ali Farooqi and Hamid Dabashi (eds), *The Adventures of Amir Hamza: Lord of the Auspicious Planetary Conjunction* by Ghalib Lakhnavi and Abdullah Bilgrami (New York: Modern Library, 2007).

[26] Robert Irwin, *The Arabian Nights: A Companion* (London: Allen Lane, 1994).

[27] Christopher Shackle, 'The Story of Sayf al-Muluk in South Asia', *Journal of the Royal Asiatic Society* (Series 3) 17, 2 (2007), pp. 115–29.

[28] West, *The East Face of Helicon*.

in the heavens, and for much of this time there has been the belief that there is a connection between movements in the heavens and human affairs.

This search for meaning in the heavens was worldwide, present no less in the Mayan civilization of Central America and the Andean of South America than in the worlds of Babylon, India, and China. In Greek hands it gained a form of scientific basis as it became linked to advances in mathematics, in particular the work of Ptolemy of Alexandria (fl. 13–70) whose *Almagest* gave a mathematical account of the movement of the heavenly bodies. It remained orthodoxy until Copernicus. The Graeco-Roman achievement in the field was inherited by the Muslim world which brought more scientific underpinning through the work of its observatories, the use of the astrolabe and the development of *Zij* tables. From here it travelled, along with those other elements of classical learning which Muslims had either preserved or developed, into late medieval Europe where it was to penetrate deeply into the intellectual and political life of the Renaissance.[29]

Astrology always had its enemies. Cicero rejected it on the commonsense grounds that inheritance and upbringing must influence a person's life more than the subtle and invisible forces from the stars.[30] Leading Christian and Muslim thinkers, for instance St Augustine and al-Ghazali, rejected it as a pagan or secular philosophy.[31] Nevertheless its influence remained powerful until the Copernican revolution began to be felt from the seventeenth century onwards. Since then, while continuing to exist, indeed flourish in Islamic lands and further east, in Europe it was increasingly the resort of the irrational and the charlatan until gaining a mild reprieve at the hands of Jungian psychology. This said, it has attracted political elites: the German High Command in the Second World War, Nancy Reagan after the failed assassination of her husband, while Indira Gandhi's devotion to astrology did not save her from being assassinated. In the United Kingdom, popular astrology has a continuing existence in the horoscope features of the red-top press and *Old Moore's Almanack*, which still sells up to half a million copies a year.[32]

To all of this one might say 'so what'! Why does it make it worthy of study by the global historian? Frankly, anything which has helped shape human understanding, or misunderstanding, across the globe and for millennia, demands our attention. I was extremely resistant to it until others showed me how it might explain the decoration of a royal tomb or the design of a major Sufi shrine complex.[33] In recent years, scholars sensitive to astrology have taught us how to interpret Timurid political thought and, most particularly, have placed aspects of the

---

[29] Peter Whitfield, *Astrology: A History* (London: The British Library, 2001), pp. 9–187.

[30] Whitfield, *Astrology*, p. 69.

[31] Whitfield, *Astrology*, pp. 81–2, 94.

[32] Whitfield, *Astrology*, pp. 188–202.

[33] For instance, for an explanation of the light symbolism on Humayun's tomb in Delhi see Glenn D. Lowry, 'Humayun's Tomb: Form, Function and Meaning in Early Mughal Architecture', *Muqarnas* 4 (1987), pp. 133–48; and for the astrological basis for the design of the shrine at Uchch, Pakistan, see Hasan Ali Khan, 'Shia-Ismaili Motifs in the Sufi Architecture of the Indus Valley 1200–1500 A.D.' (unpublished PhD thesis: School of Oriental and African Studies, University of London, 2009).

first one hundred years of Mughal rule in South Asia in a completely new light.[34] Astrology is not only a lost world of understanding, but also one in which Christians and Muslims shared a similar cosmological understanding as Serge Gruzinski has so charmingly shown recently in his exposition of the language in which a Christian in late sixteenth-century Mexico thought about the Ottoman Empire and a Turk in early seventeenth-century Istanbul thought about the Americas.[35] There is serious heuristic value in an understanding of astrology. An openness to it should be part of the armoury of any global historian wishing to reach back beyond the contemporary era.

Commodities of Global Impact

Environment, climate, diseases, and pandemics are well-established subjects for the global historian. But there are other single factors which have global reach and impact and are therefore worthy subjects for the global historian. Consider the great commodities of world history, commodities which have had a considerable impact on the societies in which they have been produced, and a considerable impact across the world as they have been consumed. Their production and consumption may well raise ethical issues. They may cause wars, make men rich, bring ill health and death. On occasion, not only have they changed individual lives, they have also shaped and continue to shape individual societies. Such commodities are: cotton, sugar, tobacco, coffee, opium, and oil. But thinking in terms of global impact, another six might have been considered—tea, alcohol, wool, gold, coal, and copper. Doubtless, there are other candidates. The first six are addressed because they have all had, and have, an impact on Muslim societies.

Looking at cotton in greater detail reveals that the first evidence of growing and processing cotton stems from *c.*3000 BC in China, India, and the Americas. At the beginning of the Christian era there was a notable cotton trade between India and the Arab lands. The Muslim conquest of Spain helped to bring cotton production into Europe. By the sixteenth century cotton cloth was highly sought after in European markets. From the seventeenth century the development of Britain's trading empire made cotton a commodity of global importance. Britain first stimulated Indian production to provide cotton goods for the European and North American markets and then destroyed it as production of cotton goods was transferred from the handloom weavers of India to the machines of Britain. In the nineteenth century, India became primarily a producer of raw cotton. Such was the centrality of cotton to the relationship between Britain and India that Mahatma Gandhi made the production of hand spun cotton cloth, *khadi*, and the wearing of clothes made of it, the symbol of Indian nationalist resistance to the British. The twentieth century saw the destruction of the British cotton industry and the transfer of mass textile manufacture to developing economies. Thus the manufacture

[34] See, for instance, A. Azfar Moin, *The Millennial Sovereign: Sacred Kingship and Sainthood in Islam* (New York: Columbia University Press, 2012).

[35] Serge Gruzinski, *What Time Is It There? America and Islam at the Dawn of Modern Times* (London: Polity Press, 2010).

of cotton goods has come to contribute to new industrial revolutions across the world, many new opportunities for exploitation, and environmental devastation such as the draining of the Aral Sea by the wanton demands of Uzbekistan's cotton monoculture.

This thumbnail sketch suggests why the global historian might take cotton seriously. Turning to a more specific Islamic angle, Richard Bulliet's recent Yarshater lectures at Harvard offer a striking demonstration of the impact of cotton on the early Islamic world. The Prophet Muhammad was opposed to luxurious apparel, so a distinct preference for cotton clothing, as opposed to silk, developed amongst Muslims. In the years after the seventh-century Arab conquest of Iran, this led to the establishment of cotton cultivation in the Iranian plateau; the transition of Iranians from being primarily Zoroastrian to being primarily Muslim can in part be measured by the spread of cotton cultivation. For the ninth and tenth century Bulliet talks of a 'cotton boom' during which Iran was transformed from a territory of landed estates and autarchic villages to one of towns, trade, and a rich cultural life. Then, there came the 'big chill', a hundred years of climate change, which hit Iran's cotton industry severely and brought a rapid decline in prosperity. The cultivated classes—rich merchants, poets, administrators, and historians—left the plateau to seek their fortunes in Muslim courts from Anatolia to Bengal. They took with them their language, Persian, and their high levels of skill in government.[36]

Like cotton, sugar has also changed the face of human history. From its early mass production in places like Tawahin as-Sukka in the eleventh-century Jordan Valley, it was to influence the formation of colonies, the development of slavery, and the composition of peoples. From the eighteenth century, it has had a substantial impact on diet particularly in the West. In consequence it keeps tens of thousands of dentists in business. Today the average human being consumes 24 kg of sugar a year. In richer societies it is recognized to be a growing general health hazard.[37]

Coffee emerged from Sufi *khanqah*s (monasteries) in fifteenth-century Yemen to become the top agricultural export of twelve countries today and the world's seventh largest legal agricultural export by value. It has been prohibited in Muslim societies from time to time but it is also the first drink one might offer a guest in contemporary Arabia. Through much of the world it helps to sustain sociability. There is no agreement as to whether its health effects are positive or negative.[38]

[36] Richard W. Bulliet, *Cotton, Climate, and Camels in Early Islamic Iran: A Moment in World History* (New York: Columbia University Press, 2009).

[37] Graham Chandler, 'Sugar Please', *Saudi Aramco World* 83, 4, (2012), pp. 36–43; Jelle Bruinsma (ed.), *World Agriculture towards 2015/2030: An FAO Perspective* (London: Earthscan Publications, 2003), p. 119.

[38] Ralph S. Hattox, *Coffee and Coffeehouses: The Origins of a Social Beverage in the Medieval Near East* (Seattle: University of Washington Press, 1985); Bennett Alan Weinberg and Bonnie K. Bealer, *The World of Caffeine: The Science and Culture of the World's Most Popular Drug* (London: Routledge, 2002), pp. 267–316.

Tobacco, as we know, is acknowledged to be a major health hazard, the direct cause of at least five million deaths a year and a contributing factor to many others. Tobacco first entered the wider world from the Americas in the early seventeenth century; it was not accepted without challenge in either the Muslim or the Western world.[39] The cultivation of tobacco is harmful to the environment in which it is produced. It also tends to make profits for large corporations rather than small producers. Its adoption by different classes and by different genders across the world over the past two hundred years can be seen as a marker of social, economic, and cultural change. Today, consumption is falling in the Western world while it rapidly increases in the developing world.[40]

The cultivation of opium poppies for anaesthetic and occasionally ritual purposes goes back at least to Neolithic times. Only in the nineteenth century was it overtaken for medical purposes by morphine and its derivative forms. Mughal emperors drank opium compounds for pleasure; they used the drink in concentrated form to execute princes without shedding blood. During the seventeenth century smoking opium with tobacco became a recreation in China. Chinese consumption led to a massive expansion of opium production in India and its trade to China, as has been so wonderfully imagined in two recent novels by Amitav Ghosh.[41] Opium thus became the cause of wars between Britain and China. In its refined form as heroin it has been entangled with wars in its three main centres of production—Mexico, Southeast Asia's 'Golden Triangle', and Afghanistan and Pakistan. Arguably, heroin production in the last region has always been a greater threat to the West than the Taleban and al-Qaeda.[42]

Nothing matches the production and consumption of oil and oil products for their impact on the Islamic world in particular and the world in general. Oil has dictated, and still dictates, the drawing of territorial boundaries; it fosters lop-sided economic development; it tends to favour dictatorships over democracy; it leads to invasions and declarations of war. But for the entanglement of oil and oil products with the workings of all world economies, we would not be consuming this carbon resource to a level that threatens the very existence of the earth as a human habitation. Oil is the greatest of the commodities that command our attention. But all six commodities that we have considered have had an impact on human history in their production and consumption which make them worthy of the attention of the global historian.

[39] Such was the debate on the acceptability of smoking in the Ottoman Empire that the great scholar of Damascus, Abd al-Ghani Nabulusi, felt impelled in 1681 to write a long treatise on the subject to say that although he did not like the practice it was perfectly legal. Samer Akkach, *Letters of a Sufi Scholar: The Correspondence of Abd al-Ghani al-Nabulusi (1641–1731)* (Leiden: Brill, 2010), pp. 105–8.

[40] Eric Burns, *The Smoke of the Gods: A Social History of Tobacco* (Philadephia: Temple University Press, 2007).

[41] Amitav Ghosh, *Sea of Poppies* (London: John Murray, 2008); *River of Smoke: A Novel* (London: Penguin Group, 2011).

[42] Pierre-Arnaud Chouvy, *Opium: Uncovering the Politics of the Poppy* (Cambridge, MA: Harvard University Press, 2010).

THE 'PROTESTANT TURN', A PROCESS
OF CHANGE WIDELY EXPERIENCED

The 'Protestant turn' was a process of change widely experienced by humankind as it has moved into the modern era. This is the 'Protestant turn' in human piety. That 'turn' in Muslim religious piety has long been a source of fascination. Its origins lie deep in the Islamic past in the tensions between revelation and the magical practices of mysticism. These came to a head in the eighteenth century in the teaching of Muhammad ibn Abd al-Wahhab in Arabia and Shah Wali Allah in India. The new 'Protestant' understandings of Islam derived from these teachings spread throughout the Muslim world in the nineteenth and twentieth centuries as it became subject to Western power. Key features of this 'Protestant' turn were: a new focussing of the believer's attention on the Quran and Hadith; translation of these texts from Arabic into the languages of the Muslim world so that there could be meaningful engagement with them; attacks on all forms of magic, in particular the idea that there could be intercession for man on earth; and a stronger emphasis than before on the horrors of the Day of Judgement. The aim was to fashion, in a world where Muslims no longer held political power, the individual human conscience as the basis of a Muslim society. Each individual was to become an active force in creating a Muslim society; belief now meant a this-worldly piety of social action. From the nineteenth century to the present these elements can be seen at work in Muslim societies from Indonesia to Morocco.

Several significant outcomes flow from these moves towards a 'Protestant' piety. The new emphasis on conscience and personal responsibility led to changes in Muslim senses of the self which Charles Taylor declares, arguing from a European Christian perspective, are associated with modernity. There is self-instrumentality, the idea of the individual human being, male and female, as the active, creative, agent on earth. This was an idea prominent in the life and ideas of men such as Sayyid Ahmad Khan, founder of South Asia's Islamic modernist thought, and Muhammad Ilyas, founder of the Tablighi Jamaat, the Preaching Society. It was no less alive in those most influential Muslim thinkers of the twentieth century, Muhammad Iqbal of British India and Ali Shariati of Iran. With the idea of man as the active agent on earth there also came the idea of action as a form of self-affirmation. Man affirms, indeed empowers, himself by increasingly fulfilling his human potential. Inevitably this leads to tension between human desire for personal fulfilment and society's concern that human desire should be kept focussed on Godly ends.[43]

The affirmation of the self leads to the affirmation of the ordinary things of the self which Taylor terms 'one of the most powerful ideas in modern civilization',[44] a process which can be seen most wonderfully and most humanly in the changing

---

[43] Francis Robinson, 'Religious Change and the Self in Muslim South Asia since 1800', in Francis Robinson, *Islam and Muslim History in South Asia* (Delhi: Oxford University Press, 2000), pp. 105–21.

[44] Charles Taylor, *Sources of the Self: The Making of the Modern Identity* (Cambridge, MA: Harvard University Press, 1989), p. 14.

ways in which Muslims have come to write the life of the Prophet. The final theme in the new Muslim self is the growth of self-consciousness and the reflective habit. A willed Islam had to be a self-conscious one. It opened up an internal landscape where the battle of the pious for the good would take place.[45]

Alongside these new senses of the self, Islamic reform, and its 'Protestant turn', undermined the old system of religious authority and opened the way to self-interpretation of the scriptures. Up to this point, as noted, religious authority rested with religious specialists, to whom knowledge had been passed down person-to-person through time and who monopolized interpretation. They transmitted knowledge to society more widely by their example, their edicts, and their sermons. Reform with its insistence on personal engagement with scripture, with its translation of scripture into vernacular languages, with its strong support for adopting print, and its fashioning of the individual human conscience, began to change all this. Reform encouraged literacy, as did colonial governments to a lesser extent. Independent Muslim states in the second half of the twentieth century came to invest in literacy to the extent that in Southeast Asia the percentage of the school-leaving cohorts is in the high nineties. Over the past thirty years this has been followed in much of the Muslim world by a move towards mass higher education. These developments have largely destroyed the old forms of religious authority and opened the way to widespread self-interpretation. A brother- and sisterhood of all believers has begun to emerge. A major feature of the modern Muslim world is the scripture-reading group in particular for women. No one now knows, it is frequently said, who speaks for Islam.[46]

A striking feature of the 'Protestant turn' is the way in which it has been carried forward in Muslim societies by rising social formations. Indeed, I would argue that this process in the twentieth century has represented a reform of Muslim society from below, some might even say a re-Islamization. The context of this has been the presence of Western power with two key outcomes: the co-option of the elites of Muslim societies to serve Western political, economic, and cultural purposes; and revolutionary economic and social change within Muslim societies with the formation of industrial, commercial, administrative, and professional classes. Ulama groups such as the Deobandis in India and the Muhammadiya in Indonesia, Islamist parties such as the Muslim Brotherhood throughout the Arab world, and the Jamaat-e-Islami throughout South Asia have found support in these social formations. As time has gone on they have tended to get the better of socialist and nationalist alternatives espoused by the elites. These ulama and Islamist groups, with their support in the middle and lower-middle social strata, are those challenging power today, as they have done with success in Turkey and Indonesia, and as they are doing with rather less success amid the complexities of the Arab world. It is helpful to compare their rise with the outcomes of the industrial transformation of Britain in the eighteenth and nineteenth centuries; the emergence of new social

---

[45] Robinson, 'Religious Change and the Self in Muslim South Asia'.
[46] Francis Robinson, 'Crisis of Authority: Crisis of Islam?' *Journal of the Royal Asiatic Society* 19, 3 (2009), pp. 339–54.

groups, the association of these groups with nonconformity and Methodism, which came in part at least to be transferred politically into the politics of the Liberal and Labour parties.

You will gather from this that I am likely to see useful comparison between the European reformation and that currently taking place in the Muslim world. Certainly, Muhammad Iqbal saw things thus: 'We are today', he declared in his *Reconstruction of Religious Thought in Islam,* 'passing through a period similar to that of the Protestant revolution in Europe.'[47] We should make this comparison in spite of the explicit disapproval of Marshall Hodgson.[48] Now, much more of what has been happening is known than Hodgson did some fifty years or so ago. However, manifestations of the 'Protestant turn' do not end here. In the nineteenth and twentieth centuries we can see a similar shift towards a faith of personal responsibility and this-worldly action in the other great religions of South Asia. The Singh Sabhas of the Sikhs in the late nineteenth century drew on the example of this-worldly action of the early Gurus to make sure that all Sikhs had the knowledge and understanding to resist Christian and Hindu missionary activity.[49] Angarika Dharmapala's 'Protestant Buddhism' pioneered a new piety in which lay folk had access to religious texts, engaged in a faith of salvation, and expressed this new private internalized piety in a life of this-worldly asceticism.[50] A similar 'Protestant turn' can be seen in the shift in the focus of nineteenth-century Hinduism from social structure to the individual human being. There was a new emphasis on personal *dharma* and individual realization. Individual Hindus had to take personal responsibility for their religion and culture, which no longer meant renunciation, but social involvement and social action.[51] In all these faiths, as well as Islam, it is possible to make a connection between their 'Protestant turn', their new this-worldliness and their pursuit of political power—even, on occasion, their use of violence.

This widespread 'Protestant turn' in the nineteenth century raises issues of origin and meaning. In the case of Islam it derived from tensions long present in the faith which came to interact with the contexts of economic, social, and ideological change presented by British India. Similar deep-rooted change exists in the case of Sikhism. In those of Hinduism and Buddhism, on the other hand, there do seem to have been specific and formative interactions with Protestant Christian missionaries which, along with the context of British India, helped fashion the new piety.

All these 'Protestant' manifestations of piety represent some of the modernities of India's religions. In the case of the 'Protestant' piety represented by reform

---

[47] Muhammad Iqbal, *The Reconstruction of Religious Thought in Islam* (Lahore: Sh. Muhammad Ashraf, 1975), p. 163.

[48] Edmund Burke III and Marshall G. S. Hodgson (eds), *Rethinking World History: Essays on Europe, Islam and World History* (Cambridge: Cambridge University Press, 1993).

[49] Triloki N. Madan, *Secularism and Fundamentalism in India: Modern Myths and Locked Minds* (Delhi: Oxford University Press, 1997), p. 187.

[50] Torkel Brekke, *Makers of Modern Indian Religion in the Late Nineteenth Century* (Oxford: Clarendon Press, 2002), pp. 63–115.

[51] Brekke, *Makers of Modern Indian Religion*, pp. 13–62; Madan, *Secularism*, pp. 203–32.

throughout the Muslim world, it is now a commonplace of modern scholarship to regard it as a profoundly modern phenomenon, being both fashioned by modernity as it also strives to shape it, protesting against the outcomes of enlightenment rationalism. It seeks to assert a moral community—transcendant and with moral absolutes—in order to confront the uncertainties and relativism of our time. In an excellent recent work Roxanne Euben has shown how much Western social theorists from Hannah Arendt to Charles Taylor have to share with the leading theorists of Islamism, Sayyid Qutb, and Mawlana Mawdudi.[52]

The 'Protestant turn' in human piety, which began just under five hundred years ago, and which has gained considerable pace over the past two hundred years, as it has mingled with worldwide economic and social change, is a great global development—a global event—one worthy of the serious attention of the global historian.

* * *

These areas have come to mind in addressing future directions in global history from an Islamic angle: the role of Muslim power and Islamic civilization itself as a factor in global history; the continuing significance of the connectedness of the Muslim world in supporting its role in global history; the shared worlds of stories and storytelling and astrology and astronomy; the impact of the production and consumption of major commodities; and the significance of the 'Protestant turn' in major world religions. There are other global issues worthy of exploration from an Islamic angle: the great move against hierarchy and patriarchy and towards equality for all human beings, surely one of the great global movements of recent times; and the issue of establishing authority (religious or civilizational) in conditions of imperialism—a problem which has beset the Muslim world over the past two hundred years and which may afflict all societies in a globalizing era. There are other subjects: global history from an Islamic angle is rich in possibilities.

---

[52] Francis Robinson, 'Islamic Reform and Modernities in South Asia', *Modern Asian Studies* 42, 2–3 (2008), pp. 259–81.

8

The Real American Empire

Antony G. Hopkins

INTRODUCTION

The 19 March 2013 marked the tenth anniversary of the invasion of Iraq.[1] The moment passed in the United States with little notice and no celebration. It is unlikely that the mood at future anniversaries will be any different. In 2003, however, the event stimulated an extraordinary outpouring of books and articles featuring the phrase 'American Empire'. Commentators ranged across the full spectrum of possibilities. For some, the notion of an American Empire was novel; for others, it was the logical culmination of the superpower status the United States had achieved since the Second World War and had consolidated after the fall of the Soviet Empire. All parties eagerly searched for comparisons that would validate their preferred view of this latest manifestation of American power. Some observers regarded the United States as the stabilizer of last resort, as Britain and Rome had been in their day; others viewed the Iraq War as evidence that the Land of the Free was loitering with intent to disturb the peace—just as Britain and other predecessors had done before their 'glad confident morning' gave way to 'life's night'.[2] Nearly everyone agreed that the United States was an empire. Amidst the rush of events, few commentators paused to reflect on the meaning of the term, or whether it was necessary to define it.

With one or two notable exceptions, historians absented themselves from this debate. Most historians like events to settle before they comment on them, and even then they are inclined to clothe their observations in qualifications, elaborations, and pleas for further research. From a historical perspective, after all, a decade is no more than a long weekend. Yet, now that invasion has turned into withdrawal and occupation has turned optimism for 'remaking the Middle East'

---

[1] This is a revised version of a keynote lecture delivered at the conference 'New Directions in Global History' held in Oxford in September 2012. I have made minor revisions and expanded the paper slightly. Given the broad range of the script, I have kept citations to a minimum, though I have referred to some of my own publications, where relevant, for the convenience of readers who wish to pursue some of the issues summarized here in greater detail. Most of the chapter, however, is derived from a larger study on the history of the American Empire I am currently completing, and is based on a much wider range of research produced by other scholars.

[2] Robert Browning, 'The Lost Leader', in Robert Browning, *Dramatic Romances and Lyrics* (London: Edward Moxon, 1845).

into predictable (and predicted) turmoil, it should be possible for historians to venture a longer and larger view of this tragic episode in contemporary international relations.[3] In this speculative spirit, I shall offer a very broad interpretation of the history of American Empire, by first outlining the parameters of the subject, then focussing on what I shall call the Real American Empire, before concluding with some remarks on the implications of my analysis for understanding the global role of the United States today.

AN OUTLINE OF AN ARGUMENT

There are various ways of taking hold of this huge, sprawling subject. I have chosen to set my account in the context of globalization by drawing on the categories set out in the book I and some Cambridge colleagues published more than a decade ago entitled *Globalization in World History*.[4] Briefly, I suggest that we can locate the history of the United States in three major crises. The first, in the late eighteenth century, was a crisis of proto-globalization as competing military fiscal states over-extended themselves while battling to control their outer domains. The second, a crisis of modern globalization, arose at the close of the nineteenth century as the residues of military-fiscal states sought to create, resist, or control new forces of nationalism and industrialization. The third crisis, the emergence of post-colonial globalization from the 1950s onwards, was marked by profound shifts in the global economy, the appearance of new regional groupings, and the influence of novel concepts of human rights, all of which helped to bring about decolonization.

I make few claims for this typology: it does little more than recast trends that are already known. Nevertheless, if it is accepted that empires transmit globalizing influences, the approach I have adopted makes it possible to link the two concepts, globalization and empire, in ways that revise or at least alter the emphasis of standard approaches to US history.[5] Historians of the United States have begun to move the frontiers of knowledge in this direction. One of the first and most prominent examples is Thomas Bender's *A Nation Among Nations: America's Place in World History*, published in 2006,[6] others could now be listed. More generally, the term 'globalization' has become almost mandatory in titles of books and articles, though it should also be said that few historians show signs of familiarity with the abundant social science literature on the subject.

[3] Antony G. Hopkins, 'Lessons of "Civilizing Missions" are Mostly Unlearned', *New York Times* (23 March 2003). This was the first of a clutch of 'op-eds' I wrote at the time and the only one to be published. Once the invasion had been launched, criticism became 'unpatriotic'. It was at least two years before eminent liberals in the United States began to ask questions that should have been put before the event. Even then, the answers tended to blame Iraqis for not responding as their 'liberators' hoped they would.
[4] Antony G. Hopkins (ed.), *Globalization in World History* (London: Pimlico, 2002).
[5] Antony G. Hopkins, 'Back to the Future: From National History to Imperial History', *Past & Present* 164 (1999), pp. 198–243.
[6] Thomas Bender, *A Nation among Nations: America's Place in World History* (New York: Hill and Wang, 2006).

All the same, there are difficulties in going global, aside from the need to master an exceptionally voluminous and complex literature. One problem for American historians is that, despite good intentions, it is hard for them to avoid bolting the world on to the United States instead of the other way round. Another is the tendency to adopt a form of refined exceptionalism that acknowledges every possible amplification and qualification, but still ends up telling the great American success story. If these observations seem too sweeping or too critical, just think of the legions of studies of the nineteenth century that contain the seemingly obligatory words 'liberty' and 'democracy' in their titles. Or consider how, after 1783, the cosmopolitan world, summarized as the Atlantic complex, is cast off and a largely domestic story, the national saga, constructed in its place. This emphasis is wholly understandable and also very familiar to historians of the ex-colonial world of the twentieth century. It is, nevertheless, misplaced.

Outsiders, like myself, on the other hand, face the formidable difficulty of trying to master the massive amount of work available on US history, with its different sub-fields and innumerable case studies produced by highly skilled specialists. The interpretation I have devised is not an attempt to rewrite a comprehensive history of the United States; that would need, minimally, to pay full attention to Native American history and the Republic's many diverse regions. It aims rather to recast those features of a capacious past that can be illuminated by the history of imperialism and empires. Viewed from this perspective, there is a case for rethinking a large slice of US history between 1783 and 1959.

Although formal independence was achieved in 1783, the process of achieving effective independence was protracted, fraught, and marked by continuing reliance on the outside world, just as it was in the case of other ex-colonies. At the close of the nineteenth century, with effective independence finally realized, the United States joined other 'late-start' powers, such as Germany, Italy, and Japan, in annexing the territory of other states and peoples. The real American Empire, that is to say the overseas territorial empire established in 1898, made the United States a formal member of the imperial club. Once created, the empire followed much the same course as other Western imperial powers. The United States decolonized at the same time, too; by 1959, when Hawai'i was incorporated as the fiftieth state of the Union, the insular empire ceased to exist, though Puerto Rico was left as it was at the outset—becalmed in the Caribbean with the contrived ambiguity of its status unresolved.

THE NINETEENTH CENTURY

The traditional master narrative, which focusses on the achievement of liberty and democracy in one country, needs to be revised.[7] The new Republic was the forerunner of other ex-colonial states in struggling to achieve economic development and political viability in a setting that remained strongly influenced by Britain. The

---

[7] Antony G. Hopkins, 'The United States, 1783–1861: Britain's Honorary Dominion?' *Britain and the World* 4, 2 (2011), pp. 232–46.

Atlantic world did not dissolve; historians have simply put it aside until the closing decades of the nineteenth century. The great debates of British politics, which centred on the perpetuation and reform of the military-fiscal state, were reproduced in the newly United States. The well-known battle between Hamiltonians and Jeffersonians reflected the controversy between protectionists who thought that government could help to deliver both liberty and development, and free-traders who were convinced that the 'big state' was part of the problem rather than of the solution. Meanwhile, British finance fuelled cotton production, supported New England's manufactures, and helped fund westward expansion. The British navy ensured that no foreign power interfered with the process. British culture continued to exercise its sway. Emerson's famous appeal for a genuine American literature remained unrealized; elite aspirations continued to copy the British model. Standard studies of US history during this period underestimate Britain's continuing and extensive influence; equally, the United States has no place in the long-standing debate on informal empire. Yet the evidence suggests that, during the first half of the nineteenth century, the United States remained part of Britain's globalizing, imperial reach.

The Republic emerges as a fragile, weak state, which, like so many other ex-colonial states, eventually became a failed state and collapsed into civil war in 1861. Recovery and reunification took much longer than was once thought. The process of rehabilitation was further complicated by new and divisive developments in the 1880s and 1890s. Expanding towns challenged the dominance of rural America; expanding factories challenged the owners of capital to control an overtly hostile urban labour force; expanding immigration, from all parts of Europe, challenged the supremacy of the established Anglo-Saxon *ethnie*. During these stressful decades, the problems the United States grappled with were very similar to those confronting the governments of Europe. Comparably, too, the United States joined the onrush of 'new' imperialism as a 'late-start' power whose interests in cementing national unity were greater than her economic motives, which were the province of special interests.

ACQUIRING THE REAL AMERICAN EMPIRE

The Spanish-American War of 1898 resulted in the creation of an American overseas empire, principally in Hawai'i, the Philippines, and Puerto Rico, with the addition of a protectorate in Cuba. The motives for the war of 1898 have generated a truly enormous literature covering every conceivable detail. Against the older view that the war was an aberration that momentarily interrupted the steady progress of liberty and democracy, we now have admirable studies of McKinley's personal motives, of political infighting in Washington, of economic interests, of the psychological needs of males whose virility was threatened by the rise of feminism, and—if needed—much more. My own view is that the war was an overseas expression of the administration's attempt to manage competing and potentially subversive domestic forces and to bring them together in ways that sealed national independence and unity. Victory over Spain celebrated the achievement, reconciled North and South, and announced the appearance of the United States as a world power.

The war, which was won by the new US navy, was the first external expression of America's industrial power applied to military purposes. Contemporaries, from Theodore Roosevelt to Woodrow Wilson, were well aware of the effect of victory in consolidating national unity. Roosevelt toured the South immediately after the war to reinforce the new spirit of solidarity. Wilson declared in 1901: 'We have come to full maturity with this new century of our national existence and to full self-consciousness as a nation.'[8]

At this point, however, something very odd happens. Once the peace treaty was signed, combatants and historians alike—to borrow Longfellow's phrase—'fold their tents, like the Arabs, and silently steal away'.[9] In what must be the most extraordinary omission in the historiography of the Western empires, the newly formed insular empire is dematerialized. Some limited work on dollar diplomacy has explored continuing informal influences in Central America, but the formal empire is left to wither on the vine. It has no place in current texts at any level; the last book that attempted to cover the period of American colonial rule in the twentieth century was published, to little notice, in Leiden in 1962, and thereafter neglected.[10]

THE TERMS OF THE TRADE

An explanation of this extraordinary omission is itself an interesting exercise, and one in which the pervasive notion of American exceptionalism plays a prominent part. The Republic had built its conception of national unity on a set of republican principles that were antithetical to the forms of imperialism associated with the European empires. The war with Spain had served its purpose in sealing national unity; the continuing presence of a visible empire was embarrassing and politically discordant. Republicans had created the empire; after the event, Democrats were keen to nail them to the cross of what they characterized as a misguided foreign policy, and they hammered away until the empire was finally demolished after the Second World War. Accordingly (after a brief flourish to establish parity with the greater European powers), the term 'empire' quickly became politically incorrect. Instead, the new colonies were referred to, euphemistically, as overseas territories or insular possessions. The sleight of hand may have deceived the public, but not those in the know. If truth were told, one Democratic Congressman observed in

[8] Woodrow Wilson, 'The Ideals of America', speech delivered 26 December 1901, published in the *Atlantic Monthly*, 90 (1902), pp. 721–34.
[9] Henry Wadsworth Longfellow, 'The Day Is Done' (1844), idem.
[10] Whitney T. Perkins, *Denial of Empire: The United States and its Dependencies* (Leyden: A. W. Sythoff, 1962).

1899, 'the titular designation of our Executive shall be President of the United States of America and Emperor of the Philippines'.[11]

A handful of scholars writing during the colonial period, that is from 1898 to 1959, used the term 'empire' to refer to the United States, and also drew attention to the long history of continental expansion that was essential to understanding the nation's imperialist history.[12] However, they were exceptions, some of them notable, but in any case now mostly forgotten. Generally speaking, the term became widely used to describe the United States only after it had achieved superpower status at the time of the Cold War and after it had decolonized its insular territories apart from Puerto Rico, which continues to linger at the door like a dependent relative. Admittedly, not everyone subscribed to the term: in the 1970s, a prominent school of international relations theorists preferred to refer to the United States as a hegemon. But from the time of the Vietnam War onwards 'empire' came into increasing use, and not only by commentators on the left. By the turn of the century, George Bush, on the campaign trail, felt obliged to engage with what had become contemporary usage: 'America has never been an empire', he declared. 'We may be the only great power in history that had the chance and refused—preferring greatness to power and justice to glory'—a phrase, it might be thought, that gives banality a bad name.[13] After the invasion of Iraq in 2003, every man and his dog, so it seemed, became an overnight expert on empire and thousands of books, now tombstones in the vast graveyard of unwanted publications, appeared with the 'e' word in the title.

The turn to empire also boosted imperial history in general, though very few historians used the inspiration to investigate the American Empire that had once existed. Those who caught the eye, like Niall Ferguson, did so because they related history to current events. Ferguson's well-known appeal was for the United States to stop being an 'empire in denial' and to face up to its imperial responsibilities. The ensuing debate about the meaning of the term baffled even scholarly authorities. Some doubted whether a superpower without territory could be called an empire; others thought that absolute and relative economic and military might were more than enough to qualify. Perhaps the United States was still an empire in the making, or a special kind of empire, or one whose future already lay behind it.

The question of whether and, if so, when, the United States became an empire depends on the definition of the term, which has changed with the empires it has described from Greece and Rome onwards. The definition I am using is now burnished with unoriginality, which gives me some confidence that it may be correct or at least applicable to the case in hand. Most empires have had a territorial base;

---

[11] Perry Belmont, 'Congress, the President and the Philippines', *North American Review* 169 (1899), p. 901. Belmont (1851–1947), a lawyer, was Congressman for New York, 1881–9, and Ambassador to Spain, 1889.

[12] For example, Scott Nearing, *The American Empire* (New York: Rand School of Social Science, 1921); Scott Nearing and Joseph Freeman, *Dollar Diplomacy: A Study in American Imperialism* (New York: B. W. Huebsch and Viking Press, 1925).

[13] Governor George W. Bush, 'A Distinctly American Internationalism', speech delivered in the Ronald Reagan Presidential Library, Simi Valley, California, 19 November 1999.

modern empires exclusively so. The maritime empires of the fifteenth to the eighteenth centuries are not significant exceptions: they had territorial ambitions but lacked the penetrative power needed to realise them fully. It was the conversion of maritime to territorial power in the eighteenth century that was both the high point of their success and the cause of their undoing. The empires that followed, however, all had extensive territorial holdings from inception to decolonization in the mid-twentieth century. It is true, as participants in the current debate have pointed out, that the British Empire in particular also had substantial areas of informal influence, and it has been argued that this fact, assuming it is a fact, validates the use of the term 'empire' when applied to the United States after the Second World War. The argument strikes me as being strained. Britain's informal influence was an adjunct to its vast territorial possessions; the United States has influence but virtually no territory.

Does this matter? Surely the means by which authority is exercised are secondary to the fact that imperialism traces a process of asymmetrical power in international relations? However, the means of exercising power do matter, and for two weighty reasons. The first is semantic, which is tedious but important. If the chosen definition is too broad, we will suppose, wrongly, that we have a licence to compare very different entities. It was this thinking that led the Pentagon to contract a prominent classicist to advise them after 2003 on how the 'lessons of the past' could help predict the future.[14] By calling the dominant powers of their day 'empires' we can then harness history to help arrest or accelerate the decline of the superpower of the moment. Purposive history of this kind is as beguiling as necromancy, and about as reliable, too. The comparison fails because we are a long way from comparing like with like.

The second reason returns us to globalization. The Western powers that created, managed, and eventually dissolved empires from the mid-eighteenth century to the mid-twentieth century established territorial empires because they were essential to their own stage of development. The pattern of global integration during the phase of modern globalization called for territorial control because the European powers, led after 1815 by Britain, launched 'civilizing' missions that sent emigrants to colonize new worlds and simultaneously attempted the wholesale transformation of indigenous societies. Economic transformation depended on the expansion of export crops and minerals, which in turn involved installing a network of communications, altering land law, and increasing labour mobility. Political transformation required institutions that, ideally, would take the form of constitutional governments, and minimally would produce co-operative partners. Cultural transformation involved various degrees of assimilation to Western values that included the creation of sets of like-minded elites, and, where possible, conversion to Christianity (for which, in the case of the United States read Protestantism). Reforms of this order were major exercises in social engineering that required a significant measure of territorial control.

---

[14] Victor Hanson Davis, Hoover Institute, Stanford University, California.

THE REAL AMERICAN EMPIRE

Modern empires, then, were globalizing forces that served a particular function during a particular stage of world development. They met the needs of emerging national-industrial states in the West, and expressed the sense of technological confidence and racial superiority that were hallmarks of the era. The United States had such an empire—what I call here a real empire—even though it is now a forgotten empire.

Even if this position is accepted, it is still possible to argue that the US empire was nevertheless exceptional or in some way so unusual as to be unrepresentative of other contemporary Western empires. If this is the case, it would invalidate the argument I want to make, namely that the territorial empire of the United States fits the category of empires produced by what I have called modern globalization. The US Empire undoubtedly had distinctive features. It consisted of a set of scattered islands which, apart from Hawai'i, were inherited from Spain and contained stocks of Spanish settlers and their descendants. However, the empire's insular quality appears to have had no effect on the formulation or implementation of policy. Spanish settlers (*peninsulares* and *criollos*), though white and Christian, were also Latin and Roman Catholic. These features assured them of a relatively lowly place in the racial hierarchy and exposed them to the same degree of paternal tuition as was applied in other colonial empires.

Moreover, the fact that politicians chose not to use the term 'empire' appears to have had no influence on their plans for ruling the territories they had acquired. On the contrary, imperial enthusiasts, like Albert Beveridge and Theodore Roosevelt, claimed that the United States would revitalize the Western civilizing mission. American energy, capital, and technological wizardry would carry to a successful conclusion the programme that old and now degenerate European powers no longer had the vitality to complete. At the turn of the twentieth century, the United States launched the first of the nation-building and development ventures that it was to repeat after 1945. The experiment was one of the earliest attempts to apply what would later be called modernization theory. It, too, has been forgotten. Today, policymakers and historians seeking to place the United States in a global historical context reach for a wide variety of historical comparisons; few, if any, refer to the nearest and most apposite precedent: the US territorial empire itself. Yet, in all important respects, the American Empire replicated the aims and claims, the successes and excesses, of its European comparators.

In attitudes and rhetoric, too, US empire-builders matched the best that Europe could offer. 'Our almost accidental possession of the Philippines', Woodrow Wilson declared in 1901, and the 'new duties now thrust upon us', provide an opportunity to 'teach them order as a condition precedent to liberty, self-control as a condition precedent to self-government'.[15] Triumphs, so policymakers declared, came quickly. As early as 1909, Theodore Roosevelt had no hesitation in advertising

---

[15] Woodrow Wilson, 'Democracy and Efficiency', *Atlantic Monthly* 87 (1901), pp. 292, 298.

the success of US policy in the Philippines, even though a long war of resistance
to American rule had still to be concluded:

> I believe I am speaking with historic accuracy and impartiality when I say that the
> American treatment of and attitude toward the Filipino people, in its combination of
> disinterested ethical purpose and sound common sense, marks a new and long stride
> forward, in advance of all the steps that hitherto have been taken, along the path of
> wise and proper treatment of weaker by stronger races.[16]

The American Empire, though small and scattered, also had sufficient diversity to
make it representative of the Western empires as a whole. Like the European
empires, the United States had colonies of settlement, trade, and concession. It
adopted policies of assimilation and association, and applied techniques of direct
and indirect rule. Colonial policy conformed to best imperial practice, which was
largely borrowed from the European empires, especially from Britain, supple-
mented by the experience of quelling and administering Native Americans on the
mainland. The US Empire, like other Western empires, developed export crops
and gave them sheltered markets. The trajectory of the American Empire fitted
that of the European empires, too, as if it were propelled by the same forces, which
it was. The insular empire was acquired at the height of 'new imperialism'; it
experienced the same oscillations of fortune during two world wars and the intervening world slump; it decolonized at the same time. The Philippines became independent in 1946; Hawaii was incorporated as a state in 1959; Cuba entered a
long, anti-colonial revolution in the same year.

OUTCOMES

Despite these similarities, it is still possible that the American Empire was exceptional in its outcomes, if not in its validating rhetoric, methods of rule, and chronological evolution. Some notable commentators, such as Warren Zimmerman, have
suggested that the US Empire was indeed an improved version of its European
counterparts either in its treatment of indigenous people or in its results.[17] Would
that it were so; the evidence, however, suggests otherwise.

The ideas were expansive; the commitment was limited. Congress quickly lost
interest in the possessions it had acclaimed with such enthusiasm. Roosevelt himself soon abandoned the 'large view' he had done so much to promote. The first
generation of imperialists failed to reproduce themselves. The new empire quickly
became a counter in the political game played between Republicans and Democrats.
Without a bipartisan policy towards the empire, the continuity the civilizing mission
needed was never established. Comprehensive, long-term policies of assimilation

---

[16] Theodore Roosevelt, 'The Expansion of the White Races', address, 18 January 1909, in Theodore
Roosevelt and Hermann Hagedorn (eds), *The Works of Theodore Roosevelt, vol. 16: American Problems*
(New York: C. Scribner's Sons, 1926), p. 264.

[17] Warren Zimmerman, *First Great Triumph: How Five Americans Made their Country a World
Power* (New York: Farrar, Straus, and Giroux, 2002).

and Americanization were tried and eventually abandoned. Congress had little incentive to give imperial affairs priority over the pressing concerns of domestic voters. The insular possessions had no right to vote in mainland elections and were too insignificant to make an impression on the wider public. The empire became a problem when, unexpectedly, it resisted the agents of freedom; once acquired, it became an increasing burden involving tariff subsidies and military commitments. Congress ignored its obligations as much as it could, and refused the funds needed to create a Colonial Office and finance development. Professionally trained personnel were in short supply; governors were appointed for political reasons, either to be rewarded or exiled; few stayed in the job for more than two or three years.

In these circumstances, crucial aspects of policy were decided not by the needs of the civilizing mission, but by the power of competing lobbies. The American colonies were typical in producing primary products, notably cane-sugar. Republicans favoured refiners on the east coast, who wanted free entry for raw sugar; Democrats supported beet and southern cane producers, who wanted protection against outside competition. The fate of colonial producers thus rested on the electoral cycle, as well as, of course, on uncontrollable changes in international demand. They competed among themselves and with global producers elsewhere in a market that was steadily weakening throughout the twentieth century as a result of overproduction. Tariff concessions provided subsidies that could make fortunes, or, if withdrawn, break them. The result was a paradox. Formally, US policy aimed at preparing its overseas territories for self-government; effectively, the insular possessions became increasingly dependent on the mainland through the tariff advantages they enjoyed in the US market.

Contemporaries were aware of these features from the outset. In 1902, Elihu Root, then Secretary of War, commented that:

> Philippine questions are so interwoven in the political game that the most curious results follow combinations of influence.... Among a large part of the gentlemen who are actually discussing the subject, the question, 'What will be good for the Philippines' plays a most insignificant part.[18]

More than a generation later, Governor Theodore Roosevelt, Jr, confirmed Root's judgement. Writing in the light of his experience in Puerto Rico and the Philippines, he stated in 1937 that he could not 'conceive of the United States having a consistent, long-range colonial policy', and added that the Republic would continue 'to fit our policies in the islands to our own internal political opinions'.[19]

Of course there were dedicated officials and some achievements: roads were built; education was encouraged; health provision was improved. It is hard, however, to argue that the American development effort was superior to that of the other Western empires. It was certainly no more popular, despite impressions to the contrary. US troops were not greeted as liberators. Fierce resistance in the Philippines lasted for a decade after the United States declared, in 1902, that it had

---

[18] Quoted in Perkins, *Denial of Empire*, p. 204.
[19] Theodore Roosevelt, *Colonial Policies of the United States* (London: Nelson, 1937), pp. 195–7.

ceased. Hawai'i, the 'island paradise', experienced massive strikes whenever the sugar industry ran into difficulties, as did Puerto Rico, Spain's former 'Enchanted Isle', while in Cuba cane-burning became a familiar act of last resort during the troubled 1930s. The assassination of leading officials was contemplated, sometimes attempted, and in at least one case succeeded. In response, the United States cracked down on dissidents with the vigour that matched that of more experienced British and French colonial officers. Continuing material hardship underlay outbreaks of mass discontent in the 1930s. Writing of these conditions, Harold Ickes, Secretary of State for the Interior, reported in 1935 to President Roosevelt that 'There is today more widespread misery and destitution and far more unemployment in Puerto Rico than at any previous time in its history.'[20] In 1946, shortly after leaving his post, he published a devastating critique of the administration of Guam and Samoa, which had been offloaded to the US Navy and had experienced half a century of alternating neglect and despotism.[21]

The decision to grant independence to the Philippines, which was taken in 1934 and implemented in 1946, is frequently cited as an example of the success of the United States in tutoring backward people in the ways of modern democracy and conferring independence before the European powers got round to it. This is a highly selective reading of the facts. The Philippines were neither viable nor democratic at the time these crucial decisions were made. Political leaders in the archipelago did not want independence on the terms offered and indeed were so concerned at the prospect that they initiated secret talks in the hope of joining the British Empire as a dominion instead. A case of out of the fire and into the frying pan, you might think, but a clear indication of the alarm and desperation nationalist leaders felt.

As for the progress of democracy, the proportion of the Filipino electorate entitled to vote in 1934 was smaller than that in India after the Government of India Act of 1935. The real problem, however, was that independence would remove the tariff advantages the Philippines enjoyed in the mainland market. Independence on these terms would be an economic disaster with dire political consequences. Franklin D. Roosevelt, however, was determined to liberate the United States from its colony to appease mainland producers and to escape the obligation of having to defend the islands in the event of war. And so the deal was done, but the motives were far from those proclaimed by his famous cousin, Theodore, and the imperial idealists of 1898.

POST-COLONIAL GLOBALIZATION

The real American Empire, then, was a wholly unexceptional empire that was fully representative of the territorial empires that came into being under the global conditions prevailing from 1850 to 1950. Yet it was not until the second half of

---

[20] Quoted in Thomas Mathews, *Puerto Rican Politics and the New Deal* (Gainesville: University of Florida Press, 1976), p. 215.
[21] 'The Navy at its Worst', *Collier's Magazine* (31 August 1946), pp. 22–3.

the twentieth century that the United States began to be called an empire. Some authors point to the extensive outer defences of fortress America, the division of the world into areas of command, and the numerous incursions into the sovereignty of independent states; others emphasize the allegedly huge informal empire the US built up through a combination of military aid and soft power. These arguments can certainly be used to illustrate the superpower status of the United States, but this is not to show that the Republic was an empire in the sense defined here. The purpose and influence of the United States as a superpower are very different from the modern empires I have described. And if it is an empire of a 'special kind', then perhaps it is not an empire at all.

Furthermore, the sources of power exerted by the United States have significant limits that are not always given the emphasis they deserve. US military might is indeed overwhelming in terms of its scale and is often used as a measure of its historic superiority over Britain, Rome, and other comparators. What matters, however, is not how much hardware you have but its effectiveness. By this measure, major victories are hard to find. If the Korean War is counted as a draw, Vietnam was a clear defeat; and, I would add, Iraq and Afghanistan too. As for the informal empire, I have yet to see its extent on a map. This is, perhaps, understandable because you would have to leave out the Soviet Union, Eastern Europe, China, India, and Western Europe, too, once it had recovered from the effects of the Second World War. We scarcely need reminding that policy in the Middle East has had mixed results; any success in backing a handful of autocrats has been negated by the reaction it eventually provoked. Interventions in Africa and Latin America, overt and covert, proved temporarily effective at various points during the Cold War, but were counterproductive in the longer run because they stoked long-lasting nationalist responses. The major long-term successes would appear to be South Korea, Indonesia, and Japan. These countries were certainly constrained in their foreign policies but, with the partial exception of South Korea, were not subjected to policies that sought to transform domestic society by administrative fiat. All of them are notable scalps to be sure, but scarcely of Roman proportions. Of course, American influence has been profound, especially in matters such as consumer tastes. But influence is not empire and can also be combined with deep-seated and continuing anti-American feelings.

We may argue about these cases, but the fundamental question they raise is why territorial empires of the kind that organized much of the world and spread globalization for almost two centuries have not reproduced themselves—or at least have not done so yet. The answer, it seems to me, lies in a profound change in the nature of globalization after 1945.[22] Here, I shall draw attention to just two fundamental shifts in the conditions that underlay earlier territorial empires.

First, the structure of the world economy altered. At a point in the 1950s, flows of world trade and finance began to change. The growth of inter-industry trade redirected commerce to what became known as the triad—North America, Europe,

---

[22] Antony G. Hopkins, 'Capitalism, Nationalism and the New American Empire', *Journal of Imperial and Commonwealth History* 35, 1 (2007), pp. 95–117; 'Rethinking Decolonization', *Past & Present* 200 (2008), pp. 211–47.

and Japan, to which we must now add China to make a 'quadrad'. This development was associated with new regional ties, notably the European Community, and later NAFTA. The corollary was the weakening of the old centre-periphery relationships that had sustained territorial empires, and a diminishing interest in what became known as the Third World as a supplier of raw materials (oil, as always, excepted).

The involvement of the great powers in the ex-colonial states was sustained during the Cold War more by ideological than by economic motives. Following decolonization, the Third World itself became differentiated, just as Karl Marx predicted, which is why the term has dropped out of favour. Today, about 75 per cent of world trade is in manufactures; Asia alone accounts for over 25 per cent of the export of manufactured goods. Territorial imperialism of the kind I have described is either impracticable or irrelevant. If Dr Strangelove were to stage his own second coming, it is surely unlikely that even he would contemplate the forcible acquisition of large swathes of Europe or Asia, at least for purposes of economic gain. He might also be persuaded that there is no point in conquering more manageable entities, such as the mini-tigers, when they are already efficient producers of cheap manufactures for American consumption—much of it the result of outsourcing. In short, thoroughgoing institutional change of the kind envisaged by imperialists and modernization theorists is no longer necessary to serve the interests of global integration.

Nor is it possible. And here is my second and final point. Of course difficulties and disputes remain. We have tariff wars and currency wars, and wish that our version of democracy could be transplanted easily and grow rapidly. However, our wishes can no longer be imposed with the degree of confidence and assertiveness that was the hallmark of the age of high imperialism. The reason for this new condition of restraint lies in the revolution in human rights that occurred after the Second World War. Whatever this did to individual rights, it validated, finally, the notion of self-determination. People do not like to have their countries invaded, even in the name of freedom and democracy, and almost certainly never have done. Now, however, they have world opinion on their side, instantaneous communications, and the means of punishing transgressors, whether by seizing their investments or by striking back across oceans and continents. We may not have been able to democratize the standard of living but we have certainly democratized the means of destruction. It is no good being Goliath if David can fell you with a sling and a stone. The exceptional global uproar over the invasion of Iraq had many sources, but one of them was the conviction that it was an anachronism—as indeed it was.

EPILOGUE

I shall close by recounting an obscure event that illustrates my concluding point.[23] On 17 January 2013, a US navy minesweeper ran aground on a coral reef, which

[23] *CNN News* (22 January 2013); *New York Times* (25 January 2013); *Washington Post* (31 March 2013); *Daily Mail Online* (5 April, 2013); *Voice of America* (19 June 2014).

was also a Unesco World Heritage site, located in Philippine waters. Vice-Admiral Scott Swift, true to his name, leapt immediately into action to express his regrets; the American Ambassador followed with a profound apology; a posse of US Congressmen arrived to reinforce both sentiments. The United States agreed to pay a substantial fine, which is currently estimated at over $2 million.

Theoretically, the United States could either crush or ignore the Philippines; practical politics determines that it can do neither. Lord Palmerston, who believed that 'half-civilized governments require a dressing down every eight to ten years', would have sent in a gunboat.[24] Today, the United States has power it cannot exercise effectively. The world has changed; the age of great empires has passed.

---

[24] Quoted in Robert J. Gavin, 'Palmerston's Policy towards East and West Africa, 1830–1865' (unpublished PhD thesis: University of Cambridge, 1958), p. 40.

9

Writing Constitutions and Writing World History

Linda Colley

INTRODUCTION

Demonstrating how new written constitutions have progressively affected most peoples across the globe can seem a straightforward enterprise.[1] Between 1776 and 1780, eleven one-time American colonies drafted state constitutions. These had an impact on the US Federal constitution of 1789 which in turn influenced the constitutions of Revolutionary France, and—along with the latter—helped precipitate new, often ephemeral constitutions in Haiti, the Netherlands, Switzerland, the Iberian and Italian peninsulas, and elsewhere. By 1820, some fifty constitutions were in being in Continental Europe, and this represented only a fraction of the total number attempted. In Northern Italy alone, at least thirteen new constitutions were drafted between 1796 and 1810. Some eighty more constitutions were formally implemented between 1820 and 1850, many of them in Latin America. In the second half of the long nineteenth century, written constitutions spread conspicuously beyond Europe and the Atlantic world. Between 1850 and 1914, they were adopted—in various forms and with varying degrees of success—in Australia, Japan, China, Tunisia, the Ottoman Empire, the Philippines, and parts of Polynesia and the Malay Peninsula; and attempts were made to introduce them in the Thai kingdom of Siam, Iran, and some Indian princely states. Both World Wars sparked intense bouts of new constitution-writing. So, dramatically, did the collapse of the Western European empires after 1945 and the fall of the Soviet empire. Of the 190 or so constitutions now in existence, by far the majority have been drafted or revised in the last sixty years. Every year, it is estimated, men and women in at least ten countries are at work on a new constitution.[2]

[1] Earlier versions of this paper were given at the 'New Directions in Global History' conference at the University of Oxford (27–29 September 2012), and the 'Constitution-writing in the long eighteenth century' symposium at Princeton University (11 April 2014). I am grateful for the responses on those occasions, and for the subsequent critiques of Jeremy Adelman, James Belich, Peter Holquist, and Jeremy Waldron.

[2] Lists of written constitutions are available in Zachary Elkins and Tom Ginsberg, *The Endurance of National Constitutions* (Cambridge: Cambridge University Press, 2009), pp. 215–30; and the database of the Comparative Constitutions Project: <http://comparativeconstitutionsproject.org> (accessed 1 February 2015). The Constitutions of the World Online database gives the texts of most of these documents, implemented and abortive, from 1776 to 1849.

So this has been a sustained and relentless alteration in human ideas, behaviour, and organization; and while its early phases coincided with the quickening spread of a mineral-based industrial revolution, at no stage was this constitutional revolution ever shaped exclusively or even overwhelmingly by developments in Europe. Yet establishing its significance in global history remains challenging.[3]

Studies of constitutions have usually focussed only on particular nations and regions. In recent decades, to be sure, some political scientists, legal scholars, and sociologists have mined databases such as the Comparative Constitutions Project in order to examine the geographical spread of constitutional ideas and practices, but works of history on these themes remain sparse.[4] Even conspicuous exceptions, like David Armitage's study of how the American Declaration of Independence served as a model for initiatives across the globe, tend still to emphasize the exemplary impact of individual nations (usually the United States).[5] Yet the diffusion of constitutional knowledge and initiatives has almost always been the outcome of influences issuing from multiple sites.

Selective history hampers understanding in another respect. Because their early proliferation was bound up in part with the American and French Revolutions, and because so many current constitutions are outcrops of decolonization and struggles for national self-determination, there has been a tendency to interpret the diffusion of these devices very much in terms of the rise of the nation state and the advance of democratic cultures. Yet nationalism and democracy are demonstrably only part of the story. Until the First World War at least, different kinds of empires remained more powerful players in the world than nation states; while, even in 1950, when codified constitutions of the modern type had been around for almost two hundred years, only twenty-two sovereign states were generally accepted as full democracies.[6]

Properly to understand their spread across the globe, then, written constitutions need to be detached from customary and sometimes overly celebratory narratives, and looked at afresh as extraordinary and protean phenomena.[7] In the limited space available, this essay addresses three areas in which global history and

[3] Though Jürgen Osterhammel offers some typically astute comments in *The Transformation of the World: A Global History of the Nineteenth Century* (Princeton: Princeton University Press, 2014).

[4] For a recent sampling, see Zachary Elkins, 'Diffusion and the Constitutionalization of Europe', *Comparative Political Studies* 43, 8–9 (2010), pp. 969–99; Denis J. Galligan and Mila Versteeg, *Social and Political Foundations of Constitutions* (Cambridge: Cambridge University Press, 2013); Benedikt Goderis and Mila Versteeg, 'The Transnational Origins of Constitutions: Evidence from a New Global Data Set on Constitutional Rights', Discussion Paper (Center for Economic Research, Tilburg University, 2013).

[5] David Armitage, *The Declaration of Independence: A Global History* (Cambridge, MA: Harvard University Press, 2007); and see George Athan Billias, *American Constitutionalism Heard Around the World, 1776–1989: A Global Perspective* (New York: New York University Press, 2009).

[6] Larry Diamond, 'A Report Card on Democracy', *Hoover Digest* 3 (2000).

[7] This should form part of a wider re-imagining of constitutional history, a subject which has been in slumberous retreat since the 1960s, and needs re-inventing as well as reviving. Constitutions can usefully be approached 'not just as abstract and self-contained juridical code and systems, but as dramatic, textual and imaginative expressions of wider [...] pressures that interact at many levels with human lives': Jose Harris, Robert Gerwarth, and Holger Nehring, 'Introduction: Constitutions, Civility and Violence', *Journal of Modern European History* 6, 1 (2008), pp. 30–7, p. 31.

constitutional history—the one an almost over-fashionable mode of enquiry, the other not fashionable at all—can profitably be pursued in tandem, and I will focus mainly on the long nineteenth century. First, I want to stress the importance of approaching written constitutions as texts, which share many points in common with other forms of manuscript and printed writing. Second, I want to argue that the rapid spread of these instruments was due in part to their capacity for serving different and by no means always emancipatory political projects and configurations. Finally, I want to glance at some of the changes in the geography, forms, and repercussions of constitutions occurring from the 1860s onwards.

SPREADING THE WORD

The contagion of constitutions has been a heterogeneous phenomenon. Written constitutions have varied markedly in length, durability, format, provisions, and in terms of the aims of their makers and the political systems embedded by them. In the United States and in much of Latin America, constitutions worked from the outset to create and perpetuate republics; but, elsewhere in the world, the majority of these instruments coexisted before 1914 with forms of monarchy. The diversity of written constitutions has unavoidably also been a product of linguistic difference. The most common Japanese word for 'constitution', *kempo*, meaning rules and regulations and itself a compound derived from two Chinese characters, does not have the same political connotations as the Anglophone term; and some regimes anyway consciously shied away from employing the word 'constitution' or close equivalents.[8] The document granted by the restored Louis XVIII in France in 1814 was explicitly a *chartre*, so as to distinguish it from its Revolutionary and Napoleonic predecessor constitutions; while the Tunisian 'constitution' enacted in 1861 and dismantled three years later was not even called a *Dustûr* (the Arabic word later used for a Constitution) but rather seen as *qanûn* (laws).[9]

Such multiple variations might seem to preclude any useful examination of constitutions across different chronologies and geographical contexts, and this kind of argument is sometimes made. A recent valuable set of essays on the Age of Revolutions explicitly rejects any 'diffusionist model' in regard to democratic movements in different parts of the world, stressing the importance rather of paying close attention to local experiences and 'differing institutional environments and political cultures'.[10] Yet this sets up too stark a binary. To a greater degree even than is usual, in regard to constitutions, states and empires 'lie

---

[8] Takii Kazuhiro, *The Meiji Constitution: The Japanese Experience of the West and the Shaping of the Modern World* (Japan: International House of Japan, 2007), p. vii.

[9] I owe this information to my Princeton colleague, M'hamed Oualdi.

[10] Joanna Innes and Mark Philp (eds), *Re-Imagining Democracy in the Age of Revolutions: America, France, Britain, Ireland 1750–1850* (Oxford: Oxford University Press, 2013), especially pp. 7 and 191.

enmeshed in each other's history'.[11] The spread of constitutions never made for anything approaching convergence in terms of content or politics, but there have always been significant interactions across countries and across continents between episodes and exponents and ideas of constitution-writing.

Moreover, for all the variations, it is possible to detect in many parts of the world a widening acceptance from the mid eighteenth century that countries and political regimes ideally needed to generate some kind of *single* legitimizing and managing text, a recognized foundational document of sorts. This development—an increasing focus among political actors in different regions on significant single political texts—proved vital in regard to diffusion.[12] As highly portable discrete documents, that were made up of words, that could be translated into any written language, and that were easily copied and transmitted in manuscript, and even more easily reproduced in pamphlets and books, and extracted in newspapers, handbills, magazines, and posters, the new single-text constitutions were superbly well adapted to a world where literacy, transport facilities, postal systems, mobility, and migration—and above all print—were expanding faster in multiple locations than ever before.

It helped too that those responsible for drafting and overseeing new constitutions often had an international audience in mind. As an intermittent US envoy in Paris between 1776 and 1783, Benjamin Franklin (himself a one-time printer and writer of Pennsylvania's radical constitution) famously helped to arrange for the translation and publication of all of the American state constitutions so as to impress Europeans with the new republic's seriousness and calibre, and hopefully secure aid against the British.[13] After 1787, American diplomats and activists were just as assiduous in distributing copies of the Federal Constitution overseas, in part so as to persuade foreign governments that the United States was now more politically stable and therefore creditworthy.[14] A desire to showcase new constitutions before international audiences, whether in order to secure diplomatic recognition or to proclaim one's political system in the hope that other countries would imitate and defer to it, helped to ensure that many of these texts were put into print very speedily. 'Let it be printed, published and circulated', ordered the makers of the 1826 Bolivian constitution. In the wake of the Meiji constitution of 1889, Japanese

---

[11] Daniel T. Rodgers, *Atlantic Crossings: Social Politics in a Progressive Age* (Cambridge, MA: Belknap Press, 1998), p. 1. For a detailed discussion of how local and transnational influences came together in a particular episode of constitution-making, see Christopher Schmidt-Nowara (ed.), 'Global Horizons and Local Interests in the Era of the Constitution of Cadiz', special issue of *Association for Spanish and Portuguese Historical Studies Bulletin* 37, 2 (2012).

[12] For some of the intellectual history of this shift, see Gerald Stourzh, 'Constitution: Changing Meanings of the Term from the Early Seventeenth to the Late Eighteenth Century', in Terence Ball and John G. A. Pocock (eds), *Conceptual Change and the Constitution* (Lawrence, KS: University Press of Kansas, 1988). This should be read in tandem with Sebastian Conrad's more wide-ranging 'Enlightenment in Global History: A Historiographical Critique', *American Historical Review* 117, 4 (2012), pp. 999–1027.

[13] Durand Echeverria, 'French Publications of the Declaration of Independence and the American Constitutions, 1776–1783', *Papers of the Bibliographical Society of America* 47 (1953).

[14] David M. Golove and Daniel J. Hulsebosch, 'A Civilized Nation: The Early American Constitution, the Law of Nations, and the Pursuit of International Recognition', *New York University Law Review* 85, 4 (2010), pp. 932–1066.

politicians went further, and commissioned a book-length commentary on the new document in both English and French, again with a view to accessing and impressing foreign centres of power.[15]

Once officially available in print, constitutions could circulate quickly in more informal media, and not only in the West. As C. A. Bayly described, by the early nineteenth century, Calcutta possessed a larger printing industry than many European capitals. Consequently, groups of Indian, British, and Portuguese reformers were able to assemble in Calcutta in August 1822 to celebrate the second anniversary of Portugal's recent liberal constitution, which had been discussed in two of the city's English-language newspapers, and possibly—though this has yet to be researched—in some indigenous language papers too.[16] As with newspapers and novels, easy availability in print allowed written constitutions *sometimes* to reach the illiterate, since extracts might be spoken out loud by individuals who could read, to men and women who could not. Thus, in 1836, at a meeting in London of 'the poorest of the working classes' held to commemorate the anniversary of Spain's Cadiz constitution of 1812, one of the organizers seized the opportunity also to read out portions of a penny pamphlet on the 'OUTLINE OF A NEW CONSTITUTION, such as should be submitted to the British nation'.[17]

Such newspaper accounts and celebratory meetings (and they were legion) suggest some of the ways in which historians can use constitutional episodes to investigate transnational and trans-continental connections. As the historian of science James A. Secord has written: 'attaining a global picture is not a question of transcending or erasing local practices but of giving more attention to practices of circulation'.[18] Investigating exactly *which* constitutions were celebrated, reported on, and extracted, at which periods of time, in what forms and locations, and amongst whom, can help pinpoint patterns of transnational influences and exchanges over time. It can also illumine how ideas about governance, power, and rights underwent modification and adaptation in the course of passing through different languages, cultural spaces, and geographies.[19] The same is true of the actual texts of constitutions, which are now widely available online and easily word-searched. An examination of the Norwegian constitution of 1814, for instance, reveals 'traces—and in some cases verbatim translations—from the French revolutionary constitutions of 1791, 1793, and 1795, the American Federal Constitution...the Polish Constitution of 1791, the Batavian [constitution] of 1798, the Swedish of 1809 and the Spanish of 1812', and from pamphlets on

---

[15] See Hirobumi Ito and Miyoji Ito (eds), *Commentaries on the Constitution of the Empire of Japan* (Tokyo: Igirisu-Horitsu Gakko, 1889).

[16] C. A. Bayly, 'Rammohan Roy and the Advent of Constitutional Liberalism in India, 1800–30', *Modern Intellectual History*, 4, 1 (2007), pp. 25–41.

[17] *The Times* (16 August 1836).

[18] James A. Secord, 'Knowledge in Transit', *Isis* 95, 4 (2004), pp. 654–72, pp. 666–7.

[19] The effects of translation on the meanings and understanding of constitutions is a major issue and remains vital today. The English version of Article 9 of the present Japanese constitution, originally drafted in the main by American officials after the Second World War, does not say exactly the same as the Japanese version, a potentially significant disparity since this is the article in which Japan renounces war: <http://www.languagerealm.com/japanese/translation_error_japan_constitution.php> (accessed 1 February 2015).

Britain's un-codified constitution.[20] As this suggests, although constitutions can supply identity stories and legitimation for particular nations, those drafting them are frequently cosmopolitan plagiarists. Consequently, these texts offer vivid, empirical evidence of the quality and extent of political and ideological transfers.

Transnational and trans-continental transfers of constitutional information over the course of the long nineteenth century were aided by the marked rise in the number of individuals choosing or obliged to travel very large distances. Professional revolutionaries (think of Tom Paine shuttling between England, North America, and France, and writing about constitutions in all three) together with lawyers, students, journalists, and missionaries were conspicuous players in this regard, and so were diplomats.[21] It was service in the Tokyo legation, San Francisco, and London that gave the Qing diplomat Huang Zunxian (1848–1905) a heightened appreciation of the differences between political systems, and later informed his treatise on Japan, which became an important handbook for Chinese activists wanting Meiji-type reforms, including a written constitution.[22] Exiles, too, could be keen trans-border communicators and absorbers of information. Some political exiles took advantage of their enforced relocation to plan fresh constitutional initiatives, often borrowing ideas from their new surroundings. Thus the Young Turk leader, Mehmet Talat (1874–1921), used his exile in Salonica to help plot what became the constitutional revolution of 1908, his access to useful international news aided by his employment as chief clerk of Salonica's telegraph office.[23] Exiles could also communicate ideas and their own local knowledge to sympathetic members of the host community. The utilitarian philosopher and legal reformer Jeremy Bentham became a notorious drafter of unofficial constitutions in part because his home city London—the biggest city in the world by 1820—was such a mecca for political exiles. Some seventy South American 'independence era leaders of the first rank' are known to have spent time in London between 1808 and 1830. Many of these men were drawn into Bentham's circle, and this helps to account for the constitutional proposals he drafted for Buenos Aires, Guatemala, Venezuela, and Colombia.[24]

Military men were also prominent transmitters of constitutional ideas, which is one reason why waves of constitutional writing and invention so often coincided

[20] Kåre Tønnesson, 'The Norwegian Constitution of 17 May 1814: International Influences and Models', *Parliaments, Estates and Representation* 21, 1 (2001), pp. 175–86, p. 179.
[21] See the significant role of individuals in linking different geographic spaces in the contributions by Mosca and Robinson in this volume.
[22] Peter Zarrow, *After Empire: The Conceptual Transformation of the Chinese State, 1885–1924* (Stanford, CA: Stanford University Press, 2012), pp. 41ff; and see Joshua A. Fogel and Peter Zarrow (eds), *Imagining the People: Chinese Intellectuals and the Concept of Citizenship, 1890–1920* (New York: M. E. Sharpe, 1997).
[23] Erik J. Zürcher, *The Young Turk Legacy and Nation Building: From the Ottoman Empire to Ataturk's Turkey* (London: I. B. Tauris, 2010), pp. 99ff.
[24] Karen Racine, '"This England and This Now": British Cultural and Intellectual Influence in the Spanish American Independence Era', *Hispanic-American Historical Review* 90, 3 (2010), pp. 423–54; David Armitage, 'Globalizing Jeremy Bentham', *History of Political Thought* 32, 1 (2011), pp. 63–82. William Smith O'Brien, transported to Van Diemen's Land [Tasmania] for his role in the Young Ireland rebellion of 1848, both drafted his own constitution for the settlement, and collaborated with activists there who wanted Tasmanian self-government.

with protracted periods of warfare and their aftermath. There were close connections between some of the army officers engaged in constitutional revolts in Spain, Naples, Russia, and parts of Latin America in the 1820s, as there were between some irregular fighters in the Russian, Iranian, and Young Turk revolutions of 1905–8.[25] Professionally mobile and invasive, provided by the nature of their trade with periods of blank time in which to read and write, frequently possessed of a sense of professional brotherhood with fellow warriors from other countries, and often multilingual, military men were well placed to gather and exchange information on constitutional matters, as on much else. The confidence and scholarship which allowed the Decembrist and Guards officer Nikita Muraviev (1796–1843) to draw on German, French, American, and British sources when drafting his attempted constitution for a federal Russia, derived in part from an Enlightenment education. But his familiarity with transnational ideas also stemmed from his time with an occupying Russian army in Paris in 1814, when he attended that city's university and befriended the liberal philosopher and theorist Benjamin Constant.[26]

Military men also participated in a trend that operated far more widely. As Walter Benjamin remarked, the more widespread the mechanical reproduction of words becomes, the more likely it is that those who read will become writers in their turn.[27] It was not only official political actors and conspicuous intellectuals and revolutionaries who acquired knowledge, ideas, and encouragement from the cross-border spread of constitutional texts. So did multitudes of unofficial and relatively minor figures, and some of these individuals also tried their hand at drafting constitutions.

Consider the career of Gregor MacGregor (1786–1845), a Scottish army officer, who fought in the Venezuelan wars of independence and married a cousin of Bolivar. Returning to Europe in the 1820s, and wanting to convince potential investors and emigrants that he was now the ruler of a new independent republic on the bay of Honduras, one of his first acts was to craft and publish a constitution for this bogus polity.[28] This was more than a stray picaresque episode. It is suggestive, to begin with, that MacGregor had been able to learn *how* to compile a feasible-seeming constitution, and that he believed—with good cause as it turned out—that he would con people more effectively if he circulated such a text. Moreover, his Central American scheme was only one of very many unofficial and imaginary constitutions, sometimes drafted by crooks as in this case, but more

[25] See, for instance, Richard Stites, 'Decembrists with a Spanish accent', *Kritika: Explorations in Russian and Eurasian History* 12, 1 (2011), pp. 5–23; Moritz Deutschmann, 'Cultures of Statehood, Cultures of Revolution: Caucasian Revolutionaries in the Iranian Constitutional Movement, 1906–1911', *Ab Imperio* 2 (2013), pp. 165–90.

[26] Andrey N. Medushevsky, *Russian Constitutionalism: Historical and Contemporary Development* (London: Routledge, 2006), pp. 86ff. For a discussion of how military men wrote across cultures, see my *Captives: Britain, Empire, and the World 1600–1850* (New York: Anchor Books, 2004), pp. 269–307.

[27] Walter Benjamin, *The Work of Art in the Age of Mechanical Reproduction*, trans. J. A. Underwood (London: Penguin Books, 2008), pp. 1–50.

[28] Gregor MacGregor, *Plan of a Constitution for the Inhabitants of the Indian Coast in Central America, Commonly Called the Mosquito Shore* (Edinburgh: Balfour and Jack, 1836).

often the work of serious reformers, revolutionaries, aspiring-empire builders, uto-pians, and gentleman scholars. Such texts offer valuable raw material for what can be styled alternative or parallel constitutional histories. As Rachel St John shows for nineteenth century Continental America, unofficial constitutions of this sort help document how national and imperial boundaries could appear to individuals in the past far more plastic and open to competing interpretations than subsequent teleological and state-centred histories may suggest.[29]

As far as I am aware however—and it would be good to be proven wrong—before 1914, very few such private political constitutions (and no official political constitutions) were drafted anywhere in the world by women who were not royal, this despite the fact that, in some regions, female participation in print culture and in certain forms of political activity was increasing sharply. In 1848, the female suffrage activists assembled at Seneca Falls, in upper New York State, famously issued their own version of the Declaration of Independence. But venturing on an explicitly styled constitution re-ordering the government of a polity, prescribing civic rights, or re-designing territory, appears to have been a step too far for women in this period, even on a purely amateur basis and in the privacy of the home.[30] Unsurprisingly, perhaps, since early written constitutions were markedly gendered texts. One of the consequences of the spread of these instruments was that women's pre-existing exclusion from much formal political activity was increasingly codified and therefore made harder to change. A worldwide view (and global history needs to look at women much more) confirms that those locations where female suffrage was achieved earliest were not in the main major polities possessed of formal written constitutions.

This was the case in parts of the Pacific world. Neither the Pitcairn Islands which allowed its sparse female population to vote at the markedly early date of 1838, nor New Zealand, which enfranchised both white and Maori women in 1893, was an independent state with an official codified constitution.[31] Both were quasi autono-mous and, from the metropole's viewpoint, very distant British colonies. By the same token, Bohemia, which became the first European country to enfranchise some women in 1864, was a subordinate kingdom of the Austrian empire. Something of a similar pattern emerges in the United States. Although the fifteenth

---

[29] Rachel St John, 'The Imagined States of America: Nation-Building in Nineteenth-Century North America', Seminar Paper, Davis Center, Department of History, Princeton University. Professor St John is currently completing a book on these themes.

[30] Even Helen Maria Williams, a committed radical and experienced writer who played a role in the French Revolution, was careful in this regard. 'Do not be alarmed', she wrote in 1801, 'I am not going to play the part of an analyser of constitutions, and act the lofty politician': quoted in Gary Kelly, *Women, Writing, and Revolution 1790–1827* (Oxford: Oxford University Press, 1993), p. 197. It needs stressing however that women's political constitution-writing (or not) in advance of the twen-tieth century has gone virtually unexplored. Women did of course occasionally draft constitutions for charitable and religious bodies, but they were always held back—not just by societal expectations—but also by their exclusion everywhere from a formal legal education.

[31] The Pitcairn Island constitution of 1838, which allowed votes for 'every native born on the is-land, male or female', and made education compulsory, is another example both of constitutional private enterprise and the role of the military. It was drafted by a passing Royal Navy officer with no sanction from London, but stuck.

amendment to the US Federal constitution, ratified in 1870, formally prohibited denying access to the franchise on the grounds of race, exclusion on the grounds of gender was allowed to continue. State constitutions were for a long time just as exclusionary. New Jersey's state constitution did give propertied women access to the vote in 1776, but this provision was rescinded in 1807. It was various American frontier territories—not recognized states of the Union equipped with formal written constitutions—that took the lead in enfranchising women: Wyoming Territory in 1869, and Utah Territory the year after.

The various ways in which constitutions have worked to *restrict* rather than expand access to active citizenship and rights, and to formalize (and sometimes invent) divisions within populations, help to explain their attraction historically for different kinds of empires. Their potential as transformative and dirigiste scripts—imposed designs circulating and influencing how a polity's inhabitants might live and think—could also make them attractive to imperialists wanting to envisage colonial lands as actual or metaphorical empty spaces upon which to impress new systems of law, beliefs, and governance.[32] It was in part their capacity to serve as tools for empire, not just for state building, that accounts for written constitutions' relentless proliferation across continents.

CONSTITUTIONS AND EMPIRES

As Beau Breslin remarks, the idea that constitutions are invariably 'devices to control arbitrary and capacious authority is powerful and comforting': and this helps to explain why their deployment by both Western and non-Western empires is often passed over.[33] Despite now intense scholarly interest in how empires have made use of systems of knowledge, archives, paperwork, and lawfare so as to consolidate territory, conquer space, organize power, and shape memory and ideas, a lingering view that written constitutions *must* be quintessentially benign—instantiations of the popular will and guarantees of rights—can still make these texts seem alien to imperial histories.[34]

Yet paying close attention to the links between matters of empire and written constitutions is essential for understanding both the evolution of these devices and their multiple roles in global history. Although the contagion of constitutions expanded markedly after 1776, there had been some significant moves towards these talismanic

[32] For an extended discussion of this point, see my 'Empires of Writing: Britain, America and Constitutions, 1776–1848', *Law and History Review*, 32, 2 (2014), pp. 237–66.
[33] Beau Breslin, *From Words to Worlds: Exploring Constitutional Functionality* (Baltimore: Johns Hopkins University Press, 2009), p. 5.
[34] For empires' deployment of legal texts in general, see John L. Comaroff, 'Colonialism, Culture and the Law: A Foreword', *Law & Social Inquiry* 26, 2 (2001), pp. 305–14. The notion that investigating imperial constitutions—because these instruments *must* somehow be benign—represents therefore a glossing over of imperial violence seems to lie behind C. A. Bayly's complaint that 'colonial historians have been concerned with the making of constitutions rather than the nature of the state'. There is no need to adopt this either/or position: C. A. Bayly, *Imperial Meridian: The British Empire and the World, 1780–1830* (London: Longman, 1989), pp. 114 and also 8–9.

political texts in the seventeenth century. Suggestively, some of these earlier initiatives were responses to developments *outside* Europe. Thus the impact of John Locke's *Two Treatises on Government* (1689) on Enlightenment political and constitutional thought is well known. But twenty years earlier, in 1669, Locke helped draft the *Fundamental Constitutions of Carolina*, a text providing both for religious freedom and a measure of slavery and serfdom, and designed for an English colonial province spanning most of the land between what is now Virginia and Florida.[35]

By the same token, it was the Seven Years War, the first near-global war, which helped render this earlier, intermittent interest in new single-document constitutions far more sustained. This was the case in parts of Europe. In 1755, for instance, Pasquale Paoli was able to safeguard Corsica's (short-lived) independence, and issue a politically advanced written constitution, because France was temporarily distracted by the early stages of the conflict; while, in 1772, Gustav III of Sweden, who had backed the wrong side in the Seven Years War, attempted both to refurbish his authority and implement judicial reforms by issuing a new 'Form of Government', ensuring it was widely distributed in print.[36] But this enhanced interest in new paper designs of government was also a response to the territorial, fiscal, and intellectual changes inflicted by the Seven Years War outside Europe. Thus, in 1764, Sir Francis Bernard, Governor of Massachusetts, presented the British government with his 'Principles of Law and Policy', an outline for a constitution for its now much expanded, and increasingly disorderly American mainland empire; while Edmund Burke's evolving schemes for a 'Magna Carta of Hindostan' was one of several attempts after the war to re-think individual rights and re-frame systems of governance in regard to millions of newly claimed imperial subjects in Asia and elsewhere who were neither white nor Christian.[37]

After the outbreak of the American Revolution, some written constitutions became notably more democratic, more rights-heavy, and more internationally discussed, but links with empire persisted and expanded. In part this was because, as Krishan Kumar argues, empires and nations have rarely in practice been absolutely contrasting and antithetical political forms.[38] Significant similarities could— and can—exist between these ostensibly divergent types of polity. Thus in France after 1789, new written constitutions undoubtedly catered to the Revolutionary regime's nationalist and emancipatory aims. Simultaneously, however, these new constitutions also functioned as instruments for internal colonialism, forming part of a wider Jacobin campaign to impose—sometimes by force—a virtuous

[35] See David Armitage, 'John Locke, Carolina, and the Two Treatises of Government', *Political Theory* 32, 5 (2004), pp. 602–27. The degree of Locke's involvement is still contested.
[36] Dorothy Carrington, 'The Corsican Constitution of Pasquale Paoli (1755–1769)', *English Historical Review* 88, 348 (1973), pp. 481–503; Gabriela Majewska, 'Sweden's Form of Government during the Reign of Gustavus III—in the Eyes of the Journals of the Polish Enlightenment', *Scandinavian Journal of History* 22, 4 (2008), pp. 291–304.
[37] Bernard Bailyn, *The Ordeal of Thomas Hutchinson* (Cambridge, MA: Belknap Press, 1974), p. 86. Professor Robert Travers is at work on some of these post-Seven Years War constitutional projects for Asia.
[38] See Krishan Kumar, 'Empires and Nations: Convergence or Divergence?' in George Steinmetz (ed.), *Sociology & Empire: The Imperial Entanglements of a Discipline* (Durham, NC: Duke University Press, 2013), pp. 279–99.

homogenization upon France's multiple linguistic, legal, and cultural enclaves. French Revolutionary leaders, and above all Napoleon Bonaparte who always 'appreciated the power of the written word', also designed and deployed numerous written constitutions to order and shape France's expanding empire in Continental Europe.[39]

On the other side of the Atlantic, written constitutions also operated simultaneously as collections of rights and national totems, and as aids to overland empire. One of the American founders' initiatives in 1787 was to ensure that treaties approved in Washington became the 'law of the land', binding on 'judges in every state'. It was partly by means of adroit, centrally devised and centrally implemented treaties that the United States was able to triple in size between 1783 and 1850.[40] The growing network of state constitutions also helped successive US governments to manage internal colonialism and to exert some control over fast-moving and expanding pioneer populations. As a one-time Ohio judge wrote in 1848: 'the introduction of the most enlightened institutions and laws into the western states, at the earliest possible stage keeps the minds of men in one track, and trains the whole population to the same habits and manners as prevail among the oldest members of the confederacy', a remark that underlines the appeal of written constitutions as didactic scripts.[41]

As happened in some other nineteenth-century settler empires, constitutions in the United States proved at once increasingly democratic and purposefully ethnically exclusive. Growing numbers of white settlers moving westwards and southwards through continental America were encouraged to draft their own state constitutions, which interlocked with the Federal constitution, and usually excluded Native Americans and blacks as well as females from full citizenship. In this way, a set of mechanisms was put in place whereby the United States became able to consolidate and represent itself as a continent-wide *nation* while at the same time implementing overland empire.[42] There was a sense—both here and in Australia, South Africa, and much of Latin America—in which an ever more extensive network of constitutions helped to erase indigenous peoples from both mental maps and maps on paper. (Indeed, exactly how, and how far the spread of written constitutions worked, like other official texts such as treaties and censuses, to marginalize peoples lacking written languages requires far more investigation.)[43]

[39] Alan Forrest, *Napoleon: Life, Legacy, and Image. A Biography* (New York: St Martin's Griffin, 2013); Stuart Woolf, *Napoleon's Integration of Europe* (London: Routledge, 1991); Juan Cole, *Napoleon's Egypt: Invading the Middle East* (New York: Palgrave Macmillan, 2007).

[40] Paul Frymer, 'Building an American Empire: Territorial Expansion in the Antebellum Era', UC Irvine Law Review, 1, 3 (2011), pp. 913–54.

[41] Frederick Grimké, *Considerations upon the Nature and Tendency of Free Institutions* (Cincinnati: H. W. Derby & Co, 1848), p. 486.

[42] For a useful summary, see Barbara Young Welke, 'Law, Personhood, and Citizenship in the Long Nineteenth Century: The Borders of Belonging', in Michael Grossberg and Christopher L. Tomlins (eds), *Cambridge History of Law in America: The Long Nineteenth Century*, 3 vols (Cambridge: Cambridge University Press, 2008), vol. II, pp. 345–86.

[43] For some of the background, see Marilyn Lake and Henry Reynolds, *Drawing the Global Colour Line: White Men's Countries and the International Challenge of Racial Equality* (Cambridge: Cambridge University Press, 2008).

When, in 1827, the Cherokee of Georgia, who did possess a written alphabet, tried to resist this kind of erasure and held a convention to draw up their own constitution, which was published in English and Cherokee, and provided for a separation of powers, trial by jury, and freedom of worship, the Georgia state legislature furiously rejected the initiative as creating an *imperium in imperio*, and in 1835 confiscated the tribe's lands.[44]

It is hard to find any overland or maritime empire in the long nineteenth century, however new-minted or well established, which did not make some use of written constitutions. When the one-time slave Jean-Jacques Dessalines succeeded in establishing an independent Haiti in 1804, he promptly declared himself an emperor and issued an imperial constitution.[45] The abortive but widely influential Cadiz constitution of 1812 proclaimed popular sovereignty and admitted some non-whites to the franchise, but this same text was also designed to keep Spain's massive Asian and Atlantic Empire intact. In John Elliott's words, 'in legislating for America as well as for Spain the [Cadiz] constitution was in effect a charter for empire'.[46] Then there was the Brazilian constitution of 1824, which survived longer than any other in nineteenth-century Latin America, and which was initiated by Emperor Pedro I who reversed customary transatlantic power flows by also imposing a new constitution on Portugal.[47] Since Britain notoriously does not possess a written constitution, it might be expected to have been an exception to this pattern of both old and new empires using and adapting written constitutions as technologies of rule, but this was emphatically not the case. The British Empire was the first fully to span the globe and, as John Darwin and others have documented, constitutions formed a persistent part of its design and organization. By 1951, it was claimed that there were 'in all something like seventy separate constitutions in the Commonwealth and most of them were made in Britain', but British constitution-writing for imperial spaces had begun much earlier.[48] During and immediately after the Napoleonic wars, for instance, constitutions were approved for areas brought under British control in the Mediterranean region, such as Corsica, Sicily, and the Ionian Islands.

TRANSITIONS

Thus far, I have been discussing the diffusion of constitutions and information about them, and how—especially from the mid eighteenth century—sponsorship

[44] William G. McLoughlin, *Cherokee Renascence in the New Republic* (Princeton: Princeton University Press, 1986).

[45] See Doris L. Garraway, 'Empire of Freedom, Kingdom of Civilization: Henry Christophe, the Baron de Vastey, and the Paradoxes of Universalism in Post-Revolutionary Haiti', *Small Axe* 16, 339 (2012), pp. 1–21.

[46] I am grateful to Professor Sir John Elliott for a copy of his unpublished essay, ' "Spaniards of Both Hemispheres": A Constitution for an Empire' (unpublished essay: University of Oxford).

[47] Gabriel Paquette, 'The Brazilian Origins of the 1826 Portuguese Constitution', *European History Quarterly* 41, 3 (2011), pp. 444–71.

[48] Frederick Madden, David Fieldhouse, and John Darwin (eds), *Select Documents on the Constitutional History of the British Empire and Commonwealth*, 8 vols (New York: Greenwood Press, 1985–2000); Kenneth C. Wheare, *Modern Constitutions* (London: Oxford University Press, 1951).

and adaption by different empires contributed to the spread of these instruments. In both respects, important changes occurred from the 1860s, that decade of truly global significance. According to the Comparative Constitutions Project database (which is not comprehensive) no official written constitution was issued or even seriously attempted by any independent polity before 1860 in Asia, South Asia, and the Middle East, or in most of Africa.[49] So while the spread of constitutions and constitutional ideas in the preceding hundred years had been striking, so were the geographical constraints. From the 1860s, however, there was an exponential rise in the geographical range and in the rate of new constitution-making. In different ways, however, issues to do with empire continued to remain central.

The outcome of the American Civil War finally put paid to projects among Southern politicians, military men, and theorists for a new slave empire that would encroach into South America and parts of the Caribbean.[50] The survival and victory of the Union were also widely understood internationally as confirming that written constitutions were here to stay. Given the limited success of most liberal constitution-making in the revolutions of 1848–9, and the brief shelf life of many early written constitutions in Latin America and some European states, conspicuously France, this had by no means seemed assuredly the case before 1861. For some observers, indeed, the outbreak of civil war in the United States, home to the most iconic written constitution, had only seemed to confirm that these devices were unstable, and possibly inherently flawed. But the defeat of the South in 1865, and the subsequent growing economic and international clout of the United States, enormously boosted the reputation of codified constitutions as viable tools for state-making (and empire-making) and as desirable emblems of modernity.

There is a further respect in which the American Civil War is likely to have had a protracted international impact, especially in the non-Western world. In 1868, five years after the thirteenth amendment to the US constitution had outlawed slavery, the fourteenth amendment admitted people of African descent to US citizenship. In practice, democracy and equal rights for American blacks would remain for a long time profoundly elusive. Nonetheless, in part because of the burgeoning trans-continental cult around Abraham Lincoln, I suspect that these constitutional changes in the United States had wide and long-term political and ideological repercussions, not least among anti-colonial activists in Africa and Asia.[51]

There were other ways too in which the more sharply competitive international system emerging from the 1860s served to widen the geographical range of constitution-writing. At one level, a growing number of non-Western polities

---

[49] To what degree, and among whom, 'unofficial' constitutions were drafted in these regions before 1860 remains under explored.

[50] For this strand of Southern thinking before 1861, see Matthew Karp, '"The Vast Southern Empire": The South and the Foreign Policy of Slavery' (unpublished PhD thesis: University of Pennsylvania, 2011).

[51] Richard Carwardine and Jay Sexton (eds), *The Global Lincoln* (New York: Oxford University Press, 2011). For a summary of recent research on the wide repercussions of the American Civil War, see Matthew Karp, 'The Transnational Significance of the American Civil War: A Global History', *Bulletin of the German Historical Institute* 52 (2013), pp. 169–76.

began to adopt written constitutions in the hope of safeguarding a measure of autonomy in the face of ever sharper Western imperial encroachment (hence in part the Johor constitution of 1895, the first ever presided over by a Malay ruler).[52] At another level, some empires themselves came under growing pressure after the 1860s, and were obliged to concede constitutions to subject and settler peoples (as with Britain's acceptance of the Australian Commonwealth constitution of 1900 and the South African constitution of 1910). At yet another level, some newer empires began to enter the constitution-writing game. Thus, having produced four ephemeral constitutions during their armed struggle against imperial Spain, Cubans received two more, in 1898 and 1901, sponsored by the United States.[53] Finally, it seems likely that the widening spread and diversity of constitutional projects after the 1860s were assisted by the increasing volume of non-white emigration, voluntary and forced. By the 1880s, for instance, Asian, black, and European reformers and radicals in Trinidad were able to acquire constitutional information and ideas not simply from their own press and imported British newspapers, but also from printed material and letters shipped in from India to service the island's expanding Asian immigrant community.[54]

But perhaps the most dramatic post-1860 development was the emergence for the first time of major constitutions drafted and instigated entirely outside the West as it was conventionally imagined. In 1876, the Ottoman sultan, Abdul Hamid II (1842–1918), approved a new constitution of 119 articles, providing for a General Assembly with an elected lower house, free education, equality before the law, and the eligibility of all Ottoman males for public office, irrespective of ethnicity or religion. This was suspended after less than two years, and only revived in modified form in 1908. Nonetheless, and despite its French, British, and Belgian borrowings, the fact that this constitution issued from the heartland of Islam ensured that it went on to exert an influence on subsequent constitution-making in Syria, Egypt, Jordan, Iraq, and elsewhere in the Arab world.[55] More immediately influential though was the Meiji constitution of 1889.

In part, this was yet another example of the close and persistent relationship between significant episodes of constitution-writing and imperial ambitions. Meiji Japan was both ruled by an emperor and increasingly an expansionist power: formally annexing Korea in 1910, and seizing outposts of the Russian and Chinese empires. The Meiji constitution was intended to signal Japan's amplified status on the world stage and—as an emblem of modernity—it was subsequently used to

[52] Iza Hussin, 'Textual Trajectories: Re-reading the Constitution and Majalah in 1890s Johor', *Indonesia and the Malay World* 41, 120 (2013), pp. 255–72.

[53] On this, see Christina Duffy Burnett, 'Contingent Constitutions: Empire and Law in the Americas' (unpublished PhD thesis: Princeton University, 2010).

[54] H. A. Will, *Constitutional Change in the British West Indies, 1880–1903* (Oxford: Clarendon Press, 1970).

[55] See Robert Devereux, *The First Ottoman Constitutional Period: A Study of the Midhat Constitution and Parliament* (Baltimore: Johns Hopkins University Press, 1963); Nathan J. Brown, *Constitutions in a Nonconstitutional World: Arab Basic Laws and the Prospects for Accountable Government* (Albany, NY: State University of New York Press, 2002).

help legitimize the Japanese imperial and civilizing mission.[56] But, for all its links with empire, the Meiji constitution nonetheless represented and confirmed a break with the past. Coming after the Ottoman constitution of 1876, its introduction further underlined that major constitutional projects were no longer overwhelmingly the preserve of Western powers, and this point was recognized at the time. 'An Oriental nation has made a sudden forward spring and that is a very remarkable event', remarked a British academic: 'In 1789 the citizens of the United States founded the first of the great modern Constitutions; a hundred years later the Japanese have come forward with the last.'[57] We still need to know more about the global impact of the Meiji constitution. We already know that political activists in Siam, China, and later Ethiopia were inspired by it, and that it was also closely scrutinized both by some Indian nationalists and by the British themselves in regard to their constitutional schemes in India.[58]

The makers of the Meiji constitution also helped to publicize a strategy that was later widely adopted by post-colonial nations. The Meiji constitution was written in the 1880s by some of Japan's top oligarchs, led by Count Itō Hirobumi (1841– 1909) a Bismarkian-type figure in energy and intelligence, who would die as a consequence of Japanese expansionism, assassinated by a Korean nationalist.[59] Along with other Japanese envoys, and in the wake of the famous Iwakura Embassy to the West, Hirobumi went on missions to the United States, Russia, and various European capitals, interviewing constitutional scholars, lawyers, and politicians. Partly because of this, the Meiji constitution was eclectic in content, incorporating American, British, French, Austrian, but above all Prussian borrowings; and some have interpreted it straightforwardly as an example of Meiji Japan's westernization.[60] Yet—as a non-specialist—I would risk the view that the thinking involved in it was more mixed and complex. What Hirobumi and his associates did was arguably follow and celebrate a strategy of pick and mix as it were. By formally touring *different* Western capitals, and appropriating a constitutional bit from here and a bit from there, and by incorporating too their own priorities and traditions, they underlined Japan's capacity to select discriminatingly from the West (especially from some more authoritarian Eastern and Central European political systems) as distinct simply from copying it.

---

[56] Kazuhiro, *Meiji Constitution, passim.*

[57] 'The New Japanese Constitution', *Macmillan's Magazine*, 70 (1894), pp. 420–8.

[58] See 'Correspondence regarding the Japanese constitution and its use as a precedent in forming constitutional reforms in India', *British Library*, IOR/L/PJ/9/12, file 536/20; for the Tokyo-Indian nationalist axis before 1914, see Harald Fischer-Tiné, 'Indian Nationalism and the "World Forces": Transnational and Diasporic Dimensions of the Indian Freedom Movement on the Eve of the First World War', *Journal of Global History* 2, 3 (2007), pp. 325–44.

[59] Kazuhiro Takii, *Itō Hirobumi: Japan's First Prime Minister and Father of the Meiji Constitution* (London: Routledge, 2014).

[60] Even before Itō's political embassies, there had been growing Japanese interest in Western constitutional texts, fostered in part by a rapidly growing press. In 1866, Fukazawa Yukichi provided translations of the American Declaration of Independence and the US Federal Constitution in his bestseller *Seijō jijō* [*The State of Affairs in the West*] (Tokyo, 1866), cited in Tadashi Aruga, 'The Declaration of Independence in Japan: Translation and Transplantation, 1854–1997', *Journal of American History* 85 (1999), pp. 1409–31.

Lest this point be missed, and as we have already seen, in 1889 the Japanese government published a commentary under Hirobumi's name on how the new Meiji constitution was to be understood. The commentary acknowledged Japan's debt to various Western constitutions, but also pronounced judgement on them, dismissing the doctrine of separation of powers embodied in the US constitution, for instance, as a mere 'close of the eighteenth century' idea. As for Britain, 'the mother country of the system of two chambers', the commentary's authors reported how all was not well with the Westminster Parliament, with growing tensions between the House of Commons and the Lords over Irish home rule. By contrast, the commentary on the Meiji constitution was explicitly represented as a 'handbook for all', its writers claiming for Japan both a prime place in the global circuit of seminal constitutional ideas and initiatives and a distinctive Asian modernity.[61]

One sees rather similar strategies at work in the making of the 1949 Indian constitution. As is well known, over 250 of the 395 articles of this constitution were taken almost word for word from the Government of India Act passed by Stanley Baldwin's British cabinet in 1935.[62] But in part to counter and offset these British retentions, the men drafting the Indian constitution again adopted a conspicuous policy of pick and mix, incorporating elements as well from the constitutions of Australia, Canada, the United States, and the Irish Republic. In addition, the constitution's main author, B. R. Ambedkar (1891–1956) brought to it his own mixed intellectual influences from Columbia University in the United States and the London School of Economics, plus crucially his personal Buddhism, Dalit connections, and strong commitment to India's underclass.[63] As with the Meiji constitution in regard to Japan, the careful and ostentatious eclecticism of India's constitution fostered and advertised the country's status as a new, discriminating, dynamic, and independent power of substance, while also positioning it as an exemplary *non-Western* political model.

CONCLUSIONS AND ISSUES

This essay has set out a research agenda. I have wanted to show how historians can ransack written constitutions for far more than their specific legal and judicial content, and how these texts possess particular value for global historians. Constitutions illumine the extent of transnational and trans-continental political transfer over time and in different locations, and do so with rich empirical and individual detail. No less significantly, they help reveal the limits and tensions of transnational and

---

[61] Ito, *Commentaries on the Constitution*, pp. 8–9, 63: Mark Ravina, 'Japanese State Making in Global Context', in Richard Boyd and Tak-Wing Ngo (eds), *State Making in Asia* (London: Routledge, 2006), pp. 31–46.

[62] The classic account by Granville Austin, *The Indian Constitution: Cornerstone of a Nation* (Oxford: Clarendon Press, 1966) needs balancing with Madhav Khosla, *The Indian Constitution* (New Delhi: Oxford University Press, 2012).

[63] For Ambedkar's ideas, see C. A. Bayly, *Recovering Liberties: Indian Thought in the Age of Liberalism and Empire* (Cambridge: Cambridge University Press, 2012); and Mohammad Shabbir, *Ambedkar on Law, Constitution, and Social Justice* (Jaipur: Rawat Publications, 2005).

trans-continental influences and borrowings, and how layering operates between the local and the universal.

Most strikingly, written constitutions have been viral, progressively a worldwide phenomenon. Global historians have often neglected political history in favour of economic history, because the former subject has traditionally been organized around nation states. But tracing the spread of constitutions shows how the political, too, has been interwoven with transnational influences, aspirations, and pressures. However powerful they were, states and empires found it increasingly impossible—and disadvantageous—to hold entirely aloof from the contagion of constitutions. The apparent exception, Great Britain with its still un-codified constitution, was in reality no exception at all. As we have seen, like other empires, Britain made prolific use of constitutions as technologies of rule. In addition, Britons increasingly made a cult of reading and writing 'constitutional history', a term that was popularized by the English historian Henry Hallam in the 1820s. Recognizing how other powers were deploying printed single-document constitutions not just for domestic governance, but to proclaim and publicize their values and political systems abroad, British apologists were obliged to produce and circulate books and pamphlets on their own real and imagined constitutional history and ideals so as to compete in a global marketplace of political ideas, a pattern that became even more pronounced from the 1860s.[64]

This has been another recurring theme of this essay: the mixed and plural nature and tendencies of written constitutions. In drawing attention to their variety, and to some of their darker, more ambivalent aspects, my concern has not been to negate their positive and democratic achievements. Indeed, part of a global history of these instruments should involve an exploration of how even authoritarian written constitutions were sometimes turned to advantage by those caught up in them, and how colonized peoples were sometimes able to exploit and demand the more emancipatory tendencies of these devices. When the American Colonization Society commissioned a Harvard law professor to advise the free black settlers of Liberia on formulating a constitution in 1847, it was put sharply in its place. 'The people of Liberia do not require the assistance of "white people" to enable them to make a Constitution for the government of themselves', declared a member of Liberia's constitutional convention on the very first day of its meeting.[65]

All that said, written constitutions in their modern form emerged during the Enlightenment, and were shaped accordingly. Whatever one thinks in general of Foucault's argument that 'the "Enlightenment" which discovered the liberties, also invented the disciplines', it certainly holds good for constitutions for much of their global history.[66] Written constitutions spread as widely and as quickly as they did

---

[64] Michael Bentley, 'Henry Hallam Revisited', *Historical Journal* 55, 2 (2012), pp. 453–73. One of Walter Bagehot's aims in writing his famous commentary on the 'English' constitution in the 1860s was to demonstrate that the British system was not *sui generis* but could be adapted and plundered by other states.

[65] James Ciment, *Another America: The Story of Liberia and the Former Slaves Who Ruled It* (New York: Hill and Wang, 2013), pp. 91–3.

[66] Michel Foucault, *Discipline and Punish: The Birth of the Prison* (New York: Random House, 1995), p. 222.

in part because, as well as sometimes enshrining rights and limits on power, and ultimately providing in most parts of the world for a measure of democracy, they were from the outset also mechanisms designed to achieve a measure of control, to publicize the contours of regimes and promote them, and to facilitate and produce certain desired mass responses.

Such tendencies have by no means vanished today. Even critics of the uses made by defunct empires of written constitutions in the past can still get caught out by some of the contradictions inherent in these devices. A *Hindutva* (Hindu nationalist) ideologue recently published online a 'draft constitution' for India, yet another example of amateur constitution-writing, and yet again the work of someone male. Like so many earlier constitution writers, this man also had an international audience in mind. His online scheme, he suggested, could easily serve as a 'template for the constitution of Bolivia ... and all third world countries'. But the writer's prime ambition was to replace 'the Indian Constitution imposed by British agents' with 'a better constitution'. Only a brand-new constitution, he insisted, was now 'suitable for super power imperial India', a new and different empire of the subcontinent.[67]

---

[67] Kalki Gaur, 'Draft Populist Constitution of India', consulted online in 2011 at <http://www.clearblogs.com/indian>.

Afterword
History on a Global Scale

John Darwin

It is now a commonplace that we live in a 'globalized' world. For a decade or more, we were encouraged to think of that world as 'flat', to imagine a world in which the free movement of capital, goods, and information (though not always people) at ever-increasing speeds would smooth cultural differences, ease geopolitical tension, and temper, if not erase, economic inequalities. We have learnt somewhat painfully that this prospectus was too optimistic, if not wildly misleading. But perhaps the naivety with which these prognostications were initially received owed something to the absence of any historical dimension to the ways in which globalization was conceived. In our crudely ahistorical culture, globalization had no past—and we lacked any perspective in which to locate our current, but all too transient, situation.

If global history has a social function, it is to help fill that gap in public understanding. That in a modest way is part of the aim of this book. There are at least four respects in which attention to its history can broaden and deepen public knowledge about globalization. The first is to recognize that globalization, minimally defined as exchange and reciprocity (in people, goods, and ideas) between different parts of the world, is a phenomenon with a very long history indeed, perhaps as far back as Homo sapiens' original migration 'out of Africa' 70,000 years ago. Historians have long been familiar with the notion that 'climate change' is far from being a uniquely contemporary preoccupation, and that periodic mutations and extinctions as well as sudden events have imposed or encouraged a variety of social, cultural, and economic adaptations in different parts of the world. Taking the long view permits us to see that globalization can be analysed more subtly if we resist treating it as an unprecedented explosion in global exchange. At the minimum, we might want to distinguish between four different phases. One: periods of vast geographic enlargement in the sphere of exchange and interaction. The European conquest of the Americas after 1500, the extension of European hegemony across much of the Afro-Asian world between 1830 and 1914, and the dramatic entry of China, the ex-Soviet bloc and (more ambiguously) India into the capitalist world (amounting to around half of the world's population) after $c.1980$ might be examples of this. Two: periods when the integration of existing geographic zones is sharply accelerated as a result of technological change in agriculture, manufacturing, or transport, the cultural changes prompted by the arrival of literacy or print, or geopolitical change. Three: periods when integration slows down or even goes into reverse, as new barriers are erected as a result of economic, religious, or ideological anxiety. Four: we might even propose that globalization (in any period) has been subject to episodes—if not whole eras—of crisis, when the interaction between its various components triggered unmanageable tensions or when the 'manic' phase of economic expansion gave way to panic, autarchy or aggression.

The second respect is to acknowledge that globalization extends far beyond the narrowly economic or financial realm. Recent experience alone should remind us that global exchange can also include the spread of diseases, the diffusion of plant life and animals, the propagation of religious beliefs and practices, the mobilization and remaking of ethnic and religious identities, and the dissemination of new forms of consumption and the cultures they promote. We might also observe the apparent connection between globalization and the acceleration of demographic and geopolitical turbulence, both in our own times and in previous periods of history. Globalization, in short, is not 'one big thing' but a complex of processes, each with its own intricate history, each susceptible to the mutual influence of the others. The briefest of glances at the historical record would suggest the scale and importance of these 'globalizing' processes far back in time and hint at the value of grasping their inter-relation.

The third, as this would imply, is that global history should also remind us that world-wide reciprocity, integration, and exchange have not just been the handiwork of bankers, multinationals, or governments. Historically, globalization has been the work of many hands, and of many agents, 'official', 'unofficial', 'formal', and 'informal', including many whose archival footprint has been light or invisible. Indeed, quite often those agents had little in common or pursued conflicting objectives, so that their 'globalizing' initiatives could induce contradictory effects or mutual antagonisms. Religious proselytization might open new doors to commercial influence, or provoke cultural antipathy and a siege mentality—the pattern in early modern Japan. Commercial penetration might prompt greater political openness, or trigger its reverse. Migrant populations might mix readily with indigenous peoples, or seek to enslave or enserf them. It was rare indeed (to take only one case) for the global ambitions of British missionaries, merchants, administrators, settlers, soldiers, and scientists to recognize a shared set of assumptions about geographical priorities or the appropriate treatment of indigenous peoples. Typically, the strategic objectives of missionaries, settlers, merchants, and military men diverged widely, and each sought different 'global' partners in their spheres of activity—although settlers often preferred sooner or later to eliminate or marginalize theirs. The globalization that resulted was necessarily 'messy', incomplete, and ideologically incoherent. If we widen our view beyond the Victorian British, the 'messiness' escalates on a dizzying scale: and the falsity of 'flatness' becomes overwhelming. Finally, an attention to history will alert us to something that perhaps ought to be obvious: that the perception of globalization, both its meanings and consequences, is likely to vary not just between agents but between cultures and civilizations as well—even if a different idiom is used to describe it. In this book, the chapters by Francis Robinson and Matthew Mosca reveal that it was not just the West that located itself (and its history) in a global perspective, or imagined for itself a compelling global future.

The long view that global history can offer helps us to see that no phase of globalization, or global connectedness, can be permanent. Globalization is always a work in progress, subject to reversals, transitions, crises, and breakdowns. No global order, whether economic or geopolitical, has been fixed for long. Each has created new frontiers and borderlands, new centres and peripheries, and incubated new sources of tension and change.

* * *

As this might suggest, global history is far from being a mere celebration of globalization in its current form, let alone a 'Whig history' of the rise and rise of the 'flat world'. Yet while global connectedness may serve as an essential context, not all those attracted to global history will see their primary aim as charting its fluctuating dimensions. There exists, perhaps, an infinite variety of ways in which global history might be rendered viable as an object of study, research, or reflection. Most will depend in the first instance (as Jürgen Osterhammel has argued) upon the intuitions and insights that historical sociology has to offer. Most though not all might be found under one of the following heads.

First 'super-human' history—the events and effects beyond human control or at best only indirectly influenced by human behaviour. Here the most obvious is climate change. While historians have long been alert to the potential impact of climate shifts on human societies—the 'medieval optimum' and the 'little ice age' have passed into common currency—advances in meteorology, in the scientific apparatus available to archaeology, and in the accessible sources, have combined to make this an exceptionally dynamic field. Both in extending our knowledge of climate change to larger and larger parts of the world, and in tracing the intricate links between climate and social behaviour, a huge task lies ahead. Some impression of its promise can be gleaned from Ronnie Ellenblum's *The Collapse of the Eastern Mediterranean*,[1] in which an array of documentary, epigraphic, scientific, and archaeological evidence is mobilized to argue for a bold hypothesis: that the repeated combination of drought and cold in the eleventh century severely damaged the stability and prosperity of the principal Near Eastern economies, reversing their lead over the more fortunate West, thriving in the sun and rain of the 'medieval warm period'. Moreover, in this case at least, climatic disaster induced demographic and religious change: the irruption of nomads into previously cultivated zones; the flight of Christian populations and their replacement by Muslims. Climatic disasters may be temporary, argues Ellenblum, but the adaptations and changes they bring in their wake can have long-lasting results.

However, the comparative history of what might be thought of as 'universal processes' is likely to remain the dominant focus for most global historians,

---

[1] Ronnie Ellenblum, *The Collapse of the Eastern Mediterranean: Climate Change and the Decline of the East, 950–1072* (Cambridge: Cambridge University Press, 2012).

drawing inspiration (if only unconsciously) from Max Weber above all. The emergence of agrarian societies; the formation of classes and castes; the varying attributes ascribed to gender; the adoption of cosmologies; the motives for state-building; the course of urbanization (and its periodic reversal); the causes and effects of population growth: all these and more form a vast field of historical enquiry, now liberated from assumptions about a European 'norm'. One of the consequences may be a less dogmatic definition of what constitutes modernity. Closely related is the investigation of 'global divergence': the wide variation in economic performance between different parts of the world. Once viewed unproblematically as the inevitable triumph of the West over the 'Rest', the methodological advances associated with the work of Kenneth Pomeranz and Robert Allen in particular, have transformed the field beyond recognition, opening up the prospect of explaining divergence not just between North-West Europe and China (where the debate began) but in the fortunes of sub-Saharan Africa, India, Latin America, and the Middle East as well. Analysing divergence requires a detailed enquiry into the links between economic fortune on the one hand and the institutions, belief systems, and consumption habits that shaped economic behaviour and choice. It also imposes the conceptual challenge of deciding on their relative significance for the outcome. Thus 'divergence' is really the entry point for exploring a multitude of possible divergences, and for the no less arduous task of estimating the varying impact of religion, law, and political order (to name only three) upon a society's prospects of escaping poverty.

A fourth kind of global history is now well established: tracking the history of commodities. As Nicholas Purcell's chapter reminds us, the circulation of commodities depends upon dense networks of information and exchange, and a crowd of agents and brokers to populate them. If we widen our gaze to include the producers and consumers, the suppliers of transport and labour, the bodies both public and private who extracted a 'rent'—or tried to—from the trade, an entire cross-section of global connectedness comes into view. What shaped the preferences of consumers in one part of the world, not just for a particular commodity but for the way they consumed it? Why did the locus of production shift, sometimes dramatically or suddenly? What social, cultural, or demographic effects can be traced to the influence of new commodity preferences, or to the availability of new items for trade? We know a good deal about trades in different parts of the world: the horse and tea trade in medieval China;[2] the global commerce in cotton;[3] as well as the trades in coffee, opium, sugar, silk—and slaves. But since the list of commodities is (almost) infinite, and their consumption has varied so widely over time and space, we are even now perhaps only at the pioneering stage of researching their history.

---

[2] See Paul J. Smith, *Taxing Heaven's Storehouse: Horses, Bureaucrats and the Destruction of the Sichuan Tea Trade 1074–1224* (Cambridge, MA: Harvard University Asia Center, 1991).
[3] See the recent studies by Giorgio Riello, *Cotton: the Fabric that Made the Modern World* (Cambridge: Cambridge University Press, 2013) and Sven Beckert, *Empire of Cotton: A New History of Global Capitalism* (London: Allen Lane, 2014).

Fifthly there is 'contagion', the global spread of diseases—and ideas. The dual role of communicable diseases is a familiar topic. Disease was a barrier, but also a battering ram. Much of the tropical and sub-tropical world was dangerous to the 'unseasoned' inhabitants of the temperate lands, and inflicted huge wastage on settlers and sojourners alike (at present our knowledge of this is heavily skewed towards the European experience). Disease might have determined the scale of the European presence in sub-Saharan Africa, the Caribbean, India, and South East Asia (and perhaps that of the Chinese in the pre-modern Nanyang). It helped to defeat the imperial reconquest of the rebellious colonies of the Americas.[4] Conversely, the intrusion of exotic diseases could decimate indigenous populations, clearing the way in temperate lands for settlers or sheep, and in the tropics for the importation of slave labour, themselves the involuntary vectors of new disease types. A large literature exists on the disease component of the 'Columbian exchange'—although the scale of depopulation has recently been challenged on the archaeological evidence for eastern North America.[5] As James Belich's chapter reminds us, the global effects of the 'Black Death' have also been closely examined. But much remains to be known about the complex relationship between society, culture, and epidemic disease.[6] Why, for example, when the risks were well known, did Europeans persist in migrating to seventeenth-century Jamaica, eighteenth-century India or nineteenth-century New Orleans, ravaged in mid-century by wave after wave of yellow fever? What was the response to epidemic disease in pre-colonial Asia or pre-literate Africa? How much do we know about the mobility of 'disease belts'—a key demographic constraint in colonial East Africa? Was it a coincidence that the devastation by rinderpest (cattle plague) of the pastoral economies of East Africa was closely followed by the imposition of colonial rule? How important (to widen the lens) is the impact of disease, epidemic or endemic, exotic or indigenous, upon religions, cosmologies, and systems of authority?

Contagion is also a useful way in which to imagine the spread of ideas. Like diseases, they needed vectors, and followed the traces of migration and trade. A fascination with the diffusion of ideas, especially religious ideas, is as old, perhaps, as historical curiosity itself. What can a 'global' perspective contribute to an already vast and sophisticated literature? Perhaps a number of viewpoints: firstly, it encourages us to see their human vectors in a comparative light, and to explore their often multiple roles as merchants, clerks, or 'crew', as well as scholars, missionaries, or teachers. In the commerce of ideas, as much as of goods or money, the part played by intermediaries, personal or institutional, is usually critical. Hence their emergence and fortunes are of great interest to the historian, not least because they varied so much across time and space. The mechanics of

    [4] See John R. McNeill, *Mosquito Empires: Ecology and War in the Greater Caribbean 1620–1914* (Cambridge and New York: Cambridge University Press, 2010).
    [5] See Audrey J. Horning, *Ireland in the Virginian Sea: Colonialism in the British Atlantic* (Chapel Hill: Omohundro Institute of Early American History & Culture, 2013), ch. 2.
    [6] For an excellent survey, Robert A. McGuire and Philip R. P. Coelho, *Parasites, Pathogens and Progress: Disease and Economic Development* (Cambridge, MA and London: MIT Press, 2011).

translation, in its literal and metaphorical senses, and the rise (and sometimes decline) of the lingua franca and pidgin that facilitated cross-cultural communication are, or should be, as intriguing to the historian as to the linguistic or literary scholar. They remind us that ideas, like most consumer items, were adapted to their local environment or hybridized by contact with other streams of influence. Yet such localization is not the whole story. In recent years, the making of what might be called a global intellectual culture has begun to draw scholarly attention to the period when (for example) the classic texts of the European Enlightenment or of Victorian Liberalism could circulate easily among Anglo-literate Indians.[7] But a global view will also alert us to the fact that in the nineteenth century, as in previous eras, the jet stream of ideas did not simply flow from west to east, or from the 'North' to the 'Global South'. Europeans consumed the ideas of other peoples and cultures, adapting and localizing them in their turn. Powerful new centres for the reception, re-making, and transmission of ideas sprang up in Asian cities like Bombay, Calcutta, Singapore, and Shanghai.

Global history does not always require us to think in globe-spanning terms, or struggle against the linguistic deficiencies that restrict all but a few to a close knowledge of two cultures at best. For many, if not most of us, the appeal of global history will lie in its capacity to enhance our knowledge of the 'local'. It was once an historical cliché, almost a default assumption, that most parts of the world, even most parts of Europe, existed before modern times in semi-, if not complete, isolation from the traffic of goods and ideas. We have learnt to mistrust this presumption. A large library now documents the existence of unsuspected connections and surprising mobilities. Much more of the world turns out to have been connected, if only spasmodically, to the electric current of ideas and shaped by the magnetism of commercial exchange. The default has shifted. Now we are more likely to assume that all but the 'remotest' (a term that has itself become suspect) communities owe their belief systems, their consumer preferences, even their choice of crops to cultivate and animals to keep, to influences far below their geographical or cultural horizon. The astonishing spread of maize cultivation across Africa and Asia is a mundane (but fascinating) example.[8] To an extent that would astonish historians of a generation or two ago, the global and the local have converged—to the intellectual benefit of both.

Global history—history on a global scale—is not an historical programme, still less a uniform approach to the history of the world. Its appeal and its value lie precisely in the multiple vistas it opens up, in the connections it suggests, in the questions it asks. 'An extensive sight or view; the view of the landscape from any position' was an early definition of 'prospect'. That might serve quite well to describe the prospect of global history.

---

[7] For a brilliant introduction to this theme, see C. A. Bayly, *Recovering Liberties: Indian Thought in the Age of Liberalism and Empire* (Cambridge: Cambridge University Press, 2012).

[8] See James C. McCann, *Maize and Grace: Africa's Encounter with a New World Crop* (Cambridge, MA: Harvard University Press, 2005).

Bibliography

PRIMARY SOURCES

British Library, IOR/L/PJ/9/12, file 536/20.

SECONDARY LITERATURE

Abbott, Andrew, *Time Matters: On Theory and Method* (Chicago and London: University of Chicago Press, 2001).

Aberth, John, *From the Brink of the Apocalypse: Confronting, Famine, War, Plague and Death in the Later Middle Ages*, 2nd edn (London and New York: Routledge, 2010).

Abramovitz, Moses, 'Catching Up, Forging Ahead, and Falling Behind', *Journal of Economic History* 46, 2 (1986), pp. 385–406.

Abulafia, David, 'Sugar in Spain', *European Review* 16, 2 (2008), pp. 191–210.

Abulafia, David, *The Great Sea: A Human History of the Mediterranean* (Oxford and New York: Oxford University Press, 2011).

Adams, Julia, Elisabeth S. Clemens, and Ann S. Orloff (eds), *Remaking Modernity: Politics, History, and Sociology* (Durham, NC: Duke University Press, 2005).

Adams, Julia, Elisabeth S. Clemens, and Ann S. Orloff, 'Introduction: Social Theory, Modernity, and the Three Waves of Historical Sociology', in Julia Adams, Elisabeth S. Clemens, and Ann S. Orloff (eds), *Remaking Modernity: Politics, History, and Sociology* (Durham, NC: Duke University Press, 2005), pp. 1–72.

Adolphsen, Mikael S., *The Gates of Power: Monks, Courtiers and Warriors in Premodern Japan* (Honolulu: University of Hawai'i Press, 2000).

Akkach, Samer, *Letters of a Sufi Scholar: The Correspondence of Abd al-Ghani al-Nabulusi (1641–1731)* (Leiden: Brill, 2010).

Alexander, John T., *Bubonic Plague in Early Modern Russia: Public Health and Urban Disaster* (New York: Oxford University Press, 2003 [1980]).

Allen, Robert C., 'The Great Divergence in European Wages and Prices from the Middle Ages to the First World War', *Explorations in Economic History* 38, 4 (2001), pp. 411–47.

Allen, Robert C., *Global Economic History: A Very Short Introduction* (Oxford: Oxford University Press 2011).

Allen, Robert C., Jean-Pascal Bassino, Debin Ma, Christine Moll-Murata, and Jan L. Van Zanden, 'Wages, Prices, and Living Standards in China, 1738–1925: In Comparison with Europe, Japan, and India', *The Economic History Review* 64 (2011), pp. 8–38.

Alston, Richard, 'Writing the Economic History of the Late Antique East: A Review', *Ancient West and East* 3, 1 (2004), pp. 124–36.

Andrade, Tonio, 'A Chinese Farmer, Two African Boys, and a Warlord: Toward a Global Microhistory', *Journal of World History* 21, 4 (2010), pp. 573–91.

Andrade, Tonio, 'Beyond Guns, Germs, and Steel: European Expansion and Maritime Asia, 1400–1750', *Journal of Early Modern History* 14, 1–2 (2010), pp. 165–86.

Ansari, Humayun, 'Islam in the West', in Francis Robinson (ed.), *The Islamic World in the Age of Western Dominance* (New Cambridge History of Islam V) (Cambridge: Cambridge University Press, 2010), pp. 686–716.

Antonson, Hans, 'The Extent of Farm Desertion in Central Sweden during the Late Medieval Agrarian Crisis: Landscape as a Source', *Journal of Historical Geography* 35, 4 (2009), pp. 619–41.

Antràs, Pol, and Hans-Joachim Voth, 'Factor Prices and Productivity Growth during the British Industrial Revolution', *Explorations in Economic History* 40, 1 (2003), pp. 52–77.

Armitage, David, 'John Locke, Carolina, and the Two Treatises of Government', *Political Theory* 32, 5 (2004), pp. 602–27.

Armitage, David, *The Declaration of Independence: A Global History* (Cambridge, MA: Harvard University Press, 2007).

Armitage, David, 'Globalizing Jeremy Bentham', *History of Political Thought* 32, 1 (2011), pp. 63–82.

Armitage, David, and Sanjay Subrahmanyam (eds), *The Age of Revolutions in Global Context, c. 1760–1840* (New York: Palgrave Macmillan, 2010).

Árnason, Jóhann P., *Civilizations in Dispute: Historical Questions and Theoretical Traditions* (Leiden: Brill, 2003).

Árnason, Jóhann P. and Björn Wittrock (eds), *Eurasian Transformations, Tenth to Thirteenth Centuries: Crystallizations, Divergences, Renaissances* (Leiden: Brill, 2004).

Artzy, Michal, 'Incense, Camels and Collared Rim Jars: Desert Trade Routes and Maritime Outlets in the Second Millennium', *Oxford Journal of Archaeology* 13, 2 (1994), pp. 121–47.

Ashtor, Eliyahu, *Histoire des prix et des salaires dans l'Orient médiéval* (Paris: S.E.V.P.E.N., 1969).

Ashtor, Eliyahu, 'Spice Prices in the Near East in the 15th Century', *Journal of the Royal Asiatic Society (New Series)* 1 (1976), pp. 26–41.

Ashtor, Eliyahu, 'The Volume of Mediaeval Spice Trade', *Journal of European Economic History* 9, 3 (1980), pp. 753–63.

Ashtor, Eliyahu, *Levant Trade in the Later Middle Ages* (Princeton: Princeton University Press, 1983).

Aslanian, Sebouh David, 'How Size Matters: The Question of Scale in History', *American Historical Review* 118, 5 (2013), pp. 1431–72.

Atwell, William S., 'Notes on Silver, Foreign Trade, and the Late Ming Economy', *Ch'ing-shih wen-t'i* 3, 8 (1977), pp. 1–33.

Atwell, William S., 'Some Observations on the "Seventeenth Century Crisis" in China and Japan', *Journal of Asian Studies* 45, 2 (1986), pp. 223–44.

Austin, Granville, *The Indian Constitution: Cornerstone of a Nation* (Oxford: Clarendon Press, 1966).

Avanzini, Alessandra (ed.), *Profumi d'Arabia* (Rome: L'Erma di Bretschneider, 1997).

Avanzini, Alessandra, *A Port in Arabia between Rome and the Indian Ocean: Khor Rori* (Rome: L'Erma di Bretschneider, 2008).

Avanzini, Alessandra, *Eastern Arabia in the First Millennium BC* (Rome: L'Erma di Bretschneider, 2010).

Azra, Azyumardi, *The Origins of Islamic Reformism in Southeast Asia: Networks of Malay-Indonesian and Middle East Ulama in the Seventeenth and Eighteenth Centuries* (Crows Nest NSU: Allen & Unwin, 2004).

Bacci, Massimo Livi, *Conquest: The Destruction of the American Indios* (Cambridge: Polity Press, 2008 [2005]).

Bailyn, Bernard, *The Ordeal of Thomas Hutchinson* (Cambridge, MA: Belknap Press, 1974).

Bairoch, Paul, and Susan Burke, 'European Trade Policy, 1815–1914', in Peter Mathias and Sidney Pollard (eds), *The Cambridge Economic History of Europe from the Decline of the Roman Empire, vol. 8: The Industrial Economies: The Development of Economic and Social Policies* (Cambridge: Cambridge University Press, 1989), pp. 1–160.

Barata, Filipe Themudo, 'Portugal and the Mediterranean Trade: A Prelude to the Discovery of the "New World"', *Al-Masaq: Islam and the Medieval Mediterranean* 17, 2 (2005), pp. 205–19.

Barkey, Karen, 'Historical Sociology', in Peter Hedström and Peter Bearman (eds), *The Oxford Handbook of Analytical Sociology* (Oxford: Oxford University Press, 2009), pp. 712–33.

Barro, Robert J., 'Economic Growth in a Cross-Section of Countries', *Quarterly Journal of Economics* 106, 2 (1991), pp. 407–43.

Barrow, Ian J., *Surveying and Mapping in Colonial Sri Lanka* (New Delhi: Oxford University Press, 2008).

Baumann, Zygmunt, *Liquid Modernity* (Cambridge: Polity Press, 2000).

Bayly, C. A., *Imperial Meridian: The British Empire and the World, 1780–1830* (London: Longman, 1989).

Bayly, C. A., 'Rammohan Roy and the Advent of Constitutional Liberalism in India, 1800–30', *Modern Intellectual History* 4, 1 (2007), pp. 25–41.

Bayly, C. A., *Recovering Liberties: Indian Thought in the Age of Liberalism and Empire* (Cambridge: Cambridge University Press, 2012).

Beaujard, Philippe, *Les mondes de l'océan Indien*, vol. 1 (Paris: A. Colin, 2014).

Beazley, C. Raymond, 'The Russian Expansion towards Asia and the Arctic in the Middle Ages (to 1500)', *American Historical Review* 13, 4 (1908), pp. 731–41.

Beckert, Sven, *Empire of Cotton: A New History of Global Capitalism* (London: Allen Lane, 2014).

Bedrosian, Robert, 'China and the Chinese According to 5th–13th Century Classical Armenian Sources', *Armenian Review* 34, 1–133 (1981), pp. 17–24.

Behl, Aditya, and Wendy Doniger (eds), *The Magic Doe: Qutban Suhravardi's Mirigavati: A New Translation by Aditya Behl* (New York: Oxford University Press, 2012).

Belmont, Perry, 'Congress, the President and the Philippines', *North American Review* 169 (1899), p. 901.

Belting, Hans, *Florence and Baghdad: Renaissance Art and Arab Science*, trans. Deborah Lucas Schneider (Cambridge, MA: Harvard University Press, 2011).

Bender, Thomas, *A Nation among Nations: America's Place in World History* (New York: Hill and Wang, 2006).

Benedictow, Ole J., *The Black Death 1346–1353: The Complete History* (Woodbridge, Suffolk: Boydell Press, 2004).

Benite, Zvi Ben-Dor, *The Dao of Muhammad: A Cultural History of Muslims in Late Imperial China* (Cambridge, MA: Harvard University Asia Center, 2005).

Benjamin, Walter, *The Work of Art in the Age of Mechanical Reproduction*, trans. J. A. Underwood (London: Penguin Books, 2008).

Bentley, Jerry H., *Old-World Encounters: Cross-Cultural Contacts and Exchanges in Pre-Modern Times* (New York and Oxford: Oxford University Press, 1993).

Bentley, Jerry H., 'Cross-Cultural Interaction and Periodization in World History', *American Historical Review* 101, 3 (1996), pp. 749–70.

Bentley, Jerry H., 'Sea and Ocean Basins as Frameworks of Historical Analysis', *Geographical Review* 89, 2 (1999), pp. 215–24.

Bentley, Jerry H. (ed.), *The Oxford Handbook of World History* (Oxford: Oxford University Press, 2011).

Bentley, Michael, 'Henry Hallam Revisited', *Historical Journal* 55, 2 (2012), pp. 453–73.

Berg, Maxine (ed.), *Writing the History of the Global: Challenges for the Twenty-First Century* (Oxford: Oxford University Press, 2013).

Biedermann, Zoltán, 'An Island under the Influence: Soqotra at the Crossroads of Egypt, Persia and India from Antiquity to the Early Modern Age', in Ralph Kauz (ed.), *Aspects of the Maritime Silk Road: From the Persian Gulf to the East China Sea* (Wiesbaden: Harrassowitz, 2010), pp. 9–24.

Billias, George Athan, *American Constitutionalism Heard around the World, 1776–1989: A Global Perspective* (New York: New York University Press, 2009).

Binbas, I. Evrim, 'Sharaf al-Din Ali Yazdi (ca. 770s–858/ca. 1370s–1454): Prophecy, Politics and Historiography in Late Medieval Islamic Historiography' (unpublished PhD thesis: University of Chicago, 2009).

Bira, Sh., *Mongolian Historical Literature of the XVII–XIX Centuries Written in Tibetan*, trans. Stanley Frye (Bloomington: Tibet Society, 1970).

Bonnett, Alastair, *The Idea of the West: Culture, Politics and History* (Basingstoke: Palgrave Macmillan, 2004).

Borsch, Stuart J., *The Black Death in Egypt and England: A Comparative Study* (Austin: University of Texas Press, 2005).

Bos, Kirsten I., et al., 'A Draft Genome of Yersinia Pestis from Victims of the Black Death,' *Nature* 478, 7370 (2011), pp. 506–10.

Bosworth, Clifford E., et al. (eds), *The Encyclopaedia of Islam*, 10 vols, 2nd edn (Leiden: Brill, 1967–2000).

Bottenburg, Maarten van, *Global Games*, trans. Beverley Jackson (Urbana, IL and Chicago: University of Illinois Press, 2001).

Bournazel, Eric, and Jean-Pierre Poly (eds), *Les féodalités* (Paris: Presses Universitaires de France, 1998).

Bowden, Brett, *The Empire of Civilization: The Evolution of an Imperial Idea* (Chicago and London: University of Chicago Press, 2009).

Bowersock, Glenn, *Roman Arabia* (Cambridge, MA: Harvard University Press 1983).

Braudel, Fernand, *Capitalism and Material Life* (London, 1973 [Paris, 1967]).

Braudel, Fernand, *Civilization and Capitalism. 15th to 18th Century*, trans. Siân Reynolds, 2 vols (London: Fontana, 1981–4).

Braudel, Fernand, *The Mediterranean and the Mediterranean World in the Age of Philip II*, 3 vols, trans. Siân Reynolds (Berkeley: University of California Press, 1995 [1972]).

Braudel, Fernand, and Frank Spooner, 'Prices in Europe from 1450 to 1750', in Edwin E. Rich and Charles H. Wilson (eds), *The Cambridge Economic History of Europe from the Decline of the Roman Empire, vol. 4: The Economy of Expanding Europe in the Sixteenth and Seventeenth Centuries* (Cambridge: Cambridge University Press, 1967), pp. 374–486.

Brekke, Torkel, *Makers of Modern Indian Religion in the Late Nineteenth Century* (Oxford: Clarendon Press, 2002).

Breslin, Beau, *From Words to Worlds: Exploring Constitutional Functionality* (Baltimore: Johns Hopkins University Press, 2009).

Briant, Pierre, *État et pasteurs au Moyen-Orient ancien* (Cambridge and Paris: Cambridge University Press and Maison des sciences de l'homme, 1982).

Broadberry, Stephen, Bruce M. S. Campbell, and Bas van Leeuwen, 'English Medieval Population: Reconciling Times Series and Cross-Sectional Evidence', University of Warwick Working Paper, 27 July 2010, <http://www2.warwick.ac.uk/fac/soc/economics/staff/academic/broadberry/wp/medievalpopulation7.pdf> (accessed 26 June 2015).

Broadberry, Stephen N., and Bishnupriya Gupta, 'The Early Modern Great Divergence: Wages, Prices and Economic Development in Europe and Asia, 1500–1800', *Economic History Review* 59,1 (2006), pp. 2–31.

Broadberry, Stephen N., and Kevin H. O'Rourke (eds), *The Cambridge Economic History of Modern Europe, vol. 2: 1870 to the Present* (New York: Cambridge University Press 2010).

Broadberry, Stephen N., 'Accounting for the Great Divergence', LSE Department of Economic History Working Paper 184 (2013).

Brocke, Bernhard vom, *Kurt Breysig: Geschichtswissenschaft zwischen Historismus und Soziologie* (Lübeck: Matthiesen, 1971).

Broodbank, Cyprian, *The Making of the Middle Sea* (London: Thames and Hudson, 2013).

Brophy, David, 'The Kings of Xinjiang: Muslim Elites and the Qing Empire', *Études Orientales: Revue Culturelle Semestrielle* 25 (2008), pp. 69–90.

Brophy, David, 'The Oirat in Eastern Turkistan and the Rise of Āfāq Khwāja', *Archivum Eurasiae Medii Aevi* 16 (2008/2009), pp. 5–28.

Brown, Nathan J., *Constitutions in a Nonconstitutional World: Arab Basic Laws and the Prospects for Accountable Government* (Albany, NY: State University of New York Press, 2002).

Browning, Robert, 'The Lost Leader', in Robert Browning, *Dramatic Romances and Lyrics* (London: Edward Moxon, 1845).

Bruinsma, Jelle (ed.), *World Agriculture towards 2015/2030: An FAO Perspective* (London: Earthscan Publications, 2003).

Bühl, Walter L., *Historische Soziologie: Theoreme und Methoden* (Münster: LIT Verlag, 2003).

Bulbeck, David, Anthony Reid, Lay Cheng Tan, and Yigi Wu, *Southeast Asian Exports since the 14th Century: Cloves, Pepper, Coffee and Sugar* (Leiden and Singapore: KITLV Press/ Institute of Southeast Asian Studies, 1998).

Bull, Marcus, 'Origins', in Jonathan S. C. Riley-Smith (ed.), *Oxford History of the Crusades* (Oxford: Oxford University Press, 1999), pp. 15–34.

Bulliet, Richard W., *Cotton, Climate, and Camels in Early Islamic Iran: A Moment in World History* (New York: Columbia University Press, 2009).

Burke, Edmund III, and Marshall G. S. Hodgson (eds), *Rethinking World History: Essays on Europe, Islam, and World History* (Cambridge: Cambridge University Press, 1993).

Burke, Peter, *Cultural Hybridity* (Cambridge and Malden, MA: Polity Press, 2009).

Burnett, Christina Duffy, 'Continent Constitutions: Empire and Law in the Americas', (unpublished PhD thesis: Princeton University, 2010).

Burns, Eric, *The Smoke of the Gods: A Social History of Tobacco* (Philadephia: Temple University Press, 2007).

Bush, George W., 'A Distinctly American Internationalism', speech delivered in the Ronald Reagan Presidential Library, Simi Valley, California, 19 November 1999.

Byrne, Joseph P., *Encyclopedia of the Black Death* (Santa Barbara: ABC-CLIO, 2012).

Caferro, William P., 'Warfare and Economy in Renaissance Italy, 1350–1450', *Journal of Interdisciplinary History* 39, 2 (2008), pp. 167–209.

Calhoun, Craig, 'The Rise and Domestication of Historical Sociology', in Terrence J. McDonald (ed.), *The Historic Turn in the Human Sciences* (Ann Arbor: University of Michigan Press, 1996).

Carannante, Alfredo and D'Acunto, Matteo (eds.), *I profumi nelle società antiche: produzione, commercio, usi, valori simbolici* (Salerno: Pandemos, 2012).

Carrington, Dorothy, 'The Corsican Constitution of Pasquale Paoli (1755–1769)', *English Historical Review* 88, 348 (1973), pp. 481–503.

Carte de l'Asie Septentrionale [...] du temps de la grande invasion [...] de Zingis-Chan, pour servir à l'histoire généalogique des Tatars (1726), <http://gallica.bnf.fr/ark:/12148/btv1b84688533> (accessed 4 June 2014).

Carwardine, Richard, and Jay Sexton (eds), *The Global Lincoln* (New York: Oxford University Press, 2011).

Casale, Giancarlo, *The Ottoman Age of Exploration* (Oxford and New York: Oxford University Press, 2010).

Caseau, Béatrice, '*Euodia*: The Use and Meaning of Fragrances in the Ancient World and their Christianization (100–900 AD)', PhD dissertation: University of Princeton, 1994.

Casparis, John, 'The Swiss Mercenary System: Labor Emigration from the Semiperiphery', *Review* (Fernand Braudel Center) 5, 4 (1982), pp. 593–642.

Castells, Manuel, *The Information Age: Economy, Society, and Culture*, 3 vols (Oxford: Blackwell, 1996–98).

Castoriadis, Cornelius, *The Imaginary Institution of Society* (Cambridge: Polity Press, 1997 [French 1975]).

Chamberlain, Michael, *Knowledge and Social Practice in Medieval Damascus, 1190–1350* (Cambridge: Cambridge University Press, 1994).

Chandler, Graham, 'Sugar Please', *Saudi Aramco World* 83, 4 (2012), pp. 36–43.

Chartier, Roger, 'La conscience de la globalité', *Annales HSS* 56, 1 (2001), pp. 119–23.

Chattopadhya, Brajadulal, *The Making of Early Medieval India* (New Delhi: Oxford University Press, 1994).

Chaudhuri, Kirti N., *Trade and Civilisation in the Indian Ocean* (Cambridge: Cambridge University Press, 1985).

Chaudhuri, Kirti N., *Asia before Europe* (Cambridge: Cambridge University Press, 1990).

Chaudhury, Sushil, 'Trading Networks in a Traditional Diaspora: Armenians in India *c.*1600–1800' in Ina B. McCabe, Gelina Harlaftis, and Ioanna P. Minoglou (eds), *Diaspora Entrepreneurial Networks: Four Centuries of History* (Oxford: Berg, 2005), pp. 51–72.

Childe, V. Gordon, *What Happened in History* (Harmondsworth: Penguin, 1942).

Chouvy, Pierre-Arnaud, *Opium: Uncovering the Politics of the Poppy* (Cambridge, MA: Harvard University Press, 2010).

Chow, Kai-Wing, 'Writing for Success: Printing, Examinations and Intellectual Change in Late Ming China', *Late Imperial China* 17, 1 (1996), pp. 120–57.

Christian, David, 'Silk Roads or Steppe Roads? The Silk Roads in World History', *Journal of World History* 11, 1 (2000), pp. 1–26.

Ciment, James, *Another America: The Story of Liberia and the Former Slaves Who Ruled It* (New York: Hill and Wang, 2013).

Clark, Gregory, *A Farewell to Alms: A Brief Economic History of the World* (Princeton and Oxford: Princeton University Press, 2007).

Clark, Gregory, Kevin H. O'Rourke, and Alan M. Taylor, 'The Growing Dependence of Britain on Trade During the Industrial Revolution', *Scandinavian Economic History Review* 62, 2 (2014), pp. 109–36.

Clark, Hugh R., *Community, Trade and Networks. Southern Fujian Province from the Third to the Thirteenth Century* (Cambridge: Cambridge University Press, 1991).

Clark, Hugh R., 'Frontier Discourse and China's Maritime Frontier: China's Frontiers and the Encounter with the Sea through Early Imperial History', *Journal of World History* 20, 1 (2009), pp. 1–33.

Clunas, Craig, Jessica Harrison-Hall, and Yu-Ping Luk (eds), *Ming China: Courts and Contacts 1400–1450* (London: British Museum Press, forthcoming 2016).

Cohn, Samuel K. Jr, *The Black Death Transformed: Disease and Culture in Early Renaissance Europe* (London: Arnold, 2002).

Cole, Arthur H., and Ruth Crandall, 'The International Scientific Committee on Price History', *Journal of Economic History* 24, 3 (1964), pp. 380–6.

Cole, Juan, *Napoleon's Egypt: Invading the Middle East* (New York: Palgrave Macmillan, 2007).

Colley, Linda, *Captives: Britain, Empire, and the World 1600–1850* (New York: Anchor Books, 2004).

Colley, Linda, 'Empires of Writing: Britain, America and Constitutions, 1776–1848', *Law and History Review*, 32, 2 (2014), pp. 237–66.

Collins, Randall, *Macrohistory: Essays in Sociology of the Long Run* (Stanford, CA: Stanford University Press, 1999).

Comaroff, John L., 'Colonialism, Culture and the Law: A Foreword', *Law & Social Inquiry* 26, 2 (2001), pp. 305–14.

Comentale, Christophe, 'Une Carte Inédite de Père Antoine Gaubil, S. J.: Chine et Tartarie', in *Chine et Europe: Évolution et Particularités des Rapports Est-Ouest de XVIe au XXe Siècle* (Paris: Institute Ricci, 1991).

Conason, Alexis, 'Is Abstinence the Best Treatment for Sugar Addiction?' *Psychology Today* (4 April 2012), <https://www.psychologytoday.com/blog/eating-mindfully/201204/sugar-addiction> (accessed 28 January 2015).

Conrad, Sebastian, 'Enlightenment in Global History: A Historiographical Critique', *American Historical Review* 117, 4 (2012), pp. 999–1027.

Conrad, Sebastian, *Globalgschichte: Eine Einführung* (München: C. H. Beck, 2013).

Conrad, Sebastian, Andreas Eckert, and Ulrike Freitag (eds), *Globalgeschichte. Theorien, Ansätze, Themen* (Frankfurt a.M. and New York: Campus, 2007).

Crone, Patricia, *Meccan Trade and the Rise of Islam* (Oxford: Oxford University Press, 1986).

Crosby, Alfred W., 'An Ecohistory of the Canary Islands', *Environmental Review* 8, 3 (1984), pp. 214–35.

Crosby, Alfred W., *Ecological Imperialism. The Biological Expansion of Europe, 900–1900* (Cambridge: Cambridge University Press, 1986).

Crowe, David M., *A History of the Gypsies of Eastern Europe and Russia* (New York: St Martin's Press, 1995).

Curta, Florin, 'Merovingian and Carolingian Gift-Giving', *Speculum* 81, 3 (2006), pp. 671–99.

Curtin, Philip D., *Cross-Cultural Trade in World History* (Cambridge: Cambridge University Press, 1984).

Dai, Yingcong, 'A Disguised Defeat: The Myanmar Campaign of the Qing Dynasty', *Modern Asian Studies* 38, 1 (2004), pp. 145–89.

Darwin, John, *After Tamerlane. The Rise and Fall of Global Empires, 1400–2000* (London: Penguin, 2007).

Davis, Edward L., *Society and the Supernatural in Song China* (Honolulu: University of Hawai'i Press, 2001).

Davis, Kathleen, *Periodization and Sovereignty: How Ideas of Feudalism and Secularization Govern the Politics of Time* (Philadelphia: University of Pennylvania Press, 2008).

Davis, Natalie Z., 'Decentering History: Local Stories and Cultural Crossings in a Global World', *History and Theory* 50, 2 (2011), pp. 188–202.

De Romanis, Federico, *Cassia, cinnamomo, ossidiana: uomini e merci tra Oceano Indico e Mediterraneo* (Rome: L'Erma di Bretschneider, 1996).

De Vries, Jan, 'The Limits of Globalization in the Early Modern World', *The Economic History Review* 63, 3 (2010), pp. 710–33.

Delanty, Gerard, and Engin F. Isin (eds), *Handbook of Historical Sociology* (London: Sage, 2003).

Deng, Kent G., 'Miracle or Mirage? Foreign Silver, China's Economy and Globalization from the Sixteenth to the Nineteenth Centuries', *Pacific Economic Review* 13, 3 (2008), pp. 320–58.

Deutschmann, Moritz, 'Cultures of Statehood, Cultures of Revolution: Caucasian Revolutionaries in the Iranian Constitutional Movement, 1906–1911', *Ab Imperio* 2 (2013), pp. 165–90.

Devereux, Robert, *The First Ottoman Constitutional Period: A Study of the Midhat Constitution and Parliament* (Baltimore: Johns Hopkins University Press, 1963).

Di, Li (ed.), *Kangxi jixia gewu bian yizhu* (Shanghai: Shanghai guji chubanshe, 1993).

Diamond, Larry, 'A Report Card on Democracy', *Hoover Digest* 3 (2000).

Duby, Georges, *The Three Orders: Feudal Society Imagined* (Chicago and London: Chicago University Press, 1980).

Dudbridge, Glen, *Religious Experience and Lay Society in T'ang China* (Cambridge: Cambridge University Press, 1995).

Dudoignon, Stéphane A., *Voyage au pays des Baloutches (Iran oriental, an XVIII–XXI siècle—de la République Islamique)* (Paris: Editions Cartouche, 2009).

Durkheim, Emile and Marcel Mauss, 'Note sur la notion de civilisation', in Marcel Mauss, *Œuvres, vol. II: Réprésentations collectives et diversité des civilisations*, ed. by Victor Karady (Paris: Minuit, 1969), pp. 451–5.

Earle, Peter, *Sailors: English Merchant Seamen 1650–1775* (London: Methuen, 1998).

Easley, David, and Jon Kleinberg, *Networks, Crowds and Markets: Reasoning about a Highly Connected World* (Cambridge: Cambridge University Press, 2010).

Echeverria, Durand, 'French Publications of the Declaration of Independence and the American Constitutions, 1776–1783', *Papers of the Biographical Society of America* 47 (1953).

Edens, Christopher, and Garth Bawden, 'History of Tayma: and Hejazi Trade during the First Millennium BC', *Journal of the Economic and Social History of the Orient* 32, 1 (1989), pp. 48–103.

Edney, Matthew H., *Mapping an Empire: The Geographical Construction of British India 1765–1843* (Chicago and London: University of Chicago Press, 1997).

Edvardsson, Ragnar, 'The Role of Marine Resources in the Medieval Economy of Vestfirðir, Iceland' (unpublished PhD thesis: City University of New York, 2010).

Eisenstadt, Shmuel N., 'Multiple Modernities', *Daedalus* 129, 1 (2000), pp. 1–30.

Eisenstadt, Shmuel N., 'Civilizations', in *International Encyclopedia of the Social and Behavioral Sciences, vol. III* (Amsterdam: Elsevier, 2001) pp. 1915–21.

Eisenstadt, Shmuel N., 'Some Observations on Multiple Modernities', in Dominic Sachsenmaier, Jens Riedel, and Shmuel N. Eisenstadt (eds), *Reflections on Multiple Modernities: European, Chinese and Other Interpretations* (Leiden: Brill, 2002), pp. 28–41.

Eisenstadt, Shmuel N., *Comparative Civilizations and Multiple Modernities*, 2 vols (Leiden: Brill, 2003).

Eliav-Feldon, Miriam, Benjamin Isaac, and Joseph Ziegler (eds), *The Origins of Racism in the West* (Cambridge and New York: Cambridge University Press, 2009).

Elkins, Zachary, 'Diffusion and the Constitutionalization of Europe', *Comparative Political Studies* 43, 8–9 (2010), pp. 969–99.

Elkins, Zachary, and Tom Ginsberg, *The Endurance of National Constitutions* (Cambridge: Cambridge University Press, 2009).

Ellenblum, Ronnie, *The Collapse of the Eastern Mediterranean: Climate Change and the Decline of the East, 950–1072* (Cambridge: Cambridge University Press, 2012).

Elliott, John, '"Spaniards of Both Hemispheres": A Constitution for an Empire' (unpublished essay: University of Oxford).

Elman, Benjamin A., 'One Classic and Two Classical Traditions: The Recovery and Transmission of the Lost Edition of the Analects', *Monumenta Nipponica* 64, 1 (2009), pp. 53–82.

Elverskog, Johan, *The Pearl Rosary: Mongol Historiography in Early Nineteenth Century Ordos* (Bloomington: The Mongolia Society, 2007).

Elverskog, Johan, 'Wutai Shan, Qing Cosmopolitanism, and the Mongols', *Journal of the International Association of Tibetan Studies* 6 (2011), pp. 243–74.

Elvin, Mark, *The Pattern of the Chinese Past* (Stanford, CA: Stanford University Press, 1973).

Elvin, Mark, *The Retreat of the Elephants: An Environmental History of China* (New Haven and London: Yale University Press, 2004).

Enthoven, Victor, 'Dutch Crossings: Migration between the Netherlands and the New World, 1600–1800', *Atlantic Studies* 2, 2 (2005), pp. 153–76.

Epplett, Christopher, 'The Capture of Animals by the Roman Military', *Greece & Rome* 48, 2 (2001), pp. 210–22.

Epstein, Stephan R., *Freedom and Growth: The Rise of States and Markets in Europe, 1300–1750* (London and New York: Routledge, 2000).

Erika, Masuda, 'The Fall of Ayutthaya and Siam's Disrupted Order of Tribute to China (1767–1782)', *Taiwan Journal of Southeast Asian Studies* 4, 2 (2007), pp. 75–128.

ESI, 'Islamic Calvinists: Change and Conservatism in Central Anatolia', Berlin/Istanbul, 19 September 2005, <http://www.esiweb.org> (accessed 31 January 2015).

Evershed, Richard P., et al., 'Archaeological Frankincense', *Nature* 390, 6661 (1997), pp. 667–8.

Fagan, Brian, *Fish on Friday: Feasting, Fasting and the Discovery of the New World* (New York: Basic Books, 2006).

Fairbank, J. K. and S. Y. Têng, 'On the Ch'ing Tributary System', *Harvard Journal of Asiatic Studies* 6, 2 (1941), pp. 135–246.

Farooqi, Musharraf Ali, and Hamid Dabashi (eds), *The Adventures of Amir Hamza: Lord of the Auspicious Planetary Conjunction* by Ghalib Lakhnavi and Abdullah Bilgrami (New York: Modern Library, 2007).

Fasolt, Constantin, 'Hegel's Ghost: Europe, the Reformation and the Middle Ages', *Viator* 39, 1 (2008), pp. 345–86.

Fasolt, Constantin, *Past Sense: Studies in Medieval and Early Modern History* (Leiden: Brill, 2014).

Febvre, Lucien, *La terre et l'evolution humaine* (Paris: Renaissance du livre, 1922).

Feinstein, Charles, 'Capital Formation in Great Britain', in Peter Mathias and Michael M. Postan (eds), *The Cambridge Economic History of Europe from the Decline of the Roman Empire, vol. 7: The Industrial Economies: Capital, Labour and Enterprise* (Cambridge: Cambridge University Press, 2008), pp. 28–96.

Ferguson, Niall, *Civilization: The West and the Rest* (London: Allen Lane, 2011).

Findlay, Ronald, and Kevin H. O'Rourke, *Power and Plenty: Trade, War, and the World Economy in the Second Millennium* (Princeton and Oxford: Princeton University Press, 2007).

Fine, John V. A., *The Late Medieval Balkans: A Critical Survey from the Late Twelfth Century to the Ottoman Conquest* (Ann Arbor: University of Michigan Press, 1987).

Finlay, Robert, 'The Pilgrim Art: The Culture of Porcelain in World History', *Journal of World History* 9, 2 (1998), pp. 141–87.

Fischer-Tiné, Harald, 'Indian Nationalism and the 'World Forces': Transnational and Diasporic Dimensions of the Indian Freedom Movement on the Eve of the First World War', *Journal of Global History* 2, 3 (2007), pp. 325–44.

Florovsky, Anthony, 'Maps of the Siberian Route of the Belgian Jesuit, A. Thomas (1690)', *Imago Mundi* 8 (1951), pp. 103–8.

Floud, Roderick, and Donald N. McCloskey (eds), *The Economic History of Britain since 1700* (Cambridge and New York: Cambridge University Press 1981).

Flynn, Dennis O., and Arturo Giráldez, 'Born with a "Silver Spoon": The Origin of World Trade in 1571', *Journal of World History* 6, 2 (1995), pp. 201–21.

Flynn, Dennis O., and Arturo Giráldez, 'Path Dependence, Time Lags and the Birth of Globalisation: A Critique of O'Rourke and Williamson', *European Review of Economic History* 8, 1 (2004), pp. 81–108.

Fogel, Joshua A., and Peter Zarrow (eds), *Imagining the People: Chinese Intellectuals and the Concept of Citizenship, 1890–1920* (New York: M. E. Sharpe, 1997).

Forrest, Alan, *Napoleon: Life, Legacy, and Image. A Biography* (New York: St Martin's Griffin, 2013).

Foss, Theodore, 'A Western Interpretation of China: Jesuit Cartography', in Charles E. Ronan and Bonnie B. C. Oh (eds), *East Meets West: The Jesuits in China, 1582–1773* (Chicago: Loyola University Press, 1988).

Foucault, Michel, *Discipline and Punish: The Birth of the Prison* (New York: Random House, 1995).

Frank, Andre Gunder, *ReOrient: Global Economy in the Asian Age* (Berkeley: University of California Press, 1998).

Freedman, Paul, 'Spices and Late-Medieval European Ideas of Scarcity and Value', *Speculum* 80, 4 (2005), pp. 1209–27.

Freedman, Paul, *Out of the East: Spices and the Medieval Imagination* (New Haven and London: Yale University Press, 2008).

Frye, Richard N., *The Golden Age of Persia: The Arabs in the East* (London: Weidenfeld & Nicolson, 1975).

Frymer, Paul, 'Building an American Empire: Territorial Expansion in the Antebellum Era', UC Irvine Law Review, 1, 3 (2011), pp. 913–54.

Fusaro, Maria, 'Maritime History as Global History? The Methodological Challenges and a Future Research Agenda', in Maria Fusaro and Amélia Polónia (eds), *Maritime History as Global History* (St John's, Newfoundland: International Maritime Economic History Association, 2010), pp. 267–82.

Fynn-Paul, Jeffrey, 'Empire, Monotheism and Slavery in the Greater Mediterranean Region from Antiquity to the Early Modern Era', *Past & Present* 205, 1 (2009), pp. 3–40.

Galligan, Denis J., and Mila Versteeg, *Social and Political Foundations of Constitutions* (Cambridge: Cambridge University Press, 2013).

Galloway, J. H., *The Sugar Cane Industry: An Historical Geography from its Origins to 1914* (Cambridge and New York: Cambridge University Press, 1989).

Garraway, Doris L., 'Empire of Freedom, Kingdom of Civilization: Henry Christophe, the Baron de Vastey, and the Paradoxes of Universalism in Post-Revolutionary Haiti', *Small Axe* 16, 339 (2012), pp. 1–21.

Gaubil, Antoine, *Correspondance de Pékin, 1722–1759*, ed. Renée Simon (Geneva: Librairie Droz, 1970).

Gavin, Robert J., 'Palmerston's Policy towards East and West Africa, 1830–1865' (unpublished PhD thesis: University of Cambridge, 1958).

Geary, Patrick J., *The Myth of Nations: The Medieval Origins of Europe* (Princeton: Princeton University Press, 2002).

Gellner, Ernest, *Plough, Sword and Book: The Structure of Human History* (London: Collins Harvill, 1988).

Gelvin, James and Nile Green (eds), *Global Muslims in the Age of Steam and Print* (Berkeley: University of California Press, 2014).

Gernet, Jacques, *Buddhism in Chinese Society: An Economic History from the Fifth to the Tenth Centuries* (New York: Columbia University Press, 1995).

Gernet, Jean, *A History of Chinese Civilization* (Cambridge: Cambridge University Press, 1982).

Ghangha-yin urusqal (Hohhot: Nei Menggu renmin chubanshe, 1980).

Ghosh, Amitav, *Sea of Poppies* (London: John Murray, 2008).

Ghosh, Amitav, *River of Smoke: A Novel* (London: Penguin Group, 2011).

Gibb, Hamilton A. R., *Encyclopaedia of Islam*, 2nd edn (Leiden: Brill, 1967).

Gibbon, Edward, *The History of the Decline and Fall of the Roman Empire* (New York: Fred de Fau and Co., 1907).

Goderis, Benedikt, and Mila Versteeg, 'The Transnational Origins of Constitutions: Evidence from a New Global Data Set on Constitutional Rights', Discussion Paper (Center for Economic Research, Tilburg University, 2013).

Godley, Michael R., *The Mandarin-Capitalists from Nanyang: Overseas Chinese Enterprise in the Modernization of China 1893–1911* (Cambridge: Cambridge University Press, 1981).

Goetz, Walter (ed.): *Propyläen-Weltgeschichte: Der Werdegang der Menschheit in Gesellschaft und Staat, Wirtschaft und Geistesleben*, 10 vols (Berlin: Propyläen, 1931–3).

Goldblatt, David, *The Ball Is Round: A Global History of Football* (London: Viking, 2006).

Goldstone, Jack A., *Why Europe? The Rise of the West in World History, 1500–1850* (Boston, MA: McGraw-Hill, 2008).

Goldthwaite, Richard A., *The Economy of Renaissance Florence* (Baltimore: Johns Hopkins University Press, 2009).

Golove, David M., and Daniel J. Hulsebosch, 'A Civilized Nation: The Early American Constitution, the Law of Nations, and the Pursuit of International Recognition', *New York University Law Review* 85, 4 (2010), pp. 932–1066.

Gommans, Jos, *Mughal Warfare: Indian Frontiers and High Roads to Empire, 1500–1700* (London and New York: Routledge, 2002).

Gongzhongdang Yongzheng chao zouzhe (Taibei: Guoli Gugong bowuyuan, 1977).

Goody, Jack, *The East in the West* (Cambridge: Cambridge University Press, 1996).

Goody, Jack, *The Theft of History* (Cambridge: Cambridge University Press, 2006).

Graf, David F., *Rome and the Arabian Frontier: From the Nabataeans to the Saracens* (Aldershot: Ashgate, 1997).

Green, Nile, *Bombay Islam: The Religious Economy of the Western Indian Ocean 1840–1915* (Cambridge: Cambridge University Press, 2011).

Green, William A., 'Periodization in European and World History', *Journal of World History* 3, 1 (1992), pp. 13–53.

Grimké, Frederick, *Considerations upon the Nature and Tendency of Free Institutions* (Cincinnati: H. W. Derby & Co, 1848).

Groom, Nigel St J., *Frankincense and Myrrh: A Study of the Arabian Incense Trade* (London: Stacey, 1981).

Gruzinski, Serge, *Les quatre parties du monde: histoire d'une mondialisation* (Paris: Martinière, 2006).

Gruzinski, Serge, *What Time Is It There? America and Islam at the Dawn of Modern Times* (London: Polity Press, 2010).

Gupta, Sunil, 'Frankincense in the 'Triangular' Indo–Arabian–Roman Aromatics Trade', in David Peacock and David Williams, *Food for the Gods: New Light on the Ancient Incense Trade* (Oxford: Oxbow, 2007), pp. 112–21.

Gurgani, Fakhraddin, *Vis & Ramin*, trans. Dick Davis (Washington, DC: Mage Publishers, 2007).

Guttmann, Allen, *The Olympics: A History of the Modern Games*, 2nd edn (Urbana, IL and Chicago: University of Illinois Press, 2002).

Haensch, Stephanie, et al., 'Distinct Clones of Yersinia Pestis Caused the Black Death', *PLoS Pathogens* 6, 10 (2010), pp. 1–8.

Halperin, Charles J., *Russia and the Golden Horde: The Mongol Impact on Medieval Russia* (Bloomington: Indiana University Press, 1987).

Hamashita, Takeshi, 'The Tribute Trade System and Modern Asia', trans. Neil Burton and Christian Daniels, in Linda Grove and Mark Selden (eds), *China, East Asia and the Global Economy: Regional and Historical Perspectives* (London: Routledge, 2008), pp. 12–26.

Hamel, Pierre, Henri Lustiger-Thaler, and Jan Nederveen Pieterse (eds), *Globalization and Social Movements* (Basingstoke: Palgrave, 2001).

Hames, Gina, *Alcohol in World History* (London and New York: Routledge, 2012).

Han, Zhong, 'Kongga'er shiliao pingzhu', *Minzushi yanjiu* 8 (2010).

Hansen, Valerie, *Changing Gods in Medieval China, 1126–1272* (Princeton: Princeton University Press, 1990).

Harcourt, Freda, and Francis Robinson, *Twentieth-Century World History: A Select Bibliography* (London: Croom Helm, 1979).

Hardy-Guilbert, Claire, 'Chihr de l'encens', *Arabian Archaeology and Epigraphy* 21, 1 (2010), pp. 46–70.

Harlaftis, Gelina, 'Maritime History or History of *Thalassa*', in Gelina Harlaftis (ed.), *The New Ways of History* (London: I. B. Tauris, 2010), pp. 213–39.

Harley, C. Knick, 'Ocean Freight Rates and Productivity, 1740–1913—the Primacy of Mechanical Invention Reaffirmed', *Journal of Economic History* 48, 4 (1988), pp. 851–76.

Haroon, Sana, 'The Rise of Deobandi Islam in the North-West Frontier Province and its Implication in Colonial India and Pakistan 1914–1996', *Journal of the Royal Asiatic Society* 18, 1 (2008), pp. 47–70.

Harper, Tim N., 'Singapore, 1915 and the Birth of the Asian Underground', *Modern Asian Studies* 47, 6 (2013), pp. 1782–811.

Harris, Jose, Robert Gerwarth, and Holger Nehring, 'Introduction: Constitutions, Civility and Violence', *Journal of Modern European History* 6, 1 (2008), pp. 30–7.

Harris, Robin, *Dubrovnik: A History* (London: Saqi Books, 2003).

Harrison, Henrietta, *The Missionary's Curse and Other Tales from a Chinese Catholic Village* (Berkeley: University of California Press, 2013).

Harvey, Susan A., *Scenting Salvation: Ancient Christianity and the Olfactory Imagination* (Berkeley: University of California Press, 2006).

Haskins, Charles Homer, *The Renaissance of the Twelfth Century* (Cambridge, MA: Harvard University Press, 1928).

Hatcher, John, *The Black Death: An Intimate History* (London: Weidenfeld & Nicolson, 2008).

Hatton, Timothy J., and Jeffrey G. Williamson, *Global Migration and the World Economy: Two Centuries of Policy and Performance* (Cambridge, MA: MIT Press, 2005).

Hattox, Ralph S., *Coffee and Coffeehouses: The Origins of a Social Beverage in the Medieval Near East* (Seattle: University of Washington Press, 1985).

Heck, Gene W., '"Arabia without Spices": An Alternate Hypothesis: The Issue of "Makkan Trade and the Rise of Islam"', *Journal of the American Oriental Society* 123, 3 (2003), pp. 547–76.

Hedström, Peter, *Dissecting the Social: On the Principles of Analytical Sociology* (Cambridge: Cambridge University Press, 2005).

Hedström, Peter, and Peter Bearman (eds), *The Oxford Handbook of Analytical Sociology* (Oxford: Oxford University Press, 2009).

Hedström, Peter, and Peter Bearman, 'What Is Analytical Sociology All About? An Introductory Essay', in Peter Hedström and Peter Bearman (eds), *The Oxford Handbook of Analytical Sociology* (Oxford: Oxford University Press, 2009), pp. 3–24.

Hedström, Peter, and Richard Swedberg (eds), *Social Mechanisms: An Analytical Approach to Social Theory* (Cambridge: Cambridge University Press, 1998).

Heitzmann, James, *Gifts of Power: Lordship in an Early Indian State* (New Delhi: Oxford University Press, 1997).

Held, David, Anthony McGrew, David Goldblatt, and Jonathan Perraton, *Globalization: Key Concepts* (London: Foreign Policy Centre, 1999).

Held, David, Anthony McGrew, David Goldblatt, and Jonathan Perraton, *Global Transformations: Politics, Economics and Culture* (Cambridge: Polity Press, 1999).

Herman, John, 'Collaboration and Resistance on the Southwest Frontier: Early Eighteenth-Century Qing Expansion on Two Fronts', *Late Imperial China* 35, 1 (2014), pp. 77–112.

Hersh, Jonathon, and Hans-Joachim Voth, 'Sweet Diversity: Colonial Goods and the Rise of European Living Standards after 1492', CEPR Discussion Paper 7386 (2009).

Hobden, Stephen, and John M. Hobson (eds), *Historical Sociology of International Relations* (Cambridge: Cambridge University Press, 2002).

Hodgson, Marshall G. S., *The Venture of Islam: Conscience and History in a World Civilization*, 3 vols (Chicago: University of Chicago Press, 1974).

Hoerder, Dirk, *Cultures in Contact: World Migration in the Second Millennium* (Durham, NC and London: Duke University Press, 2002).

Hoffman, R. C., 'Frontier Foods for Late Medieval Consumers: Culture, Economy, Ecology', *Environment and History* 7, 2 (2001), pp. 131–67.

Hoof, Thomas B. van, et al., 'Forest Re-growth on Medieval Farmland after the Black Death Pandemic: Implications for Atmospheric CO_2 Levels', *Palaeogeography, Palaeoclimatology, Palaeoecology* 237, 2–4 (2006), pp. 396–409.

Hopkins, Anthony G., 'Back to the Future: From National History to Imperial History', *Past & Present* 164 (1999), pp. 198–243.

Hopkins, Anthony G. (ed.), *Globalization in World History* (London: Pimlico, 2002).

Hopkins, Anthony G., 'Lessons of "Civilizing Missions" are Mostly Unlearned', *New York Times* (23 March 2003).

Hopkins, Anthony G., 'Capitalism, Nationalism and the New American Empire', *Journal of Imperial & Commonwealth History* 35, 1 (2007), pp. 95–117.

Hopkins, Anthony G., 'Rethinking Decolonization', *Past & Present* 200 (2008), pp. 211–47.

Hopkins, Anthony G., 'The United States, 1783–1861: Britain's Honorary Dominion?' *Britain and the World* 4, 2 (2011), pp. 232–46.

Horden, Peregrine, and Nicholas Purcell, *The Corrupting Sea: A Study of Mediterranean History* (Oxford: Blackwell Publishers, 2000).

Horning, Audrey J., *Ireland in the Virginian Sea: Colonialism in the British Atlantic* (Chapel Hill: Omohundro Institute of Early American History & Culture, 2013).

Horsburgh, James, *India Directory, or, Directions for Sailing to and from the East Indies, China, New Holland, Cape of Good Hope, Brazil, and the Interjacent Ports*, 3rd edn, (London: Parbury, Allen, and Co., 1827).

Hostetler, Laura, *Qing Colonial Enterprise: Ethnography and Cartography in Early Modern China* (Chicago: University of Chicago Press, 2001).

Huber, Valeska, 'Multiple Mobilities: Über den Umgang mit verschiedenen Mobilitätsformen um 1900', *Geschichte und Gesellschaft* 36, 2 (2010), pp. 317–41.

Hull, Bradley Z., 'Frankincense, Myrrh, and Spices: The Oldest Global Supply Chain?' *Journal of Macromarketing* 28, 3 (2008), pp. 275–88.

Humphries, Jane, and Jacob Weisdorf, 'The Wages of Women in England, 1260–1850', CEPR Discussion Paper 9903 (2014).

Hunt, Alan, *Governance of the Consuming Passions: A History of Sumptuary Law* (Basingstoke: Macmillan, 1996).

Hunt, Lynn, 'The Global Financial Origins of 1789', in Suzanne Desan, Lynn Hunt, and William Max Nelson (eds), *The French Revolution in Global Perspective* (Ithaca, NY and London: Cornell University Press, 2013), pp. 32–43.

Huntington, Samuel P., *The Clash of Civilizations and the Remaking of World Order* (New York: Simon & Schuster, 1996).

Hussin, Iza, 'Textual Trajectories: Re-reading the Constitution and Majalah in 1890s Johor', *Indonesia and the Malay World* 41, 120 (2013), pp. 255–72.

Hymes, Robert, *Statesmen and Gentlemen: The Elite of Fu Chou, Chiang-si, in the Northern and Southern Sung* (Cambridge: Cambridge University Press, 1986).

Inden, Ronald, Jonathan Walters, and Daud Ali, *Querying the Medieval: Texts and the History of Practices in South Asia* (Oxford: Oxford University Press, 2000).

Inikori, Joseph E., *Africans and the Industrial Revolution in England: A Study in International Trade and Economic Development* (Cambridge: Cambridge University Press, 2002).

Innes, Joanna, and Mark Philp (eds), *Re-Imagining Democracy in the Age of Revolution: America, France, Britain, Ireland 1750–1850* (Oxford: Oxford University Press, 2013).

Iqbal, Muhammad, *The Reconstruction of Religious Thought in Islam* (Lahore: Sh. Muhammad Ashraf, 1975).

Irwin, Robert, *The Arabian Nights: A Companion* (London: Allen Lane, 1994).

Ito, Hirobumi, and Miyoji Ito (eds), *Commentaries on the Constitution of the Empire of Japan* (Tokyo: Igirisu-Horitsu Gakko, 1889).

Jacobs, Jane, *The Economy of Cities* (New York: Random House, 1969).

Jami, Catherine, 'Western Learning and Imperial Scholarship: The Kangxi Emperor's Study', *East Asian Science, Technology and Medicine* 27 (2007), pp. 146–72.

Jennison, George, *Animals for Show and Pleasure in Ancient Rome* (Philadelphia: University of Pennsylvania, 2005 [1937]).

Jin, Noda, *Ro-Shin teikoku to Kazafu hankoku* (Tokyo: Tōkyō Daigaku Shuppankai, 2011).

Johns, A. H., 'Friends in Grace: Ibahim al-Kurani and Abd al-Rauf al-Singkili', in S. Udin (ed.), *Spectrum: Essays Presented to Sutan Takdir Alisjahbana* (Jakarta: Dian Rakyat, 1978).

Jones, Andrew, *Globalization: Key Thinkers* (Cambridge and Malden, MA: Polity Press, 2010).

Jones, Eric, *The European Miracle: Environments, Economies, and Geopolitics in the History of Europe and Asia*, 3rd edn (Cambridge and New York: Cambridge University Press, 2003).

Jong, J. W. de, 'O 'Zolotoj knige' S. Damdina; [review essay], *T'oung Pao*, 2nd Series, 54, 1 (1968), pp. 173–89.

Jordheim, Helge, 'Against Periodization: Koselleck's Theory of Multiple Temporalities', *History & Theory* 51, 2 (2012), pp. 151–71.

Kacki, Sacha, Lila Rahalison, Minoarisoa Rajerison, Ezio Ferroglio, and Raffaella Bianucci, 'Black Death in the Rural Cemetery of Saint-Laurent-de-la-Cabrerisse Aude-Languedoc,

Southern France, 14th Century: Immunological Evidence', *Journal of Archaeological Science* 38, 3 (2011), pp. 581–7.

Kalberg, Stephen, *Max Weber's Comparative-Historical Sociology* (Cambridge: Polity Press, 1994).

Kapstein, Matthew T., 'Just Where in Jambudvīpa Are We? New Geographical Knowledge and Old Cosmological Schemes in Eighteenth-century Tibet', in Sheldon Pollock (ed.), *Forms of Knowledge in Early Modern Asia: Explorations in the Intellectual History of India and Tibet, 1500–1800* (Durham, NC: Duke University Press, 2011), pp. 336–64.

Karashima, Noboru, *South Indian Society in Transition: Ancient to Medieval* (New Delhi: Oxford University Press, 2009).

Karp, Matthew, '"The Vast Southern Empire": The South and the Foreign Policy of Slavery' (unpublished PhD thesis: University of Pennsylvania, 2011).

Karp, Matthew, 'The Transnational Significance of the American Civil War: A Global History', *Bulletin of the German Historical Institute* 52 (2013), pp. 169–76.

Kauz, Ralph (ed.), *Aspects of the Maritime Silk Road: From the Persian Gulf to the East China Sea* (Wiesbaden: Otto Harrassowitz, 2010).

Kazuhiro, Takii, *The Meiji Constitution: The Japanese Experience of the West and the Shaping of the Modern World* (Tokyo: International House of Japan, 2007).

Keay, John, *The Spice Route: A History* (Berkeley: University of California Press, 2006).

Kelly, Gary, *Women, Writing, and Revolution 1790–1827* (Oxford: Oxford University Press, 1993).

Khan, Hasan Ali, 'Shia-Ismaili Motifs in the Sufi Architecture of the Indus Valley 1200–1500 A.D.' (unpublished PhD thesis: School of Oriental and African Studies, University of London, 2009).

Khosla, Madhav, *The Indian Constitution* (New Delhi: Oxford University Press, 2012).

Kim, Seonmin, 'Ginseng and Border Trespassing between Qing China and Chosŏn Korea', *Late Imperial China* 28, 1 (2007), pp. 33–61.

Kiple, Kenneth F. (ed.), *The Cambridge World History of Human Disease* (Cambridge: Cambridge University Press, 1993).

Kirby, David, *Northern Europe in the Early Modern Period: The Baltic World 1492–1772* (London and New York: Longman, 1990).

Kivelson, Valerie, '"Exalted and Glorified to the Ends of the Earth": Imperial Maps and Christian Spaces in Seventeenth- and Early Eighteenth-Century Russian Siberia', in James R. Akerman (ed.), *The Imperial Map: Cartography and the Mastery of Empire* (Chicago: University of Chicago Press, 2009), pp. 47–92.

Klapisch-Zuber, Christiane, 'Plague and Family Life', in Michael Jones (ed.), *The New Cambridge Medieval History, vol VI: c.1300–c.1415* (Cambridge: Cambridge University Press, 2000), pp. 124–54.

Klooster, Wim, *Revolutions in the Atlantic World: A Comparative History* (New York and London: New York University Press, 2009).

Knapp, Michael, 'The Next Generation of Genetic Investigations into the Black Death', *PNAS* 108, 38 (2011), pp. 15669–70.

Knöbl, Wolfgang, *Die Kontingenz der Moderne: Wege in Europa, Asien und Amerika* (Frankfurt a.M. and New York: Campus, 2007).

Knöbl, Wolfgang, 'Contingency and Modernity in the Thought of J. P. Arnason', *European Journal of Social Theory* 14, 1 (2011), pp. 9–22.

Knöbl, Wolfgang, opening remarks at the workshop 'Macrosociology and World History Writing', Freiburg Institute of Advanced Study, Freiburg i.Br. (Germany), 10 to 11 February 2012 (unpublished manuscript).

Knöbl, Wolfgang, 'Social History and Historical Sociology', *Historická Sociologie* 1 (2013), pp. 9–32.

Koenen, Gerd, *Was war der Kommunismus?* (Göttingen: Vandenhoeck & Ruprecht, 2010).

Kollmann, Nancy Shields, 'The Principalities of Rus' in the Fourteenth Century', in Michael Jones (ed.), *The New Cambridge Medieval History, vol VI: c.1300–c.1415* (Cambridge: Cambridge University Press, 2000), pp. 764–94.

Komlosy, Andrea, *Globalgeschichte: Methoden und Theorien* (Wien, Köln, and Weimar: Böhlau, 2011).

Koselleck, Reinhart, 'Einleitung', in Reinhart Koselleck (ed.), *Zeitschichten: Studien zur Historik* (Frankfurt a.M.: Suhrkamp, 2000), pp. 9–16.

Kovalev, Roman Konstantinovich, 'The Infrastructure of the Novgorodian Fur Trade in the Pre-Mongol Era (ca. 900–ca.1240)' (unpublished PhD thesis: University of Minnesota, 2003).

Krueger, John R., *The Kalmyk-Mongolian Vocabulary in Stralenberg's Geography of 1730* (Stockholm: Almqvist & Wiksell International, 1975).

Kumar, Krishan, 'Empires and Nations: Convergence or Divergence?' in George Steinmetz (ed.), *Sociology & Empire: The Imperial Entanglements of a Discipline* (Durham, NC: Duke University Press, 2013), pp. 279–99.

Lachmann, Richard, *What Is Historical Sociology?* (Cambridge: Polity Press, 2013).

Lake, Marilyn, and Henry Reynolds, *Drawing the Global Colour Line: White Men's Countries and the International Challenge of Racial Equality* (Cambridge: Cambridge University Press, 2008).

Landes, David, *The Wealth and Poverty of Nations: Why Some Are so Rich and Some so Poor* (New York: W. W. Norton, 1998).

Landes, David S., 'Why Are We so Rich and They so Poor?', *American Economic Review* 80, 2 (1990), pp. 1–13.

Lane, Frederic C., 'Pepper Prices before Da Gama', *The Journal of Economic History* 28, 2 (1968), pp. 590–7.

Lape, Peter Vanderford, 'Contact and Conflict in the Banda Islands, Eastern Indonesia 11th-17th Centuries' (unpublished PhD thesis: Brown University, 2000).

Laslett, Peter, 'Social Structural Time: An Attempt at Classifying Types of Social Change by their Characteristic Paces', in Tom Schuller and Michael Young (eds), *The Rhythms of Society* (London and New York: Routledge, 1988), pp. 17–36.

Lefebvre, Henri, *The Production of Space* (Oxford: Blackwell, 1991 [first French edition 1974]).

Lévy-Leboyer, Maurice, 'Capital Investment and Economic Growth in France, 1820–1930', in Peter Mathias and M. M. Postan (eds), *The Cambridge Economic History of Europe from the Decline of the Roman Empire, vol. 7* (Cambridge: Cambridge University Press, 1978), pp. 231–95.

Lieberman, Victor, 'Transcending East–West Dichotomies: State and Culture Formation in Six Ostensibly Different Areas', in Victor Lieberman (ed.), *Beyond Binary Histories: Re-imaging Eurasia to c.1830* (Ann Arbor: University of Michigan Press, 1999), pp. 19–102.

Liebermann, Victor, *Strange Parallels. South-East Asia in Global Context, c.800–1830, vol. 1: Integration on the Mainland, vol. 2: Mainland Mirrors: Europe, Japan, China, South Asia, and the Islands: Southeast Asia in Global Context, c.800–1830* (Cambridge: Cambridge University Press, 2003 and 2009).

Liu, Xinru, 'Silks and Religions in Eurasia, c.AD 600–1200', *Journal of World History* 6, 1 (1995), pp. 25–48.

Liu, Xinru, *The Silk Road in World History* (Oxford: Oxford University Press, 2010).

Longfellow, Henry Wadsworth, 'The Day Is Done' (1844), in Henry Wadsworth Longfellow (ed.), *The Waif: A Collection of Poems* (Cambridge: Owen, 1845).

Lorenz, Chris, and Berber Bevernage (eds), *Breaking up Time: Negotiating the Borders between Present, Past and Future* (Göttingen: Vandenhoeck & Ruprecht, 2013).

Lowry, Glenn D., 'Humayun's Tomb: Form, Function and Meaning in Early Mughal Architecture', *Muqarnas* 4 (1987), pp. 133–48.

Lucassen, Jan and Leo Lucassen (eds), *Globalising Migration History: The Eurasian Experience (16th–21st Centuries)* (Leiden: Brill, 2014).

Ludden, David, *Peasant History in South India* (Delhi: Oxford University Press, 1989).

Luhmann, Niklas, *Theory of Society*, vol. 2, trans. Rhodes Barrett (Stanford, CA: Stanford University Press, 2013 [first German edition 1997]).

Lunjiong, Chen, *Haiguo wenjian lu* (no location: no publisher, 1730), 1.28a, 41b.

Lybyer, A. H., 'The Ottoman Turks and the Routes of Oriental Trade', *The English Historical Review* 30, 120 (1915), pp. 577–88.

MacGregor, Gregor, *Plan of a Constitution for the Inhabitants of the Indian Coast in Central America, Commonly Called the Mosquito Shore* (Edinburgh: Balfour and Jack, 1836).

Mackinder, Halford, 'The Geographical Pivot of History', *The Geographical Journal* 23 (1904), pp. 421–37.

MacKinnon, Michael, 'Supplying Exotic Animals for the Roman Amphitheatre Games: New Reconstructions Combining Archaeological, Ancient Textual and Ethnographic Data', *Mouseion*, Series III, 6 (2006), pp. 137–61.

Madan, Triloki N., *Secularism and Fundamentalism in India: Modern Myths and Locked Minds* (Delhi: Oxford University Press, 1997).

Madden, Frederick, David Fieldhouse, and John Darwin (eds), *Select Documents on the Constitutional History of the British Empire and Commonwealth*, 8 vols (New York: Greenwood Press, 1985–2000).

Maddison, Angus, *The World Economy: Historical Statistics* (Paris: Development Centre of the Organisation for Economic Co-operation and Development, 2003).

Magubane, Zine, 'Overlapping Territories and Intertwined Histories: Historical Sociology's Global Imagination', in Julia Adams, Elisabeth S. Clemens, and Ann S. Orloff (eds), *Remaking Modernity: Politics, History, and Sociology* (Durham, NC: Duke University Press, 2005), pp. 92–108.

Mahan, Alfred T., *The Influence of Sea Power upon History* (London: S. Low 1890).

Mahoney, James, and Dietrich Rueschemeyer (eds), *Comparative Historical Analysis in the Social Sciences* (Cambridge: Cambridge University Press, 2003).

Maier, Charles S., *Leviathan 2.0: Inventing Modern Statehood* (Cambridge, MA and London: Harvard University Press, 2014).

Majewska, Gabriela, 'Sweden's Form of Government during the Reign of Gustavus III—in the Eyes of the Journals of the Polish Enlightenment', *Scandinavian Journal of History* 22, 4 (2008), pp. 291–304.

Makki, Fouad, 'The Spatial Ecology of Power: Long-Distance Trade and State Formation in Northeast Africa', *Journal of Historical Sociology* 24, 2 (2011), pp. 155–85.

Malanima, Paolo, *Pre-Modern European Economy: One Thousand Years (10th–19th Centuries)* (Leiden and Boston: Brill, 2009).

Mankiw, N. Gregory, David Romer, and David N. Weil, 'A Contribution to the Empirics of Economic Growth', *Quarterly Journal of Economics* 107, 2 (1992), pp. 407–37.

Mann, Michael, *The Sources of Social Power*, 4 vols. (Cambridge: Cambridge University Press, 1986–2013).

Manning, Patrick, *Navigating World History: Historians Create a Global Past* (New York: Palgrave, 2003).

Markovits, Claude, Sanjay Subrahmanyam, and Jacques Pouchepadass, 'Introduction', in Claude Markovits, Sanjay Subrahmanyam, and Jacques Pouchepadass (eds), *Society and Circulation: Mobile People and Itinerant Cultures in South Asia, 1750–1950* (New Delhi: Permanent Black, 2003), pp. 1–22.

Martin, Janet, *Treasure of the Land of Darkness: The Fur Trade and its Significance for Medieval Russia* (Cambridge: Cambridge University Press, 1986).

Martin, Janet, *Medieval Russia 980–1584*, 2nd edn (Cambridge and New York: Cambridge University Press, 2007).

Marushiakova, Elena, and Vesselin Popov, 'Gypsy Slavery in Wallachia and Moldavia', in Tomasz Kamusella and Krzysztof Jaskulowski (eds), *Nationalisms Today* (Oxford: Peter Lang, 2009), pp. 89–123.

Mathews, Thomas, *Puerto Rican Politics and the New Deal* (Gainesville: University of Florida Press, 1976).

May, Jon, and Nigel J. Thrift (eds), *Timespace: Geographies of Temporality* (London and New York: Routledge, 2001).

Maynes, Mary Jo, and Ann Waltner, *The Family: A World History* (Oxford and New York: Oxford University Press, 2012).

Mazlish, Bruce, *Civilization and Its Contents* (Stanford: Stanford University Press, 2004).

Mazlish, Bruce, and Ralph Buultjens (eds), *Conceptualizing Global History* (Boulder, CO: New Global History Press, 1993).

McCabe, Ina B., Gelina Harlaftis, and Ioanna P. Minoglou, *Diaspora Entrepreneurial Networks: Four Centuries of History* (Oxford: Berg, 2005).

McCann, James C., *Maize and Grace: Africa's Encounter with a New World Crop* (Cambridge, MA: Harvard University Press, 2005).

McGuire, Robert A., and Philip R. P. Coelho, *Parasites, Pathogens and Progress: Disease and Economic Development* (Cambridge, MA and London: MIT Press, 2011).

McLaughlin, Raoul J., *Rome and the Distant East: Trade Routes to the Ancient Lands of Arabia, India and China* (London: Continuum, 2010).

McLoughlin, William G., *Cherokee Renascence in the New Republic* (Princeton: Princeton University Press, 1986).

McNeill, John R., *Mosquito Empires: Ecology and War in the Greater Caribbean 1620–1914* (Cambridge and New York: Cambridge University Press, 2010).

McNeill, John R., and William H. McNeill, *The Human Web: A Bird's-Eye View of World History* (New York: W. W. Norton, 2003).

McNeill, William H., *Plagues and Peoples* (Garden City, NY: Anchor Press/Doubleday, 1976).

McNeill, William H., 'A Defence of World History', *Transactions of the Royal Historical Society* 5, 32 (1982), pp. 75–89.

McNeill, William H., *The Pursuit of Power: Technology, Armed Force, and Society since AD 1000* (Chicago: University of Chicago Press, 1983).

McNeill, William H., *Arnold J. Toynbee: A Life* (New York and Oxford: Oxford University Press, 1989).

Medushevsky, Andrey N., *Russian Constitutionalism: Historical and Contemporary Development* (London: Routledge, 2006).

Meijer, Fik, *The Gladiators: History's Most Deadly Sport* (London: Souvenir Press, 2004 [2003]).

Middell, Matthias, and Ulf Engel (eds), *Theoretiker der Globalisierung* (Leipzig: Leipziger Universitätsverlag, 2010).

Middell, Matthias, and Katja Naumann, 'Global History 2008–2010: Empirische Erträge, konzeptionelle Debatten, neue Synthesen', *Comparativ* 20 (2010), pp. 93–133.

Middell, Matthias, and Katja Naumann, 'Global History and the Spatial Turn: From the Impact of Area Studies to the Study of Critical Junctures of Globalization', *Journal of Global History* 5, 1 (2010), pp. 149–70.

Mitterauer, Michael, *Why Europe? The Medieval Origins of its Special Path*, trans. Gerald Chapple (Chicago and London: University of Chicago Press, 2010 [German orig. 2003]).

Moin, A. Azfar, *The Millennial Sovereign: Sacred Kingship & Sainthood in Islam* (New York: Columbia University Press, 2012).

Mokyr, Joel, *Industrialization in the Low Countries, 1795–1850* (New Haven: Yale University Press, 1976).

Mokyr, Joel, 'Demand vs Supply in the Industrial Revolution', *Journal of Economic History* 37, 4 (1977), pp. 981–1008.

Moore, Robert I., 'World History', in Michael Bentley (ed.), *Companion to Historiography* (London: Routledge, 1997).

Moore, Robert I., *The First European Revolution* (Oxford: Blackwell, 2000).

Moore, Robert I., 'The Eleventh Century in Eurasian History', *Journal of Medieval and Early Modern Studies* 33, 1 (2003), pp. 3–21.

Moore, Robert I., 'The Transformation of Europe as a Eurasian Phenomenon', in Jóhann P. Árnason and Björn Wittrock (eds), *Eurasian Transformations, Tenth to Thirteenth Centuries: Crystallizations, Divergences, Renaissances* (Leiden: Brill, 2004), pp. 77–98.

Moore, Robert I., 'Medieval Europe in World History', in Carol Lansing and Edward D. English (eds), *A Companion to the Medieval World* (Chichester: Wiley-Blackwell, 2009), pp. 563–80.

Mosca, Matthew W., *From Frontier Policy to Foreign Policy: The Question of India and the Transformation of Geopolitics in Qing China* (Stanford: Stanford University Press, 2013).

Mosca, Matthew W., 'The Qing State and Its Awareness of Eurasian Interconnections, 1789–1806', *Eighteenth-Century Studies* 47, 2 (2014), pp. 103–16.

Mottahedeh, Roy, *Loyalty and Leadership in an Early Islamic Society*, 2nd edn (London: Tauris, 2001).

Moyn, Samuel, and Andrew Sartori, 'Approaches to Global Intellectual History', in Samuel Moyn and Andrew Sartori (eds), *Global Intellectual History* (New York: Columbia University Press, 2013), pp. 3–30.

Munro, John H., 'Medieval Woollens: The Western European Woollen Industries and their Struggles for International Markets, *c.*1000–1500', in David Jenkins (ed.), *The Cambridge History of Western Textiles*, vol. I (Cambridge: Cambridge University Press, 2003), pp. 228–324.

Nappo, Dario, 'On the Location of Leuke Kome', *Journal of Roman Archaeology* 23 (2010), pp. 335–48.

Neal, Larry, and Jeffrey G. Williamson (eds), *The Cambridge History of Capitalism*, 2 vols. (Cambridge: Cambridge University Press, 2014).

Nearing, Scott, *The American Empire* (New York: Rand School of Social Science, 1921).

Nearing, Scott, and Joseph Freeman, *Dollar Diplomacy: A Study in American Imperialism* (New York: B. W. Huebsch and Viking Press, 1925).

Neville, Leonora, *Authority in Byzantine Provincial Society, 950–1100* (Cambridge: Cambridge University Press, 2004).

Newitt, Malyn, *A History of Portuguese Overseas Expansion, 1400–1668* (London: Routledge, 2005).

Nocete, F., J. M. Vargas, T. X. Schuhmacher, A. Banerjee, and W. Dindorf, 'The Ivory Workshop of Valencina de la Concepcion (Seville, Spain) and the Identification of Ivory from Asian Elephant on the Iberian Peninsula in the First Half of the 3rd Millennium BC', *Journal of Archaeological Science* 40, 3 (2013), pp. 1579–92.

Noe, Nicholas (ed.), *Voice of Hezbollah: The Statements of Sayyed Hassan Nasrallah* (London and New York: Verso, 2007).

Nolte, Hans-Heinrich, 'Zum Stand der Weltgeschichtsschreibung im deutschen Sprachraum', *Zeitschrift für Weltgeschichte* 8 (2008), pp. 89–113.

Nolte, Hans-Heinrich, *Weltgeschichte des 20. Jahrhunderts* (Vienna, Cologne, and Weimar: Böhlau, 2009).

O'Brien, Patrick, 'European Economic Development: The Contribution of the Periphery', *The Economic History Review* 35, 1 (1982), pp. 1–18.

O'Brien, Patrick K., and Caglar Keyder, *Economic Growth in Britain and France, 1780–1914: Two Paths to the Twentieth Century* (London and Boston: G. Allen & Unwin, 1978).

O'Hagan, Jacinta, *Conceptualizing the West in International Relations: From Spengler to Said* (Basingstoke: Palgrave Macmillan, 2002).

O'Rourke, Kevin H., and Jeffrey G. Williamson, 'Late Nineteenth-century Anglo-American Factor–Price Convergence: Were Heckscher and Ohlin Right?', *The Journal of Economic History* 54, 4 (1994), pp. 892–916.

O'Rourke, Kevin H., and Jeffrey G. Williamson, *Globalization and History: The Evolution of a Nineteenth-Century Atlantic Economy* (Cambridge, MA: MIT Press, 1999).

O'Rourke, Kevin H., and Jeffrey G. Williamson, 'When Did Globalisation Begin?' *European Review of Economic History* 6, 1 (2002), pp. 23–50.

O'Rourke, Kevin H., and Jeffrey G. Williamson, 'From Malthus to Ohlin: Trade, Industrialisation and Distribution since 1500', *Journal of Economic Growth* 10, 1 (2005), pp. 5–34.

O'Rourke, Kevin H., and Jeffrey G. Williamson, 'Did Vasco da Gama Matter for European Markets?' *Economic History Review* 62, 3 (2009), pp. 655–84.

O'Rourke, Shane, *The Cossacks* (Manchester and New York: Manchester University Press, 2007).

Obstfeld, Maurice, and Alan M. Taylor, *Global Capital Markets: Integration, Crisis, and Growth* (Cambridge and New York: Cambridge University Press, 2004).

Oldland, John, 'Wool and Cloth Production in Late Medieval and Early Tudor England', *Economic History Review* 67, 1 (2014), pp. 125–47.

Oliver, Roland, and Anthony Atmore, *Medieval Africa, 1250–1800*, rev. edn (Cambridge: Cambridge University Press, 2001).

Osterhammel, Jürgen, 'Transkulturell vergleichende Geschichtswissenschaft', in Heinz-Gerhard Haupt and Jürgen Kocka (eds), *Geschichte im Vergleich* (Frankfurt a.M. and New York: Campus, 1996), pp. 271–313; reprinted in Jürgen Osterhammel, *Geschichtswissenschaft jenseits des Nationalstaats: Studien zu Beziehungsgeschichte und Zivilisationsvergleich*, 2nd edn (Göttingen: Vandenhoeck & Ruprecht, 2002), pp. 11–45.

Osterhammel, Jürgen, 'Die Wiederkehr des Raumes: Geopolitik, Geohistorie und historische Geographie', *Neue Politische Literatur* 43 (1998), pp. 374–97.

Osterhammel, Jürgen, 'Gesellschaftsgeschichte und Historische Soziologie', in Jürgen Osterhammel, Dieter Langewiesche, and Paul Nolte (eds), *Wege der Gesellschaftsgeschichte* (Göttingen: Vandenhoeck & Ruprecht, 2006), pp. 81–102.

Osterhammel, Jürgen, 'Globalgeschichte', in Hans-Jürgen Goertz (ed.), *Geschichte: Ein Grundkurs*, 3rd edn (Reinbek: Rowohlt, 2007), pp. 592–610.

Osterhammel, Jürgen, 'Global History in a National Context: The Case of Germany', *Österreichische Zeitschrift für Geschichtswissenschaft* 20 (2009), pp. 40–58.

Osterhammel, Jürgen, 'Globalizations', in Jerry H. Bentley (ed.), *Oxford Handbook of World History* (Oxford: Oxford University Press, 2011), pp. 89–104.

Osterhammel, Jürgen, 'World History', in Axel Schneider and Daniel R. Woolf (eds), *Oxford History of Historical Writing, vol. V: Historical Writing since 1945* (Oxford: Oxford University Press, 2011), pp. 93–112.

Osterhammel, Jürgen, *The Transformation of the World: A Global History of the Nineteenth Century* (Princeton and Oxford: Princeton University Press 2014).

Ouerfelli, Mohamed, *Le sucre: production, commercialisation et usages dans la Méditerranée médiévale* (Leiden: Brill, 2008).

Padgett, John F., and Christopher K. Ansell, 'Robust Action and the Rise of the Medici', *American Journal of Sociology* 98, 6 (1993), pp. 1259–319.

Pagden, Anthony, *Worlds at War: The 2,500-year Struggle between East and West* (New York: Random House, 2008).

Pamuk, Şevket, 'The Black Death and the Origins of the "Great Divergence" across Europe, 1300–1600', *European Review of Economic History* 11, 3 (2007), pp. 289–317.

Panofsky, Erwin, *Renaissance and Renascences in Western Art* (Stockholm: Almqvist & Wiksell, 1960).

Paquette, Gabriel, 'The Brazilian Origins of the 1826 Portuguese Constitution', *European History Quarterly* 41, 3 (2011), pp. 444–71.

Parker, Geoffrey, *Global Crisis: War, Climate Change and Catastrophe in the Seventeenth Century* (New Haven: Yale University Press, 2013).

Parrott, David, *The Business of War: Military Enterprise and Military Revolution in Early Modern Europe* (Cambridge: Cambridge University Press, 2012).

Parthasarathi, Prasannan, 'Rethinking Wages and Competitiveness in the Eighteenth Century: Britain and South India', *Past & Present* 158 (1998), pp. 79–109.

Patai, Daphne, and Will H. Corral (eds), *Theory's Empire: An Anthology of Dissent* (New York: Columbia University Press, 2005).

Peacock, David, and Lucy Blue, 'Incense and the Port of Adulis', in David Peacock and David Williams, *Food for the Gods: New Light on the Ancient Incense Trade* (Oxford: Oxbow, 2007), pp. 135–40.

Peacock, David, and David Williams (eds.), *Food for the Gods: New Light on the Ancient Incense Trade* (Oxford: Oxbow, 2007).

Peacock, David, David Williams, and Sarah James, 'Basalt as Ships' Ballast and the Roman Incense Trade', in David Peacock and David Williams, *Food for the Gods: New Light on the Ancient Incense Trade* (Oxford: Oxbow, 2007), pp. 28–70.

Pedersen, R. K., 'The Byzantine-Aksumite Period Shipwreck at Black Assarca Island, Eritrea', *Azania* 43 (2008), pp. 77–94.

Perdue, Peter C., *China Marches West: The Qing Conquest of Central Eurasia* (Cambridge, MA: Harvard University Press, 2005).

Perkins, Whitney T., *Denial of Empire: The United States and its Dependencies* (Leyden: A. W. Sythoff, 1962).

Pernau, Margrit, *Transnationale Geschichte* (Göttingen: Vandenhoeck & Ruprecht, 2011).

Phillips, Carla Rahn, and William D. Phillips Jr, *Spain's Golden Fleece: Wool Production and the Wool Trade from the Middle Ages to the Nineteenth Century* (Baltimore and London: Johns Hopkins University Press, 1997).

Plattner, Felix A., *Jesuits Go East*, trans. Lord Sudley and Oscar Blobel (Dublin: Clonmore & Reynolds, 1950).

Pollock, Sheldon, *The Language of the Gods in the World of Men: Sanskrit, Culture and Power in Premodern India* (Berkeley: University of California, 2006).

Pomeranz, Kenneth, *The Great Divergence. China, Europe, and the Making of the Modern World Economy* (Princeton: Princeton University Press, 2000).

Pomeranz, Kenneth, 'Their Own Path to Crisis? Social Change, State-Building and the Limits of Qing Expansion, *c.*1770–1840', in David Armitage and Sanjay Subrahmanyam (eds), *The Age of Revolutions in Global Context, c 1760–1840* (Basingstoke: Palgrave Macmillan, 2010), pp. 189–208.

Ponting, Clive, *World History: A New Perspective* (London: Pimlico, 2001).

Porras, Alberto García, and Adela Fábregas García, 'Genoese Trade Networks in the Southern Iberian Peninsula: Trade, Transmission of Technical Knowledge and Economic Interactions', *Mediterranean Historical Review* 25, 1 (2010), pp. 35–51.

Proulx, Jean-Pierre, *Whaling in the North Atlantic: From Earliest Times to the Mid-19th Century* (Ottawa: Parks Canada, 1986).

Pu, Han, *Beijing lishi wenxian yaoji jieti* (Beijing: Zhongguo shudian, 2010).

Puchkovskiĭ, L. S., *Mongol'skie, Buriat-Mongol'skie Rukopisi i Ksilografy Instituta Vostokovedeniia* (Moskva: Izdvo Akademii Nauk, 1957).

Puchkovskiĭ, L. S. (ed.), *Ganga-ĭin Uruskhal: Istoriia zolotogo roda vladyki Chingisa:— sochinenie pod nazvaniem 'Techenie Ganga* (Moskva: Izdvo vostochnoĭ litry, 1960).

Purcell, Nicholas, 'Beach, Tide and Backwash: The Place of Maritime Histories', in Peter N. Miller (ed.), *The Sea: Thalassography and Historiography* (Ann Arbor: University of Michigan Press, 2013), pp. 84–108.

Purcell, Nicholas, 'On the Significance of East and West in Today's "Hellenistic" History: Reflections on Symmetrical Worlds, Reflecting through World Symmetries', in Jonathan R. W. Prag and Josephine C. Quinn (eds.), *Hellenistic West: Rethinking the Ancient Mediterranean* (Cambridge: Cambridge University Press, 2013), pp. 367–90.

Putnam, Lara, 'To Study the Fragments/Whole: Microhistory and the Atlantic World', *Journal of Social History* 39, 3 (2006), pp. 615–30.

Qi, Han, 'Cong Zhong-Xi wenxian kan Ma Guoxian zai gongting de huodong', in Michele Fatica and Francesco D'Arelli (eds), *La Missione Cattolica in Cina tra i Secoli XVIII–XIX* (Naples: Istituto Universitario Orientale, 1999), pp. 75–7.

Qing shilu (Beijing: Zhonghua shuju, 1985).

Racine, Karen, '"This England and This Now": British Cultural and Intellectual Influence in the Spanish American Independence Era', *Hispanic-American Historical Review* 90, 3 (2010), pp. 423–54.

Racz, Lajos, 'The Price of Survival: Transformation in Environmental Conditions and Subsistence Systems in Hungary in the Age of Ottoman Occupation', *Historical Studies* 24, 1 (2010), pp. 21–39.

Ravina, Mark, 'Japanese State Making in Global Context', in Richard Boyd and Tak-Wing Ngo (eds), *State Making in Asia* (London: Routledge, 2006), pp. 31–46.

Regert, Martine, Thibaut Devièse, Anne-Solenn Le Hô, and Axelle Rougeulle, 'Reconstructing Ancient Yemeni Commercial Routes during the Middle Ages Using Structural Characterization of Terpenoid Resins', *Archaeometry* 50, 4 (2008), pp. 668–85.

Reuter, Timothy, 'Medieval: Another Tyrannous Construct?' *The Medieval History Journal* 1, 1 (1998), pp. 25–45, reprinted in Timothy Reuter, *Medieval Polities and Modern Mentalities* ed. Janet L. Nelson (Cambridge: Cambridge University Press, 2006), pp. 19–37.

Revel, Jacques, *Jeux d'échelles: la micro-analyse à l'expérience* (Paris: Gallimard, 1996).

Rgya-nag chos-'byung/Hanqu Fojiao yuanliu ji (Beijing: Zhongguo Zangxue chubanshe, 2005).

Riello, Giorgio, *Cotton: The Fabric That Made the Modern World* (Cambridge: Cambridge University Press, 2013).

Riello, Giorgio, and Prasannan Parthasarathi (eds), *The Spinning World: A Global History of Cotton Textiles, 1200–1850* (Oxford and New York: Oxford University Press, 2009).

Ritzer, George, *Globalization: The Essentials* (Chichester: Wiley-Blackwell, 2011).

Robertson, Roland, and Kathleen E. White (eds), *Globalization: Critical Concepts in Sociology*, 6 vols. (London and New York: Routledge, 2003).

Robinson, Chase, *Empire and Elites after the Muslim Conquest: The Transformation of Northern Mesopotamia* (Cambridge: Cambridge University Press, 2000).

Robinson, Francis, *Atlas of the Islamic World since 1500* (Oxford: Phaidon, 1982).

Robinson, Francis (ed.), *The Cambridge Illustrated History of the Islamic World* (Cambridge: Cambridge University Press, 1996).

Robinson, Francis, 'Knowledge, its Transmission and the Making of Muslim Societies' in Francis Robinson (ed.), *Cambridge Illustration History of the Islamic World* (Cambridge: Cambridge University Press, 1996), pp. 208–49.

Robinson, Francis, 'The British Empire and the Muslim World', in Judith Brown and Wm. Roger Louis (eds.), *The Oxford History of the British Empire, vol IV: The Twentieth Century* (Oxford: Oxford University Press, 1999), pp. 398–420.

Robinson, Francis, 'Religious Change and the Self in Muslim South Asia since 1800', in Francis Robinson, *Islam and Muslim History in South Asia* (Delhi: Oxford University Press, 2000), pp. 105–21.

Robinson, Francis, *The Ulama of Farangi Mahall and Islamic Culture in South Asia* (Delhi: Permanent Black, 2001).

Robinson, Francis, 'Islamic Reform and Modernities in South Asia', *Modern Asian Studies* 42, 2–3 (2008), pp. 259–81.

Robinson, Francis, 'Crisis of Authority: Crisis of Islam?' *Journal of the Royal Asiatic Society* 19, 3 (2009), pp. 339–54.

Robinson, Francis, 'The Islamic World from World System to Religious International', in Abigail Green and Vincent Viane (eds.), *Religious Internationals in the Modern World: Globalization and Faith Communities since 1750* (Basingstoke: Palgrave Macmillan, 2012), pp. 111–38.

Robinson, Fred C., 'Medieval, the Middle Ages', *Speculum* 59, 4 (1984), pp. 745–56.

Robinson, William I., 'Globalization and the Sociology of Immanuel Wallerstein: A Critical Appraisal', *International Sociology* 26, 6 (2011), pp. 723–45.

Rockefeller, Stuart Alexander, '"Flow"', *Current Anthropology* 52, 4 (2011), pp. 557–78.

Rodgers, Daniel T., *Atlantic Crossings: Social Politics in a Progressive Age* (Cambridge, MA: Belknap Press, 1998).

Rogers, J. Daniel, 'Inner Asian States and Empires: Theories and Synthesis', *Journal of Archaeological Research* 20, 3 (2012), pp. 205–56.

Rollason, David, *Early Medieval Europe 300–1050: The Birth of Western Society* (London: Routledge, 2012).

Roosevelt, Theodore, 'The Expansion of the White Races', Address, 18 January 1909, in Theodore Roosevelt and Hermann Hagedorn (eds), *The Works of Theodore Roosevelt, vol. 16: American Problems* (New York: C. Scribner's Sons, 1926), p. 264.

Roosevelt, Theodore, *Colonial Policies of the United States* (London: Nelson, 1937).

Rossi, Pietro (ed.), *La storia comparata: Approci e prospettive* (Milan: Il Saggiatore, 1990).

Rota, Giorgio, 'Safavids and Kalmyks in the 17th Century: A Preliminary Assessment', *Proceedings of the 5th Conference of the Societas Iranologica Europæa*, vol. 2 (2006), pp. 191, 194.

Rowton, Michael B., 'Autonomy and Nomadism in Western Asia', *Orientalia* 42 (1973), pp. 247–58.

Rowton, Michael B., 'Enclosed Nomadism', *Journal of the Economic and Social History of the Orient* 17, 1–3 (1974), pp. 1–30.

Royen, Paul van, Jaap Bruijn, and Jan Lucassen (eds), *'Those Emblems of Hell?' European Sailors and the Maritime Labour Market 1570–1870* (St John's, Newfoundland: International Maritime Economic History Association, 1997).

Rozehnal, Robert, *Islamic Sufism Unbound: Politics and Piety in Twenty-First Century Pakistan* (Basingstoke: Palgrave Macmillan, 2007).

Rueschemeyer, Dietrich, *Usable Theory: Analytic Tools for Social and Political Research* (Princeton and Oxford: Princeton University Press, 2009).

Runciman, Walter G., *A Treatise on Social Theory*, 3 vols (Cambridge: Cambridge University Press, 1983–97).

Ruskin, John, *Lectures on Architecture IV, 111*, cited from the Gutenberg edition, <http://www.gutenberg.org/files/23593/23593-h/23593-h.htm> (accessed 30 January 2015).

Sachsenmaier, Dominic, *Global Perspectives on Global History: Theories and Approaches in a Connected World* (Cambridge: Cambridge University Press, 2011).

Sahlins, Marshall, *Stone Age Economics* (Chicago: Aldine-Atherton, 1972).

Said, Edward, *Orientalism* (London: Routledge and Kegan Paul, 1978).

Said, Edward, *Culture and Imperialism* (London: Vintage Books, 1993).

Salmeri, Giovanni, 'Dell'uso dell'incenso in epoca romana', in A. Avanzini, *Profumi d'Arabia* (Rome: L'Erma di Bretschneider, 1997), pp. 529–40.

Sanderson, Stephen K., *Social Transformations: A General Theory of Historical Development* (Oxford: Blackwell, 1995).

Satyal, Amita, 'The Mughal Empire, Overland Trade, and Merchants of Northern India, 1526–1707' (unpublished PhD thesis: University of California, Berkeley, 2008).

Savinetsky, A. B., and O. A. Krylovich, 'On the History of the Spread of the Black Rat (Rattus rattus L., 1758) in Northwestern Russia', *Biology Bulletin* 38, 2 (2011), pp. 203–7.

Scheele, Judith, 'Traders, Saints and Irrigation: Reflections on Saharan Connectivity', *Journal of African History* 51, 3 (2010), pp. 281–300.

Scheidel, Walter (ed.), *Rome and China Comparative Perspectives on Ancient World Empires* (Oxford and New York: Oxford University Press, 2009).

Schlögel, Karl, *Im Raume lesen wir die Zeit: Über Zivilisationsgeschichte und Geopolitik* (Munich: Hanser, 2003).

Schmid, Andre, 'Tributary Relations and the Qing-Chosŏn Frontier on Mount Paektu', in Diana Lary (ed.), *The Chinese State at the Borders* (Vancouver: UBC Press, 2007), pp 126–50.

Schmidt-Nowara, Christopher (ed.), 'Global Horizons and Local Interests in the Era of the Constitution of Cadiz', special issue of *Association for Spanish and Portuguese Historical Studies Bulletin* 37, 2 (2012).

Scholte, Jan A., *Globalization: A Critical Introduction* (Basingstoke and New York: Palgrave, 2000).

Schuenemann, Verena, et al., 'Targeted Enrichment of Ancient Pathogens Yielding the pPCP1 Plasmid of Yersinia Pestis from Victims of the Black Death', *Proceedings of the National Academy of Sciences of the United States of America (PNAS)* 108, 38 (2011), pp. 746–52.

Schützeichel, Rainer, *Historische Soziologie* (Bielefeld: Transcript, 2004).

Schwinn, Thomas, 'Multiple Modernities: Konkurrierende Thesen und offene Fragen. Ein Literaturbericht in konstruktiver Absicht', *Zeitschrift für Soziologie* 38, 6 (2009), pp. 454–76.

Scott, John, *Social Network Analysis*, 3rd edn (Los Angeles: Sage, 2012).

Scott, John, and Peter J. Carrington (eds), *The SAGE Handbook of Social Network Analysis* (Los Angeles: Sage, 2011).

Scott, Tom, *The City-State in Europe, 1000–1600: Hinterland, Territory, Region* (Oxford, Oxford University Press, 2012).

Secord, James A., 'Knowledge in Transit', *Isis* 95, 4 (2004), pp. 654–72.

Sedov, Alexander, 'The Port of Qana' and the Incense Trade', in David Peacock and David Williams, *Food for the Gods: New Light on the Ancient Incense Trade* (Oxford: Oxbow, 2007), pp. 71–111.

Seland, Eivind H., *The Indian Ocean in the Ancient Period: Definite Places, Translocal Exchange* (Oxford: Archaeopress, 2007).

Seland, Eivind H., 'The Persian Gulf or the Red Sea? Two Axes in Ancient Indian Ocean Trade, Where to Go and Why', *World Archaeology* 43 (2011), pp. 398–409.

Sewell, William H. Jr, *Logics of History: Social Theory and Social Transformation* (Chicago and London: University of Chicago Press, 2005).

Shabbir, Mohammad, *Ambedkar on Law, Constitution, and Social Justice* (Jaipur: Rawat Publications, 2005).

Shackle, Christopher, 'The Story of Sayf al-Muluk in South Asia', *Journal of the Royal Asiatic Society* (Series 3) 17, 2 (2007), pp. 115–29.

Shackley, Myra, 'Frankincense and Myrrh Today', in David Peacock and David Williams, *Food for the Gods: New Light on the Ancient Incense Trade* (Oxford: Oxbow, 2007), pp. 141–51.

Shahid, Irfan, *Byzantium and the Arabs in the Sixth Century*, vol. 2.2 (Washington, DC: Dumbarton Oaks, 2009).

Sharp, Paul, and Jacob Weisdorf, 'Globalization Revisited: Market Integration and the Wheat Trade between North America and Britain from the Eighteenth Century', *Explorations in Economic History* 50, 1 (2013), pp. 88–98.

Shunsai, Hayashi, *Ka-I hentai* (Tokyo: Tōyō bunko, 1959).

Sidebotham, Steven E., *Berenike and the Ancient Maritime Spice Route* (Berkeley: University of California Press, 2011).

Sindbaek, Søren M., 'The Small World of the Vikings: Networks in Early Medieval Communications and Exchange', *Norwegian Archaeological Review* 40, 1 (2007), pp. 59–74.

Singer, Caroline, 'The Incense Kingdoms of Yemen: An Outline History of the South Arabian Incense Trade', in David Peacock and David Williams, *Food for the Gods: New Light on the Ancient Incense Trade* (Oxford: Oxbow, 2007), pp. 4–27.

Skinner, Quentin (ed.), *The Return of Grand Theory* (Cambridge: Cambridge University Press, 1985).

Skocpol, Theda, *States and Social Revolutions* (Cambridge: Cambridge University Press, 1979).

Skocpol, Theda (ed.), *Vision and Method in Historical Sociology* (Cambridge: Cambridge University Press, 1984).

Sloane, Barney, *The Black Death in London* (Stroud: History Press, 2011).

Smith, Dennis, *The Rise of Historical Sociology* (Cambridge: Polity Press, 1991).

Smith, Paul J., *Taxing Heaven's Storehouse: Horses, Bureaucrats, and the Destruction of the Sichuan Tea Trade 1074–1224* (Cambridge, MA: Harvard University Asia Center, 1991).

Smith, Richard L., *Premodern Trade in World History* (London and New York: Routledge, 2009).

Snooks, Graeme D., *The Laws of History* (London and New York: Routledge, 1998).

Snooks, Graeme D., *Longrun Dynamics: A General Economic and Political Theory* (Basingstoke and London: Macmillan, 1998).

Snooks, Graeme D., *Global Transition: A General Theory of Economic Development* (Basingstoke and London: Macmillan, 1999).

Solow, Robert M., 'Science and Ideology in Economics', *Public Interest* 21 (1970), pp. 94–107.

Solow, Robert M., and Peter Temin, 'Introduction: The Inputs for Growth', in Peter Mathias and M. M. Postan (eds), *The Cambridge Economic History of Europe from the Decline of the Roman Empire,* vol. 7 (Cambridge: Cambridge University Press, 1978), pp. 1–27.

Sood, Gagan D. S., 'Circulation and Exchange in Islamicate Eurasia', *Past & Present* 212 (2011), pp. 113–62.

Soulis, George C., 'The Gypsies in the Byzantine Empire and the Balkans in the Late Middle Ages', *Dumbarton Oaks Papers* 15 (1961), pp. 141, 143–65.

Spier, Fred, 'Big History', in Douglas Northrop (ed.), *A Companion to World History* (Malden, MA, Oxford, and Chichester: Wiley-Blackwell, 2012), pp. 171–84.

Spohn, Willfried, 'Historical and Comparative Sociology in a Globalizing World', *Historická Sociologie* 1 (2009), pp. 9–27.

Spohn, Willfried, 'Globale, multiple und (post-) koloniale Modernen: Eine interzivilisatorische und historisch-soziologische Perspektive', in Manuela Boatcă/Willfried Spohn (eds), *Globale, multiple und postkoloniale Modernen* (Munich: Hampp, 2010), pp. 1–28.

Spohn, Willfried, 'An Appraisal of Shmuel Noah Eisenstadt's Global Historical Sociology', *Journal of Classical Sociology* 11, 3 (2011), pp. 281–301.

Squillace, Giuseppe, *I giardini di Saffo: profumi e aromi nella Grecia antica* (Rome: Carocci, 2014).

St John, Rachel, 'The Imagined States of America: Nation-Building in Nineteenth-Century North America', Seminar Paper, Davis Center, Department of History, Princeton University.

Standaert, Nicolas, *Chinese Voices in the Rites Controversy: Travelling Books, Community Networks, Intercultural Arguments* (Rome: Institutum Historicum Societatis Iesu, 2012).

Steensgaard, Niels, *The Asian Trade Revolution of the Seventeenth Century: The East India Companies and the Decline of the Caravan Trade* (Chicago: University of Chicago Press, 1974).

Stein, Burton, *Peasant State and Society in Medieval South India* (Delhi: Oxford University Press, 1980).

Stichweh, Rudolf, *Die Weltgesellschaft: Soziologische Analysen* (Frankfurt a.M.: Suhrkamp, 2000).

Stites, Richard, 'Decembrists with a Spanish Accent', *Kritika: Explorations in Russian and Eurasian History* 12, 1 (2011), pp. 5–23.

Stourzh, Gerald, 'Constitution: Changing Meanings of the Term from the Early Seventeenth to the Late Eighteenth Century', in Terence Ball and John G. A. Pocock (eds), *Conceptual Change and the Constitution* (Lawrence, KS: University Press of Kansas, 1988), pp. 35–54.

Strauch, Ingo (ed.), *Foreign Sailors on Socotra: The Inscriptions and Drawings from the Cave Hoq* (Bremen: Ute Hempen Verlag, 2012).

Strayer, Robert, *The Communist Experiment: Revolution, Socialism, and Global Conflict in the Twentieth Century* (Boston, MA: McGraw-Hill, 2007).

Struck, Bernhard, Kate Ferris, and Jacques Revel, 'Introduction: Space and Scale in Transnational History', *The International History Review* 33, 4 (2011), pp. 573–84.

Stuard, Susan Mosher, *Gilding the Market: Luxury and Fashion in Fourteenth-Century Italy* (Philadelphia: University of Pennsylvania Press, 2006).

Studnicki-Gizbert, Daviken, *A Nation upon the Ocean Sea: Portugal's Atlantic Diaspora and the Crisis of the Spanish Empire, 1492–1640* (Oxford: Oxford University Press, 2007).

Subrahmanyam, Sanjay, 'Connected Histories: Notes towards a Reconfiguration of Early Modern Eurasia', *Modern Asian Studies* 31, 3 (1997), pp. 735–62.

Subrahmanyam, Sanjay, *Explorations in Connected History: From the Tagus to the Ganges* (Delhi: Oxford University Press, 2004).

Subrahmanyam, Sanjay, and Luís Filipe F. R. Thomaz, 'Evolution of Empire: The Portuguese in the Indian Ocean during the Sixteenth Century', in James D. Tracy (ed.), *The Political Economy of Merchant Empires: State Power and Word Trade 1350–1750* (Cambridge: Cambridge University Press, 1991), pp. 298–331.

Sussman, George D., 'Was the Black Death in India and China?' *Bulletin of the History of Medicine* 85, 3 (2011), pp. 319–55.

Takahiro, Onuma, 'The Development of the Junghars and the Role of Bukharan Merchants', *Journal of Central Eurasian Studies* 2 (2011), pp. 83–100.

Takii, Kazuhiro, *Itō Hirobumi: Japan's First Prime Minister and Father of the Meiji Constitution* (London: Routledge, 2014).

Tarr, Joel A., 'A Note on the Horse as an Urban Power Source', *Journal of Urban History* 25, 3 (1999), pp. 434–48.

Taylor, Charles, *Sources of the Self: The Making of the Modern Identity* (Cambridge, MA: Harvard University Press, 1989).

Taylor, Charles, 'Modern Social Imaginaries', *Public Culture* 14, 1 (2002), pp. 91–124.

Taylor, Charles, *Modern Social Imaginaries* (Durham, NC and London: Duke University Press, 2004).

Teng, Emma, *Taiwan's Imagined Geography: Chinese Colonial Travel Writing and Pictures, 1683–1895* (Cambridge, MA: Harvard University Asia Center, 2004).

Therborn, Göran, 'At the Birth of Second-century Sociology: Times of Reflexivity, Spaces of Identity, and Nodes of Knowledge', *British Journal of Sociology* 51, 1 (2000), pp. 37–57.

Therborn, Göran, 'Entangled Modernities', *European Journal of Social Theory* 6, 3 (2003), pp. 293–305.

Tilly, Charles, *Big Structures, Large Processes, Huge Comparisons* (New York: Russell Sage Foundation, 1984).

Tilly, Charles, *Coercion, Capital, and European States, AD 990–1990* (Oxford: Blackwell, 1990).

Tilly, Charles, 'Historical Sociology', in Neil J. Smelser and Paul B. Baltes (eds), *International Encyclopedia of the Social and Behavioral Sciences*, vol. 10 (Amsterdam: Elsevier, 2001), pp. 6753–7.

Tomber, Roberta, 'Rome and Mesopotamia: Importers into India in the First Millennium AD', *Antiquity* 81 (2007), pp. 972–88.

Tong, Ma, *Zhongguo Yisilan jiaopai menhuan suyuan* (Yinchuan: Ningxia renmin chu-banshe, 1986).

Tong, Ma, 'A Brief History of the Qâdiriyya in China', trans. Jonathan Lipman, *Journal of the History of Sufism* 1, 2 (2000), pp. 547–76.

Tønnesson, Kåre, 'The Norwegian Constitution of 17 May 1814: International Influences and Models', *Parliaments, Estates and Representation* 21, 1 (2001), pp. 175–86.

Topik, Steven C., and Allen Wells, 'Commodity Chains in a Global Economy', in Emily Rosenberg (ed.), *A World Connecting, 1870–1945* (Cambridge, MA and London: Harvard University Press, 2012), pp. 593–812.

Torre, Angelo, 'Un "tournant spatiale" en histoire: paysages, regards, ressources', *Annales HSS* 63, 5 (2008), pp. 1127–44.

Totman, Conrad, *A History of Japan* (Oxford and Maldon, MA: Blackwell Publishers, 2000).

Toynbee, Arnold J., *A Study of History*, 12 vols (London: Oxford University Press, 1934–61).

Trollope, Anthony, *Barchester Towers*, ed. by John Bowen (Oxford: Oxford University Press, 2014).

Tuchscherer, Michel, *Le commerce du café* (Cairo: Institut français d'archéologie orientale, 2001).

Turner, Victor, and Edith Turner, *Image and Pilgrimage in Christian Culture: Anthropological Perspectives* (Oxford: Basil Blackwell, 1978).

Twaissi, Saad, 'Nabataean Edom: A Demographic and Archaeological Approach to Modelling Sedentarisation and Regional Dynamics', *Levant* 39 (2007), pp. 143–63.

Urry, John, 'Mobilities and Social Theory', in Bryan S. Turner (ed.): *The New Blackwell Companion to Social Theory* (Malden, MA: Wiley-Blackwell, 2009), pp. 475–95.

Vahide, Sukran, and Ibrahim M. Abu-Rabi (eds), *Islam in Modern Turkey: An Intellectual Biography of Bediuzzaman Said Nursi* (Albany: State University of New York Press, 2005).

Van der Veen, Marijke, *Consumption, Trade and Innovation: Exploring the Botanical Remains from the Roman and Islamic Ports at Quseir al-Qadim, Egypt* (Frankfurt: Africa Magna, 2011).

Villeneuve, François, 'Une inscription latine sur l'archipel Farasân, Arabie Séoudite, sud de la mer Rouge', *Comptes Rendus de l'Académie des Inscriptions* 148, 1 (2004), pp. 419–29.

[Villotte, Jacques,] *Voyages d'un Missionaire de la Compagnie de Jesus, en Turquie, en Perse, en Armenie, en Arabie, & en Barbarie* (Paris: J. Vincent, 1730).

Vink, Markus P. M., 'Indian Ocean Studies and the "New Thalassology"', *Journal of Global History* 2, 1 (2007), pp. 41–62.

Voll, John O., 'Linking Groups in the Networks of Eighteenth-Century Revivalist Scholars: the Mizjaji Family in Yemen', in Nehemia Levtzion and John O. Voll (eds), *Eighteenth-Century Renewal and Reform in Islam* (Syracuse, NY: Syracuse University Press, 1987), pp. 69–92.

Voll, John O., and Stefan Reichmuth, 'Murtada al-Zabidi (1732–91) and the Africans: Islamic Discourse and Scholarly Networks in the Late Eighteenth Century', in Scott S. Reese (ed.), *The Transmission of Learning in Islamic Africa* (Leiden: Brill, 2004), pp. 121–53.

Vries, Jan de, *The Industrious Revolution: Consumer Behavior and the Household Economy, 1650 to the Present* (Cambridge: Cambridge University Press, 2008).

Vries, Peer H. H., 'Global Economic History: A Survey', in Axel Schneider and Daniel R. Woolf (eds), *Oxford History of Historical Writing*, vol. V (Oxford: Oxford University Press 2011), pp. 113–35.

Vries, Peer H. H., *Escaping Poverty: The Origins of Modern Economic Growth* (Göttingen: Vandenhoeck & Ruprecht, 2013).

Wake, C. H. H., 'The Changing Pattern of Europe's Pepper and Spice Imports, *c.* 1400–1700', *Journal of European Economic History* 8 (1979), pp. 361–403. Reprinted in Michael N. Pearson (ed.), *Spices in the Indian Ocean World* (Aldershot: Variorum, 1996).

Walker, Bethany J., 'From Ceramics to Social Theory: Reflections on Mamluk Archaeology Today', *Mamlūk Studies Review* 14 (2010), pp. 109–57.

Wallerstein, Immanuel, 'From Sociology to Historical Social Science: Prospects and Obstacles', *British Journal of Sociology* 51, 1 (2000), pp. 25–35.

Wallerstein, Immanuel, 'Wegbeschreibung der Analyse von Weltsystemen, oder: Wie vermeidet man, eine Theorie zu werden?' trans. Hans-Heinrich Nolte, *Zeitschrift für Weltgeschichte* 2, 2 (2001), pp. 9–31.

Wallerstein, Immanuel, *The Modern World-System*, 3 vols (Berkeley, Los Angeles, and London: University of California Press, 2011).

Wallerstein, Immanuel, 'Robinson's Critical Appraisal Appraised', *International Sociology* 27, 4 (2012), pp. 524–8.

Watts, John, *The Making of Polities: Europe, 1300–1500* (Cambridge: Cambridge University Press, 2009).

Weber, Max, 'Die Objektivität sozialwissenschaftlicher und sozialpolitischer Erkenntnis' (1904), in Max Weber, *Gesammelte Aufsätze zur Wissenschaftslehre*, 2nd edn (Tübingen: Mohr, 1951), pp. 146–214.

Wei-chung, Cheng, *War, Trade and Piracy in the China Seas, 1622–1683* (Leiden: Brill, 2013).

Weinberg, Bennett Alan, and Bonnie K. Bealer, *The World of Caffeine: The Science and Culture of the World's Most Popular Drug* (London: Routledge, 2002).

Welke, Barbara Young, 'Law, Personhood, and Citizenship in the Long Nineteenth Century: The Borders of Belonging', in Michael Grossberg and Christopher L. Tomlins (eds), *Cambridge History of Law in America: The Long Nineteenth Century*, 3 vols (Cambridge: Cambridge University Press, 2008), vol. II, pp. 345–86.

Werbner, Pnina, *Pilgrims of Love: The Anthropology of a Global Sufi Cult* (London: C. Hurst & Co, 2003).

Werner, Michael, and Bénédicte Zimmermann, 'Penser l'histoire croisée: entre empirie et réflexité', *Annales HSS* 58, 1 (2003), pp. 7–36.

Werner, Michael, and Bénédicte Zimmermann, 'Beyond Comparison: *Histoire Croisée* and the Challenge of Reflexivity', *History and Theory* 45, 1 (2006), pp. 30–50.

West, Charles, *Reframing the Feudal Revolution Political and Social Transformation between Marne and Moselle, c.800–c.1100* (Cambridge: Cambridge University Press, 2013).

West, Martin L., *The East Face of Helicon: West Asiatic Elements in Greek Poetry and Myth* (Oxford: Clarendon Press, 1997).

Wheare, Kenneth C., *Modern Constitutions* (London: Oxford University Press, 1951).

Wheeler, Charles J., 'Buddhism in the Re-ordering of an Early Modern World: Chinese Missions to Cochinchina in the Seventeenth Century', *Journal of Global History* 2, 3 (2007), pp. 303–24.

White, Harrison C., *Identity and Control: How Social Formations Emerge*, 2nd edn (Princeton and Oxford: Princeton University Press, 2008).

Whitfield, Peter, *Astrology: A History* (London: The British Library, 2001).

Wickham, Chris, 'Systactic Structures', *Past and Present* 132 (1991), pp. 188–203.

Wickham, Chris, *Framing the Early Middle Ages: Europe and the Mediterranean, 400–800* (Oxford: Oxford University Press, 2005).

Wickham, Chris, *The Inheritance of Rome: A History of Europe from 400 to 1000* (London: Allen Lane, 2009).

Wiechmann, Ingrid, Michaela Harbeck, and Gisela Grupe, 'Yersinia Pestis DNA Sequences in Late Medieval Skeletal Finds, Bavaria', *Emerging Infectious Diseases* 16, 11 (2010), pp. 1806–7.

Wilder, Gary, 'From Optic to Topic: The Foreclosure Effects of Historiographic Turns', *American Historical Review* 117, 3 (2012), pp. 723–45.

Will, H. A., *Constitutional Change in the British West Indies, 1880–1903* (Oxford: Clarendon Press, 1970).

Williams, Eric E., *Capitalism & Slavery* (Chapel Hill: University of North Carolina Press, 1944).

Williams, John Bryan, 'From the Commercial Revolution to the Slave Revolution: The Development of Slavery in Medieval Genoa' (unpublished PhD thesis: University of Chicago, 1995).

Williamson, Jeffrey G., 'The Evolution of Global Labor Markets since 1830: Background Evidence and Hypotheses', *Explorations in Economic History* 32, 2 (1995), pp. 141–96.

Wilson, Woodrow, 'Democracy and Efficiency', *Atlantic Monthly* 87 (1901), pp. 292, 298.

Wilson, Woodrow, 'The Ideals of America', *Atlantic Monthly*, 90 (1902), pp. 721–34.

Wittfogel, Karl, *Oriental Despotism: A Comparative Study of Total Power* (New Haven: Yale University Press, 1957).

Wobbe, Theresa, *Weltgesellschaft* (Bielefeld: Transcript, 2000).

Wood, Ian, *The Modern Origins of the Early Middle Ages* (Oxford: Oxford University Press, 2013).

Wolf, Eric R., *Europe and the People without History* (Berkeley and London: University of California Press, 1982).

Woolf, Stuart, *Napoleon's Integration of Europe* (London: Routledge, 1991).

Wright, Donald R., *The World and a Very Small Place in Africa: A History of Globalization in Niumi, The Gambia* (Armonk, NY/London: Sharpe, 2010).

Wubs-Mrozewicz, Justyna, 'Interplay of Identities: German Settlers in Late Medieval Stockholm', *Scandinavian Journal of History* 29, 1 (2004), pp. 53–67.

Wuyunbilige, 'Guanyu Qingdai zhuming Menggu wenren Wuzhumuqin gong Gunbuzhabu de jidian xin shiliao', *Qingshi yanjiu* (2009), pp. 119–23.

Yavuz, M. Hakan, *Islamic Political Identity in Turkey* (New York: Oxford University Press, 2003).

Yeloff, Dan, and Bas van Geel, 'Abandonment of Farmland and Vegetation Succession Following the Eurasian Plague Pandemic of AD 1347–52', *Journal of Biogeography* 34, 4 (2007), pp. 575–82.

Young, Gary K., *Rome's Eastern Trade: International Commerce and Imperial Policy 31 BC–AD 305* (London: Routledge, 2001).

Yukichi, Fukuzawa, *Seijō jijō* [*The State of Affairs in the West*] (Tokyo, 1866), cited in Tadashi Aruga, 'The Declaration of Independence in Japan: Translation and Transplantation, 1854–1997', *Journal of American History* 85 (1999), pp. 1409–31.

Zarrow, Peter, *After Empire: The Conceptual Transformation of the Chinese State, 1885–1924* (Stanford, CA: Stanford University Press, 2012).

Zimmerman, Warren, *First Great Triumph: How Five Americans Made their Country a World Power* (New York: Farrar, Straus, and Giroux, 2002).

Zürcher, Erik J., *The Young Turk Legacy and Nation Building: From the Ottoman Empire to Ataturk's Turkey* (London: I. B. Tauris, 2010).

Index